Affect, Cognition, and Stereotyping

AFFECT,

COGNITION, AND

STEREOTYPING

*Interactive Processes in
Group Perception*

EDITED BY

Diane M. Mackie and David L. Hamilton

*Department of Psychology
University of California, Santa Barbara
Santa Barbara, California*

ACADEMIC PRESS, INC.
Harcourt Brace Jovanovich, Publishers
San Diego   New York   Boston
London   Sydney   Tokyo   Toronto

Copyright © 1993 by ACADEMIC PRESS, INC.

All Rights Reserved.
No part of this publication may be reproduced or transmitted in any form or by any means, electronic or mechanical, including photocopy, recording, or any information storage and retrieval system, without permission in writing from the publisher.

Academic Press, Inc.
1250 Sixth Avenue, San Diego, California 92101-4311

United Kingdom Edition published by
Academic Press Limited
24–28 Oval Road, London NW1 7DX

Library of Congress Cataloging-in-Publication Data

Affect, cognition, and stereotyping: interactive processes in group
  perception / edited by Diane M. Mackie and David L. Hamilton.
      p.   cm.
    Includes index.
    ISBN 0-12-464410-4
    1. Emotions and cognition.   2. Stereotype (Psychology)
  3. Intergroup relations.   4. Prejudices.   I. Mackie, Diane.
  II. Hamilton, David L. (David Lewis), date.
  BF311.A32   1993
  302.3–dc20   92-28250
                                                          CIP

PRINTED IN THE UNITED STATES OF AMERICA
   93 94 95 96 97   BB   9 8 7 6 5 4 3 2 1

Contents

Chapter 3

The Influence of Affect on Stereotyping: The Case of Illusory Correlations

DAVID L. HAMILTON, STEVEN J. STROESSNER, and DIANE M. MACKIE

Chapter 4

Affect and Perceived Group Variability: Implications for Stereotyping and Prejudice

STEVEN J. STROESSNER and DIANE M. MACKIE

Chapter 5

The Role of Anxiety in Facilitating Stereotypic Judgment of Outgroup Behavior

DAVID A. WILDER

Chapter 6

Cognition and Affect in Stereotyping: Parallel Interactive Networks

WALTER G. STEPHAN and COOKIE WHITE STEPHAN

Chapter 7

Values, Stereotypes, and Emotions as Determinants of Intergroup Attitudes

VICTORIA M. ESSES, GEOFFREY HADDOCK, and MARK P. ZANNA

Chapter 8

Stereotypes and Evaluative Intergroup Bias

JOHN F. DOVIDIO and SAMUEL L. GAERTNER

Chapter 9

Mere Exposure Effects with Outgroup Stimuli

ROBERT F. BORNSTEIN

Chapter 10

Applications of Emotion Theory and Research to Stereotyping and Intergroup Relations

ERIC J. VANMAN and NORMAN MILLER

Chapter 11

Negative Interdependence and Prejudice: Whence the Affect?

SUSAN T. FISKE and JANET B. RUSCHER

Chapter 12

Stereotyping and Affect in Discourse: Interpreting the Meaning of Elderly, Painful Self-Disclosure

KAREN HENWOOD, HOWARD GILES, JUSTINE COUPLAND, and NIKOLAS COUPLAND

Chapter 13

Social Identity and Social Emotions: Toward New Conceptualizations of Prejudice

ELIOT R. SMITH

Chapter 14

The Role of Discrepancy-Associated Affect in Prejudice Reduction

PATRICIA G. DEVINE and MARGO J. MONTEITH

Chapter 15

Social Stigma: The Consequences of Attributional Ambiguity

BRENDA MAJOR and JENNIFER CROCKER

Chapter 16

Affect, Cognition, and Stereotyping: Concluding Comments

DIANE M. MACKIE and DAVID L. HAMILTON

Contributors

Numbers in parentheses indicate the pages on which the authors' contributions begin.

Galen V. Bodenhausen (13), Department of Psychology, Michigan State University, East Lansing, Michigan 48824

Robert F. Bornstein (195), Department of Psychology, Gettysburg College, Gettysburg, Pennsylvania 17325

Justine Coupland (269), School of English Studies, Journalism, and Philosophy, University of Wales, College of Cardiff, Cardiff CF1 3XE, United Kingdom

Nikolas Coupland (269), School of English Studies, Journalism, and Philosophy, University of Wales, College of Cardiff, Cardiff CF1 3XE, United Kingdom

Jennifer Crocker (345), Department of Psychology, State University of New York at Buffalo, Buffalo, New York 14260

Patricia G. Devine (317), Department of Psychology, University of Wisconsin, Madison, Madison, Wisconsin 53706

John F. Dovidio (167), Department of Psychology, Colgate University, Hamilton, New York 13346

Victoria M. Esses (137), Department of Psychology, University of Western Ontario, London, Ontario, Canada N6A 5C2

Susan T. Fiske (239), Department of Psychology, University of Massachusetts at Amherst, Amherst, Massachusetts 01003

Samuel L. Gaertner (167), Department of Psychology, University of Delaware, Newark, Delaware 19711

Howard Giles (269), Department of Communication, University of California, Santa Barbara, Santa Barbara, California 93106

Geoffrey Haddock (137), Department of Psychology, University of Waterloo, Waterloo, Ontario, Canada N2L 3G1

David L. Hamilton (1, 39, 371), Department of Psychology, University of California, Santa Barbara, Santa Barbara, California 93106

Karen Henwood (269), Department of Human Sciences, Brunel University, Uxbridge UB8 3PH, United Kingdom

Diane M. Mackie (1, 39, 63, 371), Department of Psychology, University of California, Santa Barbara, Santa Barbara, California 93106

Brenda Major (345), Department of Psychology, State University of New York at Buffalo, Buffalo, New York 14260

Norman Miller (213), Department of Psychology, University of Southern California, Los Angeles, California 90089

Margo J. Monteith (317), Department of Psychology, University of Wisconsin, Madison, Madison, Wisconsin 53706

Janet B. Ruscher (239), Department of Psychology, Tulane University, New Orleans, Louisiana 70118

Eliot R. Smith (297), Department of Psychological Sciences, Purdue University, West Lafayette, Indiana 47907

Cookie White Stephan (111), Department of Sociology, New Mexico State University, Las Cruces, New Mexico 88003

Walter G. Stephan (111), Department of Psychology, New Mexico State University, Las Cruces, New Mexico 88003

Steven J. Stroessner[1] (39, 63), Department of Psychology, University of California, Santa Barbara, Santa Barbara, California 93106

Eric J. Vanman (213), Department of Psychology, University of Southern California, Los Angeles, California 90089

David A. Wilder (87), Department of Psychology, Rutgers University, New Brunswick, New Jersey 08903

Mark P. Zanna (137), Department of Psychology, University of Waterloo, Waterloo, Ontario, Canada N2L 3G1

[1]*Present address:* Department of Psychology, Barnard College, Columbia University, New York, New York 10027.

Preface

Like so many intellectual pursuits, the idea of writing this volume arose while interacting with others. For the past seven years we have participated in a weekly research meeting that includes most of the social psychology group at the University of California, Santa Barbara. Over the years, the group has had some lively intellectual brawls about various topics in intergroup perception, stereotypes, group categorization, in-group bias, social identity, stigma, and a host of other topics. At the same time, the group has debated the impact of affect, emotions, motivational goals, and self-esteem on a variety of processes and outcomes. Inevitably, in the last two years, these two sets of issues started to merge, first in our discussions, then in our laboratories. Our lines of research—on the impact of affective states on illusory correlation and on the perception of variability—evolved from these discussions of how affective and cognitive processes might interact in group perceptions.

As our research on these topics developed, we began to discover others engaged in the same task of trying to understand the integrative effects of affective and cognitive processes in intergroup contexts. The topics being investigated in these research programs were varied and diverse but all converged on the same set of issues: How do affective processes influence intergroup perception? How does affect arise from the cognitive processes involved in intergroup perception? Given this diversity around common themes, we quickly became convinced that a single volume bringing together these various research programs would be both an exciting and valuable contribution. As we talked with potential contributors, their enthusiasm matched our own. The project gathered further momentum through a symposium organized by Mark P. Zanna at the annual meeting of the Society of Experimental Social Psychology in Buffalo, 1990. Ultimately, we were able to bring together an outstanding group of authors who agreed to share their theoretical insights, to communicate their research findings, to bring different literature to bear on the issues, and to speculate on integrative themes and new directions. They suffered our extensive editorial comments with equanimity, and the present volume is the culmination of our collective efforts.

Because this project evolved from our research meetings, this book reflects the participation, to varying degrees, of many of our collaborators and colleagues in Santa Barbara: Steve Stroessner, Denise Driscoll, Arlene Asuncion, Fran Rosselli, John Skelly, Jeff Sherman, Herbert Bless, Leonel Garcia-Marques, Jose Manuel Palma-Oliveira, Stan Klein, Faith Gleicher, Daphne Bugental, Catherine Ruvolo, and Cecilia Gastardo-Conaco. Several sabbatical visitors to Santa Barbara—Mel Manis, Jim Blascovich, Brenda Major, and Bernd Simon—were regular participants in our discussions of these issues. To all of these colleagues and friends we owe a debt of gratitude.

Many thanks also go to our editor at Academic Press, Nikki Fine. Having taken our project on, Nikki has been "rewarded" by having to tolerate bypassed deadlines and missing manuscripts. But patiently and capably, she guided the project through to completion. And speaking of patience and ability, we are also grateful to Ann McDonald, not only for her clerical skills but also for remaining calm when neither of us did!

Finally, we have to thank each other for the benefits of co-editorship. At any given time, at least one of us was almost on time, somewhat organized, and close to rational.

Chapter 1

Cognitive and Affective Processes in Intergroup Perception: The Developing Interface

DAVID L. HAMILTON and DIANE M. MACKIE

Department of Psychology
University of California, Santa Barbara
Santa Barbara, California

Introduction

Two recent trends in psychology constitute the conceptual backdrop for the contributions to this volume. These two developments have evolved independently, each with its own origins and directions, and each with its own momentum. Yet they have converged at a time that offers new opportunities for advancing our knowledge of the dynamics underlying intergroup relations.

What are these developments? The first is the predominant emphasis on cognitive processes that has characterized American psychology during the last two decades. The second is a more recent revitalization of interest in the nature and role of affective processes in psychological functioning. Both of these trends have had widespread impact in diverse areas of psychological theory and research.

Separately, each of these developments has had important implications for current research on intergroup perceptions. But it is their coming together that feeds significantly into the chapters that comprise this volume, and that offers opportunities for new understanding of intergroup relations. In this introductory chapter we briefly discuss each of these evolving trends and their manifestations in and implications for intergroup research. We then preview the chapters comprising this volume, each of which reflects, in one form or another, the convergence of these developments.

Two Components of the Conceptual Backdrop

Cognition

The cognitive emphasis is evident throughout psychology and nowhere more so than in social psychology. During the last 15 years the social cognition emphasis has permeated the study of numerous substantive topics in our discipline, bringing with it a primary concern with identifying, measuring, and understanding the cognitive mediators underlying the social phenomena of interest.

From its beginning this approach was clearly evident in the literature on stereotyping and intergroup perception (cf. Allport, 1954; Hamilton, 1976). For example, the classic work of Tajfel (1969, 1970) demonstrated that intergroup discrimination, previously thought to rest on realistic conflict between groups, can derive from the mere categorization of persons into groups. Similarly Taylor's (Taylor, Fiske, Etcoff, & Ruderman, 1978) research showed that a person's context-based salience can affect observers' differential attention to majority and minority individuals, with consequent effects on how those persons are perceived. And Hamilton's (Hamilton & Gifford, 1976) research on illusory correlations showed that a cognitive bias in the way distinctive information is attended to and processed can result in the unwarranted differential perception of groups. These research programs provided an impetus to a renewed interest in the cognitive underpinnings of intergroup perception.

This early work, occurring mostly in the 1970s, was followed by more than a decade of research in which the cognitive approach to stereotyping was enthusiastically pursued. In some cases this research was designed to elucidate the role of cognitive processes underlying various intergroup judgments and behaviors. In other cases the research strategy was to push the cognitive analysis as far as it could go. That is, researchers tried to determine how well cognitive mechanisms alone could produce, and perhaps account for, judgmental and behavioral phenomena that had previously been viewed as due to more dynamic, motivational variables (cf. Dawes, 1976). This work examined the ramifications of cognitive processes for understanding intergroup differentiations, memory for group-relevant information, stereotype-based attributions, self-fulfilling prophecies, the persistence and change of stereotypic beliefs, and numerous other issues. This strategy was remarkably successful and often challenged prevailing viewpoints. The resulting literature is now voluminous (for reviews see Hamilton, Sherman, & Ruvolo, 1990; Messick & Mackie, 1989).

Affect

During this period of cognitive preeminence, the study of affective factors—emotion, motivation, mood states, arousal, and the like—and their role in social psychological processes continued, but quietly and without the prominence it had historically enjoyed. Research on these topics may have been part of the "ground," but it surely was not the "figure" on the social psychological landscape.

Recently, however, there has been a resurgence of interest in affective processes, including increased study of their role in intergroup contexts. There are probably several reasons for this resurgence. Undoubtedly, it reflects in part the proverbial swing of the scientific pendulum; any one focus will be "hot" for only so long before interest shifts to what has been relatively neglected by the predominant emphasis. However, more substantial factors have also contributed to this shift. For example, the appearance of several new theoretical positions concerned with the nature, structure, and functioning of emotions has drawn attention to these issues (Fridja, 1988; Ortony, Clore & Collins, 1988; Roseman, 1984; Shaver, Schwartz, Kirson, & O'Connor, 1987). In addition, a growing literature on affect and its impact on memory, and ultimately on cognitive processing more generally, has stirred debate (Bower, 1981; Ellis & Ashbrook, 1988; Forgas, 1990; Isen, 1984, 1987; Schwarz, 1990; Srull, 1983). And third, a major contributing factor has been the impressive technological advances made in psychophysiological measurement, permitting more precise assessment and monitoring of affectively driven variables (Cacioppo & Petty, 1983; Cacioppo, Petty, Losch, & Kim, 1986).

These developments would seem to have enormous implications for the study of intergroup perception. Despite their relative neglect in recent years, it has always seemed evident that significant affective responses arise spontaneously in many intergroup contexts. Certainly the history of intergroup relations is rich in evidence of intense emotional, even passionate, forces guiding the thoughts, feelings, perceptions, and behaviors of group members. Some intergroup contexts in and of themselves seem to generate affective reactions that can disrupt "normal" social interaction. Moreover, if our self-identities are wrapped up in our perceptions of our own and other groups, then the stereotypes we hold of outgroups are destined to be affectively laden.

These issues have not been adequately explored in empirical research. The theoretical advances and technological developments referred to earlier offer significant potential for furthering our knowledge of the affective components of stereotyping and prejudice.

The Developing Interface

Thus far we have argued that two developing emphases within psychology in recent years are important contributors to understanding intergroup perceptions. The cognitively focused research of the last decade has, in many respects, transformed our thinking about the nature and functioning of stereotypes. The renewed activity concerning affective processes promises to generate additional insights that the cognitive focus has overlooked. Thus each of these developments, as a separate approach, is generating new excitement for the social psychology of intergroup relations. But that is not enough.

Historically, affective and cognitive processes have been conceptualized as qualitatively different systems. In fact, it was not uncommon to consider the operation of these systems as mutually incompatible: the surge of impassioned affect struggled for dominance over the impassive mechanisms of cognitive calculation.

This view has also characterized much of the literature on intergroup perceptions. On the one hand, stereotypes have long been recognized as systems of beliefs about particular social groups, beliefs that could influence the nature of a perceiver's perceptions of, inferences about, and reactions to group members. On the other hand, the affect associated with our conceptions of those groups was often seen as disrupting or short-circuiting (Brigham, 1971) our normal cognitive functioning when confronted with group members. As a consequence, most research on intergroup perception has reflected a focus on either affect or cognition, but not both.

But of course any approach adopting a singular focus on a multifaceted phenomenon will ultimately reach its limits. As one of us has commented elsewhere:

> Any particular form of stereotyping or prejudice . . . is in all likelihood multiply determined by cognitive, motivational, and social learning processes, whose effects combine in a given social context to produce specific judgmental and behavioral manifestations. Therefore, any attempt to understand such phenomena as a product of one process alone is probably misguided. (Hamilton & Trolier, 1986, p. 153)

In fact, contemporary thinking about cognition and affect emphasizes a more integrative relationship between these two systems. Cognition has its impact on affect by constituting the appraisal processes that regulate the social and cultural interpretation of experienced emotion. At the same time, affect has its effects on judgments and behavior through its impact on cognitive processes. Affect activates motivations or goal states, which in turn influence the extent and nature of further processing. In addition, arousal level and affective states influence what information is attended to and what contents will be activated from memory, thereby exerting control over the raw material that becomes the grist for the information processing mill. Thus, affect and cognition are mutually interactive components of a broader system.

It is this view that is reflected in the approaches to studying intergroup relations advanced in this volume. The chapters portray a recent effort to understand how cognitive and affective variables interact and mutually influence each other in intergroup contexts. Yet when we wish to characterize this contemporary approach, we can do no better than to trace its roots back to Lippmann (1922) who eloquently captured this perspective:

> [Stereotyping] is not merely a way of substituting order for the great blooming, buzzing confusion of reality. It is not merely a short cut. It is all these things and more. It is the guarantee of our self-respect; it is the projection upon the world of our own sense of our own value, our own position and our own rights. The stereotypes are, therefore, highly charged with the feelings that are attached to them. They are the fortress of our tradition, and behind its defenses we can continue to feel ourselves safe in the position we occupy. (pp. 63–64)

Chapter Previews

The research reported in this volume represents the early fruit of this new approach. Each of the chapters reflects an integration of affective and cognitive factors as they influence intergroup perception. The richness and variety of ways in which the contributors approach this interface demonstrate its potential for generating new ways of studying—and understanding—intergroup dynamics.

The first set of chapters, Chapters 2 through 5, consider the influence of affect on a range of processes central to intergroup perception. These chapters share a common theme of specifying cognitive mechanisms known to underlie stereotyping and stereotype use, and then assessing the impact of affective and emotional states on the operation of those processes.

Galen V. Bodenhausen's chapter (Chapter 2) commences the task of specifying the motivational and cognitive consequences of affective states for information processing. Drawing on the neurological, physiological, and cognitive literatures, Bodenhausen develops the hypothesis that some affective states, but not others, produce simplified information processing. He then draws out and tests the processing implications of a range of affective states for the use of stereotypic, rather than individuating, information in social perception tasks.

Bodenhausen also introduces a useful distinction between incidental and integral affect in intergroup situations. Incidental affect arises separately from and independently of interaction between members of different groups, yet might nevertheless influence the processing of information from such interactions. For example, being in a happy or sad mood or having experienced recent frustration in a different context are affective experiences incidental to later encounters with members of different groups. In contrast, integral affect arises in the course of, and is generated by, the intergroup properties of the situation. The frustration, anger, pride, or anxiety that arise as a direct result of thinking about, anticipating, or actually engaging in intergroup interactions are examples of affect integral to the intergroup context itself. Bodenhausen's own studies manipulate incidental affect, but pose the question of whether incidental and integral affect have the same or different implications for intergroup perception.

In Chapter 3, David L. Hamilton, Steven J. Stroessner, and Diane M. Mackie take a similar approach, exploring the ways in which induced affective states impact the usual operation of cognitive mechanisms that produce differences in intergroup perception. Both the distinctiveness-based and the expectancy-based illusory correlation produce an imagined relationship between variables, but through very different processes. In specifying how affective states facilitate or interfere with these different processes, Hamilton and his colleagues demonstrate that affect may play very different roles in stereotype formation and in stereotype maintenance.

Chapter 4, by Steven J. Stroessner and Diane M. Mackie, examines the impact of affect on an even more fundamental aspect of intergroup perception: the perception of similarity and variability among group members. Most models of variability judgments cast the processing of information about individual group members in a central role. Such information either becomes the raw material for delayed memory-based judgments of group variability, or is used in an on-line fashion to produce an ongoing mental assessment of group members' variability or dispersion. These authors pose the questions: How do current affective states influence the processes underlying variability judgments? And what are their consequences for theories of intergroup contact, which often assume that increased exposure produces perceptions of increased variability?

Whereas Chapters 2 through 4 focus on incidental affect, Chapter 5, by David A. Wilder, bridges the gap between incidental and integral affect by studying the effects of both of them within the same research program. Wilder's research assesses the impact of affect on the processing of stereotypic versus individuating information about multiple group members. His work thus complements both Bodenhausen's focus on stereotypic versus individuating judgments of a single group member and Stroessner and Mackie's work on variability within groups. By inducing anxiety in a way that is either related or unrelated to the intergroup perception context, and by manipulating the processing goal with which subjects approach the interpersonal perception task, Wilder attempts to delineate the conditions under which affective states might accelerate or impede stereotype change.

The focus of interest shifts somewhat in the second set of chapters, Chapters 6 and 7. In these chapters, the authors are concerned with the interplay of different kinds of information in producing stereotypes or stereotyped judgments. In Chapter 6, Walter G. and Cookie White Stephan propose a set of structural and processing principles that allow both cognition and affect to be mutually activating and reciprocally influential. Their ideas suggest that, depending on the circumstances, different kinds of information may contribute differentially to intergroup perception, a proposition they explore in the second half of their chapter.

The informational foundation on which intergroup evaluations are based is the central concern of Chapter 7, by Victoria A. Esses, Geoffrey Haddock, and Mark P. Zanna. These authors use multiple regression techniques to test hypotheses about whether stereotyped beliefs, symbolic beliefs (about a group's impact on another group's cherished values and norms), or affective reactions are better predictors of global acceptance of and liking for various ethnic, national, and lifestyle groups. Sounding a theme that is to be echoed in later chapters, these authors make a strong argument for the importance of experienced affect and intergroup values in regulating intergroup relations.

The focus shifts once again in the next set of six chapters. Rather than assessing the impact of affect on cognitive processes, these chapters are more concerned with the mechanisms of intergroup perception that produce affect. And whereas the earlier chapters investigated affect as an antecedent in generic processes in intergroup perception, these chapters introduce the inherently evaluation-laden concepts of ingroup and outgroup membership. The chapters progress from highlighting intraindividual cognitive processes (e.g., mere activation of the concepts "we" and "they") to a focus on interindividual and intergroup interactions (e.g., being exposed to, talking with, and interacting with outgroup members) that can produce intergroup emotion.

Chapter 8, by John F. Dovidio and Samuel L. Gaertner, documents the surprisingly robust evaluative consequences of mere activation of intergroup concepts such as "we" and "they." And whereas many of the other chapters focus on the congruence between affect and cognitions (regardless of direction of the causal influence), these authors explore the dissociation between cognitive and affective components in intergroup perception. In particular, they focus on the implications of this affective–cognitive independence for attempts to reduce stereotyping and prejudice. Their analysis suggests that, whereas most theories of stereotype change have concentrated on changing beliefs, attempts to change affect directly—and quite independently—may also be necessary.

In Chapter 9, Robert F. Bornstein builds on the ingroup/outgroup theme by extending a well-studied attitudinal phenomenon into the intergroup arena. The mere exposure effect (Zajonc, 1968) suggests that increased exposure to an object—particularly without awareness of such exposure—elevates liking for that object. Does the mere exposure effect operate in intergroup interactions? Can it help explain preferences for ingroup over outgroup members? And can it mediate beneficial effects of increased exposure to outgroup members? In offering answers to these questions, Bornstein develops connections among the literatures on intergroup perception, intergroup contact, and expectancy confirmation.

In opening Chapter 10, Eric J. Vanman and Norman Miller draw a distinction between appraisal or constructionist models of emotion, in which affect derives from cognition, and biosocial theories of emotion, in which emotion causes cognition. They review evidence for both causal directions, strengthening the notion that affect and cognition are mutually interactive. In so doing, these authors suggest a number of features of intergroup interaction that serve as distal or proximal origins of the negative affect that often accompanies intergroup relations. This chapter also provides an overview of the potential benefits, and possible pitfalls, of using psychophysiological and particularly facial electromyographic techniques for tracking the arousal and dissipation of intergroup affect.

The attributes of intergroup interaction that generate negative affect are the central concern of Chapter 11, by Susan T. Fiske and Janet B. Ruscher. Their concern is with interdependence, and specifically with the nature of interdependence that causes disruption, annoyance, irritation, and anxiety when members of two different groups work together. While their analysis suggests that category differences in and of themselves can induce negative affect, social interdependence exacerbates and intensifies it. Can such category-based affect be eliminated? Or if not, are there strategies for contending with it? As the authors point out, social psychologists have often resorted to interdependence tasks to eliminate biased intergroup perceptions. But as their analysis makes clear, interdependence is not only a cure for negative intergroup relations; it can also be a cause of such outcomes.

If members of different groups are to interact at all, they do so first by speaking. Thus it should not be surprising that language embodies our social construction of reality and serves to ingrain, regulate, and eliminate relations between members of groups. But language is also the tool by which those relations are shaped in the first place, as social facts and identities are negotiated through conversation. These ideas are the driving force behind the research reported in Chapter 12, by Karen Henwood, Howard Giles, Justine Coupland, and Nikolas Coupland. In this view emotion exists only in the social nexus, and is as fluid and open to interpretation as any other socially constructed phenomenon. This chapter takes a radically different approach from the other chapters in the book, eschewing experimentation for the purpose of understanding the dynamics of intergroup conversations. By demonstrating that stereotypes are used in speech as a means of coping with affect, and that affect is negotiated through conversation to cope with stereotypic processes, the authors argue that drawing a clear-cut distinction between affect and cognition may be inadvisable.

The social nature of emotion is also the central theme in Eliot R. Smith's Chapter 13. Smith attempts to integrate social identity theory with contemporary appraisal and constructionist theories of emotion. In this analysis, emotions, like identities, stretch beyond the individual to include the group. At the same time, the group's cares and concerns become the individual's cares and concerns. Thus, the actions of outgroup members in particular situations are construed as more or less threatening to one's own group, one's social identity, and thus one's self. Depending on the implications of the other group's actions for their own group, ingroup members may feel pride, respect, anger, fear, or anxiety toward the other group. Smith's chapter presents a framework for anticipating the differentiated and situation-specific nature of intergroup emotions. Moreover, this perspective suggests strategies for prejudice reduction that recognize that emotion may be a group-based, rather than an individual-based, phenomenon.

In Chapter 14, Patricia G. Devine and Margo J. Monteith take the analysis of the reciprocal interaction between affect and cognition one step further. In previous research, Devine (1989) has argued that people low in prejudice have adopted personal standards that differ from the typically more prejudiced cultural stereotypes of outgroups. In this chapter, Devine and Monteith ask what happens when those personal standards are violated. The answer is an affective response: once again we have an example of intergroup-related cognitive processing (awareness of making a stereotypic response) producing an affective response. But Devine and Monteith continue tracing the process, and find that this affective response in turn becomes a powerful motivator for future vigilance against stereotypic responses. Thus, cognition produces affect which in turn dictates subsequent cognitive processing. These authors end their chapter with an exploration of the implications of this continuing mutual interplay for strategies of bringing about more widespread stereotype change.

Chapter 15, by Brenda Major and Jennifer Crocker, differs from all of the others in an important respect. Whereas the focus in all previous chapters was on the perceiver, the stereotype-holder, Major and Crocker's work analyzes cognitive processes and affective reactions that pertain to the target of stereotyping and prejudice, the stigmatized person in an intergroup interaction. These authors note that minority group members, cognizant of the fact that others' reactions to them may be biased by prejudice (or tempered by the desire to avoid appearing prejudiced), are faced with attributional ambiguity in interpreting the feedback they receive from others. As a consequence, both positive and negative feedback may have diminished affective impact on the minority group person, including attenuated effects on one's self-esteem. Major and Crocker report a clever series of experiments in which they document the conditions that augment and diminish this attributional ambiguity and its effects on self-evaluations.

In the final chapter (Chapter 16) we provide a commentary on the theoretical ideas, research strategies, and empirical findings represented in the contributions to this volume. In doing so, we attempt to identify some themes that emerge from this work and to suggest directions for development in future research.

Acknowledgments

Preparation of this chapter was supported by NIMH Grant MH-40058 to D. L. Hamilton and by NIMH Grant MH-43041 to D. M. Mackie.

References

Allport, G. W. (1954). *The nature of prejudice*. Reading, MA: Addison Wesley.

Bower, G. H. (1981). Mood and memory. *American Psychologist, 36*, 129–148.

Brigham, J. C. (1971). Ethnic stereotypes. *Psychological Bulletin, 76*, 15–33.

Cacioppo, J. T., & Petty, R. E. (Eds.). (1983). *Social psychophysiology: A sourcebook*. New York: Guilford Press.

Cacioppo, J. T., Petty, R. E., Losch, M. E., & Kim, H. S. (1986). Electromygraphic activity over facial muscle regions can differentiate the valence and intensity of affective reaction. *Journal of Personality and Social Psychology, 50*, 260–268.

Dawes, R. M. (1976). Shallow psychology. In J. S. Carroll & J. W. Payne (Eds.), *Cognition and social behavior* (pp. 3–11). Hillsdale, NJ: Erlbaum.

Devine, P. G. (1989). Stereotypes and prejudice: Their automatic and controlled components. *Journal of Personality and Social Psychology, 56*, 5–18.

Ellis, H. C., & Ashbrook, P. W. (1988). Resource allocation model of the effects of depressed mood states on memory. In K. Fielder & J. Forgas (Eds.), *Affect, cognition, and social behavior* (pp. 25–43). Toronto: Hogrefe.

Forgas, J. P. (1990). Affect and social judgments: An introductory review. In J. P. Forgas (Ed.), *Emotion and social judgments* (pp. 3–29). Oxford: Pergamon Press.

Frijda, N. H. (1988). The laws of emotion. *American Psychologist, 43*, 349–358.

Hamilton, D. L. (1976). Cognitive biases in the perception of social groups. In J. S. Carroll & J. W. Payne (Eds.), *Cognition and social behavior* (pp. 81–93). Hillsdale, NJ: Erlbaum

Hamilton, D. L., & Gifford, R. K. (1976). Illusory correlation in interpersonal perception: A cognitive basis of stereotypic judgments. *Journal of Experimental Social Psychology, 12*, 392–407.

Hamilton, D. L., & Trolier, T. K. (1986). Stereotypes and stereotyping: An overview of the cognitive approach. In J. F. Dovidio & S. L. Gaertner (Eds.), *Prejudice, discrimination, and racism* (pp. 127–163). New York, NY: Academic Press, Inc.

Hamilton, D. L., Sherman, S. J., & Ruvolo, C. M. (1990). Stereotype-based expectancies: Effects on information processing and social behavior. *Journal of Social Issues, 46*(2), 35–60.

Isen, A. M. (1984). Toward understanding the role of affect in cognition. In R. S. Wyer, Jr., & T. K. Srull (Eds.), *Handbook of social cognition* (Vol. 3, pp. 179–236). Hillsdale, NJ: Erlbaum.

Isen, A. M. (1987). Positive affect, cognitive processes, and social behavior. In L. Berkowitz (Ed.), *Advances in experimental social psychology* (Vol. 20, pp. 203–253). New York, NY: Academic Press, Inc.

Lippmann, W. (1922). *Public opinion.* New York: Harcourt Brace.

Messick, D. M., & Mackie, D. M. (1989). Intergroup relations. *Annual Review of Psychology,* **40,** 45–81.

Ortony, A., Clore, G. L., & Collins, A. (1988). *The cognitive structure of emotions.* New York, NY: Cambridge University Press.

Roseman, I. (1984). Cognitive determinants of emotion: A structural theory. In P. Shaver (Ed.), *Review of Personality and Social Psychology* (Vol. 5). Beverly Hills, Ca: Sage.

Schwarz, N. (1990). Feeling as information: Informational and motivational functions of affective states. In R. Sorrentino and E. T. Higgins (Eds.), *Handbook of motivation and cognition* (Vol. 2, pp. 527–561). New York, NY: Guilford Press.

Shaver, P., Schwartz, J., Kirson, D., & O'Connor, C. (1987). Emotion knowledge: Further exploration of a prototype approach. *Journal of Personality and Social Psychology, 52,* 1061–1086.

Srull, T. K. (1983). Affect and memory: The impact of affective reactions in advertising on the representation of product information in memory. In R. Bagozzi and A. Tybout (Eds.), *Advances in consumer research* (Vol. 10, pp. 520–525). Ann Arbor, MI: Association for Consumer Research.

Tajfel, H. (1969). Cognitive aspects of prejudice. *Journal of Social Issues, 25*(4), 79–97.

Tajfel, H. (1970). Experiments in intergroup discrimination. *Scientific American,* **223**(5), 96–102.

Taylor, S. E., Fiske, S. T., Etcoff, N. L., & Ruderman, A. J. (1978). Categorical bases of person memory and stereotyping. *Journal of Personality and Social Psychology,* **36,** 778–793.

Zajonc, R. B. (1968) Attitudinal effects of mere exposure. *Journal of Personality and Social Psychology Monograph Supplement,* 9(2, Pt. 2), 1–27.

Chapter 2

Emotions, Arousal, and Stereotypic Judgments: A Heuristic Model of Affect and Stereotyping

GALEN V. BODENHAUSEN

Department of Psychology
Michigan State University
East Lansing, Michigan

Introduction

After decades of disrepute, research on emotion is flourishing in contemporary psychology. Indeed, so much progress has been made in understanding the origins and consequences of emotional experience that Frijda (1988) felt sufficiently confident to enumerate a collection of empirical "laws" of emotion, describing well-validated empirical phenomena associated with emotion. Researchers have proposed numerous general theories of emotion (see, e.g., Scherer & Ekman, 1984), providing rich insights into the nature of affect. To be sure, a number of theoretical controversies continue to stir debate among emotion researchers. These debates focus on issues such as the relative importance and temporal priority of cognitive versus somatovisceral aspects of emotional experience (see Frijda, 1986), the number and nature of "basic" emotions, if such exist (see Ortony, Clore, & Collins, 1988), and the degree to which different emotional states are characterized by unique patterns of autonomic arousal (see Ekman, Levenson, & Friesen, 1983; Schachter & Singer, 1962). Whether or not such debates are ever definitively resolved, it is clear that research inspired by controversies such as these has significantly advanced our understanding of a previously neglected domain of human nature.

The interface of the affective and cognitive domains of human nature has been explored with particular enthusiasm in recent years. The theoretical integration of affective and cognitive processes promises to yield important advances in social psychology generally, but no topic of study seems likely to profit from this reunification more than the study of stereotyping and discrimination. Earlier in this century, these topics were viewed in largely motivational and affective terms derived from Freudian and Marxist thought. More recently, motivational approaches have been supplanted by a cognitive analysis focusing on common information-processing mechanisms (Hamilton, 1981). Although this cognitive analysis has been fruitful, it has become increasingly obvious that emotion is far too central a component of intergroup relations to be discarded by those who would understand intergroup phenomena. The major goal of this chapter is to present a general cognitive model of the processes involved in stereotype-based discrimination and to explore some of the principal means by which emotion affects these processes.

Before commencing with this objective, it is useful to consider the nature of emotions that characterize intergroup situations, which for the present purposes include situations in which one is thinking about members of other social groups, regardless of whether they are physically present or not. First, there is *integral affect,* or the emotion(s) elicited by the social group itself and the usual conditions and contexts with which the group is associated. For many stereotyped groups, the affect that is integral to situations involving them is decidedly negative, often involving anxiety, irritation, disgust, and other negative feelings (Dijker, 1987; Jackson & Sullivan, 1988; McConahay, 1986; Stephan & Stephan, 1985; Wilder & Shapiro, 1989). The degree, and therefore the impact, of this sort of affect should be substantially greater in actual interaction settings as opposed to situations in which one is merely thinking about outgroup members. Intergroup perceptions may also be influenced by *incidental affect,* or emotion(s) elicited by situations unrelated to the intergroup context. One of the major themes in the affect and cognition literature is the extent to which affect elicited in one context can affect memory and judgments in many other contexts (e.g., Forgas & Bower, 1988; Isen, 1987; Schwarz & Clore, 1988; Wyer & Srull, 1989). If emotion and mood can have pervasive effects on social information processing, they may affect the propensity to stereotype members of a social group even when they arise for reasons having nothing to do with the group or its members.

In the remainder of this chapter, I will explore a few of the general processes whereby integral and incidental affect impinge upon social judgments of the members of outgroups. In doing so, I will endeavor to go beyond the global distinction between positive and negative affect and consider how qualitatively different emotional states (specifically, happiness, sadness, anger, and anxiety) are related to stereotyping. I will first describe a heuristic model of the stereotyping process that is compatible with several more specific theoretical accounts. Then I will summarize evidence bearing on some of the ways that different emotional states might affect each stage of processing. Finally, I will consider several of the most interesting issues that remain for future research.

Stereotyping in Social Judgment: Stereotypes as Judgmental Heuristics

Although stereotyping is generally considered to be a simplification strategy employed by the social perceiver to facilitate her interactions with a complex social environment, a complete theoretical account of stereotyping and discrimination would have to be fairly complex. Such an account is beyond the scope of this chapter. Instead, only a few of the most central components involved in stereotyping will be examined.

When confronted with an intergroup situation, broadly defined, the social perceiver must first activate stereotypic input in long-term memory if the stereotypes are to have any impact on her social judgments. Devine (1989) has provided evidence that common stereotypes are activated automatically when members of the stereotyped group are encountered. When such input is perceived as relevant to a judgment to be made, it provides the initial basis for a discriminatory judgment. However, in most situations there is other information relevant to the judgment, so the next stage is to achieve some sort of integration of abstract (stereotypic) and concrete evidence. Two extreme patterns of response can be identified at this stage. First, the social perceiver may choose to rely primarily or exclusively on the stereotypic input in rendering a judgment, termed a heuristic strategy (Bodenhausen & Wyer, 1985; Chaiken, Liberman, & Eagly, 1989). When this "top-down" strategy is dominant, other available information may be only superficially and selectively processed in an effort to find corroboration for the stereotypic judgment (Bodenhausen, 1988). At the other extreme, the social perceiver may choose to rely primarily or exclusively on the concrete, factual data at hand, carefully assessing and integrating its implications to form a judgment. This "bottom-up" strategy (or "systematic," in the terminology of Chaiken, 1980) would tend to minimize the impact of stereotypic inputs. Many contemporary theorists envision a continuum of social information processing strategies defined by similar extremes (cf. Chaiken et al., 1989; Fazio, 1990; Fiske & Neuberg, 1990; Petty & Cacioppo, 1986).

The pioneers of cognitive psychology determined that systematic, data-driven processing is limited in two fundamental ways. First, it requires effort that people are often not willing to expend. Simon (1967) aptly characterized humans as "satisficers" rather than optimizers. Given appropriate motivation, people may rely less on stereotypes and seek a more data-based judgment (Fiske & Neuberg, 1990), but that may not be a dominant tendency. A second important limitation involves the finite capacity of working memory. Miller (1956) set that capacity at about seven chunks of information under normal conditions. Even highly motivated individuals may fall back on simpler, heuristic strategies if their capacity to engage in more systematic processing is limited by distraction (Petty, Wells, & Brock, 1976) or information overload (Pratto & Bargh, 1991; Rothbart, Fulero, Jensen, Howard, & Birrell, 1978). Moreover, complex tasks may require more capacity than is ordinarily available, leading to a greater reliance upon simplification strategies (Bodenhausen & Lichtenstein, 1987; Branscombe & Cohen, 1991). These considerations imply that processing will become more heuristic (stereotypic) as motivation and processing capacity diminish (cf. Chaiken *et al.*, 1989; Petty & Cacioppo, 1986).

Another essential component of the stereotyping process is the generation of a response. This involves taking the results of the processing at earlier stages and transforming them into a "final" overt judgment. This could involve a rather direct translation from a subjective computation to whatever response language is required. Subjects aware of a possible stereotypic bias in their judgments may disguise or distort their overt responses in order to avoid the appearance of prejudice (Gaertner & Dovidio, 1986). Furthermore, those individuals with a sincere concern about prejudice may also engage in a process that could be described as self-censorship. Devine (1989, 1990) has shown that individuals who are low in prejudice toward a social group are likely to try actively to modify their thoughts about group members in order to correct for possible stereotypic biases. This kind of process could of course be occurring prior to the response generation phase as well. However, such activity only occurs when there is sufficient processing capacity. Constraints on processing capacity may therefore not only encourage initial reliance upon stereotypic preconceptions, they may also discourage corrective actions that might be undertaken to offset possible biases.

This brief sketch of the stereotyping process is clearly incomplete. It neglects numerous important issues (e.g., the nature of stereotypic knowledge structures) that a comprehensive theory of stereotyping must address. Instead, it emphasizes the components that will be considered in more detail below, in light of the possible impact emotional states may have on them.

Emotional Arousal and Processing Capacity

Arousal plays a central role in many theories of emotion (e.g., Mandler, 1990) and even the most cognitively oriented theorists acknowledge that "the physiological concomitants of emotional experiences are of indisputable importance" (Ortony *et al.*, 1988, p. 12). Thus, a useful place to begin considering the impact of emotions on the use of stereotypes in social judgment may be with their physiological aspects. It is generally accepted that a nonmonotonic relationship exists between arousal and performance, such that performance and the cognitive systems serving performance are optimized at moderate levels of arousal but impaired at either extreme (cf. Kahneman, 1973). The cortical effects of arousal are diffuse and therefore can exert pervasive effects across a number of performance dimensions (Derryberry, 1988; Gur *et al.*, 1988). There are a number of reasons to suspect that low or high levels of arousal may also be related to the use of stereotypes in judgment. Arousal levels are related to processing efficiency (e.g., Colquhoun, 1971; Humphreys, & Revelle, 1984). Too little arousal may limit alertness and motivation, while too much arousal may prove to be distracting and may create biological interference limiting processing capacity and efficiency. At these nonoptimal levels, arousal may encourage reliance on simpler, and perhaps more dominant response strategies.

There is, in fact, evidence showing that both extremes of arousal are associated with a greater reliance on stereotypic (simplified) response strategies. In a recent study (Bodenhausen, 1990), I demonstrated that reliance upon social stereotypes is greater at the lower portions of the circadian arousal cycle. Previous research has established time-of-day differences in mental efficiency (Colquhoun, 1971) that can be related to regular, circadian fluctuations in autonomic arousal. To discover whether these fluctuations might be related to stereotyping, subjects who were identified as "morning types" or "evening types" were given social judgment tasks at different times of the day. In one task, for example, they were asked to judge the likelihood of guilt in an allegation of student misconduct. Some students were identified as members of social groups that were stereotypically associated with the alleged infraction; thus, stereotypes provided a basis for a quick judgment of guilt in such conditions. The judgments of morning types were found to be more stereotypic when rendered in the afternoon or evening, while the judgments of the evening types were more stereotypic when rendered in the morning. Arousal deficits and associated deficits in alertness and processing capacity seemed to encourage stereotypic judgments.

At the other end of the spectrum, Kim and Baron (1988) found that heightened arousal (created by exercise) led to a greater tendency to show a stereotypic pattern of responses in the expectancy-based illusory correlation paradigm (Hamilton & Rose, 1980). In this task, participants are presented with words paired with occupational labels. In some cases, a word is stereotypically associated with the occupation, but this type of association is constructed so as to be no more frequent than other associations. If the frequency of the stereotypic associations is overestimated by participants, this indicates the operation of stereotypic expectancies in the stream of information processing. Highly aroused subjects were more likely to show this kind of superficial, stereotypic thinking (see Sanbonmatsu & Kardes, 1988, for an analogous finding in a persuasion context). In line with many prominent theorists (e.g., Broadbent, 1971; Easterbrook, 1959; Hasher & Zacks, 1979), these studies suggest that too much or too little arousal decreases cognitive capacity and increases reliance upon simpler, more dominant response strategies.

In order to understand the effects of emotional arousal on stereotyping processes, it is important to come to grips with the issue of whether and how different emotions differ in their autonomic, hormonal, and other somatovisceral manifestations. It seems fairly clearly established now that there are differences in the physiological patterns associated with different emotions. Ekman, Levenson, & Friesen (1983) and others have provided compelling psychophysiological evidence to this effect (see Frijda, 1986; McNaughton, 1989). If different emotions produce different patterns of somatic activity, it may be necessary to consider the effects of discrete emotional states on information processing and social judgment separately.

Negative Emotions

Although negative affect comes in a lamentably large number of varieties, I will focus on anger/rage, anxiety/fear, and sadness. As noted previously, anxiety and anger are particularly noteworthy because they are integral to many intergroup situations. Biological evidence summarized by Henry (1986) indicates that anger and anxiety/fear, although distinguishable, are rather similar in their physiological manifestations, but both are rather different from sadness. In terms of limbic activation, both anger and fear primarily involve the amygdala, and both are associated with an increase in pulse, blood pressure, and secretion of epinephrine. Hebb (1946) noted that "fear and rage are notoriously related . . . [both involving] disruption of coordinated cerebral activity" (p. 273). Sadness, on the other hand, primarily involves the hippocampus and produces comparatively few marked changes in neuroendocrine responses. Shields (1984) provides evidence that these patterns translate fairly directly into subjectively felt body states. In particular, both anxious and angry subjects report a perception of greater cardiac activity and a general sense of restlessness. This is not true of the sad subjects, who generally do not report symptoms of elevated arousal.

These considerations raise the possibility that physiological changes associated with anger and anxiety may have disruptive effects on performance, leading people to utilize simpler, less resource-demanding strategies. The use of stereotypes in social judgment would constitute one such strategy. Sadness, however, appears not to involve elevations of arousal and may therefore not produce performance disruptions. Later I will present evidence relating to the role of anger, anxiety, and sadness on the tendency toward less systematic thinking. This evidence speaks to the prediction that sadness may differ from anger and anxiety in terms of the types of cognitive strategies it is likely to engender, but in many cases it does not compel an interpretation of this phenomenon in terms of arousal or related neuroendocrine phenomena. Discussions of other psychological mechanisms that might explain these patterns of data will be considered subsequently.

The idea that angry people are not likely to be thinking rationally is certainly commonplace. Many centuries ago, Virgil wrote that "anger carries the mind away." Contemporary theorists have similarly postulated that anger is associated with quick, heuristic processing strategies rather than careful, systematic ones (e.g., Kuhl, 1983). Yet, surprisingly little direct evidence is available bearing on this intuitively appealing hypothesis. On the other hand, there is abundant evidence available concerning the disruptive effects of anxiety and fear on performance. Darke (1988) showed that anxiety reduces both the storage capacity and the processing capacity of working memory. Gur *et al.* (1988) provided insight into the psychophysiological processes involved in anxiety. They recorded regional cerebral blood flow (rCBF), a measure of cortical activity, as well as anxiety and performance on a cognitive task. High levels of anxiety were associated with reduced performance and reduced rCBF (performance and rCBF being positively related). They conclude that the psychophysiological effects of anxiety are "diffuse . . . [suggesting] that the adverse effects of anxiety may be pervasive across aspects of human performance" (p. 398). In a more social psychological context, anxiety has been shown to promote less systematic thinking in the processing of persuasive appeals (Baron, Burgess, Kao, & Logan, 1990).

A good deal of research has also examined the impact of sadness on performance. If the impact of emotions on performance is driven by the arousal component of emotional experience, we might not expect to observe negative effects of sadness, since it is not associated with marked changes in autonomic arousal levels. In much of this research, sad subjects in fact do *not* show performance deficits. For example, Sinclair (1988) had subjects complete a performance appraisal task after experiencing a mood induction. He reports that sad subjects showed the least halo bias and the greatest accuracy. Similarly, Gotlib, McLachlan, & Katz (1988) found sad individuals to be more systematic and "evenhanded" in the information-processing strategies they deployed in a visual attention task. Finally, Bless, Bohner, Schwarz, & Strack (1990) reported that sad subjects processed a persuasive message more systematically, tending to scrutinize the message content more carefully. On the other hand, Ellis and Ashbrook (1988) report research in which depressed mood states impaired memory performance. These impairments were theoretically attributed to the tendency of depressed individuals to ruminate about the conditions provoking their sadness, thereby reducing their capacity for other tasks. Contrary to the implications of this view, however, Ellis, Seibert, & Herbert (1990, Experiment 2) observed no difference in the proportion of negative thoughts generated by depressed versus neutral subjects in a thought-listing task after engaging in a cognitive task. Whether or not sadness impairs performance may be a matter of degree. Profound sadness or depression may in fact be characterized by physiological conditions that inhibit the ability to engage in sustained, effortful processing, and by disruptive negative rumination, while milder forms of sadness may produce very little interference with concomitant cognitive tasks.

In summary, there is compelling evidence that high levels of anxiety reduce cognitive capacity and impair the performance of tasks that draw substantially on cognitive resources. Under these conditions, people often adopt simpler, more heuristic processing strategies. Similar effects can be hypothesized for anger, but there is not much in the way of direct evidence for this proposition. Sadness, with its comparatively torpid pattern of physiological activity, has often been empirically associated with more systematic and thoughtful information-processing strategies.

Positive Emotions

Although there are a number of different types of positive affect that could be identified, the prototypic positive emotion is undoubtedly happiness. Concepts such as contentment, serenity, joy, and elation seem to be variations on the same central theme. In fact, the major distinction that one might make among these terms is the level of arousal that is conveyed by them, with contentment and serenity being fairly low in arousal and joy and elation being fairly high. There is physiological evidence that happiness is accompanied by increased autonomic arousal (see, e.g., Henry, 1986). If the happiness experienced is sufficiently arousing, then it might be expected to have similar effects on cognitive capacity and information-processing strategies as those attributed to anxiety and anger. Aside from the arousal associated with it, happiness may also reduce cognitive capacity because it may trigger greater rumination on the life events that evoked the pleasant state. In an effort to maintain their mood, happy people may keep thinking happy thoughts, leaving fewer resources to be devoted to other tasks. Evidence consistent with the view that happiness limits systematic thinking will be presented here; alternative interpretations of these findings will be considered later.

A number of studies support the proposition that happiness leads to less systematic styles of thought. In one of the most influential of these studies, Isen, Means, Patrick, and Nowicki (1982) showed that happy individuals are more likely to rely on simplistic response strategies and produce erroneous judgments as a result. Specifically, happy people were prone to produce judgments that were biased by the well-known availability heuristic (Tversky & Kahneman, 1974). In persuasion situations, happy people seem to be less attentive to the substance of the arguments being advanced and instead tend to focus on the relatively superficial, heuristic cues available (Bless et al., 1990; Mackie & Worth, 1989; Worth & Mackie, 1987). Happy people generally seem to respond more quickly but less accurately, indicative of a heuristic rather than systematic strategy (Isen & Means, 1983) and consistent with the observation that phasic increases in arousal decrease reaction time but increase error rates (Derryberry, 1988). Forgas (1989) found a similar pattern, but with an important qualification: positive mood produced faster and less accurate judgments only when the outcome of the task was not personally relevant. Taken together, these results imply that happiness produces a tendency to rely on simpler, more heuristic strategies in social judgment unless one's own welfare will be affected by the quality of one's judgment.

It should be noted that if arousal is an important component in the processing biases seen among happy people, then less arousing forms of positive affect (e.g., serenity) should be unlikely to produce these effects. In line with this proposition, Clark (1981, described in Clark, 1982) reported that low-arousal positive affect produced no appreciable biases in social judgments, but higher arousal positive affect did produce a biased pattern. Positive affect involving higher levels of arousal, then, may be hypothesized to have similar effects to those negative emotions that also involve arousal.

Emotion and Cognitive Motivation

Besides having possible effects on cognitive capacity, emotional states can also have considerable impact on the motivation of organisms, a point made perhaps most forcefully by Tomkins (1984). Given that motivation is a major determinant of the processing strategies used in social cognition, it becomes essential to consider the motivational impact of the various emotional states, particularly with regard to the tendency to exert cognitive effort. In the words of Tomkins, "the affect system is. . .the primary motivational system because without its amplification, nothing else matters, and with its amplification, anything else *can* matter. . .it lends its power to memory, to perception, to thought, and to action no less than to the drives" (p. 164). If different emotional states are characteristically associated with differing motivation to engage in systematic, effortful thought, then they have another clear route whereby they can affect the propensity to stereotype others.

Negative Emotions

Schwarz (1990) has provided a provocative analysis of the motivational impact of affective states on information processing. He begins with the fundamental assumption that any particular emotion is likely to trigger processing strategies that are adaptive and functional for the types of environmental situations that elicit the emotion in question. At a global level, negative affect is associated with displeasure and distress and signals a need for remediation of some kind. Under these circumstances, it behooves the person experiencing negative affect to engage in effective problem solving, which may necessitate effortful and systematic, rather than quick and heuristic information-processing strategies. Weary (1990) reviews evidence supporting a similar argument concerning the processing strategies of depressives (specifically, mildly depressed college students). She argues that their sadness is often attributable to their experience with uncontrollability and uncertainty, leading them to be motivated to systematically seek out social information in the hope of restoring a sense of control.

Schwarz also provides a more detailed analysis of different varieties of negative affect and their likely effects on social cognition. Drawing upon Higgins's (1987) distinction between agitated and dejected emotions, he asserts that there is a fundamental asymmetry in the cognitive demands (and consequences) of different types of negative affect. Agitated emotions (such as fear) involve a threat of negative outcomes. The focus of effective problem solving in such contexts is on the avoidance of the negative outcome. To be successful in this endeavor, a person must identify and block all possible paths to the undesired outcome, a feat which presumably would require a fair amount of careful and systematic thought. Dejected emotions (such as sadness and disappointment), however, involve a lack of positive outcomes. The focus of effective problem solving in this context is on approaching and acquiring such outcomes. To be successful in this case, a person needs only to identify a single path to the desired outcome, which requires some careful thought, but presumably less than what is required under the avoidance motivation created in agitated conditions. This analysis implies that anger and fear/anxiety states may actually engender more systematic and careful thought than does sadness, in direct contrast to the implications of the arousal and performance literature previously described.

In trying to understand the differences between Schwarz's functional analysis of negative affect and the implications of the arousal perspective, the distinction between integral and incidental affect may become particularly important. When one is confronted with cognitive tasks within the same environmental setting and circumstances that have produced negative affect, the deployment of more analytic strategies should in fact be functional. However, when the current tasks are not directly relevant to the environmental circumstances that have produced negative affect (i.e., when the affect is incidental), devoting particular effort to the tasks will be unlikely to remediate the original problematic condition. So an important question that arises is whether more systematic processing strategies are utilized only when remediation of the negative affect is possible or if they are generally used even in incidental tasks. If processing resources are being used up by the individual's ruminations about possible remediation tactics, processing resources available for devotion to incidental tasks may be substantially reduced, leading to more heuristic judgment strategies in these tasks. This may be more true of agitated than dejected states. Thus, the predictions made on the basis of the arousal properties of affect may be complemented rather than contradicted by Schwarz's functional analysis, at least in the case of incidental affect.

Another issue that might profitably be borne in mind concerns the type of adaptive response system that is most likely to be activated by different varieties of negative affect. Although Schwarz's analysis of the cognitive asymmetry of approach and avoidance motivation is intuitively appealing, it might be argued that the most functional response strategy in the case of emotions like fear and anger is not carefully deliberative cognition at all. These emotions typically arise within agonistic contexts, and the most adaptive problem-solving strategies in such situations often must be invoked quickly and without much mental reflection, as in the well-known fight-or-flight response system (Scott, 1980). Situations that evoke sadness may typically be less immediately threatening, and may therefore allow for a more cognitive sort of problem solving.

Positive Emotions

Schwarz (1990) has also considered the effects of positive emotion on one's motivation to engage in systematic thought. In contrast to negative affect, positive affect signals that things are going well for the person experiencing it. Under such circumstances, there is no pressing need for extensive cognitive effort. Instead, more creative, intuitive, and heuristic strategies may be preferred. Thus, in line with predictions offered earlier, Schwarz's analysis links happiness to faster, easier, more impulsive, and less accurate response strategies (in situations where an objective standard of accuracy can be defined, e.g., Isen *et al.*, 1982). One particularly interesting source of support for this view comes from the literature on mood and helping behavior (Schaller & Cialdini, 1990). When confronted with a potential helping situation, sad individuals seem to engage in a thoughtful cost/benefit analysis in deciding whether or not to help, while happy individuals act more impulsively.

The literature cited earlier in support of the prediction that happiness may produce lower quality judgments can in most cases be explained equally well by accounts based on global motivation as by those involving cognitive capacity. For example, the fact that happy people are less likely to scrutinize persuasive messages and instead rely on heuristic cues such as source expertise in forming their opinions could be plausibly ascribed either to a lack of motivation to engage in effortful analysis of the message or to some sort of capacity limitation created by the positive emotion. As Schwarz, Bless, & Bohner (1991) note, the two interpretations generate identical predictions in many situations. However, it is possible to create situations in which the two viewpoints generate different predictions. Bless *et al.* (1990) showed that happy subjects *can* scrutinize arguments if explicitly instructed to do, suggesting that they have the mental resources to do so, but simply choose not to. This supports the motivational view. Along these lines, it is interesting to recall Forgas's (1989) finding that happy subjects only showed a "fast and loose" response style when the outcome of their judgment task was not personally relevant, again suggesting that given proper motivation, happy people can be more systematic. In contrast, Mackie and Worth (1989) showed that happy subjects could scrutinize persuasive messages just as elaborately as neutral mood subjects *if* they are given more time to do so, but not under more time-limited conditions. This suggests that happy people are in fact willing to engage in cognitive effort but they have difficulty doing so because of capacity limitations. These limits can sometimes only be overcome if additional processing resources (in this case, more time) are made available. Given these patterns of results, it is probably wisest to conclude that there is some truth to both positions; happiness is likely both to reduce the capacity for systematic, elaborative thought and to reduce the motivation for such mental activity.

The arguments that I have advanced to this point can be concisely summarized. First, I argued that stereotypic responses to outgroup members can be considered to constitute a heuristic strategy that allows for a relatively quick and easy judgment or behavioral response. In line with the thinking of many contemporary theorists, I further argued that this sort of simplified processing strategy should be utilized to a greater and greater extent as processing capacity and motivation diminish. I then reviewed recent evidence showing that some types of emotional experience, in particular anger, fear, and happiness, are likely to create just these kinds of motivation and capacity deficits. Other emotions, sadness in particular, may not have this kind of effect. It follows directly that anger, fear, and happiness should therefore increase the social perceiver's tendency to rely upon social stereotypes in making judgments, whereas sadness should not. Two aspects of this claim are particularly noteworthy. First, because outgroup stereotypes are often negative, this hypothesis implies that happiness may often produce more negative judgments of outgroup members (who are expected to be judged in negative, stereotypic terms). This contradicts intuition as well as the well-established mood congruency phenomenon. It also contradicts traditional views of the relationship between emotion and intergroup relations, which focus on negative emotions as the stuff and substance of stereotyping. A second intriguing implication of this view is that happy and angry subjects may behave more similarly than do sad and angry subjects. I will now turn to some initial empirical evidence bearing on these ideas.

Empirical Studies of Emotion and Stereotyping

The possibility that anxiety may increase reliance on stereotypes was tested directly in an interesting way by Baron, Burgess, Kao, & Logan (1990, Experiment 1). In this study, individuals awaiting dental treatment in a clinic (in some cases with a novice dentist-in-training) were given the illusory correlation task described earlier. Subjects in the high-fear condition were significantly more likely to exhibit the illusory correlation effect, a sign of stereotypic processing. Note that in this experiment, the anxiety was incidental to the task, showing that anxiety can increase reliance on social stereotypes even when it is not elicited by the outgroup in question. Another study using the illusory correlation paradigm was conducted by Mackie *et al.* (1989). Subjects were in this case either made happy by viewing a humorous film clip, made sad by viewing a depressing film clip, or were left in a neutral mood by viewing an informational film clip. Then, in the "main" study they were given the standard illusory correlation materials. Results were only partially in line with the predictions sketched above. Relative to controls, happy participants did show a greater stereotypic bias, but only when the judgments concerned negative group attributes. Also as expected, sad participants showed less stereotypic bias when their judgments concerned negative group attributes; however, they did not do so when they concerned positive group attributes.

Another recent study (Bodenhausen & Kramer, 1990a) directly examined the proposed effects of happiness on stereotyping, as well as simultaneously considering the alleged differential effects of anger and sadness. In this study, we had participants report to a laboratory for a study of emotional memories. After being greeted by an experimenter, they were told that due to the brevity of the study, it was being piggy-backed with another experiment. The experimenter explained that the first task involved having the participants recall and write about emotional events from their lives. It was explained that the researchers wanted to build a large database concerning the emotional experiences of college students. In actuality, the task served as an emotion induction procedure. In the experimental conditions, participants were asked to recall and write down an event that had made them extremely happy, extremely sad, or extremely angry. In a control condition, they were asked to write down a description of the mundane events of the previous day. The effectiveness of this sort of task in eliciting the intended emotion is implied by Frijda's (1988) "Law of Conservation of

Emotional Momentum: Emotional events retain their power to elicit emotions indefinitely" (p. 354). It has also been empirically substantiated by Strack, Schwarz, & Gschneidinger (1985) and others. We followed Strack *et al.*'s procedures for optimizing the induction by emphasizing that participants recall the event as vividly as possible and describe *how* it happened rather than *why* it happened. After participants spent about 15 minutes on this task, the experimenter collected the forms, thanked them, and left.

At this point another experimenter took over, administered a new consent form, and explained to the participants that the ostensibly unrelated second study concerned students' reactions to the behavioral transgressions of their fellow students. The task was the same one used by Bodenhausen (1990, Experiment 2). Participants were told that they would be reading about cases of alleged student misconduct and would be asked to make judgments about them. A booklet was passed out to each participant. The first page was a "Participants Characteristics Survey" which requested demographic information and, more importantly, which contained a check of the affect induction procedure imbedded within it. This check revealed the manipulations to be effective, producing significantly higher levels of the target emotion (but not the other emotions) in each case. Then participants read one of two cases. One involved a case of cheating and the other involved a physical attack on a fellow student. Half of the participants were given a case in which the offender was identified as a member of a group stereotypically associated with the offense in question (student athletes, in the case of cheating, and Hispanics, in the case of aggressive attack). In the cheating case, the student defendant was either explicitly identified as a student athlete or was not. In the assault case, the accused was either given an Hispanic name ("Roberto Garcia") or a more nondescript one ("Robert Garner"). After reading over the details of the case, which were ambiguous in their implications but identical across stereotype conditions, participants made a number of judgments, most importantly a determination of guilt.

Perceptions of the accused student's guilt showed the expected interaction pattern. Happy and angry people tended to view the case in more stereotypic terms. Those considering a stereotyped defendant saw him as significantly more likely to be guilty than those considering the same evidence when applied to a nonstereotyped defendant. This pattern did not hold for sad or neutral-mood participants, who did not appear to discriminate between stereotyped versus nonstereotyped targets. The happy and angry participants also rated the defendant to be significantly more likely to be guilty than did those in a sad or neutral mood. There was no main effect of mood on judgments; rather, the influence of mood interacted with stereotype activation to produce more negative judgments only when stereotyped targets were rated by happy or angry perceivers.

These findings are quite consistent with the claim that happiness and anger increase heuristic responding in social judgment, while sadness does not, but they do not speak directly to the underlying mechanisms. It could be, for instance, that it is the arousal or other physiological/cortical concomitants of happiness and anger that reduced cognitive capacity or impeded working memory operations. These emotions might also be associated with more task-irrelevant cognitions, which would also serve to reduce cognitive capacity for task-related processing. It may be that the mood induction procedure resulted in calling memories into awareness that were hard to put out of mind again, at least in the case of happiness and anger. That this would not also be true of sad persons may seem problematic, but Wenzlaff, Wegner, and Roper (1988) have shown that one thing differentiating depressed and nondepressed individuals is the ability of the nondepressed people to distract themselves from sad thoughts. Perhaps our participants, most of whom would presumably qualify as normal, devoted more effort to the judgment task as a way of banishing the unwanted sad memories from the center stage of consciousness. It is also possible that happy and angry people may just be less motivated to engage in more effortful processing, perhaps because quicker, more impulsive strategies are preferable under such conditions. Each of these interpretations is interesting in its own right.

We undertook a second study (Bodenhausen & Kramer, 1990b) with two major objectives in mind. First, we wanted to replicate the most provocative of these findings—that happiness can promote more negative, stereotypic judgments. Second, we wanted to shed more light on the processes at work in this effect. In the second study, we adopted a very different mood induction procedure. Instead of having subjects recall and reexperience emotion-laden events from their lives, we had them engage in a facial posing task. A good deal of evidence supports the proposition that contraction of the zygomaticus and related muscles into a smile produces the experience of happiness (Adelman & Zajonc, 1989; Laird, 1984; Strack, Martin & Stepper, 1988). Contraction of appropriate facial muscles produces not just a diffuse pleasant or unpleasant feeling, but engenders subjective emotional experiences that are specific to the differing types of emotions (Duclos et al., 1989). Interestingly, Ekman et al. (1983) found that a mood induction task involving appropriate contraction of the smile musculature was even more successful in inducing the characteristic pattern of autonomic activity associated with happiness than was a memory-based induction procedure (see also Levenson, Ekman, & Friesen, 1990). This procedure seemed ideal for our purposes because it allowed us to create a state of happiness with the concomitant pattern of physiological activity but without simultaneously filling working memory with the cognitive content of a particular life episode. If the same pattern of results were to emerge with this induction procedure, it becomes less plausible to postulate that rumination about the particular life events triggering the affective state causes a greater tendency to use a quick, heuristic response strategy. Instead, this pattern would appear to be due to something more fundamental about the experience of happiness that reduces cognitive capacity and/or motivation.

Because of the potential demand effects that might be created by explicit instructions to smile, frown, or scowl, researchers have developed more clandestine ways of getting people to engage in the desired facial pose. One popular strategy is simply to instruct participants in terms of specific muscle contractions, never mentioning terms like "smile" or "frown." We adopted this procedure with the following cover story. We explained to our participants that we were studying the "neurological basis of cognitive-motor coordination." To do this, we told the participants that we were having people engage in a number of different motor and cognitive tasks concurrently. We claimed that each task would involve different brain structures and that we wanted "to see how harmoniously these structures can work together." In the "happy" conditions, the participants were given explicit instructions about facial muscle contractions to produce the pattern characteristic of happiness. They were never told to smile but were instead asked to contract certain muscles that would "stimulate" the part of the brain involved in the control of facial muscles. In the control conditions, they were asked to contract their nondominant hand into a loose fist pose. This was expected to have no detectable effect on mood.

While maintaining these particular contractions (for several minutes), participants were asked to engage in a decision making task—the "Students' Court" task used in the previous experiment. As before, they completed a disguised affect induction check and then read about the alleged misbehavior of a college student and judged the likelihood of the student's guilt. Also as before, half of these cases involved a stereotyped target, while the other half did not. After finishing the case, participants ceased the muscle contraction and answered a questionnaire concerning the perceived difficulty of the concomitant tasks, in line with the cover story. Prior to debriefing they were probed for suspicions; none of the participants had even a vaguely accurate idea about the nature of the study, and virtually all of them accepted the cover story at face value.

The manipulation checks revealed a pattern of happiness ratings that was completely comparable to that obtained with the memory-based emotion induction procedure, with people in the smiling condition reporting significantly higher levels of happiness. Moreover, participants reported the two muscle contraction tasks (face vs. left hand) to be equally (and not particularly) distracting during the judgment task. Most importantly, they exhibited just the same pattern of case judgments as that reported in the previous study. Happy people judged stereotypic offenders to be significantly more likely to be guilty than nonstereotypic offenders; neutral mood participants did not. Taken together, the two studies show that happy people are more likely to fall back on social stereotypes in making judgments of outgroup members. Moreover, the second study lets us rule out one interpretation of this pattern. The greater reliance on stereotypes is most likely not due to rumination among happy persons on the events that produced the happy state.

These few studies only begin to explore the issues raised in the present consideration of the role of affect in stereotyping. In the remainder of the chapter, I will sketch out some of the most important avenues for future research and attempt at the same time to specify additional hypotheses that merit empirical investigation.

Issues for Future Research

In an attempt to be systematic in my consideration of issues on the agenda for future research, I will consider three broad categories: mediating processes, individual differences, and situational moderators. The nature of many of these considerations is foreshadowed by Scherer's (1984) observation that "whether emotional processes interrupt, disturb, or adaptively support cognitive or behavioral sequences depends on the specific situation, the nature of the task, the degree of arousal, and other factors" (p. 295).

Mediating Processes

As noted above, the fact that happiness, anger, and anxiety lead to more stereotypic judgments can be explained by reference to a number of different mediating processes. A challenging issue of obvious importance, then, becomes identifying the conditions under which the various processes are necessary or sufficient to produce these effects. Perhaps at the top of the agenda should be a determination of the role of arousal per se. If arousal proves to be of critical importance, then affect intensity may be the variable that should concern researchers most. Given the nonmonotonic nature of arousal's impact on performance, another question of importance is: how much is too much? Perhaps a little emotional arousal will facilitate more systematic and thorough processing while too much inhibits it. Of course laboratory mood inductions are, for the most part, relatively mild. Occasionally, creative researchers may find ways to get a really strong affective response out of research participants, such as Ax (1953), who led subjects to believe that an incompetent experimenter would be hooking them up to a defective apparatus which they observed occasionally emitting electrical sparks. For the most part, however, affective responses in the laboratory can be considered to be less intense than many of the responses elicited by real life. Given that this is so, the clear impact of the happiness and anger inductions used by Bodenhausen and Kramer (1990a,b) may indicate that even only moderately intense emotional experiences can have these effects.

It is still unclear whether it is the motivational or capacity aspects of emotional experience (or both) that tend to produce less systematic, more stereotypic thought, and it is also unclear exactly how affect-related motivational or capacity deficits enter the judgment process. Do they lead people to rely primarily on stereotypes to make judgments and to process other material only superficially and selectively (cf. Bodenhausen, 1988)? Another interesting possibility is that these deficits limit people's ability to engage in active self-censorship. As implied by the work of Devine (1989) and Devine and Monteith (Chapter 14, this volume), perhaps people automatically rely on stereotypes in making judgments, but many people are at least somewhat aware of their bias and take steps to adjust or correct for it. When processing capacity or motivation is limited, such individuals may not be able or willing to engage in this corrective action. An equally important question is how affective states are related to the initial activation of stereotypic beliefs. Clark (1982) has shown that arousal cues arousal-related material in memory, so one fairly obvious prediction is that emotional arousal, especially the negative emotional arousal that may abound in intergroup situations, will be more likely to trigger aversively arousing stereotypic beliefs about outgroup members (e.g., that they are dangerous, dishonest, violent, etc.). Perhaps less obvious is the question of whether emotional arousal might sometimes be sufficiently intense to disrupt any activation of stereotypic content in the first place. Well-learned, salient stereotypes may be automatically activated upon exposure to pertinent group members, as Devine (1989) claims (also see Fazio, 1989), but the activation of less accessible stereotypes may sometimes be undercut by emotional arousal (cf. Gilbert & Hixon, 1991). In such cases, strong emotional reactions may actually prevent reliance on stereotypes (although people may still opt for some other quick response strategy, if accessible). These and many other issues concerning mediating processes await further exploration.

Individual Differences

Social psychologists often tend to focus on generalities across individuals, but at least two classes of individual difference variables may be particularly important to investigate, as they may help shed light on the mediating processes at work, as well as possibly define subsets of people who are more or less prone to these effects. One type of measure concerns interindividual differences in stereotypic beliefs and their cognitive accessibility. In an extensive program of research, Fazio (1986, 1989) has documented that the extent and nature of an attitude's impact on perception, cognition, and behavior are a function of the attitude's accessibility in memory. This should also be true of attitudes and beliefs about social groups, and it has clear implications for the heuristic view of stereotyping. A particular stereotype (e.g., that student athletes are prone to cheating) can only serve as an effective judgmental heuristic if it is readily accessible. Many social stereotypes are commonly known and widely shared, but such beliefs are rarely universal, and some of them must vary considerably in their accessibility across individuals. If one could establish that some individuals had highly accessible stereotypes whereas another group did not, then very different predictions would be made about the impact of motivational or processing capacity deficits caused by emotional experiences (or anything else). The stereotype would be readily available as a heuristic cue for one group but not the other, who would be forced to seek some other basis for quick or easy responding. If emotions like happiness or anger produced more stereotypic judgments in the first group but not the second, it would clearly support the idea that these states encourage reliance upon stereotypes because of their heuristic value.

The chronic tendency to experience positive or negative emotional states generally (Watson & Clark, 1984) as well as specific types of emotion like anger (Novaco, 1975) and anxiety (Spielberger, Gorsuch, & Luschene, 1970) may provide the basis for a more dispositional link between affect and cognition. A recent study by Broadbent and Broadbent (1988) revealed that attentional biases associated with anxiety were most reliably found among those with trait rather than state anxiety. They interpret this to mean that the type of attentional bias they investigated "must be to some extent due to lasting personality characteristics. It is not something that happens to everybody when in a temporary state" (p. 165). This suggests that individuals who chronically experience certain types of affect should be likely to show the corresponding tendency with regard to stereotyping (i.e., greater stereotyping among anxious, angry, and happy individuals but not sad individuals) even without any mood induction procedure. Perhaps the most provocative prediction that can be derived from this reasoning is that chronically happy people should show a greater degree of stereotyping than chronically sad people.

Situational Moderators

Finally, a number of situational moderators deserve consideration. For example, the affect–stereotyping research presented above focused on tasks that involve only vicarious contact with outgroup members (i.e., reading about them) in situations involving incidental affect. A number of different considerations arise in the case of real intergroup contact and the affect that is integral to such situations. Recall Schwarz's (1990) hypothesis that anger and fear may produce more cognitive effort, at least when such effort can potentially alleviate these negative states and restore a sense of control and security. In intergroup contact situations, the agitated negative affect experienced is quite relevant to the current task environment, so if Schwarz is right, we might observe more systematic, less heuristic thinking in such situations (but see Stephan & Stephan, 1985). On the other hand, the potential impairments due to arousal should still be present in such situations, so the results might parallel the findings of Baron *et al.* (1990) and Bodenhausen and Kramer (1990a), if these impairments are sufficient to trigger a greater reliance on stereotypes.

The effects of positive affect also may be different in vicarious versus direct intergroup contact. Most theorists believe that positive affect is essential to the success of intergroup contact (see Stephan & Brigham, 1985). Ironically, if a contact strategy attempts to create a happy, celebratory context for intergroup interaction, the research described above implies that this may only fuel the tendency to think shallowly and stereotypically about the outgroup. People may become cognitively lazy when happy, or they may experience a certain degree of capacity reduction for which they are unwilling to try to compensate. However, this is probably only true when the outcome of the current task is relatively inconsequential (Forgas, 1989). Fiske and her colleagues (see Fiske & Neuberg, 1990, for a summary) have shown that when personal interests are at stake, people become less likely to rely on global stereotypes and instead attend to the specifics of the concrete data at hand. In direct intergroup contact situations, the outcomes are often of immediate personal relevance, so happy people may be willing to exert the extra effort to think more systematically and presumably thereby secure positive outcomes for themselves.

These considerations raise the general question of how able people are to compensate for the motivation and/or capacity deficits created by emotional states. In one of the earliest investigations of mood effects on performance, Sullivan (1922) concluded that in most cases, the deleterious effects of extremes of mood on performance can in fact be overcome "by increasing the output of energy" (p. 9). By this she meant that emotional impediments to high-quality performance are not insurmountable. The situational (and personal) factors that promote a willingness and desire to work harder when in various emotional states are important issues for future research. Along these lines, Petty, Cacioppo, Sedikides, and Strathman (1988) offer a number of intriguing hypotheses about the different ways that emotion can affect cognitive responses in persuasion tasks in different situational contexts. This includes its effects on the extensiveness of information-processing activity (the primary focus here) as well as others. Most of their hypotheses can be directly extrapolated to the study of affect and stereotyping.

Conclusion

The heuristic view of stereotyping emphasizes that people use their oversimplified beliefs about social groups as a basis for responding to the members of those groups whenever they lack the desire or the ability to engage in more extensive thought about the individuals. The lack of such desire and/or ability may be common enough under most everyday life circumstances (cf. Fiske & Neuberg, 1990), and it appears that conditions of heightened emotional experience (in particular, anger, anxiety, and happiness) only serve to further reduce motivation and/or processing capacity. To obtain a clear view of how emotions serve to stimulate stereotyping, much more research will need to be conducted. Other types of emotions will need to be examined. Shame, disgust, and embarrassment are prime contenders, because they may be commonly experienced in intergroup contexts. The integration of affective and cognitive (and eventually, behavioral) processes in the analysis of intergroup relations promises to yield just as many rich rewards as it does in the study of human nature generally.

Acknowledgments

I am grateful to Linda Jackson, Norbert Schwarz, Bob Wyer, and especially Diane Mackie and Dave Hamilton for their helpful comments on an early draft of this chapter.

References

Adelman, P. K., & Zajonc, R. B. (1989). Facial efference and the experience of emotion. *Annual Review of Psychology, 40*, 249–280.

Ax, A. F. (1953). The physiological differentiation between fear and anger in humans. *Psychosomatic Medicine, 15*, 433–442.

Baron, R. S., Burgess, M. L., Kao, C. F., & Logan, H. (1990, May). *Fear and superficial social processing: Evidence of stereotyping and simplistic persuasion.* Paper presented at the annual convention of the Midwestern Psychological Association, Chicago.

Bless, H., Bohner, G., Schwarz, N., & Strack, F. (1990). Mood and persuasion: A cognitive response analysis. *Personality and Social Psychology Bulletin, 16*, 311–345.

Bodenhausen, G. V. (1988). Stereotypic biases in social decision making and memory: Testing process models of stereotype use. *Journal of Personality and Social Psychology, 55*, 726–737.

Bodenhausen, G. V. (1990). Stereotypes as judgmental heuristics: Evidence of circadian variations in discrimination. *Psychological Science, 1*, 319–322.

Bodenhausen, G. V., & Kramer, G. P. (1990a, June). *Affective states trigger stereotypic judgments.* Paper presented at the annual convention of the American Psychological Society, Dallas.

Bodenhausen, G. V., & Kramer, G. P. (1990b). *Affective states and the heuristic use of stereotypes in social judgment.* Unpublished manuscript, Michigan State University, East Lansing.

Bodenhausen, G. V., & Lichtenstein, M. (1987). Social stereotypes and information-processing strategies: The impact of task complexity. *Journal of Personality and Social Psychology, 52*, 871–880.

Bodenhausen, G. V., & Wyer, R. S., Jr. (1985). Effects of stereotypes on decision making and information-processing strategies. *Journal of Personality and Social Psychology, 48*, 262–282.

Branscombe, N. R., & Cohen, B. M. (1991). Motivation and complexity levels as determinants of heuristic use in social judgment. In J. Forgas (Ed.), *Emotion and social judgments.* (pp. 145–160). Oxford: Pergamon Press.

Broadbent, D. E. (1971). *Decision and stress.* London/New York: Academic Press.

Broadbent, D., & Broadbent, M. (1988). Anxiety and attentional bias: State and trait. *Cognition & Emotion, 2,* 165–184.

Chaiken, S. (1980). Heuristic versus systematic information processing and the use of source versus message cues in persuasion. *Journal of Personality and Social Psychology, 39,* 752–766.

Chaiken, S., Liberman, A., & Eagly, A. H. (1989). Heuristic and systematic information processing within and beyond the persuasion context. In J. Uleman & J. Bargh (Eds.), *Unintended thought* (pp. 212–252). New York: Guilford.

Clark, M. S. (1982). A role for arousal in the link between feeling states, judgments, and behavior. In M. S. Clark & S. T. Fiske (Eds.), *Affect and cognition: The seventeenth annual Carnegie symposium on cognition* (pp. 263–289). Hillsdale, NJ: Erlbaum.

Colquhoun, W. P. (1971). Circadian variations in mental efficiency. In W. P. Colquhoun (Ed.), *Biological rhythms and human performance.* London: Academic Press.

Darke, S. (1988). Anxiety and working memory capacity. *Cognition & Emotion, 2,* 145–154.

Derryberry, D. (1988). Emotional influences on evaluative judgments: Roles of arousal, attention, and spreading activation. *Motivation and Emotion, 12,* 23–55.

Devine, P. G. (1989). Stereotypes and prejudice: Their automatic and controlled components. *Journal of Personality and Social Psychology, 56,* 5–18.

Devine, P. G. (1990, May). *The role of inner conflict in the study of prejudice and prejudice reduction.* Paper presented at the annual convention of the Midwestern Psychological Association, Chicago.

Dijker, A. J. M. (1987). Emotional reactions to ethnic minorities. *European Journal of Social psychology, 17,* 305–325.

Duclos, S. E., Laird, J. D., Schneider, E., Sexter, M., Stern, L., & Van Lighten, O. (1989). Emotion-specific effects of facial expressions and postures on emotional experience. *Journal of Personality and Social psychology, 57,* 100–108.

Easterbrook, J. A. (1959). The effect of emotion on cue utilization and the organization of behavior. *Psychological Review, 66,* 183–201.

Ekman, P., Levenson, R. W., & Friesen, W. V. (1983). Autonomic nervous system activity distinguishes among emotions. *Science, 221,* 1208–1210.

Ellis, H. C., & Ashbrook, P. W. (1988). Resource allocation model of the effects of depressed mood states on memory. In K. Fiedler & J. Forgas (Eds.), *Affect, cognition, and social behavior* (pp. 25–43). Toronto: Hogrefe.

Ellis, H. C., Seibert, P. S., & Herbert, B. J. (1990). Mood state effects on thought listing. *Bulletin of the Psychonomic Society, 28,* 147–150.

Fazio, R. H. (1986). How do attitudes guide behavior? In R. M. Sorrentino & E. T. Higgins (Eds.), *Handbook of motivation and cognition* (Vol. 1, pp. 204–243). New York: Guilford.

Fazio, R. H. (1989). On the power and functionality of attitudes: The role of attitude accessibility. In A. R. Pratkanis, S. J. Breckler, & A. G. Greenwald (Eds.), *Attitude structure and function* (pp. 153–179). Hillsdale, NJ: Erlbaum.

Fazio, R. H., (1990). Multiple processes by which attitudes guide behavior: The MODE model as an integrative framework. In M. P. Zanna (Ed.), *Advances in experimental social psychology* (Vol. 23, pp. 75–109). Orlando, FL: Academic press.

Fiske, S. T., & Neuberg, S. L. (1990). A continuum of impression formation from category-based to individuating processes: Influences of information and motivation on attention and interpretation. In M. P. Zanna (Ed.), *Advances in experimental social psychology* (Vol. 23, pp. 1–74). Orlando, FL: Academic Press.

Forgas, J. P. (1989). Mood effects on decision making strategies. *Australian Journal of Psychology, 41,* 197–214.

Forgas, J. P., & Bower, G. H. (1988). Mood effects on social and personal judgments. In K. Fiedler & J. Forgas (Eds.), *Affect, cognition, and social behavior* (pp. 183–208). Toronto: Hogrefe.

Frijda, N. H. (1986). *The emotions.* Cambridge: Cambridge University Press.

Frijda, N. H. (1988). The laws of emotion. *American Psychologist, 43,* 348–358.

Gaertner, S. L., & Dovidio, J. F. (1986). The aversive form of racism. In J. F. Dovidio & S. L. Gaertner (Eds.), *Prejudice, discrimination, and racism* (pp. 61–89). Orlando, FL: Academic Press.

Gilbert, D. T., & Hixon, J. G. (1991). The trouble of thinking: Activation and application of stereotypic beliefs. *Journal of Personality and Social Psychology, 60,* 509–517.

Gotlib, I. H., McLachlan, A. L., & Katz, A. N. (1988). Biases in visual attention in depressed and nondepressed individuals. *Cognition & Emotion, 2,* 185–200.

Gur, R. C., Gur, R. E., Skolnick, B. E., Resnick, S. M., Silver, F. I., Chawluk, J., Muenz, L., Obrist, W. D., & Reivich, M. (1988). Effects of task difficulty on regional cerebral blood flow: Relationships with anxiety and performance. *Psychophysiology, 24,* 392–399.

Hamilton, D. L. (Ed.). (1981). *Cognitive processes in stereotyping and intergroup behavior.* Hillsdale, NJ: Erlbaum.

Hamilton, D. L., & Rose, T. L. (1980). Illusory correlation and the maintenance of stereotypic beliefs. *Journal of Personality and Social Psychology, 39,* 832–845.

Hasher, L., & Zacks, R. T. (1979). Automatic and effortful processes in memory. *Journal of Experimental Psychology: General, 108,* 356–388.

Hebb, D. O. (1946). On the nature of fear. *Psychological Review, 53,* 259–276.

Henry, J. P. (1986). Neuroendocrine patterns of emotional response. In R. Plutchik & H. Kellerman (Eds.), *Emotion: Theory, research, and experience* (Vol. 3, pp. 37–60). Orlando, FL: Academic Press.

Higgins, E. T. (1987). Self-discrepancy: A theory relating self and affect. *Psychological Review, 94,* 319–340.

Humphreys, M. S., & Revelle, W. (1984). Personality, motivation, and performance: A theory of the relationship between individual differences and information processing. *Psychological Review, 91,* 153–184.

Isen, A. M. (1987). Positive affect, cognitive processes, and social behavior. In L. Berkowitz (Ed.), *Advances in experimental social psychology* (Vol. 20, pp. 203–253). Orlando, FL: Academic Press.

Isen, A. M., & Means, B. (1983). The influence of positive affect on decision-making strategy. *Social Cognition, 2,* 18–31.

Isen, A. M., Means, B., Patrick, R., & Nowicki, G. (1982). Some factors influencing decision-making strategy and risk taking. In M. S. Clark & S. T. Fiske (Eds.), *Affect and cognition: The seventeenth annual Carnegie symposium on cognition* (pp. 243–261). Hillsdale, NJ: Erlbaum.

Jackson, L. A., & Sullivan, L. A. (1988). Cognition and affect in evaluations of stereotyped group members. *Journal of Social Psychology, 129,* 659–672.

Kahneman, D. (1973). *Attention and effort.* Englewood Cliffs, NJ: Prentice–Hall.

Kim, H.-S., & Baron, R. S. (1988). Exercise and illusory correlation: Does arousal heighten stereotypic processing? *Journal of Experimental Social Psychology, 24,* 366–380.

Kuhl, J. (1983). Emotion, Kognition, und Motivation: II. Die funktionale Bedeutung der Emotionen für das problemlösende Denken und für das konkrete Handeln [Emotion, cognition, and motivation: II. The functional significance of emotions in perception, memory, problem solving, and overt action]. *Sprache & Kognition, 4,* 228–253.

Laird, J. D. (1984). The role of facial response in experience of emotion: A reply to Tourangeau and Ellsworth, and others. *Journal of Personality and Social Psychology, 47,* 909–917.

Levenson, R. W., Ekman, P., & Friesen, W. V. (1990). Voluntary facial action generates emotion-specific autonomic nervous system activity. *Psychophysiology, 27*, 363–384.

Mackie, D. M., & Worth, L. T. (1989). Processing deficits and the mediation of positive affect in persuasion. *Journal of Personality and Social Psychology, 57*, 27–40.

Mackie, D. M., Hamilton, D. L., Schroth, H. A., Carlisle, C. J., Gersho, B. F., Meneses, L. M., Nedler, B. F., & Reichel, L. D. (1989). The effects of induced mood on expectancy-based illusory correlations. *Journal of Experimental Social Psychology, 25*, 524–544.

Mandler, G. (1990). A constructivist theory of emotion. In N. S. Stein, B. L. Leventhal, & T. Trabasso (Eds.), *Psychological and biological approaches to emotion*. Hillsdale, NJ: Erlbaum.

McConahay, J. B. (1986). Modern racism, ambivalence, and the modern racism scale. In J. Dovidio & S. Gaertner (Eds.), *Prejudice, discrimination, and racism* (pp. 91–125). Orlando, FL: Academic Press.

McNaughton, N. (1989). *Biology and emotion*. Cambridge: Cambridge University Press.

Miller, G. A. (1956). The magical number seven, plus or minus two: Some limits on our capacity for processing information. *Psychological Review, 63*, 81–97.

Novaco, R. W. (1975). *Anger control: The development and evaluation of an experimental treatment*. Lexington, MA: Lexington Books.

Ortony, A., Clore, G. L., & Collins, A. (1988). *The cognitive structure of emotions*. Cambridge: Cambridge University Press.

Petty, R. E., & Cacioppo, J. T. (1986). The elaboration likelihood model of persuasion. In L. Berkowitz (Ed.), *Advances in experimental social psychology* (Vol. 19, pp. 123–205). New York: Academic Press.

Petty, R. E., Wells, G. W., & Brock, T. C. (1976). Distraction can enhance or reduce yielding to propaganda: Thought disruption versus effort justification. *Journal of Personality and Social Psychology, 34*, 874–884.

Petty, R. E., Cacioppo, J. T., Sedikides, C., & Strathman, A. J. (1988). Affect and persuasion: A contemporary perspective. *American Behavioral Scientist, 31*, 355–371.

Pratto, F., & Bargh, J. A. (1991). Stereotyping based on individuating information: Trait and global components of sex stereotypes under attention overload. *Journal of Experimental Social Psychology, 27*, 26–47.

Rothbart, M., Fulero, S., Jensen, C., Howard, J., & Birreli, P. (1978). From individual to group impressions: Availability heuristics in stereotype formation. *Journal of Experimental Social Psychology, 14*, 237–255.

Sanbonmatsu, D. M., & Kardes, F. R. (1988). The effects of physiological arousal on information processing and persuasion. *Journal of Consumer Research, 15*, 379–385.

Schachter, S., & Singer, J. (1962). Cognitive, social, and physiological determinants of emotional state. *Psychological Review, 69*, 379–399.

Schaller, M., & Cialdini, R. B. (1990). Happiness, sadness, and helping: A motivational integration. In E. T. Higgins & R. M. Sorrentino (Eds.), *Handbook of motivation and cognition* (Vol. 2, pp. 265–296). New York: Guilford.

Scherer, K. R. (1984). On the nature and function of emotion: A component process approach. In K. R. Sherer & P. Ekman (Eds.), *Approaches to emotion* (pp. 293–317). Hillsdale, NJ: Erlbaum.

Scherer, K. R., & Ekman, P. (Eds.). (1984). *Approaches to emotion*. Hillsdale, NJ: Erlbaum.

Schwarz, N. (1990). Feelings as information: Informational and motivational functions of affective states. In E. T. Higgins & R. M. Sorrentino (Eds.), *Handbook of motivation and cognition* (Vol. 2, pp. 527–561). New York: Guilford.

Schwarz, N., & Clore, G. L. (1988). How do I feel about it? The informative function of affective states. In K. Fiedler & J. Forgas (Eds.), *Affect, cognition, and social behavior* (pp. 44–62). Toronto: Hogrefe.

Schwarz, N., Bless, H., & Bohner, G. (1991). Mood and persuasion: Affective states influence the processing of persuasive communications. In M. P. Zanna (Ed.), *Advances in experimental social psychology* Vol. 24, pp. 161–199. Orlando, FL: Academic Press.

Scott, J. P. (1980). The function of emotions in behavioral systems: A systems theory analysis. In R. Plutchik & H. Kellerman (Eds.), *Emotion: Theory, research, experience* (Vol. 1, pp. 35–56). New York: Academic Press.

Shields, S. A. (1984). Reports of bodily change in anxiety, sadness, and anger. *Motivation and Emotion, 8,* 1–21.

Simon, H. A. (1967). Motivational and emotional controls of cognition. *Psychological Review, 74,* 29–39.

Sinclair, R. C. (1988). Mood, categorization breadth, and performance appraisal: The effects of order of information acquisition and affective state on halo, accuracy, information retrieval, and evaluations. *Organizational Behavior and Human Decision Processes, 42,* 22–46.

Spielberger, C. D., Gorsuch, R. L., & Luschene, R. E. (1970). *Manual for the State-Trait Anxiety Inventory.* Palo Alto, CA: Consulting Psychologists Press.

Stephan, W. C., & Brigham, J. C. (Eds.). (1985). Intergroup contact. *Journal of Social Issues, 41(3).*

Stephan, W. C., & Stephan, C. W. (1985). Intergroup anxiety. *Journal of Social Issues, 41(3),* 157–175.

Strack, F., Schwarz, N., & Gschneidinger, E. (1985). Happiness and reminiscing: The role of time perspective, mood, and mode of thinking. *Journal of Personality and Social Psychology, 49,* 1460–1469.

Strack, F., Martin, L. L., & Stepper, S. (1988). Inhibiting and facilitating conditions of facial expressions: A nonobtrusive test of the facial feedback hypothesis. *Journal of Personality and Social Psychology, 54,* 768–777.

Sullivan, E. T. (1922). Mood in relation to performance. *Archives of Psychology, No. 53.*

Tomkins, S. S. (1984). Affect theory. In K. R. Scherer & P. Ekman (Eds.), *Approaches to emotion* (pp. 163–195). Hillsdale, NJ: Erlbaum.

Tversky, A., & Kahneman, D. (1974). Judgment under uncertainty: Heuristics and biases. *Science, 185,* 1124–1131.

Watson, D., & Clark, L. A. (1984). Negative affectivity: The disposition to experience aversive emotional states. *Psychological Bulletin, 96,* 465–490.

Weary, G. (1990). Depression and sensitivity to social information. In B. S. Moore & A. M. Isen (Eds.), *Affect and social behavior* (pp. 207–230). Cambridge: Cambridge University Press.

Wenzlaff, R. M., Wegner, D. M., & Roper, D. W. (1988). Depression and mental control: The resurgence of unwanted negative thoughts. *Journal of Personality and Social Psychology, 55,* 882–892.

Wilder, D. A., & Shapiro, P. N. (1989). Role of competition-induced anxiety in limiting the beneficial impact of positive behavior by an out-group member. *Journal of Personality and Social Psychology, 56,* 60–69.

Worth, L. T., & Mackie, D. M. (1987). Cognitive mediation of positive affect in persuasion. *Social Cognition, 5,* 76–94.

Wyer, R. S., Jr., & Srull, T. K. (1989). *Memory and cognition in its social context.* Hillsdale, NJ: Erlbaum.

Chapter 3

The Influence of Affect on Stereotyping: The Case of Illusory Correlations

DAVID L. HAMILTON, STEVEN J. STROESSNER,
and DIANE M. MACKIE
Department of Psychology
University of California, Santa Barbara
Santa Barbara, California

Introduction

For many years the prevailing view of stereotyping and prejudice was that these phenomena are manifestations of affective processes that shape our perceptions, attitudes, and behaviors. This implicit assumption took a number of specific forms; the Freudian concepts of projection and displacement, Lippmann's (1922) views on "stereotypes as defense," the frustration-aggression hypothesis (Dollard, Doob, Miller, Mowrer, & Sears, 1939), the research culminating in *The Authoritarian Personality* (Adorno, Frenkel-Brunswik, Levinson, & Sanford, 1950), and the notion of scapegoating (Bettelheim & Janowitz, 1949) provide examples of this perspective. The common element in all of these concepts is the view that intergroup judgments are driven by affective processes. From this perspective, then, to understand stereotyping, we need to focus on these affective origins.

In response to this singular emphasis on affective determinants, attention shifted toward the cognitive antecedents of stereotyping and prejudice. The last 15 years has spawned an extensive literature viewing stereotypes as cognitive structures that influence the processing of information about social groups and their members in a variety of ways (for reviews, see Hamilton & Trolier, 1986; Hamilton, Sherman, & Ruvolo, 1990; Stroebe & Insko, 1989; Stephan, 1985). The common element in this work is the view that intergroup judgments are mediated by cognitive processes. From this perspective, then, to understand stereotyping, we need to focus on those cognitive mediators.

Each of these emphases has been effective in generating important research that has advanced our understanding of stereotyping. What has been lacking is a serious attempt to investigate the interface between affective and cognitive processes and to determine how they function interactively to influence intergroup perceptions. The research described in this chapter is an effort toward that end.

One of the difficulties in coming to grips with this interface—both conceptually and empirically—is the sheer complexity of the task one confronts. Several problems immediately arise. To begin with, the term "affect" has numerous meanings and usages in the literature, spanning the range of generalized arousal, specific emotions, transient mood states, and evaluative reactions. It would be naive to assume that "affect" in all of these senses influences cognitive processes in the same way. Similarly, the analysis of cognitive processes relevant to stereotyping is complex, including processes that occur during the initial encoding of information, the elaboration of that information through inference, evaluation, and attribution processes, the representation and storage of that information in memory, and its subsequent retrieval from memory when the judgment is made. Again, it would be naive to presume that affective factors will interact with all of these processes in the same way.

Given this complexity, the researcher of necessity must adopt some strategy for approaching this interface, inevitably selecting some subset of the overall picture on which to focus. In our research we have adopted a strategy that has two important components. First, regarding affect, we decided to focus on the role of the perceivers' temporary mood states on intergroup perceptions. And second, our strategy entails investigating the effects of those mood states on a well-defined cognitively based phenomenon that (1) has been well researched in the last decade and (2) influences intergroup perceptions. Specifically, we investigated the influence of mood on illusory correlations in judgments of groups (Hamilton, 1981).

Regarding the first aspect of our strategy, inducing mild affective states that were independent of the intergroup context had several advantages. First, we induced a mild, rather than an intense, affective state so that the affect would not completely disrupt information processing. Second, we induced mood states rather than more transitory emotional reactions so that the affective state could be expected to persist through processing of stereotype-relevant information. Third, inducing affect that was independent of the intergroup situation meant that affect could be investigated independently of particular intergroup events that might contaminate it, and independently of other motivational states that might be activated in an intergroup context.

The second component of our strategy—focusing on a well-understood cognitive system—also offers important advantages. Our goal is to determine how affect influences the processes underlying stereotypic judgments. Whatever impact affect has on judgments, it is likely to be mediated by affect's impact on the cognitive processes underlying those judgments. Therefore our focus is directed at those mediators. By conducting our research on an established cognitive phenomenon, we already know a good deal about the cognitive side of the equation (i.e., the processes underlying illusory correlations). We therefore have a good idea "where to look" in trying to determine the impact of affective states on the relevant underlying processes.

Given this strategy, we begin our analysis by considering what recent research on affect and cognitive processing has demonstrated and how these findings have been conceptualized in this literature. We then consider the implications of these findings for the specific processes underlying illusory correlations.

Influence of Affect on Cognitive Processing

Research concerned with the various ways that affective processes might interact with cognitive processes to produce social judgments has developed rapidly in recent years (for reviews see Bower, 1981; Fiedler, 1991a; Forgas, 1991; Isen, 1984, 1987; Schwarz & Clore, 1988). Despite this flurry of activity, no clear consensus has emerged as to the actual impact that different affective states have on processing, and several differing conceptual viewpoints provide viable accounts of the mechanisms by which affective states have their influence. Nevertheless, despite this general lack of clarity, some encouraging progress has been achieved. In discussing this work it is useful to consider separately the findings for positive and negative affective states.

Some convergence has emerged regarding the impact of positive mood on information processing. In a wide range of processing tasks, positive affect has been shown to spontaneously reduce the extent of deliberative or systematic processing that occurs (for reviews, see Fiedler, 1988; Schwarz, 1990; Schwarz & Bless, 1991). These tasks include attributional processing, decision making, person impression formation, forming judgments about members of a group, and processing persuasive messages. In each domain, the accumulated evidence indicates that subjects process information less analytically, while relying more on heuristic cues, decisional shortcuts, initial judgments, stereotypes, and other simplifying strategies (Abele, 1985; Bless, Hamilton & Mackie, 1992; Bodenhausen & Kramer, 1990; Isen, Means, Patrick, & Nowicki, 1982; Mackie & Worth, 1991; Sinclair, 1988; Stroessner & Mackie, 1992). *Why* these effects occur is still a matter of some debate, an issue to which we return below.

The case is less clear for the impact of negative mood. The lack of clarity is due to a couple of factors. One problem concerns inconsistencies in results for different negative moods. In contrast to positive mood states, where various positive moods seem to have similar impacts on cognitive processing, different negative moods have not shown such uniformity (see Bodenhausen, Chapter 2, this volume). Because of this variability in outcomes, it is important to specify the particular negative mood state in any discussion of these effects. Our research focused on the negative mood of sadness, and in the remainder of this chapter the term "negative mood" will refer to this particular affect.

Even given that constraint, however, the picture is far from clear. Manipulations of sadness have also produced inconsistent results. In some cases, negative mood has been found to have no detrimental effects on processing. Compared to those in a positive mood, for example, sad subjects have been found to seek and consider more information and to process persuasive messages more thoroughly (Bless *et al.*, 1990; Hildebrand-Saints & Weary, 1989; Sinclair, 1988). Thus sad subjects appear to process information at least as well as those in whom no mood state has been induced. At the same time, other results demonstrate that sad subjects exhibit decrements in memory performance, especially when the task is resource intensive (see Ellis & Ashbrook, 1988, for review). In addition, subjects in a negative mood have been found to do less attributional processing (Sullivan & Conway, 1989) and to generate and consider fewer complex hypotheses (Masters, Barden, & Ford, 1979; Silberman, Weingartner, & Post, 1983). Thus the effects of positive and negative moods sometimes produce different results, with positive mood decreasing careful processing compared to sadness. At other times, the effects of positive and negative moods appear similar, with both affective states decreasing careful processing.

Why positive and negative mood affects information processing in such ways is still a matter of debate. Most proposed explanations fall into two general classes. Although not necessarily mutually exclusive, these explanations have tended to focus either on the cognitive consequences of affective states or on their motivational consequences. Both classes of explanation characterize affect as accompanied by activation of particular kinds of content from long-term memory (Isen, 1984, 1987; Srull, 1983, 1987). Cognitive explanations of mood effects focus on the direct implications of the activation of this material, whereas motivational theories focus more on the activation of goal structures triggered by this material. We consider the cognitive and motivational approaches in turn.

Attentional Allocation Consequences of Content Activation

Both network models (Bower, 1981; Clark & Isen, 1982; Singer & Salovey, 1988) and constructionist theories (Bransford, 1979) of memory imply that affective states may result in the activation of mood-congruent material from long-term memory (Isen, 1984, 1987; Isen, Shalker, Clark, & Karp, 1978). According to a network interpretation, such activation spreads through associated nodes of similar valence, whereas according to constructionist views, a valenced probe of memory results in retrieval of similarly valenced material. In either case, the consequence is that mood states produce an initial flux of mood-congruent thoughts.

Activation of this material is likely to influence other ongoing processes, in several respects. First, affectively valenced material is inherently attention grabbing (e.g., Erdelyi & Blumenthal, 1973), thereby distracting attention from other tasks. Second, mood-induced activation of related material is likely to provide a complex cognitive context in terms of which incoming information can be encoded and interpreted (Isen, 1984; see Forgas & Bower, 1987, for related ideas). The multitude of ways in which new material can be dealt with increases both encoding and processing time (Forgas & Bower, 1987). These effects are likely to have particular impact when the information being encoded is ambiguous, difficult, or available for limited exposure. Third, even attempting to suppress such thoughts in order to continue a processing task may interfere with allocating appropriate attention to other tasks (Wegner, Schneider, Carter, & White, 1987). As a consequence of any of these three effects, the presence of affective material in working memory may interfere with attentional allocation to other tasks (Mackie & Worth, 1989, 1991).

The importance of these effects may vary according to the nature of the task at hand. With simple tasks, decrements in attention due to the activation of affective material may not impede performance. In fact, performance on tasks that require creativity or diversity of solutions may actually be enhanced by the complex cognitive context provided by affect-induced activation (Isen, 1987; Isen, Johnson, Mertz, & Robinson, 1985). However, as processing tasks increase in their requirements for concentrated, sequential, and capacity-intensive attention, they may become increasingly vulnerable to the effects of current mood state.

Activation of Motivational Goals

Motivational perspectives posit that positive and negative mood states activate very different goal structures, which in turn influence information processing. A positive mood state, on the one hand, could decrease systematic processing because of at least two different goals it might activate. First, subjects may be motivated to maintain their positive state, avoiding extensive processing (particularly of disagreeable or unpleasant information) in order to do so (Isen, 1984, 1987). Second, positive mood may inform the subject that there is little need to employ careful or effortful strategies to analyze the contingencies in an environment that seems satisfactory (Schwarz,

1990). In both cases, positive mood reduces the motivation to process information carefully.

The negative affect associated with sadness, on the other hand, is viewed as motivating more careful processing of the environment, again for a couple of possible reasons. First, subjects may be motivated to distract themselves from a negative affective state by engaging in extensive processing, particularly information of a pleasant nature (Isen, 1984, 1987). Thus increased processing results from a strategy of mood repair. Second, negative states may inform the individual that something is amiss in the environment, causing heightened information processing that is initially aimed at solving the perceived problem but then later generalizes to other processing tasks (Schwarz, 1990). In both cases, negative mood increases the desire to process systematically.

Cognitive and motivational approaches thus make different predictions about the processing consequences of positive compared to negative mood states. Motivational theories predict diametrically opposed modes of processing to be activated by positive and negative affective states. Thus motivational approaches predict asymmetric outcomes in affect-related processing: positive affect will decrease systematic processing whereas negative affect will increase deliberative processing. In contrast, to the extent that affect-induced activation interferes with attentional resources, cognitive approaches predict that positive and negative affect will produce relatively symmetric effects on processing: both should decrease systematic processing (although not necessarily to an identical degree) (Isen, 1984, 1987).

Illusory Correlations in Intergroup Perception

The goal of our research was to determine how these mood states influence the cognitive processes underlying illusory correlations, and hence, intergroup perceptions. An illusory correlation is a judgment by a perceiver that two variables are associated with each other, even though they were not associated in the information on which the judgment was based (Chapman, 1967). That is, an observer is presented with information conveying multiple instances of two categories of information, and the observer's subsequent judgments are used to determine the extent to which he or she perceived a relationship between the two categories. An illusory correlation exists when the observer "sees" a relationship that "wasn't there" in the information presented (or was there to a substantially different degree). When this happens, one can conclude that some bias in the way information was processed produced a systematic misperception of that relationship.

Research on illusory correlations has documented two bases from which these illusory correlations may derive, and these two bases rest on somewhat different processes. We refer to them as distinctiveness-based and expectancy-based illusory correlations. As applied to the study of stereo-typing (Hamilton, 1981), the two types of illusory correlation pertain to different issues in understanding intergroup perception. Specifically, *distinctiveness-based illusory correlations* are relevant to the analysis of factors contributing to the initial *formation* of stereotypic beliefs, whereas *expectancy-based illusory correlations* pertain to mechanisms by which *existing* stereotypes become self-perpetuating and resistant to change. The following sections discuss these two cases in terms of (1) the basic findings associated with each one, (2) how affect might influence the hypothesized underlying processes, and (3) our research findings pertinent to each case.

Affect and Distinctiveness-Based Illusory Correlations

Illusory correlations may arise due to the co-occurrence of distinctive stimulus events (Chapman, 1967; Hamilton & Gifford, 1976). Events that occur infrequently are distinctive and draw the attention of the observer. When two events—each of which is distinctive due to its relative infrequency—co-occur, then the observer is particularly likely to notice their co-occurrence. This information is therefore likely to become well represented in memory and hence be particularly accessible for retrieval when subsequent judgments are called for. The consequence is that the observer is likely to overestimate the frequency with which those events co-occurred. Moreover, to the extent that judgments are based on information retrieved from memory at the time, this distinctive information will have particular impact on those judgments.

In the original demonstration of this effect in social perception (Hamilton & Gifford, 1976), subjects read a series of statements, each of which described a member of one of two groups (identified only as Group A and Group B) as having performed some behavior. In the set of sentences as a whole, there were twice as many members of Group A as of Group B, and most of the behaviors described were desirable behaviors. Therefore, both Group B members and undesirable behaviors occurred with relative infrequency. However, the proportion of desirable and undesirable acts was the same for both groups, so there was no contingent relationship between group membership and behavior desirability. According to the rationale developed above, the co-occurrence of the two infrequent events (a Group B member performing an undesirable behavior) would be particularly distinctive and hence would receive differential processing. These items of information would therefore be particularly available in memory and hence, at a later time, their frequency of co-occurrence would be overestimated. In fact, Hamilton and Gifford's (1976) subjects did exactly that. They overestimated the frequency with which Group B members performed undesirable behaviors, producing an illusory correlation. In addition, this bias influenced their evaluative judgments such that members of Group B were rated less favorably than members of Group A. Thus, subjects made differential evaluations of the two groups, even though the information describing the two groups was evaluatively equivalent.

A number of subsequent studies have replicated these findings and investigated the specific mechanisms that produce them (see Hamilton & Sherman, 1989; Mullen & Johnson, 1990). There is now considerable evidence supporting the view that subjects differentially attend to and encode the distinctive items, that they are particularly well retrieved, and that the biased judgments are memory based, that is, are based largely on the information retrieved from memory at the time judgments are made (rather than on overall evaluative impressions formed as the information was being processed). Thus the processes underlying distinctiveness-based illusory correlations have been investigated extensively and are reasonably well understood (although alternative mechanisms have been proposed; see Fiedler, 1991b; Smith, 1991).

Although there is now a sizable literature on this topic, virtually all of this work has focused on the role of cognitive factors in producing illusory correlations. How might affective factors—and in particular, the perceiver's mood state at the time—influence the processes underlying these findings? And if the perceiver's affective state does influence those processes, would it also alter the formation of the illusory correlation itself?

Formation of a distinctiveness-based illusory correlation depends on the recognition of the differential frequencies of the various types of stimulus information. This recognition makes the infrequent information appear distinctive, and consequently increases the availability of this information when making subsequent judgments about the groups. The formation of this bias thus depends on at least a moderate level of processing of the information. Therefore, conditions that increase the processing of available information should increase the accuracy of group judgments and hence an illusory correlation bias should disappear (Pryor, 1986; Sanbonmatsu, Shavitt, & Sherman, 1991; Schaller & Maass, 1989). On the other hand, if processing constraints preclude the recognition that different categories of items occur with differential frequency, the bias should also be eliminated. Thus, we expect a curvilinear relationship between the thoroughness of information processing and the formation of distinctiveness-based illusory correlations. Both increased processing (fostering more accurate encoding of all information) and decreased processing (precluding recognition of differential frequencies) are expected to undermine the bias, although for different reasons.

Because the activation of affect can influence the thoroughness with which available information is processed, we (Stroessner, Hamilton, & Mackie, 1992) predicted that the presence of affect would diminish formation of distinctiveness-based illusory correlations. For positive affects, this hypothesis follows directly from both the cognitive and motivational perspectives discussed earlier. For negative mood (sadness), the two accounts make somewhat different predictions. In focusing on the attentional constraints imposed by either positive or negative mood, the cognitive interpretation would predict reduced illusory correlations in both mood conditions, in both cases due to less efficiency in processing information. On the other hand, motivational theories predict enhanced processing under negative mood. This enhancement might result in more accurate representations, and hence less bias in judgments. However, in this case the reduction in illusory correlations should be accompanied by greater accuracy in judgments.

To investigate this hypothesis, we manipulated subjects' affective states prior to their completing a standard illusory correlation task. Subjects were shown a segment of a videotape to induce a positive (i.e., happy) or a negative (i.e., sad) affective state. The positive mood video consisted of a performance by a comedian, and the negative mood video discussed a child abuse case that resulted in the child's death. The remaining subjects watched a control (i.e., neutral mood) videotape that was designed to induce no particular affective state. This video segment was part of a National Geographic program concerning the exploration of a dormant volcano.

After viewing one of the three videotape segments, subjects completed an illusory correlation task (presumably as part of a different study). Specifically, subjects read descriptions of 24 positive and 12 negative behaviors that had been performed by members of two groups. Twenty-four of the behaviors were supposedly performed by members of Group A, and twelve of the behaviors were performed by members of Group B. The ratio of desirable to undesirable behaviors for each group, however, was identical: two-thirds of the behaviors describing each group were positive in valence.

Subjects then completed two measures designed to assess whether illusory correlations had, in fact, formed. First, subjects rated how well they liked the members of each group. An illusory correlation would be evidenced by a differential evaluation of the two groups; members of Group B should be evaluated less favorably than should members of Group A. Second, subjects estimated the frequency of undesirable and desirable behaviors performed by group members. An illusory correlation would be evidenced by estimates indicating a perceived association between group membership and behavior desirability. Subjects should overestimate the frequency of undesirable behaviors performed by members of Group B as compared to Group A. In addition, because subjects overestimate the frequency of undesirable behaviors in Group B, frequency estimates for Group B should be less accurate than estimates of Group A.

Our assumption was that the control (i.e., neutral mood) condition approximated the conditions present in previous studies of illusory correlation in which mood was not explicitly manipulated. Therefore, we expected that subjects in this condition would form an illusory correlation. Specifically, subjects in a neutral mood should produce lower evaluative ratings for members of Group B, should overestimate the negative behavior of Group B, and should be less accurate in estimating the frequency of their behaviors. This is exactly what we found in our neutral mood condition (Stroessner *et al.*, 1992, Experiment 1). These results confirm that illusory correlations formed in the neutral mood condition. This condition, then, serves as an appropriate baseline for comparisons with the conditions in which positive and negative mood was induced.

What did we expect to find in the positive and negative mood conditions? We expected that subjects in the positive and negative mood conditions would not produce differential evaluative ratings or frequency estimates indicating a perceived association between group membership and behavior desirability. These hypotheses were supported in both the positive and negative mood conditions. Subjects in these conditions did not differentially evaluate the targets nor did they perceive a correlation between group membership and desirability. These findings provide preliminary evidence that distinctiveness-based illusory correlations are less likely to form following induction of happy or sad mood.

According to our rationale described above, illusory correlations can be diminished by *either* very extensive *or* very poor processing of information. To determine whether positive and negative affect increased or decreased the thoroughness of information processing, we examined the accuracy of the subjects' frequency estimates. Whereas subjects in the neutral mood condition were only inaccurate in estimating the frequency of Group B's behaviors (presumably due to the distinctiveness of this group's undesirable behaviors), subjects in the positive and negative mood conditions were inaccurate in estimating the frequency of *both* group's behaviors. This result provides evidence that subjects in the positive and negative mood conditions exhibited processing deficits compared to subjects in a neutral mood. Thus, our findings converge in showing that both positive and negative affect diminished the thoroughness of information processing, and the lower level of processing made identification of the infrequent stimulus information difficult.

This first study, however, contained no processing measure directly pertinent to these underlying mechanisms. We therefore conducted a second study (Stroessner *et al.*, 1992, Experiment 2) to collect such a processing measure. Subjects in this study viewed one of the three videotape segments used in the first study to induce a positive, negative, or no particular (neutral) mood state. In the illusory correlation phase of the study, the stimulus information was presented item-by-item on a computer screen, with the subject advancing to the next item by pressing a response key. The computer recorded the subject's processing time for each stimulus sentence. We predicted that subjects in a neutral mood would spend greater amounts of time processing the distinctive behaviors, that is, the longest processing times were expected for Group B's undesirable behaviors. We expected no such differential processing of information for subjects in the positive and negative mood conditions. These subjects were expected to process the various types of information an equal length of time. In addition, to replicate the findings of our first study and to assess the relationship between differential processing and other indices of illusory correlations, we collected the same dependent measures used in the first study.

The results of the second study replicated the findings of the first experiment, further supporting the argument that illusory correlations were less likely to form after a positive or negative mood induction. Only subjects in the neutral mood condition differentially evaluated the two groups and were differentially accurate in estimating the frequency of the two groups' desirable and undesirable behaviors. Subjects in neither the happy nor sad mood conditions produced these results. Moreover, subjects in the positive and negative mood conditions made less accurate frequency estimates overall than neutral mood subjects. Again, this finding is consistent with the view that both affective states reduced the thoroughness of processing.

The unique contribution of this study, however, was the analysis of processing times for the four types of stimulus information. As predicted, only those subjects in a neutral mood differentially processed the distinctive information. Subjects in the neutral mood condition looked longer at the undesirable behaviors of Group B than at the other types of information. In contrast, subjects in the happy and sad mood conditions did not differentially process undesirable behaviors for Group B.

We also examined the relationship between these differential processing latencies and the other indices of illusory correlations. The prevailing explanation for the formation of distinctiveness-based illusory correlations is that the distinctive information draws attention and therefore receives extended processing as the information is encoded. This differential processing then produces biased frequency estimates, and these biased estimates in turn become the basis for the differential evaluations of the groups. Thus, we expected that under standard (neutral mood) conditions, differential processing times of the distinctive information should contribute to bias in frequency estimates. In fact, the correlation between the differential processing of the infrequent information and the bias in frequency estimates was highly significant. Differential processing was also correlated with differential group evaluations. However, the partial correlation between differential processing and differential evaluations (controlling for the influence of biased frequency estimates) was not significant. These results support the argument that the bias arises from differential attention to distinctive information and its subsequent impact on frequency estimates. The differential evaluations of the groups are apparently based on biases in estimating the frequency of the groups' desirable and undesirable behaviors.

More importantly for present purposes, the same findings were *not* obtained in the positive or negative mood conditions. Differential processing of the distinctive information was not correlated with any of the other dependent measures in these conditions. In sum, it was only in the neutral mood condition that differential processing of the distinctive information affected frequency estimates and evaluations of the two stimulus groups. The failure of differential processing times to influence either frequency estimates or evaluative ratings in the positive and negative mood conditions lends additional support to the argument that mood states disrupt the processing typically underlying illusory correlations.

The symmetry of the data obtained in the positive and negative mood conditions also supports an attentional constraint interpretation of the mood effects. As was previously outlined, affect may reduce deliberative processing for either cognitive or motivational reasons. Induced affect may interfere with the resources available to process information, and this reduced processing may have undermined perception of the distinctive information in the illusory correlation task. On the other hand, an alternate explanation might suggest that positive mood subjects lack the motivation to process, which would undermine their recognition of differential frequencies in the stimulus information.

Although this latter explanation could potentially account for the data obtained in the positive mood conditions, it cannot account for the performance of subjects in a sad mood. Negative mood, according to the proponents of the motivational account, engenders careful processing of information. Thus, negative mood subjects should thoroughly process the stimulus sentences. The frequency estimate data indicate, however, that sad subjects did not do so. The fact that sad subjects exhibited the same processing deficits as happy subjects is therefore consistent with predictions made from a cognitive, rather than a motivational, perspective.

Finally, our results have implications for the role of affect in the processing of other distinctive or unusual types of information. Specifically, these results contribute to a growing body of evidence that affect reduces the impact of unusual or distinctive stimuli on judgments. Studies assessing perception of variability within a group of stimuli, for example, support this argument. In judging a set of nonsocial stimuli, subjects in whom a positive or negative affective state has been induced are more likely to rate unusual exemplars as members of a category than are subjects in a neutral mood (Isen & Daubman, 1984). In addition, subjects in a positive and negative mood also perceive a heterogeneous social group as containing less variability than do subjects in a neutral mood (Stroessner & Mackie, Chapter 4, this volume). Similarly, anxious subjects show assimilation effects in categorical judgments, seeing a favorable outgroup member as more similar to the unfavorable outgroup compared to neutral mood subjects (Wilder, Chapter 5, this volume).

Thus, there is evidence that both positive and negative affect reduce deliberative processing of available information and consequently impair the ability to perceive information as distinctive. Because identification of certain types of information as distinctive is crucial to formation of distinctiveness-based illusory correlations, affect may attenuate formation of this bias.

Affect and Expectancy-Based Illusory Correlations

The distinctiveness-based illusory correlation represents a cognitive bias that can influence the initial differential perception of groups, and thereby can contribute to the formation of diverging conceptions of groups, even where unwarranted. Once these differential conceptions are established, then beliefs that subsequently become associated with those group categories could evolve into stereotypic belief systems. In contrast, the expectancy-based illusory correlation represents a bias deriving from already established stereotypes. This type of illusory correlation is based on preexisting expectancies or associative beliefs that can then bias the observer's judgments based on newly-acquired information. For example, the observer may overestimate the frequency with which stereotypically expected associations actually co-occurred in the information provided, and if this were to happen it might then produce biased judgments of the groups described in the information.

In one illustration of this phenomenon, Hamilton and Rose (1980) presented subjects with a series of statements, each of which described a person by first name, occupation, and two trait-descriptive adjectives. Within the set of statements, three occupational groups were described equally often (e.g., there were equal numbers of accountants, doctors, and salespersons). Some of the trait-descriptive adjectives were stereotypically associated with each of these groups (e.g., timid, wealthy, and loud, respectively), but within the set of statements each adjective described two members of each occupational group. Therefore, in this set of information there was no association between occupational group and any particular attribute. Nevertheless, when subjects were subsequently asked to indicate how many times each adjective had described members of each group, they systematically overestimated the extent to which the attributes had described the group with which they are stereotypically associated. In contrast, adjectives that were not stereotypic of any of the groups were accurately judged to have described each group equally often. Apparently, then, subjects' preexisting expectancies about these occupational groups biased their judgments of frequencies of co-occurrence. Subsequent studies have replicated these findings (Kim & Baron, 1988; Slusher & Anderson, 1987; Spears, Eiser, & van der Pligt, 1987).

There are several possible mechanisms that might contribute to these expectancy-based illusory correlations. One possibility is that, because of their fit with one's a priori expectancies, it is easier to process those items that describe a group member with an attribute stereotypic of that group. If so, then these descriptions may be more likely to be represented in memory, or may become more effectively represented in memory, than nonstereotypic descriptions, and hence be more accessible for retrieval at the time judgments are made. They would then be overrepresented in subjects' frequency estimates.

An alternative possibility is that the effect is due to processes that occur solely at retrieval. That is, there may be no bias in the way information is processed and represented in memory, but the stereotype may guide one's search of memory when the judgment is called for. If so, then stereotype-consistent descriptors would be more likely to be retrieved and hence bias the resulting judgments. A variation on this theme would posit that, because of information overload, the subject is quite ineffective in representing this information in memory, so that when judgments are called for the stereotype is used as a guide for making "guesstimates" on the judgment task.

What impact might affective state be expected to have on the processes underlying expectancy-based illusory correlations? Again cognitive and motivational approaches make different predictions regarding information processing for cases in which positive as compared to negative affect is present. If mood states reduce attentional allocation to the processing task because the affect is distracting, then increased reliance on heuristic strategies in both positive and negative mood conditions could be expected. In the present case, we might expect greater use of pre-existing stereotypes in group judgments, and thus stronger illusory correlations in conditions characterized by affective state. However, it is also true that any difficulty in processing produced by attentional distraction should be exacerbated in conditions in which such processing is particularly difficult. Our experiment included conditions that allowed us to assess this possibility. Because incongruency between incoming information and the current mood state has been found to make encoding and processing more difficult (Bower, 1981; Forgas & Bower, 1988), any increased reliance on stereotypes, and thus any increased illusory correlation, could be expected to be even greater under these conditions. From the cognitive perspective then, we hypothesized that a congruent relationship between a person's mood state and the valence of the information being processed would facilitate such processing (reducing illusory correlations), whereas incongruence between affective state and information valence would make processing more difficult (exacerbating illusory correlations).

In contrast, motivational theories would predict increased reliance on the stereotype, and consequent strength of the illusory correlation, only when the affective state is positive. When subjects experience negative mood, they should process the presented information more carefully. Such careful processing might indeed undermine the impact of prior stereotypes that characterize expectancy-based illusory correlations. In these conditions, then, we would expect to see little or no illusory correlation, along with indications of relatively accurate information processing.

To examine these issues, we (Mackie *et al.*, 1989) conducted two experiments investigating the impact of induced mood state on expectancy-based illusory correlations. The same basic paradigm was used in both experiments. Subjects believed they were participating in two independent studies. In actuality, the first "study" served as a mood induction phase by showing subjects a 4-minute segment of videotape designed to induce a happy, neutral, or sad mood state. Subjects were asked to rate how the video made them feel, under the guise of pretesting these segments for possible use in a future experiment. The second "study" consisted of presenting the materials for an expectancy-based illusory correlation paradigm, as described above. The effects of mood on processing were determined by comparing the nature and extent of illusory correlation manifested in subjects' judgments in the three mood conditions.

In the illusory correlation phase of the studies, subjects read a series of 32 statements, each of which described a different person identified by first name. Within the set of sentences, eight persons were identified as members of each of four occupational groups. Each stimulus person was also described by two trait-descriptive adjectives. Eight different adjectives were used in these descriptions, two of which were stereotypic of each of the occupational groups. Two such sets were created, one using positively valanced traits and the other using negatively valenced traits. This manipulation, in combination with the mood induction conditions, permitted us to compare subject groups for whom the relationship between induced mood state and the valence of stimulus items was either congruent or incongruent.

Within the set of sentences each adjective described a member of each group equally often. Subjects were then given four questionnaire pages, each of which identified one of the occupational groups and listed the eight adjectives. Subjects were asked to estimate how often each trait had described members of each occupational group. An illusory correlation is manifested in these judgments when subjects overestimate the frequency of stereotypic, relative to stereotype-unrelated, traits for the various groups.

Analyses of these frequency estimates yielded the same results in both experiments. Overall, subjects overestimated the frequency with which the traits had characterized members of their stereotypically-associated occupational groups, thereby replicating the findings of previous studies using this paradigm (Hamilton & Rose, 1980; Kim & Baron, 1988; Slusher &

Anderson, 1987; Spears *et al.*, 1987). More importantly for present purposes, these illusory correlations were significantly *stronger* when the valence of the induced mood and of the stimulus attributes were incongruent. That is, subjects in a positive mood who read statements with unfavorable attributes, and subjects in a negative mood who read desirable characterizations of the group members, were more subject to this bias than were (1) subjects for whom these two valences were congruent, and (2) subjects in the neutral mood condition (see Mackie *et al.*, 1989, for more detailed presentation of these results).

Evidence of greater illusory correlations is indicative of increased reliance on preexisting stereotypes in making judgments. Although subjects in all conditions manifested, on average, such illusory correlations, this bias was most prominently displayed in those conditions where the mood state and the stimulus information differed in valence. These findings are compatible with the view that the incongruence between the valence of one's mood state and the valence of the current task interferes with, or makes more difficult, the processing of relevant information. As a consequence, judgments based on that information are made heuristically, in this case reflecting the influence of group stereotypes. Although this interpretation is plausible, these frequency estimates do not provide any direct evidence bearing on the ease or difficulty of processing under the various experimental conditions.

The procedure in the second study was designed to permit an examination of this issue. Specifically, we measured subjects' processing latencies by presenting the stimulus items on a computer screen and having the subject control exposure times by pressing a response key to move to the next item. The subject's processing time for each stimulus sentence was recorded by the computer. We then determined, for each subject, the average processing time for those items that included stereotypic descriptors and the average processing time for those sentences in which both traits were unrelated to the group stereotype of the person's occupation. The difference between these two processing times was calculated for each subject and analyzed as a function of mood state and valence of stimulus information (favorable or unfavorable trait descriptors).

The results clearly indicated that, when the valences of mood state and of stimulus information were incongruent, subjects spent significantly more time processing sentences that did not include attributes stereotypic of the person's occupational group. In contrast, when the sentence included a stereotypic descriptor these subjects processed the sentence more quickly, apparently relying on the stereotypic content to ease the difficulty of the processing task under these conditions. Subjects for whom the valence of mood state and the valence of the stimulus information were compatible, as well as subjects in the neutral mood condition, did not evidence any sizable difference in processing the two kinds of statements.

In addition to supporting our hypotheses, these results provide some useful evidence about the processing mechanisms underlying expectancy-based illusory correlations. Earlier we noted several possibilities. One was that these effects could be due to preferential encoding of expectancy-confirming information, making the stereotype-consistent attributes more accessible when subsequent judgments are made. Alternatively, these effects could reflect the impact of stereotypes on retrieval processes or on guessing. Although all of these mechanisms remain viable, the processing time results do provide evidence for the differential encoding of stereotypic and nonstereotypic attributes, at least under conditions of increased processing difficulty.

Summary and Implications

We began this chapter by adopting a particular strategy for experimentally approaching the interface of affective and cognitive processes in the realm of intergroup perception. Our approach was to select a well-defined cognitive phenomenon—illusory correlation biases in intergroup perception—and to investigate how induction of temporary mood states can influence the processes underlying those effects. We have investigated these issues in two different illusory correlation paradigms that pertain to different aspects of biased processing in intergroup perception. At this point it is useful to review what we have learned.

First, regarding distinctiveness-based illusory correlations, our results showed that, compared to the neutral mood condition, subjects in positive and negative induced mood states failed to manifest this form of illusory correlation. Moreover, we provided path analytic evidence that, whereas this differential attention to distinctive information (as reflected in processing times) causally mediates illusory correlations under typical (neutral mood) conditions, this causal influence was not present when more affectively toned mood states had been induced. The most plausible explanation for these findings is that induced affect (positive and negative) attenuated the subjects' ability to process the information effectively, and therefore they were less sensitive to the distinctiveness properties of the minority group and the infrequent behaviors. Without such sensitivity, and the resulting differential processing, an illusory correlation would not form.

These results are important in at least four respects. First, they provide new information about the conditions under which this type of illusory correlation is and is not likely to occur. Specifically, affectively charged mood states can undermine the kind of cognitive processing on which this bias is based. Second, the processing time results provide new evidence for the reasons why illusory correlations are formed. That is, these results document the important role played by differential attention to the distinctive stimulus category in generating these illusory correlations. Third, our findings are informative about the means by which affect influences cognitive processing in this task. As just noted, induced mood diminished subjects' sensitivity to the differential frequencies inherent in the stimulus information, thereby highlighting the influence of affect on cognitive resources for information processing. And fourth, the symmetry in our findings for the positive and negative mood conditions is of theoretical importance. Both of these groups differed from the neutral mood condition and both differed in similar ways. This symmetry implicates a greater role for cognitive, rather than motivational, mechanisms by which mood state influenced processing in our paradigms.

We also investigated the effects of these mood inductions on expectancy-based illusory correlations, a bias in judgment that derives from preexisting stereotypic beliefs. In these studies subjects overestimated the frequency with which stereotypic (relative to equally frequent nonstereotypic) attributes had described various occupational groups in the stimulus information. While this general tendency replicated previous findings, the effect was most strongly obtained under those conditions where the subjects' positive or negative mood state was incongruent with the evaluative tone of the stimulus attributes. That incongruency was postulated to make information processing more difficult, creating conditions wherein subjects' judgments might be more likely to reflect a heuristic reliance on stereotypic beliefs. The assumption of greater processing difficulty was supported by the analysis of subjects' processing times. Specifically, in those conditions for which there was incongruency between the valence of the mood state and the valence of the stimulus attributes, subjects spent significantly more time processing the stimulus items that did not contain a stereotypic attribute, compared to sentences that did contain stereotypic content. With increased processing difficulty, then, subjects found it easier to process stereotype-confirming information, and this in turn produced the overestimation of stereotype-consistent attributes that is observed in expectancy-based illusory correlations. Thus one's affective state, in conjunction with properties of the information being processed, created conditions under which subjects' judgments were more likely to reflect pre-existing stereotypes.

Again, these results seem more compatible with attentional than with motivational interpretations of affect's influence on information processing and judgment. This conclusion is based on two considerations. First, these results are consistent with other findings indicating that stereotypes have greater influence on judgments under conditions of increased cognitive demand and task difficulty (e.g., Bodenhausen & Lichtenstein, 1987; Pratto & Bargh, 1991). This similarity supports the interpretation that mood states influence the allocation of cognitive resources for complex information processing tasks. Second, as in the previous studies, our results were symmetric for the positive and negative mood conditions, again implicating cognitive rather than motivational effects of affective state.

We have summarized two sets of studies investigating the effects of mood state on biases that contribute to the unwarranted perception of intergroup differences. The distinctiveness-based illusory correlation contributes to the initial differentiation between groups (in the absence of preconceptions of those groups), whereas the expectancy-based illusory correlation reflects the influence of already established stereotypes on judgments. Taken together, these studies illustrate the complexities involved in understanding the impact of affective states on intergroup perceptions. In the first case, subjects in the positive and negative mood conditions failed to manifest a distinctiveness-based illusory correlation bias, suggesting that under these conditions affect might serve to attenuate a process contributing to stereotype formation. In contrast, in the second case induced mood resulted in the greater use of pre-existing beliefs in social judgments, suggesting conditions under which stereotypic responding is likely to be enhanced.

In light of these findings, it becomes clear that there is no simple answer to the question of whether affect has an augmenting or an ameliorating effect on stereotype-related outcomes. Our findings reveal both of these effects, though in different forms and in different paradigms that refer to different aspects of the overall stereotyping process. That is, affect diminished the likelihood that a cognitive bias would *create* differential group perceptions, but it also contributed to the greater *use* of already existing stereotypes. Affect, then, can have different effects on intergroup perceptions, depending on the conditions.

At the same time, the results of these experiments illustrate the value of investigating the impact of affective states not simply on intergroup judgments but on the cognitive processes that mediate those judgments. That is, despite the differing outcomes just noted, the evidence suggests that affect had the same effect on underlying mechanisms in both cases. Specifically, our findings are most easily interpreted by viewing affect as constraining the observer's capacity for thorough and efficient processing of information about group members. In the case of distinctiveness-based illusory correlations, this constraint undermines detection of the differential frequencies of stimulus items, thereby undermining the typically observed bias in group perceptions. In the case of expectancy-based illusory correlations, the increased demands imposed by the incongruency between mood state and valence of stimulus information result in greater reliance on the simplifying strategy of using preexisting group stereotypes as a basis for judgment. Thus, by focusing on measures of underlying cognitive processes, we are able to determine not only *what* effects affective states have on intergroup perceptions, but also *how* those effects come about.

Acknowledgments

Preparation of this chapter was supported by NIMH Grant MH-40058 to D. L. Hamilton and by NIMH Grant MH-43041 to D. M. Mackie. The research reported here was conducted while S. J. Stroessner was a Jacob K. Javits National Graduate Fellow.

References

Abele, A. (1985). Thinking about thinking. Causal, evaluative and finalistic cognitions about social situations. *European Journal of Social Psychology, 15,* 315–332.

Adorno, T. W., Frenkel-Brunswik, E., Levinson, D. J., & Sanford, R. N. (1950). *The authoritarian personality.* New York: Harper.

Bettelheim, B., & Janowitz, M. (1949). Ethnic tolerance: A function of social and personal control. *American Journal of Sociology, 55,* 137–145.

Bless, H., Bohner, G., Schwarz, N., & Strack, F. (1990). Mood and persuasion: A cognitive response analysis. *Personality and Social Psychology Bulletin, 16,* 331–345.

Bless, H., Hamilton, D. L., & Mackie, D. M. (1992). Mood effects on the organization of person information. *European Journal of Social Psychology.*

Bodenhausen, G. V., & Kramer, G. P. (1990). *Affective states trigger stereotypic judgments.* Paper presented at the American Psychological Society Convention, Dallas, Texas.

Bodenhausen, G. V., & Lichtenstein, M. (1987). Social stereotypes and information processing strategies: The impact of task complexity. *Journal of Personality and Social Psychology, 52,* 871–880.

Bower, G. H. (1981). Mood and memory. *American Psychologist, 36,* 129–148.

Bransford, J. D. (1979). *Human cognition.* Belmont, CA: Wadsworth.

Chapman, L. J. (1967). Illusory correlation in observational report. *Journal of Verbal Learning and Verbal Behavior, 6,* 151–155.

Clark, M. S., & Isen, A. M. (1982). Towards understanding the relationship between feeling states and social behavior. In A. H. Hastorf & A. M. Isen (Eds.), *Cognitive social psychology* (pp. 73–108). New York: Elsevier-North Holland.

Dollard, J., Doob, L. W., Miller, M. E., Mowrer, O. H., & Sears, R. R. (1939). *Frustration and aggression.* New Haven: Yale University Press.

Ellis, H. C., & Ashbrook, P. W. (1988). Resource allocation model of the effects of depressed mood states on memory. In K. Fiedler & J. P. Forgas (Eds.), *Affect, cognition, and social behavior* (pp. 25–43). Toronto: Hogrefe.

Erdelyi, M. H., & Blumenthal, D. G. (1973). Cognitive masking in rapid sequential processing: The effect of an emotional picture on preceding and succeeding pictures. *Memory and Cognition, 1,* 201–204.

Fiedler, K. (1988). Emotional mood, cognitive style, and behavior regulation. In K. Fiedler & J. P. Forgas (Eds.), *Affect, cognition, and social behavior* (pp. 100–119). Toronto: Hogrefe.

Fiedler, K. (1991a). On the task, the measures and the mood in research on affect and social cognition. In J. Forgas (Ed.), *Emotion and social judgments* (pp. 83–104). Elmsford, NY: Pergamon.

Fiedler, K. (1991b). The tricky nature of skewed frequency tables: An information loss account of "distinctiveness-based illusory correlations." *Journal of Personality and Social Psychology, 60,* 24–36.

Forgas, J. P. (Ed.). (1991). *Emotion and social judgments.* Elmsford, NY: Pergamon.

Forgas, J. P., & Bower, G. H. (1987). Mood effects on person perception judgments. *Journal of Personality and Social Psychology, 53,* 53–60.

Forgas, J. P., & Bower, G. H. (1988). Affect in social and personal judgments. In K. Fiedler & J. P. Forgas (Eds.), *Affect, cognition, and social behavior* (pp. 183–208). Toronto: Hogrefe.

Hamilton, D. L. (1981). Illusory correlation as a basis for stereotyping. In D. L. Hamilton (Ed.), *Cognitive processes in stereotyping and intergroup behavior* (pp. 115–144). Hillsdale, NJ: Erlbaum.

Hamilton, D. L., & Gifford, R. K. (1976). Illusory correlation in interpersonal perception: A cognitive basis of stereotypic judgments. *Journal of Experimental Social Psychology, 12,* 392–407.

Hamilton, D. L., & Rose, T. L. (1980). Illusory correlation and the maintenance of stereotypic beliefs. *Journal of Personality and Social Psychology, 39,* 832–845.

Hamilton, D. L., & Sherman, S. J. (1989). Illusory correlations: Implications for stereotype theory and research. In D. Bar-Tal, C. F. Graumann, A. W. Kruglanski, & W. Stroebe (Eds.), *Stereotyping and prejudice: Changing conceptions* (pp. 59–82). New York: Springer-Verlag.

Hamilton, D. L., & Trolier, T. K. (1986). Stereotypes and stereotyping: An overview of the cognitive approach. In J. Dovidio & S. L. Gaertner (Eds.), *Prejudice, discrimination, and racism* (pp. 127–163). New York: Academic Press.

Hamilton, D. L., Sherman, S. J., & Ruvolo, C. M. (1990). Stereotype-based expectancies: Effects on information processing and social behavior. *Journal of Social Issues, 46*(2), 35–60.

Hildebrand-Saints, L., & Weary, G. (1989). Depression and social information gathering. *Personality and Social Psychology Bulletin, 15,* 150–160.

Isen, A. M. (1984). Toward understanding the role of affect in cognition. In R. S. Wyer, Jr., & T. K. Srull (Eds.), *Handbook of social cognition* (pp. 179–236). Hillsdale, NJ: Erlbaum.

Isen, A. M. (1987). Positive affect, cognitive processes, and social behavior. In L. Berkowitz (Ed.), *Advances in experimental social psychology* (Vol. 20, pp. 203–253). New York: Academic Press.

Isen, A. M., & Daubman, K. A. (1984). The influence of affect on categorization. *Journal of Personality and Social Psychology, 47,* 1206–1217.

Isen, A. M. Shalker, T., Clark, M., & Karp, L. (1978). Positive affect, accessibility of material in memory, and behavior: A cognitive loop? *Journal of Personality and Social Psychology, 36,* 1–12.

Isen, A. M., Means, B., Patrick, R., & Nowicki, G. (1982). Some factors influencing decision-making and risk taking. In M. S. Clark & S. T. Fiske (Eds.), *Affect and cognition* (pp. 243–261). Hillsdale, NJ: Erlbaum.

Isen, A. M., Johnson, M. M. S., Hertz, E., & Robinson, G. F. (1985). The effects of positive affect on the unusualness of word associations. *Journal of Personality and Social Psychology, 48,* 1413–1414.

Kim, H., & Baron, R. S. (1988). Exercise and the illusory correlation: Does arousal heighten stereotypic processing? *Journal of Experimental Social Psychology, 24,* 366–380.

Lippmann, W. (1922). *Public opinion.* New York: Harcourt, Brace.

Mackie, D. M., & Worth, L. T. (1989). Processing deficits and the mediation of positive affect in persuasion. *Journal of Personality and Social Psychology, 57,* 27–40.

Mackie, D. M., & Worth, L. T. (1991). "Feeling good but not thinking straight": Positive mood and persuasion. In J. P. Forgas (Ed.), *Emotion and social judgments* (pp. 201–220). Oxford: Pergamon Press.

Mackie, D. M., Hamilton, D. L., Schroth, H. A., Carlisle, C. J., Gersho, B. F., Meneses, L. M., Nedler, B. F., & Reichel, L. D. (1989). The effects of induced mood on expectancy-based illusory correlations. *Journal of Experimental Social Psychology, 25,* 524–544.

Masters, J. C., Barden, R. C., & Ford, M. E. (1979). Affective states, expressive behavior, and learning in children. *Journal of Personality and Social Psychology, 37,* 380–390.

Mullen, B., & Johnson, C. (1990). Distinctiveness-based illusory correlations and stereotyping: A meta-analytic integration. *British Journal of Social Psychology, 29,* 11–28.

Pratto, F., & Bargh, J. A. (1991). Stereotyping based on apparently individuating information: Trait and global components of sex stereotypes under attention overload. *Journal of Experimental Social Psychology, 27,* 26–47.

Pryor, J. B. (1986). The influence of different encoding sets upon the formation of illusory correlations and group impressions. *Personality and Social Psychology Bulletin, 12,* 216–226.

Sanbonmatsu, D. M., Shavitt, S., & Sherman, S. J. (1991). The role of personal relevance in the formation of distinctiveness-based illusory correlations. *Personality and Social Psychology Bulletin, 17,* 124–132.

Schaller, M., & Maass, A. (1989). Illusory correlation and social categorization: Toward an integration of motivational and cognitive factors in stereotype formation. *Journal of Personality and Social Psychology, 56,* 709–721.

Schwarz, N. (1990). Feelings as information: Informational and motivational functions of affective states. In R. Sorrentino & E. T. Higgins (Eds.), *Handbook of motivation and cognition: Foundations of social behavior* (Vol. 2, pp. 527–561). New York: Guilford.

Schwarz, N., & Bless, H. (1991). Happy and mindless, but sad and smart? The impact of affective states on analytic reasoning. In J. Forgas (Ed.), *Emotion and social judgments* (pp. 55–71). Elmsford, NY: Pergamon.

Schwarz, N., & Clore, G. L. (1988). How do I feel about it? Informative functions of affective states. In K. Fiedler & J. Forgas (Eds.), *Affect, cognition, and social behavior* (pp. 44–62). Toronto: Hogrefe.

Silberman, E. K., Weingartner, H., & Post, R. M. (1983). Thinking disorder in depression: Logic and strategy in an abstract reasoning task. *Archives of General Psychiatry, 40,* 775–780.

Sinclair, R. C. (1988). Mood, categorization breadth, and performance appraisals: The effects of order of information acquisition and affective state on halo, accuracy, information retrieval, and evaluations. *Organizational Behavior and Human Decision Processes, 42,* 22–46.

Singer, J. A., & Salovey, P. (1988). Mood and memory: Evaluating the network theory of affect. *Clinical Psychology Review, 8,* 211–251.

Slusher, M. P., & Anderson, C. A. (1987). When reality monitoring fails: The role of imagination in stereotype maintenance. *Journal of Personality and Social Psychology, 52,* 653–662.

Smith, E. R. (1991). Illusory correlation in a simulated exemplar-based memory. *Journal of Experimental Social Psychology, 27,* 107–123.

Spears, R., Eiser, J. R., & van der Pligt, J. (1987). Further evidence for expectancy-based illusory correlations. *European Journal of Social Psychology, 17,* 253–258.

Srull, T. K. (1983). Affect and memory: The impact of affective reactions in advertising on the representation of product information in memory. In R. Bagozzi and A. Tybout (Eds.), *Advances in consumer research* (Vol. 10, pp. 520–525). Ann Arbor, MI: Association for Consumer Research.

Srull, T. K. (1987). Memory, mood, and consumer judgment. In M. Wallendorf & P. Anderson (Eds.), *Advances in consumer research* (Vol. 14, pp. 404–407). Provo, UT: Association for Consumer Research.

Stephan, W. G. (1985). Intergroup relations. In G. Lindzey & E. Aronson (Eds.), *Handbook of social psychology* (Vol. 2, pp. 599–658). New York: Random House.

Stephan, W. G., & Stephan, C. W. (1985). Intergroup anxiety. *Journal of Social Issues, 41*(3), 157–175.

Stroebe, W., & Insko, C. A. (1989). Stereotype, prejudice, and discrimination: Changing conceptions in theory and research. In D. Bar-Tal, C. F. Graumann, A. W. Kruglanski, and

W. Stroebe (Eds.), *Stereotyping and prejudice: Changing conceptions* (pp. 3–34). New York: Springer-Verlag.

Stroessner, S. J., & Mackie, D. M. (1992). The impact of induced affect on the perception of variability in social groups. *Personality and Social Psychology Bulletin, 18,* 546–554.

Stroessner, S. J., Hamilton, D. L., & Mackie, D. M. (1992). Affect and stereotyping: The effect of induced mood on distinctiveness-based illusory correlations. *Journal of Personality and Social Psychology, 62,* 564–576.

Sullivan, M. J. L., & Conway, M. (1989). Negative affect leads to low-effort cognition: Attributional processing for observed social behavior. *Social Cognition, 7,* 315–337.

Wegner, D. M., Schneider, D. J., Carter, S., III, & White, L. (1987). Paradoxical effects of thought suppression. *Journal of Personality and Social Psychology, 53,* 5–13.

Chapter 4

Affect and Perceived Group Variability: Implications for Stereotyping and Prejudice

STEVEN J. STROESSNER and DIANE M. MACKIE

Department of Psychology
University of California, Santa Barbara
Santa Barbara, California

> *Most of the business of life can go on with less effort if we stick to-gether with our own kind. Foreigners are a strain . . .*
> —Allport, *The Nature of Prejudice*

Introduction

Affect is an inexorable force in intergroup relations. Encounters with members of different groups might activate beliefs and thoughts, but they are also likely to activate feelings and emotions (Fiske & Pavelchak, 1986). In fact, contact with outgroup members is likely to be characterized by heightened levels of both arousal and affect (Dijker, 1987; Pettigrew, 1986; Stephan & Stephan, 1985).

Unfortunately (as Allport's quote makes clear) the feelings that arise during intergroup contact are often negative in nature. This is especially true when prior intergroup contact is characterized by a history of conflict (Sherif, 1966) or if interactants have negative stereotypes about outgroup members (Stephan & Stephan, 1985). In one recent study, for example, students who were asked to imagine the emotions that they would experience when conversing with a member of another race reported expecting to feel irritation, dislike, apprehension, and anxiety (Vanman & Miller, Chapter

10, this volume). Similar results are found when heterosexual males experience or imagine the presence of homosexual males (Jackson & Sullivan, 1987). Such feelings may be heightened when actual contact between groups is minimal, leaving perceivers with little knowledge of or experience with outgroup members (Stephan & Stephan, 1985).

Of course, there are situations in which intergroup contact might produce positive emotions. When interactions between group members are successful, members are likely to feel happy, jovial, or satisfied (Amir, 1969). If groups successfully cooperate to obtain a superordinate goal, positive affect is likely (Sherif, 1966). In addition, if attitudes about a group are ambivalent, that is, they contain both positive and negative evaluations of the group, then both positive and negative emotions may be simultaneously evoked by intergroup contact (Katz, Wackenhut, & Haas, 1986). Whether positive, negative, or ambivalent in valence, emotion appears to be an integral and inevitable part of intergroup interaction.

Despite the likely presence of affect during intergroup encounters, relatively little empirical work has directly addressed the impact of affective states on intergroup perceptions, judgments, and behaviors. Because affect has been shown to have consequences on information processing in a number of different contexts (Fiedler & Forgas, 1988; Forgas, 1991a; Isen, 1987), it should come as no surprise that affect also influences the cognitive processes underlying intergroup perception. The breadth of chapters in this volume testifies to the impact or affect on a wide range of processes implicated in intergroup judgments and behaviors. In this chapter, we describe a series of studies assessing the influence of affect on one important process underlying stereotyping of group members: the formation of judgments about a group's variability.

Perceived Variability and Stereotyping

Until recently, perception of the differences within a group was not of primary interest to stereotype researchers. Traditionally, research on stereotyping focused on measuring the perceived central tendencies of social groups on various attributes (Dovidio, Evans, & Tyler, 1986; Gilbert, 1951; Karlins, Coffman, & Walters, 1969; Katz & Braly, 1933). Erroneous perceptions of central tendencies, such as "Jews are shrewd" or "Blacks are lazy" (Katz & Braly, 1933), were thought to be the primary obstacle to harmonious relations between groups.

Several theorists have speculated that an equally pernicious consequence of stereotypes—as much as their negative nature—is the consequential stripping of stigmatized groups of variability (Linville, Salovey, & Fischer, 1986; Park & Hastie, 1987; Park & Judd, 1990). Because stereotypes contain attributes that are assumed to be characteristic of group members in general, stereotypes discourage recognition of differences among members of targeted groups. As Gordon Allport pointed out, "the category saturates all that it contains with the same ideational and emotional flavor" (1954, p. 21). Thus, stereotypes are damaging not only because they contain negative beliefs about group members but also because these beliefs are generalized to all group members. It is for this reason that Linville and her colleagues argue that lack of intragroup differentiation is "at the heart of the stereotype concept" (Linville, Salovey, & Fischer, 1986, p. 165).

What are the negative consequences associated with reductions in perceived intragroup variability? Research on this topic has primarily focused on differential perceptions of intragroup variability within ingroups and outgroups. One consistent finding, termed the outgroup homogeneity effect, is that outgroups are perceived as more homogeneous than ingroups (Judd & Park, 1988; Linville, Fischer, & Salovey, 1990; Linville et al., 1986; Park & Rothbart, 1982; Quattrone & Jones, 1980; Wilder, 1984). This effect has been associated with polarized evaluations of outgroup members, presumably because perceivers' homogeneous representations of outgroups are noncomplex (Linville & Jones, 1980). Perceivers are also more likely to make generalizations about members of homogeneous outgroups (Nisbett, Krantz, Jepson, & Kunda, 1983; Quattrone & Jones, 1980) and are more likely to discriminate against a homogeneous outgroup's members (Wilder, 1978).

One intuitively obvious strategy for countering the negative consequences of perceived homogeneity is to increase perceptions of intragroup variability by encouraging members of different groups to interact with one another. This suggestion, of course, lies at the heart of the contact hypothesis (Allport, 1954; Cook, 1978; see Miller & Brewer, 1984, for a review). As intergroup contact increases, representations of groups should become more differentiated, and perceptions of intragroup variability should increase (Brewer & Miller, 1984; Linville et al., 1986; Wilder, 1978). Contact between groups should thus decrease the insidious consequences of perceived homogeneity.

But does it do so? In fact, assessments of stereotype and prejudice reduction following contact reveal mixed results, and the conditions under which intergroup contact does and does not work continue to provoke both empirical and theoretical debate (Brewer & Miller, 1984; Hewstone & Brown, 1986; Pettigrew, 1986; Stephan, 1987). Conspicuously absent from many such discussions, however, is the role that affect or emotion could play in promoting or inhibiting the potential benefits of contact (McClendon, 1974; Stephan & Stephan, 1984, 1985 are exceptions). Yet, if intergroup interaction, either actual or anticipated, is marked by affect, the impact of affect on intergroup perceptions might be pervasive. More specifically, affect could be expected to influence the perceptions of variability intended to break down stereotypes. This, then, was the issue that motivated our investigation: How does the presence of affect impact perceptions of the variability within a group?

How Do People Judge Group Variability?

Until recently, relatively little was known about how people make judgments of intragroup variability. In the last ten years, however, a number of models have developed that focus on how judgments of intragroup variability are made. The models differ primarily with regard to what type of information serves as the primary basis for making variability judgments and with regard to the timing of these judgments. Some models argue that information about group variability is abstracted from individual group member exemplars on-line (i.e., as they are encountered and processed) and the abstracted information serves as the basis for making variability judgments. Other models posit that representations of exemplars are stored in memory and retrieved when a judgment of intragroup variability is required. Despite the differences among the existing models, all place a great emphasis on attention to and processing of exemplar information.

According to the first type of model, variability information is abstracted on-line. Fried and Holyoak (1984) have proposed a model positing the on-line abstraction of both central tendency and variability information. As perceivers are exposed to individual members of a category, summary representations reflecting both the category's central tendency and variability on a variety of attributes are formed. Both central tendency and variability information are used to make subsequent decisions about the category as well as about new exemplars, and both types of information are updated as new exemplars are encountered. Although specific exemplars may be stored in memory along with the abstracted information, these exemplars play no role in judgments about the category. However, thorough processing of the exemplars is important in such models because it allows the initial on-line abstraction of variability information.

The second set of models argues that judgments of variability are made in a memory-based fashion. In these models, group-level judgments about variability are not abstracted as group members are encountered, but rather are computed from stored exemplar information retrieved some time later. Thorough processing of exemplars is also crucial in these models, however, because the efficient encoding of exemplars allows subsequent retrieval of this information from memory when judgments of variability need to be made.

One such model was proposed by Linville and her colleagues (Linville *et al.*, 1986, 1990). They argue that group information is represented in memory by both individual exemplars and abstracted types and subtypes. Abstracted information has no special status in this model, however, and abstractions simply serve as additional exemplars. Variability is computed by retrieving a set of exemplars and observing the distribution of the exemplars on an attribute dimension.

Another exemplar-based model, termed the dual predictor model (Kashima & Kashima, 1991), argues that the perception of variability within a group is a function of the perceived similarities and differences within a set of retrieved exemplars. Consistent with the arguments of Tversky (1977), differences among a set of retrieved exemplars should increase and similarities among the exemplars should decrease the perception of variability. When information about both similarities and differences exists within a set of exemplars, then differences and similarities will have additive effect, and perceived variability will depend on the relative salience of each type of information. Thorough processing is necessary to allow the encoding of an exemplar's features so that this information will be available to compute the similarities and differences within a set of retrieved exemplars.

In contrast to the models discussed above, Park and her colleagues (Judd & Park, 1988; Park & Hastie, 1987; Park & Judd, 1990) have proposed a model that explicitly recognizes the influence of both abstracted and exemplar information on variability judgments. Consistent with Fried and Holyoak's (1984) position, the model argues that judgments of a group's variability are made as exemplars are encountered. This model, however, also recognizes the role of stored exemplars in updating or "correcting" the stored variability judgment. For example, if the stored judgment is that the group is homogeneous, but the retrieved exemplars appear to represent more diversity, the judgment will be modified to reflect the variability inherent within the set of exemplars. Processing of exemplar information is doubly important in this model because it determines both what is abstracted on-line and what is available to supplement, update, or verify that group-level information later.

How Might Affect Influence Judgments of Group Variability?

Any factor that influences how exemplar information is processed is therefore likely to influence variability judgments. Perceivers' affective states have been shown to strongly influence how information is processed in a number of different contexts (e.g., Fiedler & Forgas, 1988; Forgas, 1991a; Isen, 1984, 1987; Schwarz, 1990). In regard to positive affect, there is accumulating evidence that positive mood reduces deliberate processing of information. Because deliberate and thorough processing is undermined by positive affect, perceivers tend to rely on intuitive and heuristic cues to make judgments about a group's members (Bodenhausen & Kramer, 1990; Mackie *et al.*, 1989). In addition, positive affect can undermine biases requiring relatively deliberative processing (Stroessner, Hamilton, & Mackie,

1992). Thus, people in a positive mood often fail to process available information in a thorough fashion.

Negative mood, specifically sadness, has not produced such unequivocally clear results. Sadness has been argued to both leave unaffected (Schwarz, 1990) and undermine (Ellis & Ashbrook, 1988) the thoroughness with which information is processed. Compared to positive mood, negative mood appears to increase the careful processing of information about performances (Sinclair, 1988) and about judgments of criminal guilt (Bodenhausen & Kramer, 1990). On the other hand, both experimentally saddened and clinically depressed subjects perform poorly in memory tasks, especially when the task is complex (Ellis, Thomas, & Rodriguez, 1984). They also appear to do less systematic processing of material from which inferences can be drawn and hypotheses deduced (Silberman, Weingartner, & Post, 1983; Sullivan & Conway, 1989). In addition, sad subjects show no signs of an illusory correlation bias, a bias which depends on relatively thorough information processing (Stroessner et al., 1992). Thus there is some evidence to suggest that both positive and negative affect can have detrimental effects on careful information processing.

Considering the impact of affect on information processing in these varied contexts, both positive and negative mood might be expected to influence perceivers' judgments of variability within social groups. Positive moods, by interfering with the deliberative processing and encoding of group exemplars, would make veridical identification of intragroup variability difficult. Negative moods might also interfere with the processes necessary to correctly judge variability.

In fact, one series of studies demonstrated just these effects on the perception of variability within groups of nonsocial stimuli, specifically, words and colors (Isen & Daubman, 1984). In these studies, positive affect was experimentally induced before subjects rated the category fit of a variety of exemplars in a number of different ways. Regardless of the variety of means by which positive affect was induced, subjects in a positive mood created and used broader, more inclusive categories than did control (neutral mood) subjects. Happy subjects formed fewer categories when they were asked to group stimuli together to form groups, and they were more likely to rate unusual exemplars as category members compared to those in a neutral mood. Happy subjects were thus more likely to see everything as similar and as "going together" and much less likely to reflect exemplar variability in their judgments.

In two of these studies, Isen and Daubman (1984) induced negative affect by showing subjects a documentary film of Nazi concentration camps. Subjects in whom a negative mood had been induced showed similar effects on the categorization tasks as did subjects in the positive mood conditions, although the findings did not reach customary levels of statistical significance. Subjects in a negative mood were marginally more likely than neutral mood subjects to rate unusual exemplars as category members and were more likely to group diverse colors together.

In summary, then, it appears that both positive and negative affective states might interfere with the accurate processing of individual exemplars and, as a result, influence the perception of intragroup variability. Our research tested this hypothesis with perceivers judging social stimuli, namely, a group of individuals. We hypothesized that both positive and negative affect would undermine perceivers' ability to accurately perceive the variability within a social group. Specifically, we expected that subjects in these mood conditions would not accurately perceive a heterogeneous group as being more variable than a homogeneous group. This hypothesis was based on the belief that the presence of affect during encoding of group exemplar information interferes with the thoroughness with which the information is processed. Consequently, the ability to accurately perceive intragroup variability is adversely affected.

Affect and the Perception of Intragroup Variability

In our first experiment (Stroessner & Mackie, 1992, Experiment 1), male and female undergraduates were asked to watch a brief videotape segment, supposedly to rate its suitability for use in a classroom project. Subjects saw either a humorous segment from a television comedy special, a poignant excerpt from a documentary about a camp for children with cancer, or a neutral piece on the corking of fine wines. These excerpts were intended to induce a positive mood, a sad mood, or to have no particular affective consequences, respectively. Our cover story allowed us to ask the subjects to rate the videotapes on a variety of items. In this way, we were able to ensure that the video segments successfully induced the intended affective states without arousing subjects' suspicions about the purpose of the experiment.

Following the mood induction, subjects read about the members of a hypothetical group of males whose behaviors were either quite homogeneous or rather heterogeneous. Each subject saw 28 different sentences, each of which described an activity engaged in by a single group member (we borrowed the stimulus set from Park & Hastie, 1987). Half of the sentences described activities related to sociability and half described behaviors that pertained to intelligence.

One group of students saw a set of sentences in which the variability of the behaviors described was rather low. That is, there were no extremely intelligent, extremely stupid, extremely sociable, or extremely unsociable behaviors; the activities of the 28 members all suggested a moderate degree of both intelligence or sociability.

Subjects in the high variability condition, however, read a set of behaviors reflecting a high degree of variability on these traits. Some of the group members were described as behaving in highly intelligent or sociable ways, whereas others engaged in rather unintelligent and introverted activities. One member, for example, was described as having "joined a group of strangers playing frisbee," whereas another "went to a Saturday matinee alone." Although one member of the group "presented the paper to experts in his field," another "failed the written driver's test."

It is important to note that the average sociability and intelligence values represented in the two behavior sets were identical; the sets differed only in the degree of variability around this central tendency. The subjects in both the high and low variability conditions were asked to read each behavioral statement carefully and, after having done so, to indicate "how similar the members of the group were to one another" by checking a 9-point scale. They answered this question three times: once with regard to the group members' general similarity, once with regard to their sociability, and once with regard to their intelligence. These three measures of similarity were highly correlated and so were reverse scored and averaged to form a variability index with higher scores representing greater perceived variability. We then examined this index to see how the experimental manipulations of affective state influenced subjects' perceptions of variability.

These results appear in Figure 1. As can be seen, affective state had a dramatic effect on ratings of variability. Only those in the neutral-mood conditions accurately perceived the heterogeneous group as more variable than the homogeneous group. In contrast, subjects in both the positive- and negative-mood conditions saw targets in both groups as being equally (and highly) similar to one another. Although ratings of the homogeneous group were comparable regardless of affective state, the presence of either positive or negative mood made perceivers less aware of the variability in the heterogeneous group. Thus, our results are consistent with previous studies that used nonsocial stimuli (e.g., Isen & Daubman, 1984) and support the argument that both positive and negative affect can influence the accuracy of judgments regarding intragroup variability.

What produced these differences? Why were those experiencing either positive or negative mood so immune to the variability information? Recall that we had predicted these results would occur if affective states decrease deliberative processing of the material. Although we collected no measures in this study bearing directly on this question, one of our other measures did reveal results consistent with this idea. We asked subjects to indicate how sociable and intelligent the group members were as a whole. Recall that based on pretesting of the individual items the central tendencies of the groups on these two traits were equated. When asked to make judgments about the group as a whole, however, subjects in a neutral mood perceived the heterogeneous targets as less intelligent and less sociable than the homogeneous group, apparently reflecting the greater weight they gave to ex-

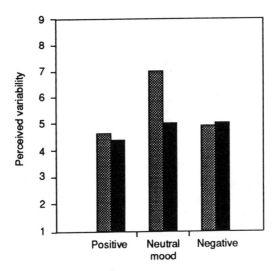

Figure 1 Ratings of intragroup variability by induced mood and variability condition, Experiment 1. Higher scores (of a possible 9) indicate greater perceived variability. HV, High variability (▨); LV, low variability (■).

tremely negative items when combining behaviors into an overall impression. [Subjects in Park and Hastie's (1987) experiment who did not experience a mood induction showed the same effect.] In contrast, judgments made by subjects in a positive or negative mood appeared unaffected by the presence of extreme behaviors in the heterogeneous behavior set. By apparently decreasing the perceived diversity of presented behaviors, affect simultaneously inflated similarity judgments and reduced the impact of extreme behaviors on judgments.

Although these results were consistent with our hypotheses, we were aware of some alternative mechanisms that might have contributed to our findings. First, our study was not the first to demonstrate that mildly elated subjects report seeing more similarities among presented stimuli than do subjects in a neutral mood. Similar findings were reported by Murray, Sujan, Hirt, and Sujan (1990). After receiving a positive-, negative-, or neutral-mood induction, subjects in their study performed a sorting task similar to the one used by Isen and Daubman (1984). Subjects were asked to focus on differences between stimuli, focus on similarities between stimuli, or were given no explicit processing instructions. In the no processing goal condition, subjects in a positive mood formed fewer categories than did subjects in the neutral- or negative-mood conditions. These findings are consistent with our results for subjects in a positive mood, although subjects in their negative-mood condition formed as many categories as did neutral-mood subjects.

The findings obtained in the other processing goal conditions, however, suggest an alternate interpretation of effects of positive mood. When subjects in a positive mood were instructed to focus on intraitem similarity, they formed relatively few categories compared to the subjects in the negative- or neutral-mood conditions. However, when these same subjects were told to focus on differences between items, they formed more categories than the other subjects. Murray *et al.* (1990) speculated that positive affect increased one's flexibility in processing exemplars so that subjects in a positive mood saw more similarities *and* more differences between items in a judgment task, depending on their processing goal.

These results suggest that subjects in our positive-mood condition might have reported seeing little heterogeneity in the high-variability group because the labeling of the variability scales (i.e., the primary dependent measure) asked them to focus on judging the similarity within the group. This interpretation contrasts with our argument that the inaccurate ratings of the heterogeneous group reflected a lack of thorough processing of the exemplars. It was possible that elated subjects would also report inflated intragroup *differences* compared to subjects in a neutral mood if they were asked to judge the variability, rather than the similarity, within the group. To assess this possibility, we asked subjects in a second study to indicate how *different,* rather than how *similar,* group members were to one another.

We were also interested in eliminating a second alternate explanation of our results, namely, that mood may have influenced judgments only because subjects read about a meaningless, unfamiliar, and uninvolving group. It has been suggested, for example, that mood effects are most apparent under conditions of low involvement or motivation (Forgas, 1991b). In our second study (Stroessner & Mackie, 1992, Experiment 2), therefore, we assessed the impact of affective states on perceptions of variability in a familiar and strongly stereotyped outgroup: a college sorority. Sororities are comprised of undergraduate female students who plan and participate in social and philanthropic activities and who frequently share residential facilities. Like most college populations, our students at University of California, Santa Barbara have well-ingrained stereotypes about sorority members, including the view that they are sociable but not very intelligent. Replicating the effects of the first experiment with this target group would indicate that mood can affect variability judgments even when the group is both meaningful and familiar. A demonstration of mood effects on estimations of variability in such groups would also be more germane to our contention that mood may interfere with the intended results of contact with stereotyped groups. In such cases, for example, one has to deal with the issue of whether the presence of stereotypic beliefs would enhance or undermine perceptions of variability.

Affect and Perceived Variability of Real Groups

To assess these issues, we asked female undergraduates, none of whom belonged to a campus sorority, to watch one of our mood-inducing videotapes and to read some information about the members of an unidentified campus sorority. The procedure and cover story for showing the videotapes were the same as in our earlier study, but the actual content of the segments was changed to provide converging evidence for the mood induction. A segment from the television comedy show, "The Simpsons," was used to induce a positive mood; excerpts from an evening news show about a bus accident, a deadly disease, and ethnic strife were used to induce a negative mood; and a documentary segment on the history of Yellowstone Park was used as the nonaffective control. Responses to the manipulation check questions indicated that the tapes had been successful in inducing happiness, sadness, and affective neutrality, respectively.

Subjects then received a booklet of information about members of a single campus sorority. As in the earlier experiments, subjects saw behaviors that were either relatively homogeneous or quite variable, again pertaining to both intelligence and sociability. Behavioral items were presented one to a page, and subjects were given five seconds to read the item before being asked to turn to the next page.

After reading the behaviors, subjects were asked to indicate "How different are the members of this group from one another?" Their responses can be seen in Figure 2. As before, subjects in the neutral mood condition perceived the heterogeneous group's members as quite different from one another as compared to the members of the homogeneous group. Results in the two mood conditions also paralleled those in the earlier experiment: no distinction was made between the homogeneous and heterogeneous groups by subjects in either the positive- or negative-mood conditions. Subjects in these conditions saw targets in both groups as being equally lacking in variability.

Having established that both happiness and sadness interfered with the perception of variability in the sorority groups, we turned our attention to understanding the processes underlying this effect. We had asked subjects both to recall as many of the behavior sentences they could and to make several trait judgments about the targeted group of sorority members. Reasoning that less deliberative processing should reduce free recall and increase stereotypical judgments, we expected subjects in a positive and negative mood to recall fewer behaviors, and to make stereotype-congruent judgments of the sorority members, regardless of the information they had seen.

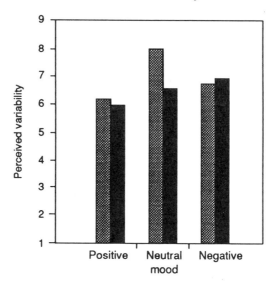

Figure 2 Ratings of intragroup variability by induced mood and variability condition, Experiment 2. Higher scores (of a possible 9) indicate greater perceived variability. HV, high variability (▨); LV, low variability (■).

As expected, subjects in a positive mood recalled few (only 15%) of the sociable and intelligent behaviors. However, subjects in the negative mood condition recalled as many behaviors as did those in the control condition (26% and 23% of the behaviors, respectively). Although the failure of happy subjects to perceive variability information may well have been due to their failure to process the information carefully, this did not necessarily appear to be true for those subjects experiencing sadness.

We also asked subjects to rate the sorority group's sociability, intelligence, promiscuity, and irresponsibility. The results of pretesting indicated that sociability and intelligence represented positive stereotypic and nonstereotypic attributes, respectively, whereas promiscuity and irresponsibility represented negative stereotypic and nonstereotypic traits, respectively. Examination of these ratings indicated that, as expected, subjects in a positive mood judged the stereotype-consistent traits to be highly characteristic of the group of sorority members and stereotype-inconsistent traits to be quite uncharacteristic of the group, regardless of whether they had seen the high or low variability set of behaviors. Although the trait ratings of subjects in the negative conditions showed a somewhat similar pattern, their ratings did not differ significantly from those of subjects in the neutral-mood conditions.

Our first two studies provided results generally consistent with our hypotheses. For positive mood, our results proved quite replicable and consistent with our predictions about affect undermining accurate perceptions of variability. Perceivers in a happy mood processed the available information in a less deliberate fashion than did those in a neutral mood (Mackie & Worth, 1991; Schwarz, 1990). First, they failed to differentiate the amount of variability present in the heterogeneous from that present in the homogeneous group. Second, this failure arose largely because these subjects made decreased estimates of variability in the heterogeneous group. Third, they recalled relatively few of the presented behaviors, and finally, they showed considerable reliance on a stereotype when making their judgments (see also Bodenhausen, Chapter 2, this volume). All of these results are consistent with the view that those in a happy mood did less deliberative processing of available information. What they do not tell us, however, is *why* these subjects show processing deficits of this kind. We return to this point below.

In addition, it is clear that the findings obtained in the positive-mood conditions are inconsistent with a cognitive flexibility interpretation of positive mood (Murray et al., 1990). Subjects in a positive mood in the first study who were asked to judge intragroup similarity reported seeing a high degree of similarity in both the behavioral sets. However, these same subjects did not report a high degree of differentiation when asked to indicate intragroup differences in the second study. Rather than increasing cognitive flexibility, positive mood appeared to make processing less thorough. As a consequence, it apparently reduced accurate perception of intragroup variability.

Consistent with prior research, the results for subjects in the sad-mood condition were less clear. We did find that sad subjects failed to correctly differentiate the variability present in the homogeneous and heterogeneous groups' behaviors, and that they underestimated the variability in the heterogeneous group. In fact, on these measures, they performed as poorly as the happy subjects. However, sad subjects showed no recall deficit and did not rely on the stereotype when judging the stimulus group (see also Bodenhausen & Kramer, 1990). Thus it was not clear whether saddened subjects were processing more or less deliberately than neutral-mood subjects.

In an attempt to better understand the processing deficit found in positive-mood conditions, and in the hope of clarifying the processes at work in the negative-mood conditions, we designed a study to more definitively test the mechanisms underlying the results obtained in the first two studies. Our reasoning was as follows: if subjects in a positive mood failed to make differentiated variability judgments because they were unable to process group-relevant information thoroughly, then giving them the opportunity to more thoroughly process the exemplar information should diminish the adverse impact of affect on perceived variability. If subjects feeling sad experience a processing deficit similar to that experienced by happy subjects, increasing the time they had to process the information might be expected to have a similar effect on sad subjects' judgments. Alternatively, if sad subjects do not experience a processing deficit in dealing with variability information, their responses might be expected to look more like those of neutral-mood subjects.

Reduced Perceived Variability: Motivation and Cognitive Mechanisms

In our third study (Stroessner & Mackie, 1990), then, we sought more direct evidence of the mechanisms underlying the apparent reduction of processing of variability-relevant information by observers in a good mood. Various theories of the impact of mood have suggested that such deficits could result for both motivational or cognitive reasons. According to the first view, positive mood decreases systematic processing because extensive processing detracts from the subjective experience of being in a good mood. Not surprisingly, being in a good mood is a positive and rewarding state. Individuals may well be motivated to maintain this positive state, selectively engaging in those activities that enhance their mood and avoiding those activities that threaten to destroy it (Isen & Levin, 1972; Isen & Simmonds, 1978; Mischel, Ebbesen, & Zeiss, 1973). Alternatively, positive mood could signal perceivers that there is no need to thoroughly process information in the environment (Schwarz, 1990). In this view, then, reduced systematic processing by people in a positive mood reflects a lack of desire or lack of need to process extensively.

Alternatively, positive mood may decrease systematic processing and increase "satisficing" strategies because it disrupts attentional allocation, interfering with performance on other capacity-intensive processing tasks (Mackie & Worth, 1989; see also Isen, 1984 and Isen et al., 1982, for related views). If positive affect is characterized by the activation of considerable amounts of affective material from memory, the affective nature of this information might consequently draw attention to itself, and detract from the capacity available to thoroughly process incoming information. In addition, the focus of attention might be broadened or diffused, leading to a continual allocation and reallocation of processing capacity. If so, focusing attention on tasks that require thorough or analytical processing would be difficult. From this perspective, then, those in a positive mood may not thoroughly process because they are less able to maintain the attentional focus necessary for such processing.

To assess the impact of motivational and cognitive antecedents of the mood-induced processing deficits found in our studies, we created experimental situations in which capacity and motivational explanations would make different predictions. Specifically, we manipulated the amount of time that subjects were given to look at the information presented. Some subjects were given only 3 seconds to see each behavioral item about the group—even less time than subjects were allotted to process information in the first two studies. If happy perceivers had difficulties processing the information, then subjects in the 3-seconds condition might be expected to do as poorly as, and perhaps even more poorly than subjects did in the previous studies. Other subjects were given 7 seconds to read each behavioral item. This was more than enough time to read the item and thus should diminish the effects of any processing difficulties created by affective state.

This manipulation of exposure time should thus be informative about the role of cognitive and motivational factors in our earlier results. On the one hand, if our earlier findings were the result of attentional difficulties, subjects in a positive mood should fail to differentiate high- and low-variability groups in the 3-second condition but should make such distinctions in the 7-second condition. On the other hand, if the earlier findings were due to motivational deficits, we should replicate our earlier findings in both the fast and the relatively leisurely processing condition. Inclusion of a negative-mood condition allowed us to determine whether results in this condition were more similar to those produced by the positive- or by the neutral-mood subjects.

Almost all of the procedures in our third study duplicated those used in the first two studies. Happy, neutral, and sad moods were induced in male and female subjects by having them watch the same video tapes employed in Experiment 1. As before, the responses to manipulation check items on the postvideo questionnaire revealed that watching the respective segments produced the intended affective states. Subjects were then exposed to one of the two sets of behaviors previously described, so that they read about either a highly variable or a rather homogeneous group. The important new manipulation in this study was exposure time: the items appeared one at a time on a computer monitor screen for either 3 seconds or 7 seconds. After the 28 items had appeared, subjects were asked to estimate the similarity of the group members to one another.

We tested our hypotheses with a series of planned comparisons. First, we tested whether subjects in the positive- and negative-mood conditions were able to distinguish between the high- and low-variability sets when subjects were under a processing constraint (i.e., processing the behaviors at a 3-second pace). As can be seen in Figure 3, both happy and sad subjects in the 3-second-pace condition saw both groups as being relatively homogeneous. Not surprisingly, then, this contrast did not even approach significance, $F(1, 205) = .61$, $p = .44$. We also predicted that those who had time to process the information *and* those in a neutral mood would produce different variability judgments for the two sets. This planned contrast was significant, $F(1, 205) = 16.83$, $p < .001$. Happy and sad subjects who viewed the behaviors at a 7-second pace produced different variability ratings for the two sets, as did subjects in the neutral-mood conditions. Finally, we

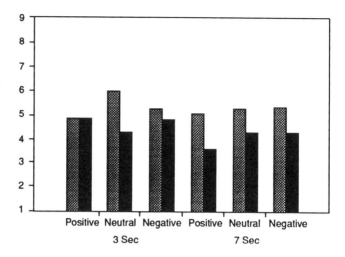

Figure 3   Ratings of intragroup variability by induced mood, variability condition, and pace of presentation, Experiment 3. Higher scores (of a possible 9) indicate greater perceived variability. HV, high variability ( ); LV, low variability ( ).

compared the ratings of the high- and low-variability sets made by happy and sad subjects in the 3-second and the 7-second conditions. As expected, this contrast was significant, $F(1, 205) = 6.6, p < .05$. Given enough time to thoroughly process the information, subjects in the positive- and negative-mood conditions produced variability judgments as differentiated as the judgments of subjects in a neutral mood, even though they had failed to differentiate the homogeneous and the heterogeneous groups when processing time was limited. The results from this study were thus more consistent with a processing constraint interpretation in both the positive- and the negative-mood conditions.

Taken together, the results of the three studies provide considerable evidence that both happy and sad moods decrease perceivers' abilities to make intragroup differentiations, an important process contributing to stereotypical judgments and behavior. In three different studies, subjects in a happy mood did not perceive the differential amounts of variability present in homogeneous and heterogeneous social groups. These subjects also produced evidence of decreased deliberative processing of group information and increased reliance on a stereotype when judging the group. Only when happy subjects were given enough time to process the behavioral information did they produce differentiated estimates of intragroup variability.

With regard to sad mood, the results were somewhat mixed. Subjects who were in a sad mood did not accurately perceive the greater variability present in the heterogeneous set of behavioral descriptions, unless adequate time to process was available. In this regard, responses from sad subjects were identical to those produced by happy subjects. Sad subjects, however, did not reveal processing deficits in the amount of recalled information or the tendency to stereotype outgroup members. Although the mechanisms underlying these findings are less clear, the results demonstrate that negative affect can undermine differential perception of variability to the same degree as positive affect, and that increasing processing time can ameliorate this situation.

Affect and the Contact Hypothesis: Implications for Stereotype Change

We began this chapter by discussing several of the negative consequences associated with a lack of perceived variability. We also briefly described the contact hypothesis: the belief that increasing exposure to members of various groups can increase perceptions of variability and consequently avoid these negative consequences. Despite the appealing simplicity of contact as a solution to stereotyping and prejudice, many factors have been found to qualify the conditions under which contact can have benefits for intergroup perception, as noted above.

The present studies suggest an additional factor that may make group differentiation difficult to achieve through intergroup contact. The presence of affect as group-relevant information is encoded appears to moderate or even undermine the potential benefits of contact between group members (Amir, 1969; Miller & Brewer, 1984). In fact, our data indicate that both positive and negative affect can *increase* the likelihood of stereotyping of outgroup members. Although intuition suggests that the presence of positive affect during intergroup contact should improve intergroup relations (cf. Amir, 1969), our data suggest that some undesirable effects are likely to arise under such conditions. In fact, positive mood heightened two manifestations of stereotyping: a reliance on perceived central tendencies in making judgments and perceptions of group homogeneity. Negative mood also had at least one potential undesirable effect on intergroup perception: groups were perceived as homogeneous entities.

Because of these effects, the affective states of perceivers may be an important consideration for intervention strategies aimed at increasing perceptions of intracategory differentiation. The potential costs of experiencing negative emotions such as anger, fear, and hate during intergroup interaction have always been clear. The more sobering implication of our results, however, is that those attempting to increase differentiation through intergroup contact may also need to consider the possible adverse consequences of positive affect on perceptions of variability and stereotyping.

Our studies demonstrate that mild states of happiness and sadness induced independently of the intergroup situation can nevertheless influence perceptions of intragroup variability. These results raise the issue of generalizability; would the obtained results generalize across other positive and negative affective states, and would they generalize to situations in which affect is an integral aspect of intergroup interaction? These questions are not of mere theoretical interest, since emotions such as anger, jealousy, fear, or pride may typically arise during interactions with members of different groups. The first issue of generalizability, whether different affective states influence processing in the same way, is an empirical question, and some early answers are described in other chapters in this volume (see Chapters 2, 10, and 5 by Bodenhausen, Vanman & Miller, and Wilder, respectively). In our studies, predictions were made about the motivational and cognitive consequences of two affective states. To the extent that other affective states have different motivational and cognitive consequences, different predictions would be made and different outcomes perhaps obtained. Pride, for example, could motivate one to see ingroups as richly varied and outgroups as sadly homogeneous. Threat could motivate the perception of solidarity-enhancing homogeneity in the ingroup while encouraging the perception of disorganized and splintered heterogeneity in the outgroup (Simon & Brown, 1987).

One factor likely to influence the cognitive and motivational implications of a particular affective or emotional state is its intensity. As intensity increases, the cognitive consequences of experiencing the emotion become more severe, with total disruption of processing being the upper bound. The intensity of manic euphoria, terror, or complete depression might have such effects. The relation between motivation and intensity, however, may be more complex. With both very low and very high levels of affective intensity, motivation to process may be low. In the former case the "signal" sent by the mood state or the motivation to overcome fairly low levels of processing impairment might be minimal. In the latter case, the intensity of the emotion might overwhelm motivation to process; attempts to cope may be seen as pointless, or applications of effort may be insufficient to cope with the cognitive consequences of intense emotion. All of this suggests that the maximal impact of motivational consequences of affect might be seen at intermediate levels of affective intensity. Because different emotions vary in intensity in the intergroup situation, different motivational and cognitive consequences will influence the processing of group relevant information.

The second issue of generalizability focuses on the potentially different impact of affect that is induced incidental to the intergroup interaction and affect that arises in the course of that interaction (see Bodenhausen, Chapter 2, this volume). We induced incidental affect—affect that arose prior to and independently of subjects reading the group information. Integrally induced affect may introduce motivational concerns not present in situations where perceivers are experiencing incidentally induced affect. A group member may, for example, feel happiness and good will toward an outgroup member following a particularly positive interaction. This may consequently motivate the perceiver to get to know the outgroup member better. Subsequent interactions could expose the perceiver to distinguishing features of the outgroup member and potentially increase the perceived variability of the outgroup as a whole.

Little is currently known about the differential effects of incidental and integral affect on intergroup perception. One program of research, however, does support the idea that affect that arises integrally in interaction can have effects very similar to those of affect induced independently of the intergroup situation. In a series of studies, Wilder and Shapiro (1989a,b; see Wilder, Chapter 5, this volume) showed that subjects who were anxious manifested assimilation effects in group-relevant judgments. Anxiety was induced by putting subjects in competition with members of an outgroup (integral affect) or by having subjects expect to present a highly embarrassing speech on the aspect of their body that they would like to change (incidental affect). In one study, subjects then judged the similarity of a favorably described outgroup member to a majority of other outgroup members presented in a negative light. In another study, they rated the competency of groups with a majority of competent or incompetent members.

In both studies, assimilation effects were found. In comparison with nonanxious subjects, anxious subjects saw a favorable outgroup member as more similar to the unfavorable outgroup (Wilder & Shapiro, 1989a). In addition, they rated incompetent members of competent groups more favorably and competent members of incompetent groups less favorably than did subjects who were not anxious (Wilder & Shapiro, 1989b). Thus regardless of how it was induced, anxiety increased the tendency to see similarities within a social group. These results provide some preliminary evidence that integral and incidental affect can operate in the same way. They also suggest that our findings regarding the impact of happy and sad mood on intergroup perception may also obtain with other affective states. Consistent with our interpretation of happy and sad moods, Wilder and Shapiro argue that anxiety interferes with accurate processing of social information. Consequently, anxious subjects did not accurately identify group members that differed from their group's central tendencies.

Our results may have a number of implications for changing stereotypes and reducing prejudice in contexts involving heightened affect. On the one hand, we have already discussed some of the negative consequences associated with reduced perceived variability. It is not the case, however, that the prospect for stereotype change under conditions of heightened affect is completely bleak. If fact, there are a number of potentially positive consequences that might result from reduced perceptions of variability.

First, consider the consequences of subjects failing to see or being relatively unaffected by exemplars that differ greatly from a group's central tendency. If happy and sad individuals are relatively immune to perceiving unusual exemplars, then they might be less likely to subtype group members who exhibit stereotype-disconfirming behaviors. Subtyping is assumed to occur when a member of a social group exhibits behaviors that disconfirm the group stereotype. This member is then seen as a poor exemplar of the social group, and the member is "subtyped" into a subordinate and individuated subcategory. Although the formation of subtypes introduces some variability into the representation of the category, it also insulates the original category from the subcategory, and thus from modification (Rothbart & John, 1985; Weber & Crocker, 1983).

What are the consequences of failing to subtype stereotype-disconfirming exemplars? Because the disconfirming instances of the group are not subtyped, they remain as viable group members and could contribute to a relatively heterogeneous representation of the general category. To the extent that at least some stereotype-disconfirming information about these exemplars is noticed by the perceiver, some modification of the group stereotype would be expected. In fact, stereotype change is most likely when exemplars are categorized and accepted as members of a group but also exhibit some stereotype-disconfirming behavior (Rothbart & Lewis, 1988; Wilder, 1984). If affect decreases the likelihood of subtyping, it may result in *greater* modification of beliefs about the general category. Thus, one positive aspect of our findings is that affect may allow for stereotype change in at least some conditions where an absence of affect would preclude such an alteration.

Second, affect may influence stereotyping by increasing perceived similarity not only within groups but also between members of different groups. For example, it is possible that identification of differences between groups or between the self and a group may be diminished. Thus, while decreasing perceptions of variability *within* outgroups, affect may simultaneously reduce perception of differences *between* the ingroup and the outgroup. We know of no empirical evidence that speaks to this issue of how affective states might influence perception of two different groups or perception of individual members of two different groups. There is, however, a related issue about which some data are available. One of the individual ingroup members that can be compared to members of other groups is the self. On the one hand, it is possible that affect will increase perceptions of similarity to the ingroup, and ingroup biases may be exacerbated. On the other hand, perceived similarity to outgroups may also increase, and biases favoring the ingroup may be ameliorated.

Although we did not collect judgments of perceived similarity of the target groups to the self, one set of findings indicates that affect can increase perceived similarity to the self when processing information about disliked individuals. In one study (Boden, Marcus-Newhall, Gross, & Miller, 1990), subjects underwent a manipulation designed to induce a positive mood. Some subjects then had this mood eliminated, with the intention of returning them to a relatively neutral state. Following these procedures, subjects were asked to make judgments of three targets as well as judgments about the self. The targets differed in terms of their reported abilities; whereas one target was reported as being "definitely above average," the other targets were described as "definitely average" and "definitely below average."

Subjects intended to be in a neutral mood distinguished among the described targets, reporting themselves as most similar to the above-average target and least similar to the below-average target. In contrast, subjects in a positive mood did not differentiate among the targets; they saw themselves as equally similar to all three targets. Although many interpretations of these results remain viable, they are consistent with the idea that positive affect can influence similarity judgments between the self and others, and in this case, even unattractive (low-ability) others. How affectively based perceptions of similarity between the self and groups influence stereotype change is an intriguing question for future research.

When the contact hypothesis was first introduced, it "aspired to the role of dragon slayer" (Stephan, 1987, p. 15). As conditions specifying its sphere of successful operation accumulated, however, it became more like "bag lady . . . encumbered with extra baggage" (Stephan, 1987, p. 17). In suggesting that affective states have both negative and positive consequences for the stereotype change that intergroup contact seeks to produce, we don't wish to weight down the theoretical structure even further. However, our results, and those reported in many other chapters in this volume, are testament to the need to incorporate an emerging understanding of affective states into well-established cognitive models of intergroup perception, stereotype change, and intergroup behavior. We look forward to greater understanding of the complexities of intergroup relations as social psychologists discover how affect and cognition interact when members of different groups do so.

Acknowledgments

This research was supported by a Jacob K. Javits National Graduate Student Fellowship awarded to S. Stroessner and by NIMH Grant MH-43014 to D. Mackie. We thank David L. Hamilton for his helpful comments on earlier drafts of this manuscript.

References

Allport, G. W. (1954). *The nature of prejudice*. Cambridge, MA: Addison-Wesley.
Amir, Y. (1969). Contact hypothesis in ethnic relations. *Psychological Bulletin, 71,* 319–342.

Boden, J., Marcus-Newhall, A., Gross, S., & Miller, N. (1990). *Social outlook theory as an explanation for anchored high subjects.* Paper presented at the Western Psychological Association Convention, Los Angeles, CA.

Bodenhausen, G. V., & Kramer, G. P. (1990). *Affective states trigger stereotypic judgments.* Paper presented at the American Psychological Society Convention, Dallas, TX.

Brewer, M. B., & Miller, N. (1984). Beyond the contact hypothesis: Theoretical perspectives on desegregation. In N. Miller & M. B. Brewer (Eds.), *Groups in contact: The psychology of desegregation* (pp. 281–302). New York: Academic Press.

Cook, S. W. (1978). Interpersonal and attitudinal outcomes in cooperating interracial groups. *Journal of Research in Developmental Education, 12,* 97–113.

Dijker, A. G. M. (1987). Emotional reactions to ethnic minorities. *European Journal of Social Psychology, 17,* 305–326.

Dovidio, J. F., Evans, N., & Tyler, R. B. (1986). Racial stereotypes: The contents of their cognitive representations. *Journal of Experimental Social Psychology, 22,* 22–37.

Ellis, H. C., & Ashbrook, P. W. (1988). Resource allocation model of the effects of depressed mood states on memory. In K. Fiedler & J. Forgas (Eds.), *Affect, cognition, and social behavior* (pp. 25–43). Toronto: Hogrefe.

Ellis, H. C., Thomas, R. L., & Rodriguez, I. A. (1984). Emotional mood states and memory: Elaborative encoding, semantic processing, and cognitive effort. *Journal of Experimental Psychology: Learning, Memory, and Cognition, 10,* 470–482.

Fiedler, K., & Forgas, J. (Eds.). (1988). *Affect, cognition, and social behavior.* Toronto: Hogrefe.

Fiske, S. T., & Pavelchak, M. A. (1986). Category-based versus piecemeal-based affective responses: Developments in schema-triggered affect. In R. M. Sorrentino & E. T. Higgins (Eds.), *The handbook of motivation and cognition: Foundations of social behavior* (pp. 167–203). New York: Guilford Press.

Forgas, J. P. (Ed.). (1991a). *Emotion and social judgments.* Oxford: Pergamon Press.

Forgas, J. P. (1991b). Affect and social judgments: An introductory review. In J. P. Forgas (Ed.), *Emotion and social judgments* (pp. 3–29). New York: Pergamon Press.

Fried, L. S., & Holyoak, K. J. (1984). Induction of category distributions: A framework for classification learning. *Journal of Experimental Psychology: Learning, Memory, and Cognition, 10,* 234–257.

Gilbert, G. M. (1951). Stereotype persistence and change among college students. *Journal of Abnormal and Social Psychology, 46,* 245–254.

Hewstone, M., & Brown, R. (Eds.). (1986). *Contact and conflict in intergroup encounters.* Oxford/New York: Basil Blackwell.

Isen, A. M. (1984). Toward understanding the role of affect in cognition. In R. S. Wyer & T. K. Srull (Eds.), *Handbook of social cognition* (pp. 179–236). Hillsdale, NJ: Erlbaum.

Isen, A. M. (1987). Positive affect, cognitive processes, and social behavior. In L. Berkowitz (Ed.), *Advances in experimental social psychology* (Vol. 20, pp. 203–253). New York: Academic Press.

Isen, A. M., & Daubman, K. A. (1984). The influence of affect on categorization. *Journal of Personality and Social Psychology, 47,* 1206–1217.

Isen, A. M., & Levin, P. F. (1972). The effect of feeling good on helping: Cookies and kindness. *Journal of Personality and Social Psychology, 21,* 384–388.

Isen, A. M., & Simmonds, S. (1978). The effect of feeling good on a task that is incompatible with good mood. *Social Psychology Quarterly, 41,* 346–349.

Isen, A. M., Means, B., Patrick, R., & Nowicki, G. (1982). Some factors influencing decision-making and risk taking. In M. S. Clark & S. T. Fiske (Eds.), *Affect and cognition* (pp. 243–261). Hillsdale, NJ: Erlbaum.

Jackson, L. A., & Sullivan, L. A. (1987). *Cognition and affect in evaluations of stereotyped group members.* Paper presented at the Society for Experimental Social Psychology meeting, Charlottesville, VA.

Judd, C. M., & Park, B. (1988). Out-group homogeneity: Judgments of variability at the individual and group levels. *Journal of Personality and Social Psychology, 54,* 778–788.

Karlins, M., Coffman, T. L., & Walters, G. (1969). On the fading of social stereotypes: Studies in three generations of college students. *Journal of Personality and Social Psychology,* **13,** 1–16.

Kashima, E. S., & Kashima, Y. (1991). *Perceptions of general variability of social groups.* Unpublished manuscript, La Trobe University, Australia.

Katz, D., & Braly, K. (1933). Racial stereotypes in one hundred college students. *Journal of Abnormal and Social Psychology, 28,* 280–290.

Katz, I., Wackenhut, J., & Hass, R. G. (1986). Racial ambivalence, value duality, and behavior. In J. Dovidio and S. L. Gaertner (Eds.), *Prejudice, discrimination, and racism.* New York: Academic Press.

Linville, P. W., & Jones, E. E. (1980). Polarized appraisals of out-group members. *Journal of Personality and Social Psychology, 38,* 689–703.

Linville, P. W., Fischer, G. W., & Salovey, P. (1990). Perceived distributions of the characteristics of in-group and out-group members: Empirical evidence and a computer simulation. *Journal of Personality and Social Psychology, 57,* 165–188.

Linville, P. W., Salovey, P., & Fischer, G. W. (1986). Stereotyping and perceived distributions of social characteristics: An application to ingroup–outgroup perception. In J. F. Dovidio & S. L. Gaertner (Eds.), *Prejudice, discrimination, and racism* (pp. 127–163). Orlando, FL: Academic Press.

Mackie, D. M., & Worth, L. T. (1989). Processing deficits and the mediation of positive affect in persuasion. *Journal of Personality and Social Psychology, 57,* 27–40.

Mackie, D. M., & Worth, L. T. (1991). "Feeling good but not thinking straight": Positive mood and persuasion. In J. P. Forgas (Ed.), *Emotion and social judgments* (pp. 201–220). Oxford: Pergamon Press.

Mackie, D. M., Hamilton, D. L., Schroth, H. A., Carlisle, C. J., Gersho, B. F., Meneses, L. M., Nedler, B. F., & Reichel, L. D. (1989). The effects of induced mood on expectancy-based illusory correlations. *Journal of Experimental Social Psychology, 25,* 524–544.

McClendon, M. J. (1974). Interracial contact and the reduction of prejudice. *Sociological Focus, 7,* 47–65.

Miller, N., & Brewer, M. B. (1984). *Groups in contact: The psychology of desegregation.* New York: Academic Press.

Mischel, W., Ebbesen, E., & Zeiss, A. (1973). Selective attention to the self: Situational and dispositional determinants. *Journal of Personality and Social Psychology, 27,* 129–142.

Murray, N., Sujan, H., Hirt, E. R., & Sujan, M. (1990). The influence of mood on categorization: A cognitive flexibility interpretation. *Journal of Personality and Social Psychology,* **59,** 411–425.

Nisbett, R. E., Krantz, D. H., Jepson, C., & Kunda, Z. (1983). The use of statistical heuristics in everyday intuitive reasoning. *Psychological Review, 90,* 339–363.

Park, B., & Hastie, R. (1987). The perception of variability in category development: Instance- versus abstraction-based stereotypes. *Journal of Personality and Social Psychology, 53,* 621–635.

Park, B., & Judd, C. M. (1990). Measures and models of perceived group variability. *Journal of Personality and Social Psychology, 59,* 173–191.

Park, B., & Rothbart, M. (1982). Perception of out-group homogeneity and levels of social categorization: Memory for subordinate attributes of in-group and out-group members. *Journal of Personality and Social Psychology, 42,* 1051–1068.

Pettigrew, T. F. (1986). The intergroup contact hypothesis reconsidered. In M. Hewstone & R. Brown (Eds.), *Contact and conflict in intergroup encounters.* New York: Basil Blackwell.

Quattrone, G. A., & Jones, E. E. (1980). The perception of variability within in-groups and out-groups: Implications for the law of small numbers. *Journal of Personality and Social Psychology, 38,* 141–152.

Rothbart, M., & John, O. P. (1985). Social categorization and behavioral episodes: A cognitive analysis of the effects of intergroup contact. *Journal of Social Issues, 41*(3), 81–104.

Rothbart, M., & Lewis, S. (1988). Inferring category attributes from exemplar attributes: Geometric shapes and social categories. *Journal of Personality and Social Psychology, 55,* 861–872.

Schwarz, N. (1990). Feelings as information: Informational and motivational functions of affective states. In R. Sorrentino & E. T. Higgins (Eds.), *Handbook of motivation and cognition: Foundations of social behavior* (Vol. 2, pp. 527–561). New York: Guilford.

Sherif, M. (1966). *Group conflict and cooperation.* London: Routledge and Kegan Paul.

Silberman, E. K., Weingartner, H., & Post, R. M. (1983). Thinking disorder in depression: Logic and strategy in an abstract reasoning task. *Archives of General Psychiatry, 40,* 775–780.

Simon, B., & Brown, R. (1987). Perceived intragroup homogeneity in minority-majority contexts. *Journal of Personality and Social Psychology, 53,* 703–711.

Sinclair, R. C. (1988). Mood, categorization breadth, and performance appraisals: The effects of order of information acquisition and affective state on halo, accuracy, information retrieval, and evaluations. *Organizational Behavior and Human Decision Processes, 42,* 22–46.

Stephan, W. G. (1987). The contact hypothesis in intergroup relations. In C. Hendrick (Ed.), *Review of personality and social psychology* (Vol. 8, pp. 13–40). Newbury Park, CA: Sage.

Stephan, W. G., & Stephan, C. W. (1984). The role of ignorance in intergroup relations. In N. Miller & M. B. Brewer (Eds.), *Groups in contact: The psychology of desegregation* (pp. 229–255). New York: Academic Press.

Stephan, W. G., & Stephan, C. W. (1985). Intergroup anxiety. *Journal of Social Issues, 41*(3), 157–175.

Stroessner, S. J., & Mackie, D. M. (1990). *Distinguishing motivational and cognitive explanations of reduced perceived variability under affect.* Unpublished manuscript, University of California, Santa Barbara, CA.

Stroessner, S. J., & Mackie, D. M. (1992). The impact of induced affect on the perception of variability in social groups. *Personality and Social Psychology Bulletin.*

Stroessner, S. J., Hamilton, D. L., & Mackie, D. M. (1992). Affect and stereotyping: The effect of induced mood on distinctiveness-based illusory correlations. *Journal of Personality and Social Psychology, 62,* 564–576.

Sullivan, M. J. L., & Conway, M. (1989). Negative affect leads to low-effort cognition: Attributional processing for observed social behavior. *Social Cognition, 7,* 315–337.

Tversky, A. (1977). Features of similarity. *Psychological Review, 84,* 327–352.

Weber, R., & Crocker, J. (1983). Cognitive processes in the revision of stereotypic beliefs. *Journal of Personality and Social Psychology, 45,* 961–977.

Wilder, D. A. (1978). Reduction of intergroup discrimination through individuation of the outgroup. *Journal of Personality and Social Psychology, 36,* 1361–1374.

Wilder, D. A. (1984). Prediction of belief homogeneity and similarity following social categorization. *British Journal of Social Psychology, 23,* 323–333.

Wilder, D. A., & Shapiro, P. N. (1989a). Role of competition-induced anxiety in limiting the beneficial impact of positive behavior by an out-group member. *Journal of Personality and Social Psychology, 56,* 60–69.

Wilder, D. A., & Shapiro, P. N. (1989b). Effects of anxiety on impression formation in a group context: An anxiety-assimilation hypothesis. *Journal of Experimental Social Psychology, 25,* 481–499.

Chapter 5

The Role of Anxiety in Facilitating Stereotypic Judgments of Outgroup Behavior

DAVID A. WILDER

Department of Psychology
Rutgers University
New Brunswick, New Jersey

. . .when our actions do not, Our fears do make us traitors.
—*Shakespeare,* Macbeth

Introduction

Fearful of murderous Macbeth, Macduff has fled Scotland without stopping to pick up his wife and children. On hearing this, his wife reproaches him for abandoning the family. Whether it be Macduff's anxious flight or Othello's jealous rage, strong affect can move hands in ways cool heads would not. Powerful emotions such as fear, anxiety, or jealousy seem to compel behavior that is less rational and appropriate than that exhibited when we are cooler and our wits more collected. Dramatists have earned their bread and butter by forging conflicts around the ability of feelings to overpower good sense. While literary examples are purposefully extreme to maximize dramatic tension, affect can more subtly influence our judgments of others, often without our awareness. This chapter looks at some ways in which anxiety increases our reliance on social stereotypes and makes us traitors to our objective reason.

In discussing the influence of subjective anxiety on stereotypes, the following line of reasoning will be pursued: When anxiety distracts persons from careful attention to the environment, they rely more on available cognitive structures such as social stereotypes in making judgments of others. Increased reliance on stereotypes manifests itself in two ways. First, stereotypes supply best guesses to complete gaps in information created by anxiety. Second, counterstereotypic information loses impact when persons are anxious and their attention is restricted.

In the research discussed in this chapter, stereotypes are beliefs about the characteristics or behaviors of most members of a social group. Note this definition does not necessarily imply that stereotypes are erroneous or unfavorable beliefs, but merely that they are generalizations about members of a group. (See Ashmore and DelBoca, 1981, and Hamilton, 1979, for other definitions of social stereotypes.) While stereotypes may differ in the extent to which they apply to all group members and the degree to which they are well articulated, at minimum, a social stereotype is a statement that can be applied to most members of the social category or group in question.

Past research on stereotypes has concentrated on three issues. Historically, many researchers have focused on the content of stereotypes. From Katz and Braley (1933) forward, subjects have been asked to indicate the characteristics they associate with a variety of social groups. A second topic area, the process of forming stereotypes, has received increasing attention over the years (e.g., Rothbart, Fulero, Jensen, Howard & Birrell, 1978). For example, Hamilton (1981) has noted that stereotypes can be formed from illusory correlations in which distinctive characteristics associated with distinctive groups are thought to co-occur more often than is actually the case. A third line of research has addressed the question of how stereotypes change in response to disconfirming information (e.g., Weber & Crocker, 1983). This chapter focuses on a subset of that third line of research—how the impact of counterstereotypic information is influenced by a person's level of anxiety.

Before delving directly into the relevant research, a few comments need to be made about the circumstances under which stereotypes are likely to manifest themselves. Counterstereotypic information is likely to have maximum impact when persons make the linkage between that information and the stereotype it challenges.

Stereotype Usage

To begin with, stereotypes are likely to be employed when they are the only relevant constructs a person has available to help interpret and predict the actions of others. Stereotypes are likely to be used as a default in the absence of other relevant information. Indeed, specific information about a target individual may sometimes override stereotypic expectations (e.g.,

Locksley, Borgida, Brekke, & Hepburn, 1980; Locksley, Hepburn, & Ortiz, 1982).

Second, stereotypes should become salient when observing persons who engage in actions that are relevant to those stereotypes. In other words, actions that cue the stereotypes ought to increase their likelihood of influencing social perception and behavior (Bodenhausen & Wyer, 1985; Fazio, 1986, 1990). Evidence from social cognition research suggests that cognitive schemas (such as stereotypes) can channel a person's attention to notice and process more fully information that is consistent with those schemas (Hamilton & Trolier, 1986). As a result, an individual's recollections and judgments are shaped to respond in a more schema-consistent manner than may have been the case had those expectations not led in that direction. Similarly, Berman, Read, & Kenny (1983) have reported evidence for preferential processing of information consistent with cognitive schemas/expectations.

Third, one might expect stereotypes to be cued by the set with which the perceiver enters the setting. For instance, if I enter a situation feeling unpleasant (e.g., anxious or uncomfortable) and interact with members of an outgroup of which I have unfavorable stereotypes, then those negative stereotypes may be cued by my unpleasant mood or set. Furthermore, those negative stereotypes may well exacerbate or, at least, reinforce my unpleasant expectations. There is ample research to indicate that persons favorably process information that confirms existing expectations and schemas as discussed in the preceding paragraph (e.g., Fiske & Taylor, 1984; Hamilton & Troiler, 1986).

Fourth, stereotypes may be relied on as a cognitive short cut, an efficient use of time and resources. Stereotypes allow me to get on with my agenda. If I have categorized a person as a member of a group of which I have definite stereotypes, I need not commit my limited attentional resources to a careful monitoring of that individual's behavior. In areas relevant to the stereotypes, I may assume that the category member fits my expectations without my assessing the accuracy of that assumption.

Fifth, stereotypes can be relied on to replace information lost because of distortion or oversight. When attention is diverted from careful observation of another's behavior, stereotypes can provide the missing information. For instance, a sudden noise or passing object may distract me during a conversation. Rather than interrupt the conversation, I can hazard an "educated guess" as to what I have missed and continue on as if nothing were missed. Similarly, a stereotype about a group member may be employed to plug an information gap caused by a diversion of attention.

One potential source of distraction is a person's level of arousal. There is evidence to indicate that arousal leads to an increase in self-focused attention which may distract a person from a thorough processing of the external social environment (Smith, Ingram, & Brehm, 1983; Wegner & Giuliano, 1980). Moreover, one should expect a diminution of available attention when persons are angry, anxious, or fearful since these negative emotions often require an immediate, active response. The next two sections focus on the relationship between emotional arousal, anxiety, and stereotyping. They are, in turn, followed by a discussion of the effects of anxiety on the processing of stereotype-disconfirming information. Because the focus of this chapter is on the role of anxiety in the use of stereotypes, research involving anxiety is discussed separately from research concerned with other emotional arousal (e.g., sadness, mirth).

Affect, Arousal, and Stereotyping

Research on arousal and performance indicates that arousal facilitates the performance of well-learned responses (Kahneman, 1973; Zajonc, 1965). Inasmuch as stereotypes are well-learned expectations, reliance on them should increase when persons are highly aroused. Kim and Baron (1988) reported that subjects made stereotypic responses when they had just finished an exercise regimen that had raised their levels of arousal. Employing an illusory correlation procedure (Hamilton & Rose, 1980), subjects read sentences characterizing members of several occupational groups. Subjects then estimated the frequency with which those traits had occurred. When aroused, subjects overestimated the presence of adjectives that were consistent with their occupational stereotypes.

Turning to research with specific emotions, there is mixed evidence regarding the effect of sadness on information processing. Persons appear to be more reliant on well-learned responses to the extent sadness disrupts rumination or reflective thought. If the sad person is preoccupied with the source of that affect or immobilized by attempts to cope with the unpleasant feeling, then that distraction will likely interfere with processing of current, on-line information. But there is also some evidence that sadness may focus the person and encourage a careful, more systematic analysis of the situation (Fiedler & Forgas, 1988; Schwarz, 1990).

Some recent research more directly addresses the relationship between affect and stereotyping. Mackie *et al.* (1989) employed film excerpts to induce happiness or sadness in subjects. Happy subjects showed more evidence of stereotyping on an illusory correlation task than did control (neutral) subjects, but only on negative group attributes (see Hamilton, Stroessner, & Mackie, Chapter 3, this volume).

Bodenhausen & Kramer (1990) asked subjects to recall events that were either happy, sad, or angry as a means of inducing affective arousal. Then subjects read cases of a student accused of cheating or assault and who either fit subjects' stereotypes for that infraction or not. (Hispanics and

athletes were operationalized as stereotypic defendants in assault and cheating cases, respectively.) Happy and angry subjects rated the stereotypic defendant (athlete for cheating, Hispanic for assault) as more likely to be
guilty than did subjects in the unaroused, neutral condition. To add to the
strength of these findings, the authors reported the same effect for a positive
emotion (happiness) with a different induction technique. In a follow-up
study subjects were given directions to arrange facial muscles to create a
smile without that expression being identified as a smile. Those subjects
were more likely to make a stereotypic judgment than were subjects who
had not been induced to smile.

Anxiety and Stereotyping

Anxiety has been shown to foster a deterioration of performance (Gur
et al., 1988). Darke (1988) reported memory decrements due to anxiety. As
a consequence, the anxious individual may display greater reliance on dominant heuristics and habits.

Baron, Burgess, Kao, & Logan (1990) reported a relationship between
anxiety and superficial processing of information. Subjects in their first experiment, who were anxious while waiting for dental work, exhibited more
pronounced illusory correlation effects. Those subjects significantly overre-
ported the number of associations between stereotypic traits and members
of the corresponding occupational groups (stewardesses and librarians). In
a second experiment subjects evaluated the adequacy of a persuasive message. The authors cleverly constructed the message to contain weak arguments that were presented in a forceful way, interrupted by applause from
the audience on the tape. So while a person who carefully examined the arguments in the message would judge it to be weak and unpersuasive, a person who focused on superficial cues such as presentation style and audience
reaction would conclude that the message had merit. As predicted, the authors reported that subjects who had been exposed to a high-fear-inducing
message about dental procedures rated the message as more effective than
did subjects who were exposed to a low-fear-inducing message.

Taken together, the experiments reviewed in the last two sections indicate that arousal (whether induced by a neutral stimulus such as exercise or
by affectively charged stimuli) can facilitate the use of entrenched schemas
including stereotypes when making social judgments. The process by which
this occurs is less clear, although two hypotheses seem reasonable.

Affective Consistency Hypothesis

On one hand, something about the affect and accompanying arousal
may directly promote the use of stereotypes. If so, then the valence of the

affect may be important because it cues similarly valenced schemas. Thus, a person experiencing negative (positive) affect might be expected to be cued into negative (positive) stereotypes more so than positive (negative) stereotypes. Some research (Clark, Milberg, & Erber, 1984; Isen, 1987; Isen & Levin, 1972) indicates a consistency of affect cuing such that a positive mood induces positive thoughts while negative moods engender negative thoughts.

Distraction Hypothesis

On the other hand, the valence of the affect may be less important than the interference the affect has on the locus and amount of attention available for monitoring and evaluating the external field. If affect-induced stereotyping is due to distraction, then the valence of the affect may be of less importance than the degree to which the arousal interferes with the perception of ongoing, current information. Such interference should foster increased dependence on preexisting stereotypes. Some recent research can be marshaled to support this argument.

In a recent set of clever experiments, Gilbert and Hixon (1991) reported that cognitively active or "busy" perceivers are likely to rely on stereotypes to help interpret and recall the actions of a target. But, interestingly, being "busy" at the onset of social perception, when the interaction or observation begins, may actually inhibit the use of stereotypes as the cognitive activity interferes with or prevents initial activation of the stereotype. If, however, the stereotype is activated, subjects are likely to draw upon it when further pressed by mental demands. In their studies subjects were asked to make a series of judgments in the presence of either a Caucasian or Oriental experimenter. They found that when subjects had to attend to multiple tasks (overload condition), they were not likely to stereotype the Asian experimenter. But they were more likely to stereotype her when they were overloaded with task demands later in the experiment, after they had the opportunity to categorize the Asian experimenter.

The affective consistency and distraction hypotheses differ in one important prediction. According to the consistency hypothesis, if negative-valenced affect cues negative cognitions, then anxiety should facilitate negative stereotypes. But according to the distraction hypothesis, the valence of the affect is of less importance than its role as a source of cognitive interference. Anxiety should facilitate all relevant stereotypes, both positive and negative. Information that is consistent with the relevant stereotypes receives preferential processing while inconsistent information (e.g., instances of counterstereotypic behavior) has diminished impact. These arguments are developed more fully in the next section and become the focus for the remainder of the chapter.

Anxiety and the Impact of Counterstereotypic Information

The research program described in the remainder of this chapter has explored the role of anxiety in processing counterstereotypic information. This work spanned about ten years including initial pilot studies. Three graduate students (Warren Cooper, John Thompson, and Peter Shapiro) were involved, along with a number of undergraduate assistants. We began with an interest in how successful contact with a member of a disliked outgroup can be generalized to attitudes and beliefs about the outgroup as a whole.

Glancing at everyday instances of intergroup contact, a casual observer would conclude that pleasant or favorable intergroup encounters do not always lead to a lessening of outgroup bias. Indeed, as Allport (1954) and others since have argued (e.g., Amir, 1969; Pettigrew, 1986), pleasant contact between members of antagonistic groups is most effective in lessening bias under some fairly stringent conditions. The most prominent of these conditions are that the contact be (1) between persons of equal status, (2) intimate as opposed to superficial, (3) cooperative in pursuit of a superordinate goal, and (4) sanctioned by institutions or agencies outside of the groups. To these should be added the proviso that the cooperative encounter must be seen as representative of how other group members would behave in that setting (Hewstone & Brown, 1986; Wilder, 1984b). Otherwise, the contact experience may be readily (and perhaps accurately) dismissed as attributable to the specific contact person and not indicative of the outgroup as a whole (i.e., an exception to the rule). Under this circumstance, the favorable contact may cause a softening in evaluation of that contact person without significantly affecting beliefs and affect toward the outgroup as a whole.

Unfortunately, many aspects of the contact situation work against those factors that are important in ensuring its success as a means to alter more general evaluations of the outgroup. When dealing with conflict between groups, the prospect of contact with an outgroup member may be sufficient to provoke a variety of negative emotions: anxiety, loathing, fear, disgust, anger (Stephan & Stephan, 1985).

There is a fair amount of evidence, although often indirect, indicating that anxiety at the prospect of an impending negative event affects social perception and judgment. When applied to intergroup relations, the anticipation of contact with a member of a disliked outgroup should generate anxiety and reduce the likelihood for a successful contact experience. Three arguments support this prediction. First, anxiety may draw attention away from a careful analysis of another's actions. Attention may be directed toward monitoring and coping with the anxiety. Behavior by outgroup members may be scrutinized less carefully when persons are anxious in an intergroup context. As a result, the anxious person will have a less detailed representation of the outgroup members in memory. On later recall, gaps in information would likely be filled with plausible stereotypes associated with the outgroup. When the outgroup member's behavior is positive and the stereotypes of the outgroup are negative, anxious observers should underrate the favorability of the member's actions. The net effect will be a less favorable contact experience than a nonanxious observer would have experienced.

Easterbrook (1959) and Kahneman (1973) have shown that arousal restricts one's attention span, thereby reducing the amount of information available for analysis. Mandler (1975) suggested that arousal activates the autonomic nervous system and that the resultant internal cues compete with external cues (e.g., task demands) for processing. Anxious subjects may replace the missed external stimulation with information derived from their schemas of how the outgroup members should behave (Schank & Abelson, 1977; Stephan & Stephan, 1985). In addition, anxiety can interfere with the subsequent learning of information, such as in retrograde amnesia (e.g., Detterman, 1975). Thus, specific information about a given outgroup member may be less accessible to anxious than to nonanxious subjects.

Second, as an aversive experience, anxiety may poison interpretation of the interaction. Several perspectives support this argument. From cognitive consistency theory, one would expect that negative feelings generated by anxiety would color judgment of the contact person's actions in a manner consistent with the negative feelings. From basic principles of conditioning, one might expect some response generalization of negative feelings to actions. In addition, anxiety may serve as a prime for interpretation of later information. Persons experiencing anxiety should feel more negative about other things going on around them due to generalization of the negative affect.

Some research indicates that learning is facilitated when the valence of the information is congruent with the perceiver's mood (Bower, 1981). Encoding positive information is easier when one is in a positive mood than when in a negative mood. Therefore, positive acts by a member of a hostile outgroup may have limited impact on an anxious perceiver because the latter's negative mood matches the negative behavior of the majority better than the favorable behavior of the positive member.

Third, anxiety generated by the prospect of an unpleasant or, at least, uncertain encounter with an outgroup member may be threatening to the self. Social identity theory posits that feelings of well-being are derived from favorable comparisons persons make between ingroups and outgroups (Tajfel & Turner, 1979, 1985). Motivation to differentiate oneself positively from outgroup members should be accentuated when social comparison threatens and provokes anxiety. An unpleasant interaction with members of an outgroup can result in a negative evaluation of oneself because of verbal criticism, goal blockage, or even physical threat (Stephan & Stephan, 1985). Motivation to denigrate the outgroup should, therefore, be accentuated when persons are anxious about an upcoming unpleasant interaction in order to preserve a positive identity vis-à-vis that outgroup. Thus, anxiety should enhance the motivation to make social comparisons that are favorable to the self (Wills, 1981). This can be accomplished by minimizing any positive actions of outgroup members. Note that this argument assumes we are motivated to maintain a positive view of ourselves relative to others. The following paragraph outlines a different, more cognitive explanation that focuses on our limits as processors of information.

That less information is used by the anxious perceiver may be of little consequence when information is redundant or homogeneous. If several persons behave similarly, an anxious observer may not miss much. But if they behave differently from one another, then a restriction of available information may yield a less detailed and accurate impression of them. More concretely, when forming an impression of one member of a group, anxious observers may be more influenced by easily noticed contextual cues (e.g., how the rest of the interactants behave) and judge the member more like the others than would nonanxious perceivers who can attend more closely to details of the specific target (anxiety-assimilation hypothesis). These predictions were tested in a series of investigations conducted with Peter Shapiro (Wilder & Shapiro, 1989a).

In our experiments some subjects were made anxious while others were not, and then all subjects received information about a member of an outgroup who behaved favorably toward the subject's ingroup in the context of a generally unfavorable set of expectations and actions by the majority of the outgroup. We assessed subjects' perceptions and evaluations of the positive contact person as well as reactions to the outgroup as a whole.

Before plunging into a description of our work, it should be noted that we expected a modest, though significant, impact of anxiety on social perception. We did not anticipate that anxious subjects would totally disregard the positive actions of an outgroup member. Rather, any interference that anxiety creates for accurate monitoring of the pleasant contact person would be most evident when that person's actions were embedded in the context of expected, negative behavior by other members of the outgroup. Thus, in our first series of experiments the outgroup member who behaved in a counterstereotypic manner did so amongst other outgroup members who reinforced the prevailing stereotypes. This procedure provided a strong test of our predictions. With most group members' behavior supporting the negative stereotypes, the deviant member ought to stand out like the proverbial sore thumb and be closely watched. Nevertheless, based on our anxiety-assimilation hypothesis, we predicted that anxious subjects would distort their impression of the positive outgroup member in the direction of the negative outgroup majority.

We manipulated subjects' anxiety by creating a competitive or cooperative relationship between the subject's ingroup and an outgroup. We expected that competition between groups would produce greater anxiety than cooperation for a number of reasons. First, competition with an outgroup often elicits hostile feedback from that group. Second, feedback from fellow ingroup members may be more negative under conditions of intergroup competition. Poor performance by an individual may benefit the outgroup. Consequently, anxiety caused by ingroup evaluation should be heightened in a competitive setting. Third, individuals may have learned to associate competition with anxiety. Because competition in various contexts has been associated with unpleasantness, a network or schema of competition develops that includes negative feelings and arousal (e.g., Clark *et al.*, 1984). Negative feeling states generally produce unfavorable impressions. This conclusion has been suggested by researchers coming from either a cognitive or motivational orientation (Bower, 1981; Wills, 1981). Based on these arguments as well as pretesting, we concluded that anticipation of intergroup competition would successfully manipulate subjects' levels of anxiety. Moreover, our pilot work indicated that a competitive relationship between the groups enhanced experimental realism by actively engaging the subjects' interest.

In the main experiments small groups of subjects worked on a group project that was to be evaluated by the four members of another group. Subjects anticipated face-to-face interaction with members of the outgroup in either a competitive or a cooperative context. In the competitive condition the group from each session that performed better would be eligible for a reward. In the cooperative condition, eligibility for the reward was contingent on the combined performance of the groups. Before the contact occurred subjects received an evaluation of their ingroup product. Three of the outgroup members gave critical, negative evaluations, and one member responded favorably. We expected that, relative to the cooperative condition, the competitive context would generate more anxiety and result in the positive outgroup member being perceived more unfavorably and more like the outgroup majority. Moreover, subjects in the competitive condition would recall less information about the favorable outgroup member than would those in the cooperative condition.

Results were largely consistent with these expectations. Compared to subjects given the cooperative set, those expecting competition made fewer differentiations between the positive contact person and the negative others from the outgroup. When viewed in the competitive context, the favorable outgroup member was evaluated more negatively, perceived to have made arguments more similar to the others, thought to have delivered more harmful criticisms, and was incorrectly attributed more of the negative comments of the others. In short, the actual positive behavior of the deviant outgroup member was substantially tainted by the anticipated, negative actions of the majority when subjects were anxiously awaiting a competitive encounter with the outgroup.

Furthermore, the pattern of correlations between subjects' self-reports of anxiety and the other measures strongly suggested that anxiety mediated the biases in judgments of the favorable outgroup member. The less comfortable subjects indicated they felt, the less positively they evaluated the pleasant outgroup member, the less favorable and less constructive they found his comments to be, the more similar they judged him to be to the other outgroup members, and the more they committed errors in recall of his behavior. When the contribution of subjective anxiety was statistically removed using analyses of covariance, differences between the cooperative and competitive conditions in judgments and recall of the target were substantially reduced or completely eliminated.

In a follow-up experiment (Wilder & Shapiro, 1989a, Experiment 2) an additional condition was added to test more directly for the causal role of anxiety in producing assimilation of the favorable outgroup member to the negative majority. In this condition subjects were made anxious in the manner employed in the first experiment. But prior to viewing the outgroup members' evaluations of their ingroup product, some subjects performed a task designed to lessen their anxiety. These subjects read a series of amusing cartoons selected by pilot subjects. The cartoons should lessen anxiety by eliciting the incompatible response of humor (Baron, 1977). Therefore, these subjects would not be as anxious when receiving feedback from the outgroup as those who did not see the cartoons, even though both sets of subjects had been led to expect an unpleasant encounter with the outgroup.

Results of the second experiment corroborated the major findings of the first study. Subjects reported feeling less comfortable and more anxious when they expected to compete with the outgroup than when they anticipated cooperation. In addition, contact with the positive outgroup member had less impact on subjects expecting a hostile encounter. They judged the outgroup member less favorably and less differently from the negative majority and made more errors in recalling the positive member's behavior. When anxiety was lowered prior to contact, subjects responded to the positive outgroup member in a more favorable and veridical manner, comparable to the reaction when they expected a cooperative, less anxious encounter. Reports of subjective anxiety were significantly correlated with the major dependent variables such that greater anxiety was associated with a more stereotypic, less differentiated response to the target outgroup member.

Overall, these experiments offer a strong case for the hypothesized link between anxiety and outgroup perception. Using both direct manipulations of level of anxiety and correlational analyses, anxiety appeared to be a causal agent in determining the effectiveness of disconfirming information on judgments of outgroup behavior. When subjects were anxious and an outgroup member's favorable actions contradicted unfavorable expectations, they biased judgments in the direction of the expected negative stereotypes—an assimilation of the deviant in the direction of how he "should" have acted.

We conducted another set of experiments looking at the relationship between subjective anxiety and social perception using different manipulations of anxiety, a different cover story, and a different procedure (Wilder & Shapiro, 1989b). In the first experiment of this series, subjects were exposed to a videotape of a 4-member jury discussing a court case. Behavior of the majority was designed to create an expectation of group competence while one member (deviant) behaved incompetently. Anxiety was manipulated by the threat of embarrassment. We hypothesized that, compared to nonanxious subjects, anxious ones should evaluate the deviant member more like the rest of the group (anxiety-assimilation hypothesis). Furthermore, anxious perceivers should recall less detailed information about the deviant than should nonanxious subjects.

To manipulate anxiety, subjects were told that they would be expected to develop and deliver a speech. In the anxiety condition the speech would be about some aspect of their bodies that they would like to change. In the control condition they were to talk about the need for a dress code on campus. Subjects participated in mixed-sex groups of four, so they believed that they would present the speech to an audience of peers as well as the experimenter. All students in a pretest sample agreed that talking about one's body is anxiety provoking, particularly in the presence of peers of the opposite sex, whereas the question of campus dress is quite banal. After the manipulation of anxiety, subjects viewed a portion of a videotape in which 4 male confederates discussed a legal case. The tape portrayed a lively discussion with three members presenting confident and reasoned arguments in support of their views while one member (deviant) wavered in his opinions. After viewing the discussion, subjects had the opportunity to evaluate the performance of the deviant who had behaved quite differently, and less competently, than the others. Subjects rated the determination, intelligence, and skillfulness of the deviant outgroup member and recalled as much as they could about what he had said.

Although all subjects had viewed the same stimulus materials, those in the high-anxiety condition judged the target (member four) to be more intelligent, skillful, and determined than subjects in the low-anxiety condition. Moreover, subjects in the low-anxiety condition recalled more correct pieces of information (e.g., physical descriptions of the members, arguments made by them) than subjects in the high-anxiety condition. But there was no difference in the accuracy of what was recalled. Relative to the control subjects, anxious subjects did not make more errors in what they recalled, but they did report less of what had occurred on the tape.

To test for generalizability of these findings, the previous experiment was replicated with a different manipulation of anxiety. Rather than making a speech, subjects were told that they would pose for pictures that would be used in a subsequent experiment dealing with unexpected stimuli. In the anxiety condition they were asked to wear baby clothes and pose in a playpen. Because a public record would be made (photograph) to be viewed by peers, subjects felt embarrassed and nervous at the prospect of donning the baby outfit. In the low-anxiety condition they were asked to wear a Halloween mask that would disguise their identity. As expected, subjects felt less anxious at the prospect of this task. Otherwise the procedure was the same as described for the preceding experiment. The pattern of results was also the same.

In a third study anxiety was again operationalized differently. This time subjects were threatened with a series of electric shocks as part of a measure of stress tolerance. For subjects in the high-anxiety condition, this series of shocks would be administered during the second part of the experiment after they viewed the group's discussion. Subjects in the low-anxiety condition did not expect to receive any shocks. Four new items were added to the measures completed after subjects had observed the group. They were asked to indicate the extent to which they thought about the following topics while viewing the tape of the group discussion: the anticipated second task, their feelings and emotions, other objects in the room, and events or things outside the experiment.

Results of the third experiment fit well with those reported from the earlier studies. Compared to control subjects, those in the high-anxiety conditions (1) felt more anxious, (2) rated the target as more competent, intelligent, determined, and skillful, (3) recalled less information about the target, and (4) thought more about their feelings and the anticipated noxious task (receiving shocks). Furthermore, distortions in social perception of the target group member were significantly correlated with both self-reports of anxiety and time spent thinking about their feelings and the imminent anxiety-provoking task.

Finally, a fourth experiment replicated the third experiment with one important change. Rather than presenting the target as "incompetent" and the majority as "competent," the tables were turned and the majority was portrayed as less competent whereas the deviant appeared to be intelligent, skillful, and determined. Again, results paralleled those of the other three studies.

Outcomes from the experiments in this research program were consistent and complementary to those reported for the earlier set of experiments (Wilder & Shapiro, 1989a). Induction of anxiety resulted in less differentiation between a deviant member of the group and modal members, less recall of information about the deviant, and increased thought by subjects about their feelings and the upcoming noxious task. Correlational evidence indicated that anxiety distracted subjects from attending fully to the behavior of the deviant which fostered reliance on expectations generated by the majority's behavior.

While distraction appears to have contributed to the findings, the location of that distraction is not clear. One possibility is that distraction occurred early when subjects were attending to the stimulus tape. Anxiety at the prospect of the upcoming negative contact distracted subjects from the task at hand, so less information was gleaned about the target. In making later judgments, gaps were filled in with the impression subjects had of the group as a whole.

Alternatively, subjects may have attended to the behavior of the target equally well in all conditions. Arousal may have distracted them, not at the stage of gathering information, but at the point of retrieval when subjects were asked to complete the dependent measures. Arousal could have peaked at that point because subjects completed the measures just before they expected the face-to-face contact with the outgroup. To help sort out encoding and retrieval contributions, anxiety may be manipulated before or after exposing subjects to the target. An encoding argument would be supported if an increase in anxiety following exposure to the target does not affect judgments.

Assimilation or Contrast

Despite the strength of the replications, we have been struck by the plausibility of a different pattern of results. If subjects narrow attention when anxious, why do they not focus more closely on the deviant outgroup member and recall his actions more accurately? Moreover, if any distortion occurs, should it not be in the direction of judging greater differences between the deviant and the others in the outgroup? It should be noted, however, that in our research program the experimenter did not instruct subjects to focus on one particular outgroup member. Most likely, then, subjects did not focus their attention only on the deviant. Rather, they attended more or less equally to all the comments made by the various outgroup members. Such a set would favor assimilation of the deviant's behavior in the direction of the majority of the group (Martin, 1986). A contrast of the deviant away from the majority would have been more likely had subjects been told to focus specifically on the deviant. In effect, the deviant would have become the figure relative to the ground of the majority. These issues have been addressed in a couple of recent experiments (Wilder & Shapiro, 1991).

Our follow-up studies have examined conditions under which anxious observers contrast a counterstereotypic outgroup member from the outgroup majority. Three conditions came to mind as sufficient to restructure the social field so that anxious subjects would focus more closely on the different outgroup member and not show the assimilation to the majority reported in our earlier studies. First, subjects can be asked to focus their attention on the stereotype-disconfirming outgroup member from the outset. Second, the deviant outgroup member can be presented explicitly as atypical of other members of the group. Third, and more extreme, the deviant outgroup member can be presented as a member of a different outgroup than the one to which the other stimulus persons belong. We have obtained data bearing on each of these three possibilities.

If attention were clearly directed toward the disconfirming outgroup member at the outset, observers should continue to focus available attention on the deviant even when highly anxious. Attention to the others in the field would suffer most when they are distracted by anxiety. Employing the procedures from some of our earlier experiments (Wilder, Cooper, & Thompson, 1981; Wilder & Shapiro, 1989b), anxiety was manipulated by informing subjects that they would be making a public speech. Then they witnessed a group of 4 confederates discussing a civil suit. The actions of one group member were programmed to be quite different from the others. To this point, the design replicated the first experiment of Wilder & Shapiro (1989b). In addition, a third of the subjects were told explicitly to focus on the deviant's behavior, a third were instructed explicitly to focus on forming an impression of the group as a whole, and a third were given no instructions as to how to channel their attention. Results showed that subjects who were either given no attention instructions or who were asked to focus on the group as a whole displayed the same pattern of findings as reported in Wilder & Shapiro (1989b). When anxious, they showed a significant assimilation of the deviant toward the majority. But when subjects were instructed to focus on the deviant, the anxiety manipulation did not lead to an assimilation effect. On the contrary, anxious subjects rated the deviant even more differently from the majority.

In a second experiment using the procedure just described, we manipulated the apparent typicalness of the stereotype-disconfirming group member. For half of the subjects, the deviant member appeared to be a member in good standing, like the others, except for his divergent opinions. For the other subjects, however, the deviant was explicitly described by the experimenter as a marginal group member, atypical of most members of that group. Then all subjects' anxiety levels were manipulated by using the speech expectation described in preceding research. Following the induction of anxiety, subjects evaluated the outgroup members' comments on a civil suit. Analyses of subjects' judgments about the outgroup members and recall of their behaviors revealed the assimilation effect reported in past research when subjects were anxious and the deviant outgroup member appeared to be otherwise like others in the group. But when subjects were initially informed that the deviant was not a typical member of the outgroup, recall and judgments about him were not significantly altered by the anxiety manipulation. Data suggested that pointing out his atypicalness drew attention to him, resulting in subjects psychologically cleaving him from the outgroup at the outset.

To test this possibility more explicitly, in a follow-up study some subjects were told that they would rate the behavior of members of two different outgroups. Three were members of the same group while the fourth (the deviant in past research) was described as a member of a different outgroup. To reinforce this separation, when subjects began to speak they introduced themselves and indicated the group to which they belonged. Otherwise their behavior was the same as described in the preceding two experiments. A control group of subjects observed the same behavior by the confederates, but the outgroup members allegedly belonged to the same group. As in previous research, there was a significant relationship between reported anxiety and assimilation of the deviant in the direction of the majority when all confederates allegedly belonged to the same outgroup. But when the deviant hailed from a different outgroup, anxious subjects evaluated him as even more different from the others than did nonanxious subjects. In short, differences among members of separate outgroups were accentuated when subjects were anxious.

Taken together, the pattern of findings from these follow-up investigations along with our other work (Wilder & Shapiro, 1989a,b) suggest that anxiety encourages an accentuation of the field. The anxious observer tends to assimilate within salient cognitive categories, so discrepancies within groups are underestimated. In a complementary fashion, anxiety fosters accentuation of differences between categories, so members of different groups who behave differently are viewed as even more different when observers are anxious.

Working Propositions

The results of these experiments may be summarized by a few propositions that can also accommodate much of the related research reviewed earlier in this chapter. First, anxiety generates arousal and self-focused attention that distracts the perceiver, thereby decreasing capacity to make fine differentiations of the external social world. As a result, the perceiver relies to a greater extent on dominant schemas and heuristics to interpret the behavior of others. When observing or interacting with members of an outgroup, these schemas may include stereotypes based on what many outgroup members are presently doing or have done in the past.

The first leg of the model posits that arousal induced by anxiety serves as a source of distraction from the external world. Clearly there is evidence that arousal can distract by focusing attention on the self (e.g., Wegner & Giuliano, 1980). It should be noted, as mentioned earlier, that most of the research suggesting a role between arousal and distraction has manipulated arousal as an incidental variable (see Chapter 2 by Bodenhausen). That is, the initial arousal is not generated by the stimulus that the subjects observe and judge. If the stimulus of interest is also the clear source of the subject's arousal, one might expect the arousal to concentrate attention on that stimulus. Thus, I may pay particular attention to a person who is making me anxious by his threatening gestures directed at me.

Second, distraction induced by arousal encourages a more superficial or peripheral processing of information from the environment. This follows from the fact that persons have a finite, limited amount of conscious attention to allocate among monitoring events internally and externally. Superficial processing induced by anxiety may manifest itself in a variety of ways. For example, persons may process persuasive arguments in a more limited manner and judge them to be of a quality superior to that normally perceived (Baron *et al.*, 1990). Alternatively, observers may rely on stereotypic expectations when making judgments of others to whom they have been exposed, as in the illusory correlation studies of Kim and Baron (1988) and Mackie *et al.* (1989).

Third, in our studies (Wilder & Shapiro, 1989a,b) this superficial processing manifested itself in the assimilation of differences among group members when subjects were preoccupied by anxiety. The anxious perceiver's reliance on existing schemas and stereotypes may reflect a more general principle. When aroused, persons simplify their perceptions by reducing variability in the external field. Details are leveled and sharpened to form a simpler, coherent percept such that similarities within and differences between categories are exaggerated. Stereotypes will be employed if they aid in simplifying the external percept. But if simplification of the field can be brought about through greater differentiation between some elements, then that will also occur, as indicated by the follow-up studies summarized briefly in the last section (Wilder & Shapiro, 1991). When the deviant was focused on carefully at the onset or when the target was initially categorized differently from the others (atypical of the group or a member of a different group), then anxiety accentuated differences between the deviant and the other members of his group.

Applications and Discussion

As our everyday experience indicates, anxiety can have a number of effects on us. Although the subjective experience of anxiety is usually unpleasant, it can be quite functional if we are aroused and motivated to constructive action. However, anxiety can be debilitating when we freeze or vacillate between undesirable alternative courses of action. More subtly, anxiety can create a negative mood that colors our judgments, thereby encouraging further conflict and distress. And anxiety can distract us so that we are not fully aware of all that is happening in our environment. These latter, often subtle consequences have been of chief concern in this chapter.

Two effects of anxiety on person perception have been examined in our research. First, anxiety may actively trigger other unpleasant, negative cognitions (affective consistency). As a result, persons should be prone to make negative, unfavorable judgments when anxious. Alternatively, anxiety may increase reliance on existing expectations and schemas regardless of whether these are affectively positive or negative (distraction). In our studies, anxious subjects generally relied more on expectations of the outgroup when making judgments about a deviant member regardless of the valence of the stereotype. But support for the distraction hypothesis in this particular paradigm does not preclude the validity of the affective consistency hypothesis in other situations.

Furthermore, while our findings suggest that subjects did not use all the information available to them in evaluating the outgroup targets, it is not clear whether "distortions" occurred at the point of gathering information (attention) or in the act of making judgments (informational integration and evaluation). In the former case, distortions result in less information being taken in; in the latter case information may be attended to but interpreted to fit prevailing expectations. Certainly both types of biases can occur and either is sufficient to generate an assimilation of an outgroup member in the direction of the outgroup stereotypes.

Before considering some of the implications of this research for person perception and intergroup relations, a few caveats need to be kept in mind. First, we have examined the consequences of manipulating one affective state (anxiety) on judgments of outgroups. Anxiety has been induced in several ways, ranging from dread of an unpleasant interaction with an outgroup to social embarrassment to noxious shocks. Regardless of the induction, consequences of anxiety for judgments of outgroup members were the same. We felt that arousal induced by anxiety would be most relevant to intergroup encounters as they are often characterized by hostility (Stephan & Stephan, 1985). Second, in many "natural" intergroup encounters, the groups have had some history of association and persons may rely on stereotypes that they have held for some time. In our studies, however, expectations and stereotypes were created during the experiment.

The research reviewed here has implications for the evaluation of counterstereotypic information in general and the contact hypothesis in particular (e.g., Hewstone & Brown, 1986; Pettigrew, 1986). When relations between groups are poor, anticipation of intergroup contact may generate anxiety (Stephan & Stephan, 1985). The success of positive contact with a member of an outgroup may be limited by biases induced by anxiety. In turn, these errors can be mitigated by reducing anxiety in the contact setting as the results of one of our experiments indicate (Wilder & Shapiro, 1989a). Nevertheless, it would be rash to conclude that making persons less anxious or more happy will guarantee the success of intergroup contact. Recall that one of Sherif's (1967) unsuccessful attempts to reduce conflict between his belligerent campers involved bringing them together for an ostensibly enjoyable camp party. Reducing anxiety or injecting joy into the contact experience will not resolve conflict, but it can reduce distortions of information processing (e.g., distraction, cueing of negative cognitions) that characterize the anxious perceiver. However, contact that is engulfed with extreme joy may also distract and distort social perception.

To the extent that a reduction in anxiety helps to restore accurate perception of a favorable outgroup member, it opens the opportunity for successful contact between group members and effective integration of counterstereotypic information. The ultimate outcome will depend on the nature of the contact experience itself. Even if a counterstereotypic outgroup member is perceived veridically, she or he may still be dismissed as an exception to the rule. The relationship between anxiety and intergroup judgments augurs poorly for the effectiveness of positive outgroup models when intergroup relations are poor and anxiety is high. Under such circumstances positive models face a disturbing dilemma. On the one hand, because they are few, they may be dismissed as exceptions. Indeed, as our follow-up studies suggest, once an outgroup member is labeled an exception, judgments of that member are contrasted away from more typical members and discounted. In a complementary manner, the positive outgroup model may be dismissed by underweighting differences with the majority. Whether discounted by assimilation or contrast, the positive model may be rendered ineffective as an influence to counter existing intergroup expectations. To prevent that, steps must be taken (1) to ensure that the outgroup member is perceived to be typical of the group and (2) to encourage multiple contacts with that member as well as others who also are counterstereotypic (Rothbart, 1981; Weber & Crocker, 1984; Wilder, 1984b).

In addition to promoting accurate social judgments, reducing anxiety in intergroup settings can break two cycles of self-fulfilling prophecies. First, to the extent anticipation of unpleasant contact generates anxiety, it biases social perception in the direction of a more negative evaluation of what occurs. That, in turn, reinforces negative stereotypes of the outgroup and can enhance intergroup anxiety. Second, distortions in the direction of the outgroup stereotypes should increase the perceived homogeneity of the outgroup (Mullen & Hu, 1989; Park, Judd, & Ryan, 1991; Park & Rothbart, 1982; Quattrone & Jones, 1980; Wilder, 1984a). That, in turn, reduces the empathic benefits of individuating or personalizing outgroup members

(Wilder, 1978; Zimbardo, 1970). Thus, while cool heads do not guarantee warm hearts, they do encourage clear eyes.

Finally, a brief note should be made about the role of conscious decision making in the research reported in this chapter. We have made no assumptions about subjects' awareness that their judgments of the outgroup have been affected by their stereotypes. Certainly, persons often consciously consider their stereotypes, as when they list characteristics of groups in the manner popularized by Katz and Braly (1933). But individuals can also be influenced in a more subtle, nonconscious way by their stereotypes. Expectations can guide the way in which we select, integrate, and remember social information (e.g., Fiske & Taylor, 1984; Snyder, 1981). The effects of anxiety on judgments of an outgroup member appear to be of this latter, nonconscious type. While subjects in our studies reported feeling uncomfortable and being distracted by the anxiety manipulations, they did not realize that they were relying more heavily on outgroup expectations when making judgments of an individual group member. Thus, anxious subjects did not actively choose to rely more on outgroup stereotypes. Most subjects that we spoke with believed that their anxiety had no impact on the judgments they were required to make. While it may be of no consolation to Lady Macduff, not only do our feelings sometimes betray our beliefs, but we are also sometimes unaware that the betrayal has occurred.

References

Allport, G. W. (1954). *The nature of prejudice.* Cambridge, MA.: Addison-Wesley.

Amir, Y. (1969). Contact hypothesis in ethnic relations. *Psychological Bulletin, 71,* 319–341.

Amir, Y. (1976). The role of intergroup contact in change of prejudice and ethnic relations. In P. A. Katz (Ed.), *Towards the elimination of racism* (pp. 73–123). New York: Plenum Press.

Ashmore, R. D., & DelBoca, F. K. (1981). Conceptual approaches to stereotypes and stereotyping. In D. L. Hamilton (Ed.), *Cognitive processes in stereotyping and intergroup behavior* (pp. 1–35). Hillsdale, NJ: Lawrence Erlbaum Associates.

Baron, R. A. (1977). *Human aggression.* New York: Plenum Press.

Baron, R. S., Burgess, M. L., Kao, C. F., & Logan, H. (1990). *Fear and superficial social processing: Evidence of stereotyping and simplistic persuasion.* Paper presented at the Midwestern Psychological Association convention, Chicago.

Berman, J. S., Read, S. J., & Kenny, D. A. (1983). Processing inconsistent social information. *Journal of Personality and Social Psychology, 45,* 1211–1224.

Bodenhausen, G. V. (1988). Stereotypic biases in social decision making and memory: Testing process models of stereotype use. *Journal of Personality and Social Psychology, 55,* 726–737.

Bodenhausen, G. V. (1990). Stereotypes as judgmental heuristics: Evidence of circadian variations in discrimination. *Psychological Science, 1,* 319–322.

Bodenhausen, G. V., & Kramer, G. P. (1990). *Affective states trigger stereotypic judgments.* Paper presented at the annual convention of the American Psychological Society, Dallas.

Bodenhausen, G. V., & Wyer, R. S., Jr. (1985). Effects of stereotypes on decision making and information-processing strategies. *Journal of Personality and Social Psychology,* **48,** 262–282.

Bower, G. H. (1981). Mood and Memory. *American Psychologist,* **36,** 129–148.

Clark, M. S. (1982). A role for arousal in the link between feeling states, judgments, and behavior. In M. S. Clark & S. T. Fiske (Eds.), *Affect and cognition: The seventeenth annual Carnegie symposium on cognition* (pp. 263–289). Hillsdale, NJ: Erlbaum.

Clark, M. S., Milberg, S., & Erber, R. (1984). Effects of arousal on judgments of others' emotions. *Journal of Personality and Social Psychology,* **46,** 551–560.

Darke, S. (1988). Anxiety and working memory capacity. *Cognition and Emotion,* **2,** 145–154.

Detterman, D. K. (1975). The von Restorff effect and induced anxiety: Production by manipulation of sound intensity. *Journal of Experimental Psychology: Human Learning and Memory,* **1,** 614–628.

Easterbrook, J. A. (1959). The effect of emotion on cue utilization and the organization of behavior. *Psychological Review,* **66,** 183–201.

Fazio, R. H. (1986). On the power and functionality of attitudes: The role of attitude accessibility. In A. R. Pratkanis, S. J. Breckler, & A. G. Greenwald (Eds.), *Attitude structure and function* (pp. 153–179). Hillsdale, NJ: Erlbaum.

Fazio, R. H. (1990). Multiple processes by which attitudes guide behavior: The MODE model as an integrative framework. In M. P. Zanna (Ed.), *Advances in experimental social psychology* (Vol. 23, pp. 75–109). Orlando, FL.: Academic Press.

Fiedler, K., & Forgas, J. (1988). *Affect, cognition, and social behavior.* Toronto: Hogrefe.

Fiske, S. T., & Neuberg, S. L. (1990). A continuum of impression formation from category-based to individuating processes: Influences of information and motivation on attention and interpretation. In M. P. Zanna (Ed.), *Advances in experimental social psychology* (Vol. 23, pp. 1–74). Orlando, FL: Academic Press.

Fiske, S. T., & Taylor, S. E. (1984). *Social cognition.* Reading, MA: Addison-Wesley.

Forgas, J. P. (1989). Mood effects on decision making strategies. *Australian Journal of Psychology,* **41,** 197–214.

Forgas, J. P., & Bower, G. H. (1988). Mood effects on social and personal judgments. In K. Fiedler & J. Forgas (Eds.), *Affect, cognition, and social behavior* (pp. 183–208). Toronto: Hogrefe.

Gilbert, D. T., & Hixon, J. G. (1991). The trouble of thinking: Activation and application of stereotypic beliefs. *Journal of Personality and Social Psychology,* **60,** 509–517.

Gur, R. C., Gur, R. E., Skolnick, B. E., Resnick, S. M., Silver, F. I., Chawluk, J., Muenz, L., Obrist, W. D., & Reivich, M. (1988). Effects of task difficulty on regional cerebral blood flow: Relationships with anxiety and performance. *Psychophysiology,* **24,** 392–399.

Hamilton, D. L. (1979). A cognitive-attributional analysis of stereotyping. In L. Berkowitz (Ed.), *Advances in experimental social psychology* (Vol. 12, pp. 53–84). NY.: Academic Press.

Hamilton, D. L. (Ed.). (1981). *Cognitive processes in stereotyping and intergroup behavior.* Hillsdale, NJ: Erlbaum.

Hamilton, D. L., & Rose, T. L. (1980). Illusory correlation and the maintenance of stereotypic beliefs. *Journal of Personality and Social Psychology,* **39,** 832–845.

Hamilton, D. L., & Trolier, T. K. (1986). Stereotypes and stereotyping: An overview of the cognitive approach. In J. F. Dovidio & S. L. Gaertner (Eds.), *Prejudice, discrimination and racism* (pp. 127–163). New York: Academic Press.

Hewstone, M., & Brown, R. (1986). Contact is not enough: An intergroup perspective. In M. Hewstone & R. Brown (Eds., pp. 1–44), *Contact and conflict in intergroup encounters.* Oxford: Basil Blackwell.

Isen, A. M. (1987). Positive affect, cognitive processes, and social behavior. In L. Berkowitz (Ed.), *Advances in experimental social psychology* (Vol. 20, pp. 203–253). Orlando, FL: Academic Press.

Isen, A. M., & Levin, P. F. (1972). The effect of feeling good on helping: Cookies and kindness. *Journal of Personality and Social Psychology, 21,* 384–388.

Isen, A. M., & Means, B. (1983). The influence of positive affect on decision-making strategy. *Social Cognition, 2,* 18–31.

Kahneman, D. (1973). *Attention and effort.* Englewood Cliffs, NJ: Prentice-Hall.

Katz, D., & Braly, K. W. (1933). Racial stereotypes of 100 college students. *Journal of Abnormal and Social Psychology, 28,* 280–290.

Kim, H. S., & Baron, R. S. (1988). Exercise and illusory correlation: Does arousal heighten stereotypic processing? *Journal of Experimental Social Psychology, 24,* 366–380.

Locksley, A., Borgida, E., Brekke, H., & Hepburn, C. (1980). Sex stereotypes and social judgment. *Journal of Personality and Social Psychology, 39,* 821–831.

Locksley, A., Hepburn, C., & Ortiz, V. (1982). Social stereotypes and judgments of individuals: An instance of the base rate fallacy. *Journal of Experimental Social Psychology, 18,* 23–42.

Mackie, D. M., Hamilton, D. L., Schroth, H. A., Carlisle, C. J., Gersho, B. F., Meneses, L. M., Nedler, B. F., & Reichel, L. D. (1989). The effects of induced mood on expectancy-based illusory correlations. *Journal of Experimental Social Psychology, 25,* 524–544.

Mandler, G. (1975). *Mind and emotion.* New York: Wiley.

Martin, L. L. (1986). Set/reset: Use and disuse of concepts in impression formation. *Journal of Personality and Social Psychology, 51,* 493–504.

Miller, N., & Brewer, M. B. (1984). *Groups in contact: The psychology of desegregation.* New York: Academic Press.

Mullen, B., & Hu, L. (1989). Perceptions of ingroup and outgroup variability: A meta-analytic integration. *Basic and Applied Social Psychology, 10,* 233–252.

Park, B., & Rothbart, M. (1982). Perception of out-group homogeneity and levels of social categorization: Memory for the subordinate attributes of in-group and out-group members. *Journal of Personality and Social Psychology, 42,* 1051–1068.

Park, B., Judd, C. M., & Ryan, C. S. (1991). Social categorization and the representation of variability information. In W. Stroebe & M. Hewstone (Eds.), *European review of social psychology,* (Vol. 2, pp. 211–245). New York, NY: John Wiley & Sons.

Pettigrew, T. F. (1986). The intergroup contact hypothesis reconsidered. In M. Hewstone & R. Brown (Eds.), *Contact and conflict in intergroup encounters* (pp. 169–195). Oxford: Basil Blackwell.

Quattrone, G. A., & Jones, E. E. (1980). The perception of variability within in-groups and out-groups: Implications for the law of small numbers. *Journal of Personality and Social Psychology, 38,* 141–152.

Rothbart, M. (1981). Memory processes and social beliefs. In D. L. Hamilton (Ed.), *Cognitive processes in stereotyping and intergroup behavior* (pp. 145–181). Hillside, NJ: Erlbaum.

Rothbart, M., Fulero, S., Jensen, C., Howard, J., & Birrell, P. (1978). From individual to group impressions: Availability heuristics in stereotype formation. *Journal of Experimental Social Psychology, 14,* 237–255.

Schank, R. L., & Abelson, R. P. (1977). *Scripts, plans, goals, and human understanding: An inquiry into human knowledge structures.* Hillsdale, NJ: Erlbaum

Schwarz, N. (1990). Feelings as information: Informational and motivational functions of affective states. In E. T. Higgins & R. M. Sorrentino (Eds.), *Handbook of motivation and cognition* (Vol. 2, pp. 527–561). New York: Guilford.

Sherif, M. (1967). *Group conflict and co-operation: Their social psychology.* London: Routledge & Kegan Paul.

Smith, T. W., Ingram, R. E., & Brehm, S. S. (1983). Social anxiety, anxious self-preoccupation, and recall of self-relevant information. *Journal of Personality and Social Psychology,* **44**, 1276–1283.

Snyder, M. (1981). On the self-perpetuating nature of social stereotypes. In D. L. Hamilton (Ed.), *Cognitive processes in stereotyping and intergroup behavior* (pp. 183–212). Hillsdale, NJ: Erlbaum.

Stephan, W. C., & Stephan, C. W. (1985). Intergroup anxiety. *Journal of Social Issues,* **41**, 157–175.

Tajfel, H., & Turner, J. C. (1979). An integrative theory of intergroup conflict. In W. G. Austin & S. Worchel (Eds.), *The social psychology of intergroup relations.* Monterey, CA: Brooks/Cole.

Tajfel, H., & Turner, J. C. (1985). The social identity theory of intergroup behavior. In S. Worchel & W. G. Austin (Eds.), *Psychology of intergroup relations* (pp. 7–24). Chicago: Nelson-Hall.

Turner (1975). Social comparison and social identity: Some prospects for intergroup behavior. *European Journal of Social Psychology,* **45**, 961–977.

Weber, R., & Crocker, J. (1983). Cognitive processes in the revision of stereotypic beliefs. *Journal of Personality and Social Psychology,* **45**, 961–977.

Wegner, D. M., & Giuliano, T. (1980). Arousal-induced attention to self. *Journal of Personality and Social Psychology,* **44**, 290–293.

Wilder, D. A. (1978). Reduction of intergroup discrimination through individuation of the out-group. *Journal of Personality and Social Psychology,* **36**, 1361–1374.

Wilder, D. A. (1984a). Prediction of belief homogeneity and similarity following social categorization. *British Journal of Social Psychology,* **23**, 323–333.

Wilder, D. A. (1984b). Intergroup contact: The typical member and the exception to the rule. *Journal of Experimental Social Psychology,* **20**, 177–194.

Wilder, D. A., & Shapiro, P. N. (1989a). Role of competition-induced anxiety in limiting the beneficial impact of positive behavior by an out-group member. *Journal of Personality and Social Psychology,* **56**, 60–69.

Wilder, D. A., & Shapiro, P. (1989b). Effects of anxiety on impression formation in a group context: An anxiety-assimilation hypothesis. *Journal of Experimental Social Psychology,* **25**, 481–499.

Wilder, D. A., & Shapiro, P. (1991). Polarization of intergroup judgments induced by anxiety. (Manuscript in preparation.)

Wilder, D. A., Cooper, W. E., & Thompson, J. E. (1981). Effects of anxiety on perceptions of differences among group members. Paper presented at the American Psychological Association Convention, New York.

Wills, T. A. (1981). Downward comparison principles in social psychology. *Psychological Bulletin,* **90**, 245—271.

Zajonc, R. B. (1965). Social facilitation. *Science* **149**, 269–274.

Zimbardo, P. (1970). The human choice: Individuation, reason, and order versus deindividuation, impulse, and chaos. In W. Arnold & D. Levine (Eds.), *Nebraska symposium on motivation* (Vol. 17, pp. 237–307). Lincoln, NE: University of Nebraska Press.

Chapter 6

Cognition and Affect in Stereotyping: Parallel Interactive Networks

WALTER G. STEPHAN
Department of Psychology
New Mexico State University
Las Cruces, New Mexico

COOKIE WHITE STEPHAN
Department of Sociology
New Mexico State University
Las Cruces, New Mexico

Introduction

Few problems have fascinated and bedeviled psychologists as much as the relationship between cognition and affect. Many psychologists have devoted their professional lives to the study of one or the other, but few have gambled their reputations by trying to join the two. Attempts to consider their interrelationships are fraught with seemingly insurmountable barriers, for they do not appear to be made of the same stuff. Reason and emotion have been counterpoised in our culture for as long as these topics have been contemplated (Isen, 1982). One is cold, the other hot. One by its very nature can be analyzed: the rules of logic can be applied to it, and it is susceptible to scientific investigation. The other is so slippery that most attempts to analyze it have foundered on the shoals of the scientific method. Affect and emotions appear irrational and illogical. Affect and emotions are the quintessential hypothetical constructs: we know them by their antecedents and their consequences. Attempts to delineate them physiologically have mostly met with failure (Rime, Philippot, & Cisamolo, 1990). Yet the problem of the interrelations of cognition and affect is so intriguing and so challenging that there continue to be a few brave or foolish souls willing to build elaborate theoretical sand castles, only to see them washed away by the counterarguments of those who follow them.

In this article we will construct a modest sand castle conceptualizing the structure of cognitive and affective information in stereotypes. We begin by presenting a network model of cognitive information processing in stereotypes, and then extrapolate this model to the structure and processing of affect. Evidence from previous studies supporting a model of interrelated cognitive and affective networks is reviewed along the way. We end by presenting a study that offers support for some aspects of our model.

A Network Model of Stereotype-Related Cognitions

Cognitive Models

There are a variety of ways of conceptualizing the representation of category information, but two basic types of models appear to be most widely used: prototype models and exemplar models. In prototype models, categories are defined in terms of the average features of the category (Posner & Keele, 1968). Information about individual category instances may or may not be stored, but it is not used in making judgments about the category. Assessments of category membership are based on the similarity of the new instances to the prototype.

In exemplar models, categories are defined in terms of individual exemplars of the category (Medin & Shaffer, 1978). Judgments about the category are assumed to be based on integrating information about individual exemplars. Assessments of category membership are based on comparing the similarity of new instances to available exemplars.

In addition, mixed models have been proposed that combine elements of prototype and exemplar models. In mixed models, category labels are thought to be linked to both prototype features and to individual instances (Medin, Altom, & Murphy, 1984; Smith & Zarate, 1990). In such models, judgments about the category may be based on central tendency or on category exemplars. In both cases, judgments of category membership are based on featural comparisons. When using prototypes, instances are compared to a prototype consisting of the average features of the category, but when using exemplars new instances are compared to the features of category exemplars. In the domain of social categories, mixed models appear to be more useful than pure prototype or pure exemplar models (Messick & Mackie, 1989; Park & Hastie, 1987).

The model we will propose is a mixed model of stereotype information processing. We first discuss stereotype networks and their structure, then we consider the processing of cognitive information in stereotype networks. In discussing cognitive networks we draw heavily on previous research and theory to create a radial model of the cognitive processing of stereotype information. Although none of the components of this model is novel, the resulting radial model is unique.

Stereotype Networks

The mixed model we propose here assumes that stereotypes consist of nodes connected by links that vary in strength (cf. Anderson, 1983; Rumelhart, Hinton, & McClelland, 1986). The strength of the links depends on the frequency and consistency with which they have been activated (Bargh, 1988; Smith & Lerner, 1986).

The basic types of information represented by the nodes in stereotype networks consist of group labels, defining features, characteristic features, behaviors, and individual exemplars. The *defining features* of a category consist of the criteria used to define group membership (Smith, Shoben, & Rips, 1974). For instance, to be defined as an "American" a person must be born in the United States, be born of an American parent, or be naturalized through a legal proceeding. Many social categories are "fuzzy": the defining features are imprecise and category members are not necessarily expected to possess all of the defining features. In the case of fuzzy social categories, group membership may be defined by such criteria as (1) possessing a sufficient number of defining features, (2) possessing a certain pattern of defining features, or (3) possessing a sufficient level of one defining feature. For example, in the first instance (1), to define a person as a Protestant might require two of the following four features: membership in a Protestant church, baptism in the church, church attendance, and obeying the commandments. In the second instance (2), baptism and weekly attendance might be required (i.e., a nonpracticing Protestant may not be defined as a Protestant). In the third instance (3), a minimum of weekly attendance might be required.

The *characteristic features* do not define the category, but they are probabilistically associated with it. For stereotypes, the characteristic features consist primarily of the traits associated with the category. For American students' stereotype of Russians, the characteristic features consist of such traits as disciplined, hard working, strong, proud, obedient, and serious (Stephan *et al.*, 1990). Defining and characteristic features of social categories are qualitatively different. To be identified as a category member, an individual must possess all or a subset of the defining features. However, an individual may possess none of the characteristic features of a category and still be a category member.

The *behaviors* of relevance to stereotypes are primarily those linked to the characteristic features (traits). Exhibiting self-control, putting effort into one's job, resilience in the face of adversity, and self-respect might be examples of behaviors that would be related to traits in the Russian stereotype. Behaviors are usually subordinated to traits in stereotypes—we expect category members to behave in ways that are consistent with the traits associated with the category. Distinguishing the traits and behaviors in stereotypes is valuable for understanding stereotype change. For instance, counterstereotypical behaviors that are not attributed internally to traits do not contribute to stereotype change (Crocker, Hannah, & Weber, 1983).

Exemplars consist of individual members of the category a person has directly or indirectly encountered (the particular Russians one has met, seen in movies, or read or heard about). Category exemplars are important in stereotyping because they may be used in categorizing new instances and because stereotype change often depends on observing a number of different individuals who behave in counterstereotypical ways (Weber & Crocker, 1983).

The Structure of Stereotype Networks

Although it is possible that the networks relating these five types of nodes in stereotypes are hierarchical in character, it is likely that these networks are more complex. In Figure 1 we present a radial model of stereotype networks. This model differs from strictly hierarchical models in several respects. First, the defining features "fan in" to the group label node, instead of "fanning out" from it. Fanning in refers to multiple nodes that are directly linked to a single node. For instance, to activate the group node for "man," such defining features as the presence of masculine clothing, a (potentially) bearded face, and sex-appropriate nonverbal behavior or large physical size may have to be activated. The defining features are more likely to activate the group label (fan in) than vice versa (fan out).

Second, there are different types of nodes set at one level removed from the group label. Defining features, characteristic features, and exemplars are all directly linked to the group node and are not subsumed under one another. Third, links exist that extend across more than one level in the hierarchy. For instance, the group label "man" might be directly linked to some expected behaviors (leaves socks in the living room) without being linked to a related trait (slovenliness).

Fourth, there may be numerous links between nodes at the same level in the hierarchy. Thus, aggressiveness, coldness, lack of emotional expressiveness, and competitiveness may be linked to each other in the masculine stereotype. Those traits that are most central to the stereotype will have strong links to one another and weaker links to more peripheral traits (Schul & Burnstein, 1990). The links between the peripheral traits may be

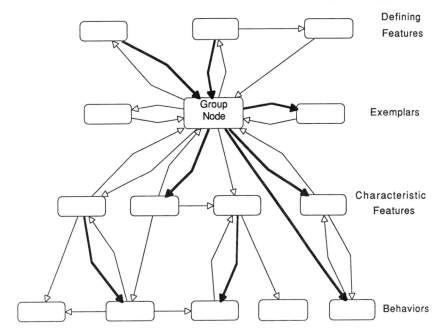

Figure 1   A radial model of cognitions in stereotypes.

weak or nonexistent. Also, in stereotype networks some of the links between traits may be stronger than the links between the traits and the group
label (linkage strength is represented by the thickness of the lines in Figure
1). An example of this type of linkage occurred in a study of the stereotypes
of Russians held by Americans (Stephan *et al.*, 1990). The traits of "obedient" and "hard working" were more closely related to the trait of "disciplined" than they were to the group label.

Finally, hierarchical structures encourage people to think of knowledge
representation in two-dimensional terms. The figures in this article would
lead to the same conclusion, but this is not our intent. We encourage you to
think of these networks as being at least three-dimensional. We now turn to
the flow of information through stereotype networks.

Processing in Stereotype Networks

Although it is customary to discuss networks in terms of "top down"
and "bottom up" processing, these terms lose some of their meaning in radial networks. We will adopt the terms "centrifugal" and "centripetal" to
refer to processing that flows away from the group node and processing

that flows toward the group node, respectively. In Figure 1, the links in a network are represented as being unidirectional; the centrifugal links are separate from the centripetal links.

In stereotypes, centrifugal processing probably dominates centripetal processing, with the exception of processing along the links between defining features and the group node. During centrifugal activation, the group node activates the stereotype-related traits, and through them, the trait-related behaviors. As each of these nodes is activated, it will, in turn, activate the other nodes to which it is connected. That is, activation will spread outward through the network along whatever links exist among the nodes. During centripetal activation, the observation of behavior would activate nodes associated with these behaviors, which would, in turn, activate the related trait nodes. If a sufficient number of the trait nodes are activated, the group node may then be activated.

As a consequence of their greater frequency of use, the strength of the centrifugal links is probably stronger than the centripetal links (cf. Andersen & Klatzky, 1987). Thus, the links from the group node "male" to the characteristic traits of aggressiveness, coldness, lack of emotional expressiveness, and competitiveness are probably stronger than the links from these traits to the group node. There is a higher probability that a male will possess these traits than there is that a person possessing any one of these traits will be male. Being male is more diagnostic of aggressiveness than aggressiveness is of being male. If this were not the case, the trait of aggressiveness probably would not be part of the stereotype of men. That is, only traits that are more closely associated with a group node than with people in general are likely to be considered characteristic of that group (cf. McCauley & Stitt, 1978).

There are two types of activation that can spread across the links: excitatory or inhibitory (cf. Klatzky, Martin, & Kane, 1982). A person holding a traditional stereotype of women may perceive women as warm, gentle, empathic, and emotional (Spence & Helmreich, 1978). If a person is identified as a woman, the group node for women will be activated and the links to the associated traits will receive excitatory activation. At the same time, the link to the group node for men will most likely receive inhibitory excitation. The result would be that the individual would expect behaviors consistent with the traits that had received excitatory activation and would not expect behaviors linked to the group node that had received inhibitory activation (i.e., masculine behaviors).

The processing that occurs in stereotype networks is often automatic and the activation that spreads through the networks is usually passive (Bargh, 1988). In real social settings, defining features are probably activated automatically (Bargh, 1984) and definitional issues rarely arise ("Are you a real Count?") Thus, other people are quickly categorized, stereotype-related expectancies are generated, and related actions are undertaken. At the same time, the behavior of the other is being attended to and inferences are being made and stored, but again with only a minimum of attentional resources being devoted to this task. Of course, it is also possible for people to exercise active control over the processing of stereotype information. Devine (1989) and Devine and Monteith (Chapter 14, this volume) have suggested that people who are low in prejudice may do so often.

To summarize briefly, the model of the cognitive aspects of stereotypes we are proposing suggests that five types of information (group nodes, defining features, characteristic features, exemplars, and behaviors) are linked in a radial network in which excitatory and inhibitory activation flow primarily in the centrifugal direction. This network model of stereotypes, as complex as it may seem, is almost certainly a major simplification of the actual functioning of the cognitive aspects of stereotype networks. In the next section we will extend our radial network model to the structure and processing of affect. We will argue that affective networks exist in parallel to cognitive networks and interact with them.

A Network Model of Affect and Cognition

Because there are perplexing differences in the usage of terms in the affective lexicon, it seems appropriate at the outset to clarify our own use of the terms affect, evaluation, arousal, and emotion. *Affect* refers to feeling states that may range from strongly positive to strongly negative. *Evaluations* are cognitive representations of affect. *Arousal* refers to the level of activation of the central nervous system and it can vary from very low to very high. *Emotions* are labeled changes in arousal that involve deviations from homeostatic activation levels. For instance, the feeling state associated with the statement by a white person "I feel uncomfortable when I am with blacks" is an affective state. The statement by this person "I dislike blacks" refers to an evaluation. The statement by the same person "I hate blacks" refers to an emotion, but only when it is associated with a change in physiological arousal, otherwise it is an evaluation. Note that negative evaluations of social groups are expressions of prejudice.

Our primary concern in this article is with affect, particularly with the affect associated with stereotyped traits and group labels. Clark and Isen (1982) argue that affective states, unlike emotions, typically do not become the focus of attention and do not interrupt behavior, although they can influence cognition. As the term "state" implies, affect is transitory. Affective states can involve arousal, but frequently they do not (Clark & Isen, 1982). As a result, it is difficult to directly assess affective states. Instead, we measure evaluations, under the assumption that they reflect affective states. Fortunately, affective states can be effectively manipulated, which has greatly aided our understanding of their functioning.

The Relationship between Cognition and Affect

Perhaps the most basic issue to address concerning the relationship between cognition and affect in stereotyping is whether the two are independent, form a unitary system, or operate as parallel systems. Independence would seem to be unlikely, except under special circumstances. If the cognitive and affective networks of stereotypes were independent, the affective responses to a stimulus would not be mediated by categorization. Instead, they would be primitive responses to the appearance and behavior of others. Independence is plausible in the case of some spontaneous positive and negative affective reactions. For instance, classically conditioned positive and negative affect may be elicited by members of social groups (e.g., dentists) and this process does not necessarily involve labeled cognitive categories. However such reactions are likely to be consistently related to only a small number of social categories. It is possible that negative affective reactions to the stigmatized may not be mediated by categorization, but instead represent a direct response to the anxiety created by their appearance. The primitiveness of this response is suggested by the finding that white infants as young as 4 months display anxiety and avoidance responses to blacks (Feinman, 1980). In spite of the limited applications of the position that cognition and affect are independent in stereotyping, it is held by some researchers. For instance, Taylor and Falcone (1982) made this argument based on the finding that prejudice against women and the tendency to treat males and females categorically were uncorrelated.

Cognition and affect are also unlikely to be a totally unitary system in which the cognitive and the affective nodes completely overlap. In such a system cognition and affect would be indistinguishable. It would mean that eliciting the category would simultaneously elicit affect—a position that seems plausible. However, it would also mean that eliciting the affect would simultaneously elicit the category—a position that is less plausible. In the latter case, it would imply that every time a person experienced positive affect all cognitive nodes associated with positive affect would be simultaneously activated, a state of affairs that could be very confusing. A unitary system would also seem to limit the extent to which the cognitive and affective networks could evolve and change independently of one another, something that almost certainly occurs as we gain experience with other groups and their members.

In Figure 2 we depict the relationship between cognition and affect as a set of interconnected parallel systems. According to this approach, affect can be associated with any node in a network (defining features, group labels, characteristic features, behaviors, or exemplars). Any type of affective (or emotional) reaction may be associated with the various types of nodes in stereotypes. In fact, more than one type of affective or emotional reaction may be associated with a single node, an idea consistent with the supposi-

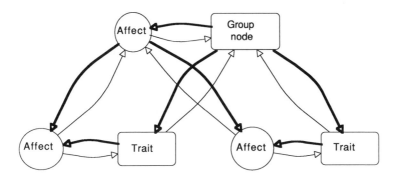

Figure 2 Parallel affective and cognitive networks in stereotypes.

tion that affective reactions to stigmatized groups are ambivalent (Katz, Wackenhut, & Haas, 1986). The affect associated with group labels is of special interest. If the affect is negative and leads to a negative evaluation of that group, then the person is prejudiced toward that group.

Obviously, affective reactions can vary in intensity. Also, the strength of the link between cognitive and affect nodes can vary, such that some categories or traits are strongly linked to affect, while others are weakly linked. In general, it would seem more likely that activating the cognitive nodes in a stereotype would elicit the associated affect than that activating an affective response would elicit the associated cognitive nodes, but both can clearly occur. One reason for thinking that cognitions are more likely to elicit affect than vice versa is based on classical conditioning, one of the primary mechanisms by which cognition and affect become associated. During classical conditioning, an unconditioned affective or emotional response becomes associated with a conditioned stimulus that is potentially cognizable. For instance, experiencing pain at the hands of dentists makes most of us apprehensive when we encounter dentists in their offices. Although no semantic cognitions need be involved in this process, we are capable of labeling the group of people who cause this apprehension. Thus, thinking of dentists can make us feel apprehensive. However, experiencing apprehension does not typically make us think of dentists, although it could. Apprehension is probably weakly linked to a wide variety of semantic cognitions, but dentists are strongly linked primarily to one affective state.

As in the case of links between cognitive nodes, the strength of the links between cognitive and affective nodes should depend on the frequency and consistency with which they have been associated. Thus, a naive visitor to a foreign country would have a more accessible positive reaction to the country the greater the number of positive interactions and the higher the ratio of positive to negative interactions.

Activation

When a cognitive node for a category is activated, it activates the affective nodes to which it is linked. Activation then spreads through the associated cognitive and affective networks. Evidence consistent with these propositions comes from a study conducted by Millar and Tesser (1986, Study 1). They found that when subjects who had initially evaluated individuals based on trait information were subsequently asked to think about these people, their later evaluations were polarized in the direction of the initial evaluations. This effect occurred for complex schemata, but not for simple ones (cf. Chaiken & Yates, 1985). Our interpretation of this finding is that processing complex schema activates more nodes that are affectively consistent with the initial evaluation than does processing less complex schema. Thus, when a second evaluation is called for, more affect consistent with the initial evaluation is present, leading to polarized evaluations.

In a similar vein, activation of the trait nodes activates the associated affect nodes. For instance, one study found that briefly exposing subjects to varying numbers of hostility-related words such as "hostile," "unkind," and "unfriendly" subsequently influenced their evaluations of an ambiguous stimulus person (Bargh & Pietromonaco, 1982). The more hostility-related words to which they were exposed, the more negative were their subsequent ratings. The hostility-related words were presented below the level of conscious awareness suggesting that the effects occurred as a result of automatic processing. Our interpretation of this finding is that the presentation of greater numbers of hostility-related words activated more negative affect, which then influenced the evaluations of the stimulus person.

As in cognitive networks, the activation in affective networks may be either excitatory or inhibitory. In one study supporting this idea, positive and negative category labels (animals, foods, social groups, nations) were used as primes for positive and negative adjectives (Fazio, Sanbonmatsu, Powell, & Kardes, 1986). It was found that strong positive primes facilitated the processing of positive adjectives and inhibited the processing of negative adjectives, while the reverse was true for strong negative primes. Our interpretation of these findings is that activating the category label elicited the associated positive or negative affect, which then facilitated access to affectively consistent traits and inhibited access to affectively inconsistent traits. Evidence consistent with these results has also been obtained for racial stereotypes in several studies reported by Gaertner and Dovidio (1986). In one of these studies, the group labels "white" and "black" were briefly flashed on a screen. The presentation of the group labels differentially facilitated judgments concerning positive and negative stereotyped-related traits among white subjects (Dovidio, Evans, & Tyler, 1986). Similar effects have been found for responses to the "old" and the "young" among young people (Perdue & Gurtman, 1990). In a related study, briefly presenting words associated with the ingroup (we, us, ours) facilitated reaction times to positive traits, while inhibiting reaction times to negative traits (Perdue, Dovidio, Gurtman, & Tyler, 1990; see Dovidio & Gaertner, Chapter 8, this volume). In these studies, after the group label was briefly flashed on the screen, a visual mask was presented to prevent the group label from being consciously processed. These findings suggest that the facilitating and inhibiting effects of the group labels were entirely automatic. Thus, the activation of the group label automatically activated traits that were affectively consistent with the evaluation of the group and inhibited the activation of affectively inconsistent traits. The group label was presented semantically to the subjects in the Dovidio studies, but the presentation of faces as primes has a parallel effect (Baker & Devine, 1988).

Another set of studies providing evidence consistent with the proposition that affective activation may be facilitory or inhibitory was conducted by Dutta, Kanungo, and Freibergs (1972). English Canadian subjects who were prejudiced toward French Canadians read lists of traits attributed to French Canadians or English Canadians. They subsequently recalled more of the negative than positive traits that were attributed to French Canadians, while the opposite was true for traits attributed to English Canadians. According to our theory, at the time of recall, the group label "French Canadian" should have elicited negative affect among these prejudiced subjects and thus facilitated access to negative trait information associated with the group label in memory and inhibited access to positive trait information associated with the group label.

Although it is possible that the results of the Dutta *et al.* (1972) studies could have been due to strong links between the affect associated with the group label and the affectively related traits, due to the extensive prior experiences of the subjects with these groups, this explanation is rendered less plausible by a study conducted by Higgins and Rholes (1978). In this study subjects made evaluative inferences about the character of a stimulus person after reading information about the person. Subsequent measures of recall indicated that subjects tended to recall information that was affectively consistent with the positive or negative inferences they had drawn about the characteristics of the stimulus person. At the time of recall, activating the person node probably elicited positive or negative affect that then facilitated access to the affectively related information (cf. Taft, 1954). Taken together, the implication of these findings is that during intergroup interaction, traits that are affectively consistent with the evaluation of the group will be automatically activated and may consequently be used as a basis for expectancies, attributions, behaviors, and subsequent judgments.

Interactions between Cognition and Affect

As the discussion above indicates, cognitive and affective networks interact with one another. Under some conditions, cognitive and affective networks operate in concert with one another, but under others they interfere with one another.

A number of studies have found that induced positive and negative affective states can interfere with the systematic processing of cognitive information (Leight & Ellis, 1981; Mackie & Worth, 1989). In one set of studies relevant to stereotypes, induced positive and negative affect interfered with subjects' perceptions of the distinctively low frequencies with which certain traits and groups had been associated in the stimulus materials presented to them (Stroessner, Hamilton, & Mackie, 1990; Hamilton *et al.*, Chapter 3, this volume). In another study, subjects recalled that stereotype-related traits which were affectively inconsistent with their moods had been more frequently associated with group members than were traits unrelated to the stereotype, although the actual frequencies of association were equal (Mackie *et al.*, 1989). Apparently, the induced moods made it difficult for the subjects to attend accurately to mood-inconsistent information, and they relied more on their preexisting stereotypes in making frequency estimates. This study suggests that moods interfere with systematic processing primarily when they are affectively inconsistent with the information to be processed.

In support of this proposition, a study by Forgas and Bower (1986) found that positive and negative moods led to mood-consistent evaluations and greater recall of mood-consistent than mood-inconsistent information. In a related study, induced positive or negative moods resulted in mood-consistent perceptions of the behavior of self and others (Forgas, Bower, & Krantz, 1984). It has also been found that when subjects' mood at recall is consistent with their mood during memorization, recall is better than when the two moods are inconsistent (Bower, 1981), although subsequent research has not always replicated this effect (for a review see Mayer, 1989). In general, induced affect increases attention to, and facilitates the encoding of, cognitive information that is mood consistent. This differential encoding influences subsequent recall, evaluations, and other judgments (Mayer, 1989; Mayer, Gayle, Meehan, & Haarman, 1990). One implication of these studies is that during intergroup interactions, people may have difficulty processing mood-inconsistent information. For instance, when negative affect is elicited in an intergroup context, positive information about outgroup members may not be effectively processed, limiting its capacity to alter stereotypes and prejudices.

Interestingly, not only may negative affect interfere with systematic processing, but when this processing is disrupted, the disruption itself may lead to negative affect. Several studies have found that the processing of stereotype-inconsistent behaviors elicits negative affect (Costrich, Feinstein, Kidder, Maracek, & Pascale, 1975; Deaux & Lewis, 1984; Jackson & Cash, 1985, but not Jackson, MacCoun, & Kerr, 1987). For instance, in one study people who violated gender stereotypes were less well liked than people who did not (Jackson & Cash, 1985). According to the model presented here, the process of making such judgments begins with categorization of the stimulus person, which then elicits stereotype-based expectancies. When these expectancies are violated, they lead to negative affect, which is then associated with the stimulus person or group causing a negative evaluation. The reason that violated expectations lead to negative affect is unclear, but it may be that the extra effort required to process stereotype-inconsistent information (Srull, Lichtenstein, & Rothbart, 1985) is experienced as aversive. Alternatively, it may be that violations of stereotype-based expectancies are one of the types of disruptions in anticipated sequences of behavior that Mandler (1984) has argued lead to negative emotional reactions.

Although we know of no evidence bearing directly on the issue, our model also has implications for processing in the absence of induced affective states. Processing should be facilitated in stereotypes containing affectively consistent information, but should be hindered in stereotypes containing inconsistent affect. For instance, when the affect associated with the traits in a stereotype is consistent with the affective reactions to the group, processing should occur smoothly and evaluations of the group should be made rapidly. However, when the affect associated with the traits is mixed or is not consistent with the affective reactions to the group, processing should be hindered and evaluations should be slowed.

Differences between Cognitive and Affective Networks

We have been arguing that affective networks operate according to the same rules that apply to cognitive networks (cf. Bower, 1981; Posner & Snyder, 1975), but it is also important to note some of the ways in which the two types of networks differ. First, it is likely that the processing in affective networks is predominantly automatic, while there is probably a greater balance between controlled and automatic processing in cognitive networks. People have relatively little insight into the internal processes associated with affect, except when affective intensity levels are quite low or quite high. Self-reports of emotional states are often unreliable and inaccurate (Rime, Philippot, & Cisamolo, 1990). The lack of insight into affective reactions limits the controlled processing that can occur within these networks. In contrast, people are capable of using their cognitive networks to solve problems and they can analyze their contents more thoroughly than the contents of affective networks. Of course, controlled cognitive processing can also be used to influence affective states (e.g., daydreaming about a romantic partner), but the reverse is probably much less common (i.e., creating an affective state to influence one's cognitions).

Second, affective networks are probably less complex than cognitive networks because the domain of affective responses is limited, while the domains of cognitive networks are almost unlimited. The automaticity and simplicity of affective networks may account for the findings that affective reactions precede cognitive reactions under many circumstances (Zajonc, 1980).

Third, arousal may have a different impact on the processing of cognitive and affective information. Arousal refers to the level of activation of the system and as such differs from both the affective and cognitive networks we have been discussing, although it has an impact on both types of networks (for a discussion of some of these issues, see Johnson-Laird & Oakley, 1989). A number of researchers have suggested that arousal causes a reduction in cognitive capacity that can have a detrimental effect on encoding, retention, and subsequent judgments (Broadbent, 1971; Kahneman, 1973; Mandler, 1984). For instance, Kim and Baron (1987) found that arousal (produced by running in place) interfered with the processing of cognitive information as indicated by an increase in one type of illusory correlation effect (the tendency to overestimate the frequency of stereotype-consistent adjectives in a set of stimulus materials).

With respect to the impact of arousal on affect, Clark, Milberg, & Erber (1984) and Stangor (1990) have argued that arousal facilitates the processing of extreme evaluative constructs. When aroused subjects evaluate a moderately positive or a moderately negative stimulus person, they give more extreme evaluations than nonaroused subjects (Stangor, 1990). Stangor (1990) also found that positive arousal led to more positive evaluations of a neutral stimulus person than negative arousal. When arousal is accompanied by positive affect, extreme positive constructs are activated, and when arousal is accompanied by negative affect, extreme negative constructs are activated. The activation of extreme constructs then biases evaluations of stimulus persons in a positive or negative manner (Clark, Milberg, & Ross, 1983). These studies suggest that affect and arousal often work in concert. When affect is associated with arousal, polarized evaluations that are consistent with the valence of the affect result.

Comparisons to Other Models

The model we have presented is compatible with models developed by Bower (1980), Clark and Isen (1982), Isen (1982, 1984), Posner and Snyder (1975), Fiske (1982), Fiske and Pavelchak (1986) and Fiske and Neuberg (1989). Because our model is most similar to Fiske's, it may be valuable to note some of the differences between them.

Fiske argues that each of the nodes in a cognitive network can have a positive or negative affective tag associated with it. Nodes become linked to affect by conditioning, communications from others, or by combining the affective responses to related nodes. When another person is categorized as a member of a group, the affect associated with the category is activated and it will dominate evaluations of the other person. If attempts to categorize another person are not successful, evaluative reactions to the other person will be built up piecemeal from the affective tags associated with the traits the person is perceived to possess (Fiske, Neuberg, Beattie, & Milberg, 1987; Fiske & Neuberg, 1989).

Our approach to the cognition–affect relationship differs in five important ways from the approach taken by Fiske. First, in our approach, affect nodes are treated the same way as cognitive nodes, while in Fiske's approach, affect is treated as a tag that can be associated with a cognitive node. Second, in our approach affective nodes can be interconnected, and both affective and cognitive nodes can have multiple connections. No interconnections or multiple connections occur in Fiske's approach. Third, we have included both excitatory and inhibitory activation in our model, while it appears that Fiske's model includes only excitatory activation. Fourth, in Fiske's model no distinction is made between the defining and characteristic features of a category, but in our model these features are treated separately. Fifth, we have explicitly considered the relationship of arousal to cognitive and affective processing, while Fiske has not.

Next, we present a study in which the evaluative responses to characteristic features of national stereotypes are used to predict evaluative responses to these nations.

Stereotypes and Prejudice: An Empirical Study

Stereotypes and Prejudice

A basic issue in intergroup relations concerns the relationship of stereotypes and prejudice. Our model predicts that stereotypes and prejudice are related through the cognitive and affective networks associated with the group label. Prejudice consists of negative evaluations of social groups. Thus, prejudice is a cognitive representation of the affective responses associated with group nodes. Group nodes are also linked to the characteristic features (traits) in the stereotype of the group, and these features are linked to their own affective responses. There are also links between the affect associated with the group node and the related affective responses associated with the traits (Figure 2). In the study to be presented here, we attempt to determine if the affective responses to the group can be predicted by the affective responses to traits associated with the group.

In most previous studies investigating the relationship between prejudice and stereotypes, prejudice has been measured with simple attitude scales and the percentage technique has been used to measure stereotypes. For instance, subjects were asked to indicate their attitudes toward a given group and then asked what percentage of the members of that group possessed each of a list of traits. These studies have obtained mixed results, but they typically find only a small relationship between prejudice and stereotyping. Brigham (1971) reported that only 7 of 15 individual traits in the stereotypes of blacks were significantly correlated with attitudes toward blacks. The average correlation in this study was .15. In one of our previous studies, the correlation between prejudice toward Caucasians and stereotyping of Caucasians was –.05 in a sample of Asian Americans, while the correlation between prejudice toward Asian Americans and stereotyping of Asian Americans was .05 in a sample of Caucasians (Stephan & Stephan, 1989). In another study, the correlation between ethnocentrism (favorableness of ingroup vs. outgroup evaluation) and stereotyping of Hispanics was –.16 in a sample of Anglo-Americans (Stephan & Stephan, 1985). In another of our studies we examined the correlation between the stereotypes of Japan, the then Soviet Union, and the United States and attitudes toward these countries in 6 nations (Stephan et al., 1991). Of the 18 possible correlations, 5 were significant. For the attitudes toward the Japanese the correlations in the 6 samples ranged from –.08 to .16 and averaged .03. For attitudes toward the Soviets the correlations ranged from –.03 to .30 and averaged .10. For attitudes toward the Americans the correlations ranged from .04 to .41 and averaged .19.

Higher correlations have been obtained when the evaluations of the characteristic features are considered along with the degree to which these features characterize the group. Eagly and Mladinic (1989) found that attitudes toward Republicans and Democrats were significantly correlated with a stereotype measure in which the trait percentages were multiplied by the evaluations of the traits on a good–bad dimension (.55 for both groups). In this study, the correlations for attitudes toward women and men and a parallel stereotype measure were considerably lower (.32 for women and .26 for men).

A somewhat similar index was used in a much earlier study by Katz and Braly (1933). In one sample, they asked students to indicate the traits that characterized ten different national groups. A second sample evaluated the traits on their desirability in friends and associates. A third sample ranked the groups on the basis of preference for association with its members. A stereotype/evaluation index was created by multiplying the percent of students nominating a trait as characteristic of the group by the desirability of the traits and summing over the traits for each national group. The groups were then ranked using the stereotype/evaluation index. Katz and Braly noted the similarity in the ranking of the groups on the stereotype/evaluation index and the ranks on the preference index, but it was left to Stroebe and Insko (1989) to calculate the rank order correlation (.89).

The stereotyping/evaluation indices employed in these studies are conceptually related to the expectancy × value approaches proposed by Rosenberg (1960) and Fishbein (1967). In these approaches beliefs are weighted by their importance or evaluation. In the current study, beliefs about the prevalence of traits in social groups are weighted by the evaluative reactions to these traits on a positive–negative dimension. The correlation between these stereotype/evaluation ratings and evaluative responses to the group are then examined.

Overview

In this study, we attempted to predict the evaluative responses of two samples of students to 6 national groups (Americans, Moroccans, Russians, Indians, Japanese, and Chinese). One sample, the Semester-at-Sea sample, consisted of 85 students participating in an international exchange program that included short (4–7 days) visits to 10 countries, including all of those mentioned above. The other sample, the New Mexico sample, consisted of 63 students who had little or no experience with the foreign countries the other students had visited. We hoped that the use of national groups, instead of racial groups, would lead to fewer attempts at the kind of controlled processing that limits the expression of negative affect toward social groups. In addition, the students provided these data anonymously to encourage them to respond honestly.

Hypotheses

Based on our model, we predicted that evaluative reactions to these national groups would be correlated with a stereotype/evaluation index composed of evaluations of traits associated with the group weighted by the strength of the links between these traits and the groups. These correlations were expected to be higher than the correlations of the evaluative reactions to the national groups and pure stereotype measures (the strength of the trait linkages only). In addition, we anticipated that the correlation of the evaluative reactions to the national groups and the stereotype/evaluation index would be greater in the Semester-at-Sea sample than in the New Mexico sample. This last prediction is based on the premise that when impressions of a group are built up in a piecemeal fashion, by encountering members of the group, there should be a relatively close correspondence between evaluations of the traits attributed to the group and evaluations of the group as a whole. As Pavelchak has noted, when evaluations of social categories are based on piecemeal processing, they are computed from the trait evaluations (Pavelchak, 1989). However, when impressions of the group are based on information acquired from the media, family, peers, and educational materials, evaluations of the group may not be as closely related to the traits attributed to the group. In the latter instance, the category itself is likely to be labeled and evaluated as such, whereas when the impression is built up through experience, it is individual members of the group who are encountered, rather than a labeled group.

In addition, there should be more extensive controlled processing and hence greater correspondence between category evaluations and trait evaluations for experience-based impressions than for those based on indirect exposure. Also, the greater personal relevance of experience-based impressions should lead to more attention being devoted to the attributes of the group (Brewer, 1988). The greater accuracy of the resultant impressions and evaluations would be expected to increase the correspondence between group evaluations and trait evaluations. As a result of these considerations, we expected to find higher correlations between the stereotype/evaluation measure and the attitude measure in the Semester-at-Sea sample than in the New Mexico sample.

Method

The degree to which the groups were stereotyped was assessed by asking both samples of students to indicate the percent of 6 national groups who possessed each of the following 20 traits: disciplined, group oriented, proud, status oriented, kind, competitive, traditional, independent, materialistic, friendly, rigid, concerned with dignity, hard working, cold, inefficient, conforming, individualistic, artistic, trustworthy, and unattractive. This list was composed of traits derived from previous studies of the stereotypes of Americans and Russians and from a study of values in Eastern cultures (Stephan *et al.*, 1990; The Chinese Cultural Connection, 1987). An attempt was made to include traits from all of the personality domains outlined by Peabody (1987) and to balance positive and negative traits. The response scale consisted of 10 points increasing in 10-point increments from 0–100%. The responses to these questions were used as an index of the strength of the link between the country node and the trait node. Although this is not a direct measure of strength, it seems justified in view of research suggesting that frequency judgments are based on the strength of the memory traces (Jonides & Nevah-Benjamin, 1987).

The affect nodes were assessed by asking subjects to indicate their evaluative reactions to each of the 20 stereotype traits. The format for this measure consisted of a 9-point scale running from "Extremely Negative" to "Extremely Positive." Using the same scale, the evaluations of the country nodes were assessed by asking the subjects to indicate their evaluative reaction to people from each of these countries.

Results

We first obtained correlations between the evaluative reactions to each country and a stereotype/evaluation index consisting of a weighted sum of the evaluative reactions to the traits and the stereotype ratings. In calculating the stereotype/evaluation index, the percentage rating for each trait was multiplied by the evaluative reaction to that trait. These scores were summed across all 20 traits to obtain a summary stereotype/evaluation index for each country for each subject.

The correlations between these stereotype/evaluation measures and the evaluative reactions to the group were then calculated separately for all 6 countries in the New Mexico sample and the Semester-at-Sea sample (Table I). In the New Mexico sample these correlations ranged from .26 to .45 and averaged .37. In the Semester-at-Sea sample the correlations ranged from .29 to .54 and averaged .36.

To create a comparison set of correlations, the correlations between a pure stereotyping index and the evaluative reactions to the groups were also calculated. The stereotyping index was created by summing the

TABLE I
Correlations of Stereotype and Group Affect Measures

Samples	Stereotype/evaluation measure	Pure stereotype measure
Semester-at-Sea Sample		
Moroccans	.30**	.01
Russians	.29**	.07
Japanese	.54**	.41**
Chinese	.32**	.10
Americans	.32**	.09
Indians	.39**	.16
New Mexico Sample		
Moroccans	.38**	.22
Russians	.26*	.16
Japanese	.29*	.20
Chinese	.41**	.28*
Americans	.40**	.23
Indians	.45**	.29*

$*, p < .05; **, p < .01.$

stereotype ratings across all 20 traits for each group for each subject. These stereotypes were then correlated with the evaluative reactions of the subject to the groups. The resulting correlations are similar to the prejudice-stereotype correlations obtained in previous research. For the New Mexico sample these correlations ranged from .16 to .29 and averaged .23. For the Semester-at-Sea sample the correlations ranged from .01 to .41 and averaged .14.

As expected, the correlations for the stereotype/evaluation measures and the evaluations of the groups are generally higher than the correlations for the pure stereotypes and the evaluations of the groups in both samples. The difference between the correlation using the stereotype/evaluation index and the correlation using the pure stereotype measure is significant in the Semester-at-Sea sample for the Moroccans, the Russians, the Chinese, the Americans, and the Indians (Fisher's Z, 1.96, p's < .05). None of the differences in the size of the correlations is significant in the New Mexico sample.

Discussion

The results of this study indicate that affect and cognition are interrelated in intergroup perception, as our model suggests. In this test of the model, evaluative reactions to national groups were found to be correlated with an index in which the strength of the links between traits and national groups were multiplied by the evaluations of these traits. Although these correlations were only moderate, there are several possible factors that may have attenuated their strength. Devine (1989) has argued that low levels of prejudice are largely a product of controlled processing, whereas stereotypes tend to be automatically processed. As a result, people who are low in prejudice may or may not stereotype social groups, depending on their socialization. She suggests, for example, that many feminists hold traditional stereotypes of women acquired through socialization that can be activated automatically, but they do not exhibit a corresponding prejudice against women because of their conscious ideological commitments. If the low-prejudiced subjects in our samples did not stereotype the countries they were rating, this would have attentuated the correlations between the stereotype/evaluation measure and the evaluations of the countries.

Second, it has been customary in the research on stereotypes and prejudice to deal with evaluations as a unitary construct that varies from positive to negative. This conception of evaluations is probably an oversimplification. For many social groups, the evaluative responses are likely to include a variety of reactions that vary in valence (Eagly & Mladinic, 1989). The theorists who argue that whites' attitudes toward blacks are ambivalent have provided data indicating that attitudes toward blacks are often a mixture of sympathy and aversion (Katz *et al.*, 1986). We have also made this point in our model. According to the model, the affective responses associated with a category may be interconnected among themselves in complex ways and each may be connected to other related affective responses as well. The affective measures used in this and other studies are summary indices that may not capture the complexity of the affective responses to social groups.

There was no evidence for the hypothesis that students with recent experiences in these countries would display higher correlations between the stereotype/evaluation measure and the group evaluation measure than students who had little experience with these countries. Further evidence against this hypothesis comes from the finding that in the New Mexico sample the correlation for Americans (where the stereotypes were presumably experience based) was not significantly higher than the correlations for the other countries. These nonsignificant effects suggest that the accessibility of stereotype information does not aid in the prediction of evaluative responses to social groups. This conclusion is consistent with the results obtained by Eagly and Mladinic (1989). They found that the correlations of their stereotype/affect measure and evaluations of social groups were higher for Republicans and Democrats than for females and males. Since it seems reasonable to argue that the stereotypes of males and females are based on direct experience to a greater degree than those of Republicans and Democrats, it appears that in this instance also experience-based stereotypes do not produce higher correlations with evaluative responses to groups.

In addition, in the present study it was found that among students with stereotypes based on personal experience, taking into consideration their evaluations of the traits in their stereotypes generally resulted in significantly better predictions of their evaluations of the groups than simply using their stereotypes. Significant differences were not obtained among students whose stereotypes were not experience based. One interpretation of this finding is that with direct experience, links may be forged between the affect associated with the traits in the stereotype and the affect associated with the group node. Because they are based on controlled processing, these links are likely to be evaluatively consistent in accordance with the idea that stereotypes tend toward evaluative consistency (Ehrlich, 1973; Ehrlich & Van Tubergen, 1971; LeVine & Campbell, 1972, p. 192). Thus, in these networks, predictions of group evaluations are improved by considering the affect associated with the characteristic features. However, in networks that are not based on experience, it is primarily the characteristic features that are linked to the affective reactions to the groups. In these networks, taking into consideration the affect associated with the characteristic features does not appreciably improve the prediction of group evaluations.

Conclusion

In this article we have presented a model that delineates the relationships between cognition and affect in stereotyping and we have reported supportive evidence for some aspects of the model. The evidence indicated that evaluations of social groups are related to evaluations of the traits associated with the group weighted by the strength of the links between the traits and the group nodes. It seems possible that the model applies to other domains involving cognition and affect, as well as to stereotyping, but we have not attempted to make these leaps of faith. The model is limited in several important ways. A more comprehensive model would integrate episodic and iconic memory structures with the semantic and affective structures we have discussed. And, a comprehensive model would specify the relations of cognition and affect to behavior. We hope that the model we have proposed takes us a few steps toward this untrodden terrain.

Acknowledgments

The authors thank Lisa Coates-Shrider for her assistance in gathering the data and for reading an earlier version of the manuscript. They also thank Jim McDonald and the editors for their comments on earlier versions of the manuscript.

References

Andersen, S. M., & Klatzky, R. (1987). Traits and social stereotypes: Levels of categorization in person perception. *Journal of Personality and Social Psychology, 53*, 235–246.

Anderson, J. R. (1983). *The architecture of cognition.* Cambridge: Harvard University Press.

Baker, S. M., & Devine, P. G. (1988). *Faces as primes for stereotype activation.* Paper presented at the Midwestern Psychological Association, Chicago, IL.

Bargh, J. A. (1984). Automatic and conscious processing of social information. In R. S. Wyer & T. K. Srull (Eds.), *Handbook of social cognition* (pp. 1–44). Hillsdale, NJ: Erlbaum.

Bargh, J. A. (1988). Automatic information processing: Implications for communication and affect. In L. Donophew, H. E. Sypher, & T. E. Higgins (Eds.), *Communication, social cognition and affect* (pp. 9–32). Hillsdale, NJ: Erlbaum.

Bargh, J. A., & Pietromonaco, P. (1982). Automatic information processing and social perception: The influence of trait information presented outside of conscious awareness on impression formation. *Journal of Personality and Social Psychology, 43*, 437–449.

Bower, G. H. (1981). Mood and memory. *American Psychologist, 36*, 129–148.

Brewer, M. B. (1988). A dual process model of impression formation. In R. S. Wyer & T. K. Srull (Eds.), *Advances in Social Cognition* (pp. 1–36). Hillsdale, NJ: Erlbaum.

Brigham, J. C. (1971). Ethnic stereotypes. *Psychological Bulletin, 76*, 15–38.

Broadbent, D. E. (1971). *Decision and stress.* New York: Academic Press.

Chaiken, S., & Yates, S. (1985). Affective-cognitive consistency and thought induced polarization. *Journal of Personality and Social Psychology, 49*, 1470–1481.

Chinese Cultural Connection. (1987). Chinese values and the search for culture-free dimensions of culture. *Journal of Cross-Cultural Psychology, 18,* 143–163.

Clark, M. S., & Isen, A. M. (1982). Toward understanding the relationship between feeling states and social behavior. In A. Hastorf and A. M. Isen (Eds.), *Cognitive social psychology* (pp. 73–108). NY: Elsevier North-Holland.

Clark, M. S., Milberg, S., & Ross, J. (1983). Arousal cues material in memory with a similar level of arousal: Implications for understanding the effects of mood on memory. *Journal of Verbal Learning and Verbal Behavior, 22,* 633–649.

Clark, M. S., Milberg, S., & Erber, R. (1984). Effects of arousal on judgments of others' emotions. *Journal of Personality and Social Psychology, 46,* 551–560.

Costrich, N., Feinstein, J., Kidder, L., Maracek, J., & Pascale, L. (1975). When stereotypes hurt: Three studies of penalties for sex-role reversal. *Journal of Experimental Social Psychology, 11,* 520–530.

Crocker, J., Hannah, D. B., & Weber, R. (1983). Person memory and causal attributions. *Journal of Personality and Social Psychology, 44,* 55–66.

Deaux, K., & Lewis, L. L. (1984). Structure of gender stereotypes: Interrelationships among components and gender label. *Journal of Personality and Social Psychology, 46,* 991–1004.

Devine, P. G. (1989). Stereotypes and prejudice: Their automatic and controlled components. *Journal of Personality and Social Psychology, 56,* 5–18.

Dovidio, J. F., Evans, N., & Tyler, R. B. (1986). Racial stereotypes: the contents of their cognitive representations. *Journal of Experimental Social Psychology, 22,* 22–37.

Dutta, S. R., Kanungo, N., & Freibergs, V. (1972). Retention of affective material: effects of intensity of affect on retrieval. *Journal of Personality and Social Psychology, 23,* 64–80.

Eagly, A. H., & Mladinic, A. (1989). Gender stereotypes and attitudes toward men and women. *Personality and Social Psychology Bulletin, 15,* 543–558.

Ehrlich, H. J. (1973). *The social psychology of prejudice.* New York: John Wiley.

Ehrlich, H. J., & Van Tubergen. (1971). Exploring the structure and salience of stereotypes. *Journal of Social Psychology, 83,* 113–127.

Fazio, R. H., Sanbonmatsu, D. M., Powell, M. C., & Kardes, F. R. (1986). On the automatic activation of attitudes. *Journal of Personality and Social Psychology, 50,* 229–238.

Feinman, S. (1980). Infant responses to race, size, proximity, and movement of strangers. *Infant Behavior and Child Development, 3,* 187–204.

Fishbein, M. (1967). A behavior theory approach to relations between beliefs about an object and the attitude toward the object. In M. Fishbein (Ed.), *Readings in attitude theory and measurement* (pp. 389–400). New York: Wiley.

Fiske, S. T. (1982). Schema-triggered affect: Applications to social perception. In M. S. Clark and S. T. Fiske (Eds.), *Affect and cognition* (pp. 55–74). Hillsdale, NJ: Erlbaum.

Fiske, S. T., & Neuberg, S. L. (1989). A continuum of impression formation, from category-based to individuating processes: Influences of information and motivation on attention and interpretation. In M. Zanna (Ed.), *Advances in experimental social psychology* (pp. 1–74). San Diego: Academic Press.

Fiske, S. T., & Pavelchak, M. A. (1986). Category-based versus piecemeal-based affective responses: Developments in schema-triggered affect. In R. M. Sorrentino and E. T. Higgins (Eds.), *The handbook of motivation and cognition: Foundations of social behavior* (pp. 167–203). New York: Guilford Press.

Fiske, S. T., Neuberg, S. L., Beattie, A. E., & Milberg, S. J. (1987). Category-based and attribute-based reactions to others: some informational conditions of stereotyping and individuating processes. *Journal of Experimental Social Psychology, 23,* 399–427.

Forgas, J. P., & Bower, G. H. (1986). Mood effects on person-perception judgments. *Journal of Personality and Social Psychology, 53,* 53–60.

Forgas, J. P., Bower, G. H., & Krantz, S. E. (1984). The influence of mood on perceptions of social interactions. *Journal of Experimental Social Psychology, 20,* 497–513.

Gaertner, S. L., & Dovidio, J. F. (1986). The aversive form of racism. In J. F. Dovidio & S. L. Gaertner (Eds.), *Prejudice, discrimination, and Racism* (pp. 61–90). Orlando, FL: Academic Press.

Higgins, E. T., & Rholes, W. S. (1978). "Saying is believing:" effects of message modification on memory and liking for the person described. *Journal of Experimental Social Psychology, 13,* 141–154.

Isen, A. M. (1982). Some perspectives on cognitive social psychology. In A. H. Hastorf & A. M. Isen (Eds.), *Cognitive social psychology* (pp. 1–31). New York: Elsevier.

Isen, A. M. (1984). Toward understanding the role of affect in cognition. In R. S. Wyer, Jr. & T. K. Srull (Eds.), *Handbook of social cognition* (Vol. 3, pp. 179–236). Hillsdale, NJ: Erlbaum.

Jackson, L. A., & Cash, T. F. (1985). Components of gender stereotypes and their implications for stereotype and nonstereotype judgments. *Personality and Social Psychology Bulletin, 11,* 326–344.

Jackson, L. A., MacCoun, R. J., & Kerr, N. L. (1987). Stereotypes and nonstereotype judgments. *Personality and Social Psychology Bulletin, 13,* 45–52.

Johnson-Laird, P. N., & Oakley, K. (1989). The language of emotions: An analysis of a semantic field. *Cognition and Emotion, 3,* 81–123.

Jonides, J., & Nevah-Benjamin, M. (1987). Estimating frequency occurrence. *Journal of Experimental Psychology: Learning, Memory and Cognition, 13,* 230–240.

Kahneman, D. (1973). *Attention and effort.* Englewood Cliffs, NJ: Prentice-Hall.

Katz, D., & Braly, K. N. (1933). Verbal stereotypes and racial prejudice. *Journal of Abnormal and Social Psychology, 133,* 280–290.

Katz, I., Wackenhut, J., & Hass, G. R. (1986). Racial ambivalence, value duality, and behavior. In J. F. Dovidio and S. L. Gaertner (Eds.), *Prejudice, discrimination, and racism* (pp. 35–61). New York: Academic Press.

Kim, H., & Baron, R. S. (1987). Exercise and the illusory correlation: Does arousal heighten stereotypic processing? *Journal of Experimental Social Psychology, 24,* 366–380.

Klatzky, R. L., Martin, G. L., & Kane, R. A. (1982). Influence of social-category activation and processing of visual information. *Social Cognition, 1,* 95–109.

Leight, K. A., & Ellis, H. C. (1981). Emotional states, strategies, and state-dependent memory. *Journal of Verbal Learning and Behavior, 20,* 251–266.

LeVine, R. A., & Campbell, D. T. (1972). *Ethnocentrism.* New York: John Wiley.

Linville, P. W., Salovey, P., & Fischer, G. W. (1986). Stereotyping and perceived distributions of social characteristics: An application to ingroup–outgroup perception. In J. F. Dovidio & S. L. Gaertner (Eds.). *Prejudice, discrimination, and racism.* Orlando, FL: Academic Press.

Mackie, D. M., & Worth, L. T. (1989). Processing deficits and the mediation of positive affect in persuasion. *Journal of Personality and Social Psychology, 57,* 27–40.

Mackie, D. M., Hamilton, D. L., Schroth, H. A., Carlisle, C. J., Gersho, B. F., Meneses, L. M., Nedler, B. F., & Reichel, L. D. (1989). The effects of induced mood on expectancy-based illusory correlations. *Journal of Experimental Social Psychology, 25,* 524–544.

Mandler, G. (1984). *Mind and body.* New York: Norton.

Mayer, J. D. (1989). How mood influences cognition. In N. E. Sharkey (Ed.), *Advances in cognitive science* (Vol. I, pp. 290–313). New York: Wiley.

Mayer, J. D., Gayle, M., Meehan, M. E., & Haarman, A. (1990). Toward better specification of the mood-consistency effect in recall. *Journal of Experimental Social Psychology, 26,* 465–480.

McCauley, C., & Stitt, C. L. (1978). An individual and quantitative measure of stereotypes. *Journal of Personality and Social Psychology, 36,* 929–940.

Medin, D. L., & Schaffer, M. M. (1978). Context theory of classification learning. *Psychological Review, 85,* 207–238.

Medin, D. L., Altom, M. W., & Murphy, T. D. (1984). Given versus induced category representations: Use of prototype and exemplar information in classification. *Journal of Experimental Psychology: Learning, Memory, and Cognition*, 10, 333–352.

Messick, D. M., & Mackie, D. M. (1989). Intergroup relations. *Annual Review of Psychology*, 40, 45–81.

Millar, M. G., & Tesser, A. (1986). Thought-induced attitude change: The effects of schema complexity and commitment. *Journal of Personality and Social Psychology*, 51, 259–269.

Park, B., & Hastie, R. (1987). The perception of variability in category development: Instance-versus abstraction-based stereotypes. *Journal of Personality and Social Psychology*, 53, 621–635.

Pavelchak, M. A. (1989). Piecemeal and category-based evaluation: An ideographic analysis. *Journal of Personality and Social Psychology*, 56, 354–363.

Peabody, D. (1987). Selecting representative trait adjectives. *Journal of Personality and Social Psychology*, 52, 59–71.

Perdue, C. W., & Gurtman, M. B. (1990). Evidence of the automaticity of ageism. *Journal of Experimental Social Psychology*, 26, 199–216.

Perdue, C. W., Dovidio, J. F., Gurtman, M. B., & Tyler, R. B. (1990). "Us" and "them": Social categorization and the process of intergroup bias. *Journal of Personality and Social Psychology*, 59, 475–486.

Posner, M. I., & Keele, S. W. (1968). On the genesis of abstract ideas. *Journal of Experimental Psychology*, 77, 353–363.

Posner, M. I., & Snyder, C. R. R. (1975). Attention and cognitive control. In R. L. Solso (Ed.), *Information processing and cognition* (pp. 55–86). Hillsdale, NJ: Erlbaum.

Rime, B., Philippot, P., & Cisamolo, D. (1990). Social schemata of peripheral changes in emotion. *Journal of Personality and Social Psychology*, 59, 38–49.

Rosenberg, M. J. (1960). An analysis of affective-cognitive consistency. In C. I. Hovland & M. J. Rosenberg (Eds.), *Attitude organization and change* (pp. 15–64). New Haven, CT: Yale University Press.

Rumelhart, D. E., Hinton, G. E., & McClelland, J. L. (1986). A general framework for parallel distributed processing. In D. E. Rumelhart, J. L. McClelland, and the PDP research group (Eds.), *Parallel distributed processing* (pp. 45–76). Cambridge, MA: MIT Press.

Schul, Y., & Burnstein, E. (1990). Judging the typicality of an instance: Should the category be accessed first? *Journal of Personality and Social Psychology*, 58, 964–974.

Smith, E. R., & Lerner, M. (1986). Development of automatism of social judgments. *Journal of Personality and Social Psychology*, 50, 246–259.

Smith, E. E., Shoben, E. J., & Rips, L. J. (1974). Structure and process in semantic memory. *Psychological Review*, 81, 214–241.

Smith, E. R., & Zarate, M. A. (1990). Exemplar and prototype use in social categorization. *Social Cognition*. 8, 243–262.

Spence, J. T., & Helmreich, R. L. (1978). *Masculinity and femininity*. Austin, Tx: University of Texas Press.

Srull, T. K., Lichtenstein, M., & Rothbart, M. (1985). Associative storage and retrieval processes in person memory. *Journal of Experimental Psychology: Learning, Memory, and Cognition*, 11, 316–345.

Stangor, C. (1990). Arousal, accessibility of trait constructs, and person perception. *Journal of Experimental Social Psychology*, 26, 305–321.

Stephan, W. G. (1985). Intergroup relations. In G. Lindzey and E. Aronson (Eds.), *Handbook of social psychology* (Vol. III, pp. 599–658). New York: Addison-Wesley.

Stephan, W. G., & Stephan, C. (1985). Intergroup anxiety. *Journal of Social Issues*, 41, 157–176.

Stephan, W. G., & Stephan, C. W. (1989). Antecedents of intergroup anxiety in Oriental-Americans and Hispanics. *International Journal of Intercultural Relations*, 13, 203–219.

Stephan, W. G., Ageyev, V. S., Stephan, C. W., Abalakina, M., Stefanenko, T., & Coates-Shrider, L. (1990). *Soviet and American stereotypes: A comparison of methods.* Unpublished manuscript, New Mexico State University.

Stephan, W. G., Abalakina, M., Ageyev, V., Blanco, A., Bond, M., Saito, I., Stephan, C. W., Turcinovic, P., & Wenzel, B. (1991). *Perceptions of the superpowers: An international study.* Unpublished manuscript, New Mexico State University.

Stroebe, W., & Insko, C. (1989). Stereotype, prejudice, and discrimination: Changing conceptions in theory and research. In D. Bar-Tal, C. F. Graumann, A. W. Kruglanski, & W. Stroebe (Eds.), *Stereotyping and prejudice: Changing conceptions* (pp. 3–36). New York: Springer-Verlag.

Stroessner, S. J., Hamilton, D. L., & Mackie, D. M. (1990). *Affect and stereotyping: The effect of induced mood on distinctiveness-based illusory correlation.* Unpublished manuscript, University of California, Santa Barbara, CA.

Taft, R. (1954). Selective recall and memory distortion of favorable and unfavorable material. *Journal of Abnormal and Social Psychology, 49,* 23–28.

Taylor, S. E., & Falcone, H. (1982). Cognitive bases of stereotyping: The relationship between categorization and prejudice. *Personality and Social Psychology Bulletin, 8,* 426–432.

Weber, R., & Crocker, J. (1983). Cognitive processing in the revision of stereotype beliefs. *Journal of Personality and Social Psychology, 45,* 961–977.

Zajonc, R. B. (1980). Feeling and thinking: Preferences need no inferences. *American Psychologist, 35,* 151–175.

Chapter 7

Values, Stereotypes, and Emotions as Determinants of Intergroup Attitudes*

VICTORIA M. ESSES

Department of Psychology
University of Western Ontario
London, Ontario, Canada

GEOFFREY HADDOCK and MARK P. ZANNA

Department of Psychology
University of Waterloo
Waterloo, Ontario, Canada

Introduction

When we are asked about our attitude toward a social group, we are as likely to express our feelings toward and beliefs about members of the group as we are to provide a summary evaluation of the group. For example, we may say that we admire Native Canadians, that we believe they make a significant contribution to our society, and that we hold a favorable view of the group. Although potentially related, these three pieces of information are distinct, providing separate classes of information. Thus, our everyday experience suggests that intergroup attitudes are rather complex, involving affective and cognitive components as well as overall evaluations.

*Editor's Note: This chapter was selected as the 1992 winner of the Otto Klineberg Intercultural and International Relations Award, given by the Society for the Psychological Study of Social Issues. In making its selection, the award committee cited the chapter for offering a "substantial advance in our understanding of basic psychological processes underlying racism, stereotyping, and prejudice".

Researchers have long acknowledged this multifaceted nature of intergroup attitudes. However, depending on the theoretical framework in which they were operating, they have tended to focus on either the affective or cognitive underpinnings of these attitudes, rather than on the joint role of affect and cognition. Disparities in the measurement of intergroup attitudes have contributed to this rift.

In this chapter, we will begin to redress this problem by providing a framework for thinking about the contribution of both affect and cognition in determining attitudes toward groups. We will discuss how previous findings fit within this framework and will then describe recent research designed to examine the interplay between affect and cognition. Specific questions to be addressed include: (1) to what extent do affect and cognition predict overall evaluations of groups? (2) are there individual differences in the weighting of affective and cognitive information? and (3) are there also situational determinants of whether affect or cognition dominates? In parallel with societal trends, research in this area has progressed from a focus on attitudes toward social groups at the level of ethnic groups (especially attitudes toward blacks in the United States) to a broader scope which includes attitudes toward groups based on such varied characteristics as sex, sexual orientation, political affiliation, and age. In addition to reviewing previous literature and discussing current findings in some detail, we will suggest some future directions for research.

Framework and Terminology

Attitudes toward social groups can be defined within the framework of approaches to attitudes in general. A recent development in the attitude literature has been the recognition that evaluations, cognitions, and affect are separable yet interconnected aspects of the attitude concept. In this vein, Zanna and Rempel (1988) have suggested that an attitude be defined as an overall evaluation of a stimulus object which is, in turn, based on three separable components or sources of information: cognitive information (beliefs), affective information (specific feelings or emotions), and information concerning past behavior. Attitudes toward social groups can be defined in a similar way. The summary attitude can be defined as a favorable or unfavorable overall evaluation of a social group, with an unfavorable overall evaluation being labeled prejudice (Stephan, 1985). The cognitive component can be divided into (1) stereotypes: beliefs about the specific characteristics possessed by members of a social group (Stephan, 1985), and (2) more general beliefs about a social group, including symbolic beliefs (Zanna, Haddock, & Esses, 1990). The affective component can be defined as specific feelings or emotions toward a social group. And finally, information concerning past behavior can be defined as how we have behaved toward, or, at least, believe that we have behaved toward members of a social group in the past.

Within this framework, we will focus on the affective and cognitive components of attitudes toward social groups, as well as on the summary attitudes themselves. In discussing the affective component of intergroup attitudes we will be looking at the emotions elicited by social groups. In contrast to global mood states, emotions can be defined by the fact that they generally have clear targets and possess specific labels (Schwarz & Clore, 1988). Thus, one can experience many different types of positive emotions, such as admiration or pride, as well as many different types of negative emotions, such as fear or anger.

In discussing the cognitive component of intergroup attitudes, we will talk about stereotypes and symbolic beliefs. Stereotypes will be dealt with at both the consensual and individual level. Consensual stereotypes are shared beliefs about the characteristics possessed by members of a social group, that is, ascribed characteristics for which there is considerable agreement. In contrast, individual stereotypes include all characteristics that an individual attributes to members of a social group, whether consensual or idiosyncratic. For example, an individual may share the popular belief that men are self-confident (consensual stereotype) but may also believe that they are lazy, a characteristic for which there is less agreement (idiosyncratic stereotype). If we were examining consensual stereotypes we would focus only on the characteristic "self-confident," but in examining individual stereotypes we would include both "self-confident" and "lazy." We suggest that both consensual stereotypes and individual stereotypes are worthy of investigation. Consensual stereotypes, because of their prevalence in society, may have a significant impact on the status and treatment of social groups (Gardner, 1973, 1993). Individual stereotypes, on the other hand, may be especially useful in helping us to understand the basis of individuals' attitudes toward groups.

In addition to beliefs about the specific characteristics possessed by members of a social group, more general, abstract beliefs, such as symbolic beliefs, may contribute to intergroup attitudes. Based on the concept of symbolic racism (McConahay & Hough, 1976; Sears & Kinder, 1971), we use the term symbolic beliefs to refer to beliefs that social groups violate or uphold cherished values and norms (Zanna *et al.*, 1990).[1] For example, an individual may hold the symbolic belief that homosexuals threaten the value of the family and family life.

We will reserve the term intergroup attitudes to refer to overall evaluations of social groups on a global dimension, such as favorable–unfavorable

---

[1] By using the term symbolic beliefs, we wish to emphasize the abstract, moral nature of these cognitions. However, in contrast to symbolic racism, we currently make no claims as to the origin and function of these beliefs.

or positive–negative. Perhaps the best measure of intergroup attitudes to date is the evaluation thermometer, which uses a graphical depiction to assess favorable or unfavorable perceptions of groups (Campbell, 1971). Because the thermometer does not contain specific dimensions on which to rate groups, it allows subjects to base their attitudes on whatever cognitions and/or emotions are relevant and important to them. Unfortunately, this measure has not been uniformly utilized in assessing attitudes toward groups. Therefore, in reviewing previous literature, we will try to apply our definition of intergroup attitudes to measures used at the time. However, some judgment calls have had to be made in determining whether certain measures assess evaluations of groups at a global level.

Affect and Intergroup Attitudes

Affect has long been considered to be a major determinant of intergroup attitudes. In particular, negative emotions have played key roles in theories of prejudice. For example, the scapegoat theory of prejudice (Dollar, Doob, Miller, Mowrer, & Sears, 1939; Zawadzki, 1948) postulated that prejudice was the expressed outlet of displaced hostility. In his definitive work, *The Nature of Prejudice,* Allport (1954) discussed the role of projected guilt in exacerbating prejudice.

More recently, researchers have begun to recognize the potential role of positive emotions as well as negative emotions in determining attitudes toward social groups. This is of importance because an individual may experience both negative and positive emotions toward a group, either simultaneously or sequentially (Kaplan, 1972; Katz, 1981). Researchers have also begun to assess specific emotions as they contribute to intergroup attitudes, rather than postulating emotions as intervening variables. For example, Dijker (1987) examined the relation between emotions and attitudes toward two minority groups in the Netherlands: Surinamers and immigrant workers from Turkey and Morocco. Subjects were asked to indicate how often they had felt each of 11 negative and 7 positive emotions in response to members of the two target groups. They were also asked to evaluate the target groups on a thermometer measure. Factor analysis of responses to the emotions measure revealed four emotion categories which were quite similar across target groups: positive emotions (e.g., admiration), irritation (e.g., annoyance), anxiety (e.g., fear), and concern (e.g., worry). Regression analyses revealed that, irrespective of target group, each of the four emotion categories made a significant contribution to attitudes toward the group. In addition, perhaps because Surinamers were evaluated more favorably than were immigrant workers from Turkey and Morocco, the positive emotions category was more predictive of attitudes toward Surinamers, and two of the negative emotion categories, irritation and concern, were more predictive of attitudes toward Turks and Moroccans. Similarly, Stangor, Sullivan, and Ford (1991, Study 1) investigated the relation between positive and negative emotional responses and attitudes toward the majority group and seven minority groups in the United States. They found that both positive and negative emotions predicted attitudes toward the groups.

Based on these two studies, it is apparent that emotions can make a significant contribution to the prediction of intergroup attitudes. Because the focus has shifted from understanding prejudice to understanding group attitudes, whether they are unfavorable or favorable, the role of both negative and positive emotions has emerged as a topic for consideration.[2]

Cognition and Intergroup Attitudes

Stereotypes

Historically, it has been assumed that stereotypes and attitudes toward social groups are highly related, either because stereotypes are used to rationalize unfavorable intergroup attitudes (Zawadzki, 1948), or because stereotypes contribute to overall evaluations of groups (Katz & Stotland, 1959). However, research seeking to support this assumption has met with mixed success.

Perhaps due to the seminal work of Katz and Braly (1933), which looked at the degree of agreement of Princeton students in assigning traits to various racial groups, stereotypes have traditionally been examined at the level of consensual stereotypes—shared beliefs about the characteristics of groups. In assessing the extent to which individuals subscribe to consensual stereotypes, measurement strategies have consistently been based on the use of lists of characteristics or bipolar adjective scales. Variation has occurred in the type or responses that subjects are asked to make on these measures and the technique for transforming responses into numerical values.

Studies that have examined the relation between the tendency for individuals to subscribe to consensual stereotypes of groups and their attitudes toward the groups have obtained seemingly conflicting findings. When one looks further, however, it becomes evident that the level of analysis is crucial. In general, the tendency to endorse the consensual stereotypes for groups has been found to be minimally related to overall evaluations of the groups. That is, merely looking at the degree to which an individual

---

[2]This research on emotion examines the relation between specific emotional reactions to a group and attitudes toward that group. From a rather different perspective, researchers have also investigated the effects of global mood state on the use and expression of intergroup beliefs and attitudes.

expresses stereotypes of groups that are in accord with the stereotypes expressed by others often tells us little about the individual's overall evaluations of the groups. For example, Brigham (1971a, 1972) reports nonsignificant correlations between the tendency to endorse consensual stereotypes of blacks and attitudes toward blacks. Using factor-analytic techniques, Gardner and his colleagues (e.g., Gardner, 1973; Gardner, Lalonde, Nero, & Young 1988; Gardner, Wonnacott & Taylor, 1968) have shown that the tendency to attribute consensual stereotypes to various ethnic groups is largely independent of attitudes toward these groups. In both of these cases, it is likely that, for most subjects, attitudes toward outgroups were being examined. When attitudes toward ingroups and outgroups are specifically differentiated, it is found that endorsement of ingroup stereotypes shows a significant positive relation to attitudes toward ingroups, whereas endorsement of outgroup stereotypes shows little relation to attitudes toward outgroups (Lalonde & Gardner, 1989).

Despite the fact that stereotypes are considered to be part of the cognitive component of intergroup attitudes, they, like most other beliefs, have valences associated with them. That is, stereotypes usually involve an evaluative dimension ranging from negative to positive. The consensual stereotypes of an outgroup may vary in valence, including both positive and negative characteristics. This would explain why a measure that takes into account only the extent to which consensual stereotypes of an outgroup are endorsed, irrespective of the proportion of these that are positive or negative, is a poor predictor of attitudes toward the group. That is, a measure that lumps positive and negative consensual stereotypes together without taking into account their valence is unlikely to predict attitudes toward a group. In contrast, consensual stereotypes of an ingroup may be more homogeneous in valence, predominantly positive, so that the more of these stereotypes that are endorsed, the more positive one's attitude will likely be. This suggestion is supported by research that takes into account the valence of endorsed consensual stereotypes. Several studies have demonstrated that the tendency for an individual to attribute positive consensual stereotypes to an outgroup is related to a more positive attitude toward the group, whereas the tendency to attribute negative consensual stereotypes to an outgroup is related to a more negative attitude toward the group (Brigham, 1971b, 1972; Smith & Clark, 1973).

In comparison to consensual stereotypes, individual stereotypes may be especially useful in predicting an individual's attitude toward a social group because they include beliefs that are not necessarily shared with others about the characteristics of the group. Thus, they go beyond consensual stereotypes in providing information about an individual's view of a group. In seeking an adequate measure of individual stereotypes, we found that the traditional techniques for assessing stereotypes were unsuitable for our purposes. That is, we found that the adjective checklist and bipolar scales that are often used to assess consensual stereotypes were inappropriate for our assessment of individual stereotypes. Not only do these procedures prime particular dimensions rather than eliciting spontaneous attributions, but they are bound to overlook many of the idiosyncratic stereotypes held by individuals. As a result of our inability to discover a satisfactory established measure, we found it necessary to develop our own open-ended procedure to assess individual stereotypes.

We wished to develop a procedure that would not only get at the characteristics that come to mind when an individual thinks about a social group, but that would also take into account the meaning that the individual invests in the characteristics when using them to describe that particular group. We believed this to be important because the same characteristic can differ in valence depending on the individual making the attribution and the target group to which it is directed (see Peabody, 1968, and Saenger & Flowerman, 1954, for similar arguments). For example, the characteristic "rich" can be considered positive, neutral, or negative depending on one's perspective (and perhaps one's own wealth) and the group to which it is being attributed. Thus, if we wish to use individual stereotypes to predict attitudes toward social groups, it would seem advantageous to take into account the connotative aspect of these characteristics. We also wished to take into account the percentage of the group to which the characteristics are attributed. It seems likely that a characteristic that is attributed to many members of a group is more likely to predict one's evaluation of the group than a characteristic that is attributed to fewer members of the group.

We have developed a measure of individual stereotypes based on these considerations (Esses & Zanna, 1989). Subjects are asked to provide descriptions of various groups as follows. First, they are asked to list characteristics, using single adjectives or short phrases, that they would use to describe typical members of each group. They are told to provide as many characteristics as necessary to convey their impression of each group and to describe each group adequately. Then, they are asked to look at the characteristics that they have listed for each group and assign a valence to each characteristic as they have used it to describe members of that particular group (− −, −, 0, +, + +, adapted from Karlins, Coffman & Walters, 1969). Finally, they are asked to once again look at the characteristics that they have provided for each group and indicate the percentage of the group to which each characteristic applies (0% to 100%, adapted from Brigham, 1971b).

What is particularly striking about the outcome of this procedure is the actual characteristics that people are willing to spontaneously attribute to members of social groups at the present time. It is not uncommon to elicit extremely negative characteristics, such as "smelly" and "dirty," that we thought people were no longer willing to express. This stands in contrast to the assumption that social desirability now inhibits the expression of blatantly negative stereotypes (e.g., Crosby, Bromley & Saxe, 1980; McConahay, 1986). In order to transform subjects' responses into numerical values, the valences and percentages they themselves provide are utilized. Valences (V) are transformed into numbers ranging from -2 $(--)$ to $+2(++)$ and percentages (P) are divided by 100 so that they range from 0 to 1. A stereotype score is then computed for each subject for each group as

$$\sum_{i=1}^{n} (P_{ig} \times V_{ig})/n$$

where n equals the number of characteristics attributed to the group.[3]

How well do these individual stereotype scores predict overall evaluations of social groups? We conducted a study at the Ontario Science Centre in Toronto, Canada to examine this issue (Esses & Zanna, 1990). Adult members of the general public were asked to complete an ethnic attitudes poll containing our individual stereotypes measure and evaluation thermometers (ranging from 0 = extremely unfavorable to 100 = extremely favorable) used to assess overall evaluations of groups (adapted from Campbell, 1971). Perceptions of six ethnic groups were examined, with the order of presentation of the individual stereotypes measure and the evaluation thermometer measure balanced across subjects.[4]

Results obtained from 205 subjects (age range: 16 to 73 years) demonstrated that individual stereotypes do indeed predict attitudes toward ethnic groups (see Table I). Irrespective of target ethnic group, the correlation between our two measures is statistically significant. Perhaps not surprisingly, the weakest relation is obtained for most subjects' own ethnic group, English Canadian. It may be that people express favorable evaluations of their own group for motivational reasons (e.g., Tajfel & Turner, 1979, 1985) that have little to do with the specific characteristics they attribute to the group. In addition, when we separate the valence of the characteristics from the percent-

---

[3]It is a bit unclear whether an averaging or additive formula is most appropriate in this context. We use the averaging formula because it seems to correspond best to the conceptual variable of interest, namely, the typical (or average) characteristic used to describe a group. In addition, in a related context, research on information integration in impression formation favors averaging models over additive models (Anderson, 1981). This is a moot point because averaging scores and additive scores (where we do not divide by n) are very highly correlated (> .80 in all studies to date).

It is also the case that subjects occasionally provide descriptions that seem to reflect more on how a group is treated by others than on characteristics of the group (e.g., "mistreated," "given many opportunities"). When these descriptions are excluded, stereotype scores are not appreciably altered.

[4]The group labels were selected on the basis of pretesting, which indicated that our subject population understood these labels, believed these groups to be distinct, and could express attitudes toward these groups.

TABLE I
The Relation between Individual Stereotypes and Attitudes toward Six Ethnic Groups[a]

Target ethnic group	Mean attitude	Stereotype-attitude relation (r)
English Canadian	77.61	.37
Chinese	68.61	.55
Jewish	67.19	.61
Native Indian	66.19	.45
Pakistani	53.62	.45
Arabic	46.34	.50

[a]$N = 205$. All correlations are significant at the $p < .001$ level (two-tailed test). We present results collapsed across order of presentation of measures because our analyses indicate that order of presentation had no significant effects on results obtained.

age of the groups to which they are attributed, we find that the valences play a more potent role in the prediction of attitudes than do the percentages. That is, despite the fact that there is considerable range in the percentages utilized, there is no systematic relation between attitudes and the percentages that subjects assigned to characteristics of different valences.[5]

Eagly and Mladinic (1989) utilized a similar measure of individual stereotypes to examine the relation between gender stereotypes and attitudes toward men and women. They found that individual stereotypes provide weak, though significant, predictions of attitudes toward the sexes. Two other target groups, Democrats and Republicans, were included in their study in order to reduce demand and provide comparison data. Individual stereotypes also significantly predict attitudes toward these groups.

Thus, researchers have begun to utilize individualized measures of stereotypes rather than relying on consensual stereotypes to predict individuals' intergroup attitudes. Although these stereotypes account for a

---

[5]This point is relevant to a recent critique of the use of multiplicative composites in correlational analyses (Evans, 1991). It is suggested that the use of simple correlations to analyze the relation between a multiplicative composite, such as our

$$\sum_{i=1}^{n} (P_{ig} \times V_{ig})/n$$

and a criterion variable can sometimes provide erroneous information about the magnitude of the relation. This does not seem to be a problem in analyzing our data because the magnitude of the correlations shows little change when we replace the composite measure with a simple measure of average valence,

$$\sum_{i=1}^{n} V_{ig}/n$$

$(.00 < $ change in $r < .04)$.

significant proportion of variance in group attitudes, there is substantial variance left to be explained. Besides the potential contribution of emotions, as already discussed, part of this variance may be taken up by cognitions other than those that comprise stereotypes. Symbolic beliefs may play an important role in this regard.

Symbolic Beliefs

Cognitions about social groups are not based solely on stereotypes. Indeed when we think about various groups, many thoughts may come to mind other than those relating to characteristics of members of the groups. One type of thought that may be particularly relevant to our attitudes toward groups may be our perception of how they fit into society and help to make it a better or worse place in which to live. Our beliefs about how society should be organized and operate are rooted in our basic values and norms.

Interest in the role of values in determining intergroup attitudes can be traced back to Rokeach's belief-congruence model of prejudice which suggested that prejudice toward members of other ethnic groups is mediated primarily by perceived dissimilarity of beliefs, rather than by ethnicity per se (Rokeach, 1968; Rokeach & Mezei, 1966; Rokeach, Smith, & Evans, 1960). In testing this model, Rokeach examined the effect of manipulated ethnicity and belief similarity on evaluations of target individuals, often using beliefs that he initially described as important and later labeled values. In support of the belief-congruence model, it has been demonstrated that perceived similarity can be more important than ethnicity in determining interpersonal attraction, at least when social pressures to discriminate are minimal (see Insko, Nacoste, & Moe, 1983, for a review).[6]

Values and norms were assigned a more central role in intergroup attitudes during the 1970s under the rubric of symbolic racism (McConahay & Hough, 1976; Sears & Kinder, 1971), aversive racism (Gaertner, 1976; Kovel, 1970), and racial ambivalence (Katz, 1970; Katz, Glass, & Cohen, 1973). It was observed that despite an apparent decline in the expression of stereotypes of blacks in the United States, beliefs were still a critical element of whites' expressed racial views. These beliefs were often couched in terms of values and norms as they provided justifications for attitudes toward such civil rights issues as quotas and forced integration. The salience of val-

---

[6]Schwartz and Struch (1989) have recently proposed that the perceived belief dissimilarity that is central to intergroup antagonism involves beliefs about groups' value hierarchies, that is, beliefs about groups' basic guiding principles. Schwartz and Struch (1989) also suggest that assumed dissimilarity between own group and other groups' value hierarchies leads to antagonism because of a lack of feeling of shared humanity (i.e., because this dehumanizes the members of the other groups).

ues in public expressions of attitudes toward blacks prompted researchers to more fully incorporate values into their theories of prejudice and discrimination.

Although similar in their emphasis on values, the concepts of symbolic racism, aversive racism, and racial ambivalence diverge in their specification of how values fit into the conglomeration comprising attitudes toward blacks. Symbolic racism is proposed to be a new form of prejudice based on a combination of negative affect and beliefs that blacks violate cherished American values, especially those embodied in the Protestant work ethic.[7] This racism is considered to be symbolic in that it is based on individuals' abstract beliefs and standards of morality, rather than on issues having strong personal relevance (Kinder, 1986; Sears, 1988). In order to assess this new form of prejudice, measurement tools, such as the Modern Racism Scale (McConahay, 1986), have been developed. These measures have typically assessed negative feelings about the current role of blacks in society and have been used for the most part as overall assessments of prejudice.

Aversive racism and racial ambivalence are both predicated on the notion of an intrapsychic conflict. The concept of aversive racism is used to describe the conflict between whites' beliefs in an egalitarian value system and their unacknowledged negative feelings and beliefs about blacks. Aversive racism is not conducive to effective questionnaire measures because aversive racists are considered to be strongly motivated to protect a nonprejudiced self-image (Gaertner & Dovidio, 1986). Racial ambivalence is used to describe the conflict within an individual of two sets of values that are particularly relevant to intergroup relations: humanitarianism-egalitarianism and the individualistic Protestant work ethic. To date, measures of this ambivalence have involved the construction of pro- and anti-black scales which are significantly related to measures of humanitarian-egalitarian and Protestant work ethic value orientations, respectively (Katz & Hass, 1988; Katz, Wackenhut, & Hass, 1986).

In a broader context, it is likely that, to a greater or lesser extent, beliefs incorporating values and norms contribute to attitudes toward many social groups. These beliefs may, at times, be rather idiosyncratic and may concern both the perceived violation and promotion of values and norms. Following the lead of symbolic racism, we use the term symbolic beliefs (Zanna et al., 1990) to refer to all thoughts about the relation between social groups and basic values and norms, whether the relation is negative or positive. In order to more systematically and distinctly assess symbolic beliefs about a variety of social groups, we have developed a measure similar to the one we use to assess individual stereotypes. Research on how these sym-

---

[7]Recently, Sears and Kosterman (1991) have suggested that egalitarian values, in particular, *resistance* to black equality, may be more central to symbolic racism than are Protestant work ethic values.

bolic beliefs relate to overall evaluations of groups will be discussed in the next section on the interplay of affect and cognition.

The Interplay of Affect and Cognition

Emotions, Stereotypes, and Symbolic Beliefs

It is evident from the studies discussed up to this point that emotions and stereotypes contribute significantly to intergroup attitudes. However, because these two components of intergroup attitudes have been examined in separate studies, it is yet to be determined whether one or the other tends to have more predictive power. In addition, it is unclear whether they share their influence on intergroup attitudes, that is, whether, to some extent, intergroup attitudes are explained by common variance of emotions and stereotypes. The role of symbolic beliefs in determining intergroup attitudes may also be of significance. Thus, the first question we will address is: what are the relative roles of affect and cognition in determining intergroup attitudes?

Of course, this question may be overly simplistic in implying that attitudes toward all target groups are based on a similar weighting of affective and cognitive information. It would not be unreasonable to suggest that, in contrast, the structure of intergroup attitudes may vary depending on the target group (see Ehrlich, 1973, for a similar argument). One obvious feature of the target group that may play a role is the general favorability of the attitude toward that group. Thus, depending on the attitude to be predicted, emotions, stereotypes, or symbolic beliefs may predominate. For example, symbolic beliefs may be especially likely to predict unfavorable intergroup attitudes because our values may be most salient, and thus influential, when they seem to be threatened.

In order to examine these issues, we conducted a study at the University of Waterloo in which we measured components of attitudes toward four ethnic groups, English Canadians, French Canadians, Native Indians, and Pakistanis, and one additional social group to which we expected to obtain rather interesting and sometimes extreme responses, homosexuals (Zanna *et al.*, 1990). Seventy-one students (47 females and 24 males) were presented with questionnaires regarding their perceptions of different groups in the community. All subjects completed four measures for each of the target groups. First, all subjects evaluated the target groups on the 0 to 100 thermometer measure in order to determine their attitudes toward these groups. Then, they completed measures of individual stereotypes, symbolic beliefs, and emotions, with the order of presentation of these three measures counterbalanced across subjects.

Our individual stereotypes measure has already been described in considerable detail. The symbolic beliefs and emotions measures were constructed to be consistent with the stereotypes measure. Thus, in order to assess symbolic beliefs, subjects were asked to list values, customs, and traditions that they believed were blocked or facilitated by the group, to indicate the extent to which each was blocked or facilitated (- - to + +, V), and to specify the percentage of the group to which this applied (0 to 100%, P). In order to assess emotions, subjects were asked to list emotions and feelings that they experienced when they saw, met, or thought about members of the group, to indicate the valence of each emotion toward that particular group (- - to + +, V), and to specify the percentage of group members who made them feel this way (0 to 100%, P). As with the stereotypes measure, scores were computed for each subject for each group as

$$\sum_{i=1}^{n} (P_{ig} \times V_{ig})/n$$

where n equalled the number of symbolic beliefs or emotions listed for each group.[8]

Although our individual stereotypes, symbolic beliefs, and emotions measures were separate, this did not guarantee that subjects' responses to these measures would be independent. Fortunately, as indicated in Table II, the measures are not completely redundant. Stereotypes and emotions do seem to be rather highly correlated, although, on average, only 39% of their variance is shared. In addition, symbolic beliefs seem to be largely independent of stereotypes and emotions, with a few exceptions. Thus, although there is some overlap among our measures, they are also eliciting somewhat different pieces of information.[9]

As expected, the target groups varied considerably in overall evaluations (see Table III). Subjects' attitudes were most favorable toward the ethnic group to which most of them belonged, English Canadians, and least favorable toward a typically stigmatized group in society, homosexuals.[10] Are stereotypes, symbolic beliefs, and emotions all useful predictors of these attitudes? To begin to answer this question, we first looked at the

---

[8]Consistent with the stereotypes measure, averaging scores and additive scores are highly correlated for symbolic beliefs (> .76) and emotions (> .82).

[9]There is no indication that subjects are unwilling to express negative information on any of the measures. Rather, subjects provide a wide range of negative and positive responses to each measure. For example, for the target group French Canadians, stereotypes include "self-centered" and "friendly," symbolic beliefs include "disrupt Canadian unity" and "promote personal freedom," and emotions include "disgust" and "pride." It is also clear that the content of responses differs considerably among the measures.

[10]Fifty-three of the 71 subjects identified themselves as English Canadian. Attitudes toward the target groups did not differ significantly as a function of subjects' own ethnic identity.

TABLE II
Intercorrelations among Individual Stereotypes, Symbolic Beliefs, and Emotions
toward Five Social Groups[a]

Target group	St-SB[b]	St-E	SB-E
English Canadian	.11	.55***[b]	.20
French Canadian	.44***	.61***	.40***
Native Indian	.25*	.54***	.25*
Pakistani	.20	.72***	.15
Homosexual	.33**	.69***	.23

[a]$N = 71$. The numbers indicate Pearson product-moment correlation coefficients. We present results collapsed across order of presentation of measures because our analyses indicate that order of presentation had no significant effects on results obtained.
[b]St, stereotypes; SB, symbolic beliefs; E, emotions.
*, $p < .05$; **, $p < .01$; ***, $p < .001$ (two-tailed tests).

simple correlations between our predictor variables and our criterion measure of attitudes. As shown in Table III, emotions seem to be most consistently related to attitudes, although symbolic beliefs and stereotypes also seem to have some predictive power. Examination of the pattern of correlations suggests that emotions are most predictive of attitudes toward English Canadians, French Canadians, and Native Indians. In contrast,

TABLE III
The Relation between Individual Stereotypes, Symbolic Beliefs, Emotions,
and Attitudes toward Five Social Groups[a]

Target group	Mean attitude	St-Att[b]	SB-Att[b]	E-Att[b]
English Canadian	81.42	.11	.09	.25*
French Canadian	69.07	.49***	.49***	.59***
Native Indian	66.20	.24*	.17	.44***
Pakistani	58.88	.30*	.58***	.32**
Homosexual	44.13	.48***	.50***	.43***

[a]$N = 71$. The numbers indicate Pearson product-moment correlation coefficients. We present results collapsed across order of presentation of measures because our analyses indicate that order of presentation had no significant effects on results obtained.
[b]St, stereotypes; SB, symbolic beliefs; E, emotions; Att, attitudes.
*, $p < .05$; **, $p < .01$; ***, $p < .001$ (two-tailed tests).

TABLE IV

Simultaneous Multiple Regressions Using Individual Stereotypes, Symbolic Beliefs,
and Emotions To Predict Attitudes toward Five Social Groups[a]

Target group	Variable	Unstandardized regression coefficient (b)
English Canadian	Stereotypes	−0.97
	Symbolic Beliefs	0.80
	Emotions	5.82
	Multiple $r = .25$, *ns*	
French Canadian	Stereotypes	3.77
	Symbolic Beliefs	6.82*
	Emotions	11.64***
	Multiple $r = .66, p < .001$	
Native Indian	Stereotypes	−0.03
	Symbolic Beliefs	1.54
	Emotions	12.21**
	Multiple $r = .45, p < .01$	
Pakistani	Stereotypes	1.18
	Symbolic Beliefs	17.61***
	Emotions	6.68
	Multiple $r = .63, p < .001$	
Homosexual	Stereotypes	7.58
	Symbolic Beliefs	10.04***
	Emotions	5.62
	Multiple $r = .62, p < .001$	

[a]$N = 71$. We present results collapsed across order of presentation of measures because our analyses indicate that order of presentation had no significant effects on results obtained.
*, $p < .05$; **, $p < .01$; ***, $p < .001$.

symbolic beliefs are most predictive of attitudes toward Pakistanis and homosexuals.[11]

Although the correlations are suggestive, their utility is limited by the fact that there is some intercorrelation among the predictor variables. Therefore, a series of multiple regressions were performed in which the

[11]Once again, the magnitude of the correlations shows little change when we replace the composite measures with measures of average valence,

$$\sum_{i=1}^{n} V_{ig} / n$$

($.00 <$ change in $r < .09$).

three predictors were entered simultaneously in order to determine the unique contribution of each to attitudes toward the groups. As shown in Table IV, emotions provide the greatest unique contribution to the prediction of attitudes toward French Canadians and Native Indians. In contrast, symbolic beliefs are most uniquely predictive of attitudes toward Pakistanis and homosexuals. In this series of simultaneous multiple regressions, stereotypes stand out as having no unique role to play.

It is interesting to note that, in contrast to attitudes toward the four other target groups, attitudes toward the English Canadian target group were minimally predicted by stereotypes, symbolic beliefs, or emotions. This is consistent with our earlier suggestion that evaluations of this group may develop on the basis of motivational forces relevant to one's own membership in the group. Not only did the English Canadian target group receive the highest mean evaluation, but the variance in this evaluation was less than that of any other group. This range restriction alone reduces the magnitude of correlations with predictor variables.

For the four target groups to which subjects did not belong, it is interesting to speculate on the correspondence between mean favorability of attitudes and the component that best predicts these attitudes. On the basis of the correlations and the multiple regressions, it seems that there is a tendency for symbolic beliefs to play the greatest unique role in predicting attitudes toward groups that are perceived in a relatively unfavorable light. In contrast, emotions seem to play the greatest unique role in predicting attitudes toward groups that are regarded more favorably. Our speculations aside, results from this study suggest that, in general, emotions and symbolic beliefs both uniquely contribute to attitudes toward social groups. Depending on the group, emotions or symbolic beliefs may dominate.

Our findings regarding the role of stereotypes in predicting intergroup attitudes are also noteworthy. Our initial study focusing solely on stereotypes (Esses & Zanna, 1990) and this more extensive study examining the role of stereotypes, symbolic beliefs, and emotions (Zanna *et al.*, 1990) both find that stereotypes are significantly correlated with intergroup attitudes. However, in examining the unique contribution of each predictor, there is a marked lack of predictive utility of stereotypes when emotions and symbolic beliefs are taken into account.[12]

This pattern of findings may indicate that stereotypes play a more indirect role in determining intergroup attitudes. More specifically, given that stereotypes and emotions are rather highly correlated and that emotions uniquely predict attitudes, one possibility is that stereotypes in part deter-

---

[12]A somewhat similar result has subsequently been obtained by Stangor *et al.* (1991, Study 2). Using measures of emotions, consensual stereotypes, and our individual stereotypes to predict attitudes toward four social groups, they found that both consensual stereotypes and individual stereotypes had little unique role to play.

mine our emotional reactions to members of other groups which then more directly influence our attitudes toward the groups. That is, the characteristics that we attribute to members of a group may influence how we feel about these people and thus our evaluation of the group. This suggestion receives some support from a study by Dijker and Frijda (1988) which examined reported antecedents or causes of emotional reactions to Surinamers and immigrant workers from Turkey and Morocco in the Netherlands. Many of the reported causes of emotions were related to characteristics of members of the groups (e.g., positive traits, ethnic appearance). In addition, Dijker and Frijda (1988) performed regression analyses in which emotional reactions and their reported antecedents were used to predict attitudes. Results are consistent with the suggestion that characteristics attributed to groups influence attitudes because of their emotional implications. Of course, other causal connections between stereotypes, emotions, and attitudes cannot be ruled out on the basis of any of these findings. Further research involving causal modeling will be required in order to disentangle this issue.

The Role of Individual Differences

The second question that we would like to address is whether the measurement of individual differences can help us in using affect and cognition to predict intergroup attitudes. That is, are there individual differences in the weighting of affective and cognitive information? In order to begin to answer this question, we included three individual difference measures in the Zanna *et al.* (1990) study just discussed. Two of these measures, Need for Cognition (Cacioppo & Petty, 1982) and self-esteem (Rosenberg, 1979), proved to have no predictive utility. However, the third measure, Right-Wing Authoritarianism (Altemeyer, 1982, 1988, 1993), played a significant role in moderating the relation between affect, cognition, and attitudes toward the groups.

The Right-Wing Authoritarianism scale is designed to assess three related components of the original authoritarian construct (Adorno, Frenkel-Brunswik, Levinson, & Sanford, 1950): authoritarian submission (e.g., "Obedience and respect for authority are the most important virtues children should learn"), conventionalism [e.g., "There is nothing wrong with premarital sexual intercourse" (reverse scored)], and authoritarian aggression (e.g., "Once our government leaders and the authorities condemn the dangerous elements in our society, it will be the duty of every patriotic citizen to help stomp out the rot that is poisoning our country from within"). High right-wing authoritarians are described as extremely self-righteous individuals who feel threatened by outgroups (Altemeyer, 1988). Using an abbreviated version of the scale, we divided subjects into high and low right-wing authoritarians on the basis of a median split of our sample. In line with Altemeyer's earlier findings, high and low authoritarians' attitudes

TABLE V

The Relation between Individual Stereotypes, Symbolic Beliefs, Emotions,
and Attitudes toward Five Social Groups for Low and High Right-Wing Authoritarians[a]

Target group[a]	Mean attitude	St-Att[b]	SB-Att[b]	E-Att[b]
Low RWA				
English Canadian	81.35	−.14	.16	.14
French Canadian	71.19	.65***	.51**	.71***
Native Indian	68.11	.25	.13	.54***
Pakistani	63.16	.60***	.51**	.47**
Homosexual	51.35	.65***	.44**	.66***
High RWA				
English Canadian	81.50	.29	.04	.35*
French Canadian	66.76	.36*	.50**	.47**
Native Indian	64.12	.30	.23	.40*
Pakistani	54.12	.08	.63***	.23
Homosexual	36.26	.27	.46**	.20

[a]Low RWA, N = 37; High RWA, N = 34. The numbers indicate Pearson product-
moment correlation coefficients.
[b]St, stereotypes; SB, symbolic beliefs; E, emotions; Att, attitudes.
*, $p < .05$; **, $p < .01$; ***, $p < .001$ (two-tailed tests).

toward their own group (English Canadians) did not differ, but their attitudes toward the four other groups showed a consistent pattern of differences (see Table V). For all four groups, high authoritarians demonstrated
more negative attitudes than did low authoritarians.[13] These differences
were especially evident for the two groups that generally received the least
favorable evaluations (Pakistanis and homosexuals).

These differences in attitudes correspond to differences in the predictive
power of emotions, symbolic beliefs, and stereotypes. Examination of the
simple correlations shown in Table V suggests that emotions and stereotypes are most highly related to the attitudes toward other groups held by
low authoritarians. In contrast, symbolic beliefs stand out as being most
highly related to the attitudes toward other groups held by high authoritarians. Once again, simultaneous multiple regressions were performed in
order to determine the unique contribution of each of the three predictors.
As shown in Table VI, for low authoritarians, emotions provide the greatest
unique contribution to attitudes toward other groups, with stereotypes also
contributing uniquely to attitudes toward homosexuals. In contrast, as
shown in Table VII, symbolic beliefs are most uniquely predictive of the attitudes toward other groups held by high authoritarians.

[13]The correlation between scores on the Right-Wing Authoritarianism scale and
attitudes toward the four groups is highly significant, $r(69) = -.33$, $p < .01$.

TABLE VI
Simultaneous Multiple Regressions for Low Right-Wing Authoritarians
Using Individual Stereotypes, Symbolic Beliefs, and Emotions
To Predict Attitudes toward Five Social Groups

Target group[a]	Variable	Unstandardized regression coefficient (b)
English Canadian	Stereotypes	−9.44
	Symbolic Beliefs	4.81
	Emotions	6.22
	Multiple $r = .36$, *ns*	
French Canadian	Stereotypes	3.27
	Symbolic Beliefs	7.21
	Emotions	14.86**
	Multiple $r = .76$, $p < .001$	
Native Indian	Stereotypes	3.38
	Symbolic Beliefs	3.46
	Emotions	18.22**
	Multiple $r = .57$, $p < .01$	
Pakistani	Stereotypes	12.11
	Symbolic Beliefs	8.32
	Emotions	6.93
	Multiple $r = .64$, $p < .001$	
Homosexual	Stereotypes	11.68*
	Symbolic Beliefs	2.84
	Emotions	11.83*
	Multiple $r = .73$, $p < .001$	

[a]$N = 37$.
*, $p < .05$; **, $p < .01$.

We would like to return briefly to our speculation about the role of symbolic beliefs and emotions in predicting relatively unfavorable and favorable attitudes toward other groups. It is worth noting that symbolic beliefs were generally the best unique predictors of the relatively unfavorable attitudes toward other groups expressed by high authoritarians. In contrast, emotions were generally most uniquely predictive of the more favorable attitudes toward other groups expressed by low authoritarians. In a relative sense, this is consistent with our earlier observation that symbolic beliefs seem to play a greater role in predicting attitudes toward groups that are perceived in a negative light, and that emotions seem to play a greater role in predicting attitudes toward all other groups. In addition, for both high and low authoritarians, attitudes toward English Canadians were minimally predicted by any of our component measures.

TABLE VII
Simultaneous Multiple Regressions for High Right-Wing Authoritarians
Using Individual Stereotypes, Symbolic Beliefs, and Emotions
To Predict Attitudes toward Five Social Groups

Target group[a]	Variable	Unstandardized regression coefficient (b)
English Canadian	Stereotypes	3.32
	Symbolic Beliefs	0.40
	Emotions	6.49
	Multiple r = .38, ns	
French Canadian	Stereotypes	4.28
	Symbolic Beliefs	8.02*
	Emotions	6.88
	Multiple r = .58, p < .01	
Native Indian	Stereotypes	0.25
	Symbolic Beliefs	1.13
	Emotions	8.77
	Multiple r = .40, ns	
Pakistani	Stereotypes	−2.66
	Symbolic Beliefs	18.39***
	Emotions	7.66
	Multiple r = .66, p < .001	
Homosexual	Stereotypes	0.64
	Symbolic Beliefs	12.12**
	Emotions	6.11
	Multiple r = .51, p < .05	

[a]N = 34.
*, p < .05; **, p < .01; ***, p < .001.

The Role of Situational Factors

The third and final question that we would like to address in this section is whether salient incidents can alter the weighting of affective and cognitive information in determining intergroup attitudes. Although attitudes, once formed, are generally considered to be rather stable over time (Ajzen, 1984; Ostrom, 1984), significant events may occur that lead people to reassess their attitudes, or, at least, that may influence the components on which their attitudes are based. One such situation arose for many Canadians at a time in which our examination of the role of cognitions and affect in determining intergroup attitudes was in progress. The Zanna *et al.* (1990) study that we have been discussing was conducted in the winter of 1989–1990. Data from an additional 65 students at the University of Waterloo were collected during the summer of 1990 (Haddock, Zanna, & Esses, 1991). The situation that became newsworthy at the time of collection of our second set of data was a crisis at Oka, Canada involving Native Indian people.

In the spring of 1990, members of the paramilitary Mohawk Warrior Society had erected a barrier in Oka, Quebec (30 km northwest of Montreal) in response to the town's planned extension of a local golf course. The land in question had been a source of dispute for a long period of time because both local Native Canadians and the municipality claimed its ownership ("Chronology," 1990). The barrier was generally ignored by the national media until a Quebec Superior Court injunction to tear down the barrier was disregarded. At that point, the Quebec Provincial Police attacked the barrier, leading to the death of a police officer and a bitter standoff that lasted two months. During that time, Canadians were bombarded with media images of the Warriors, who were typically clad in army fatigues and armed with weapons, often shown standing defiantly while surrounded by members of the Quebec Provincial Police and, eventually, the Canadian Armed Forces. The Warriors were labeled "criminals" and "terrorists" by Canada's political leaders (e.g., Canadian Prime Minister Brian Mulroney and Quebec Premier Robert Bourassa) and front page headlines and stories describing the blockade became the norm (Picard & Platiel, 1990). The events in Oka also touched off a series of additional Native barricades, the most notable being a barrier that shut down the Mercier bridge, a major artery into Montreal. Following considerable negotiation, the barricades were finally removed five months after the initial crisis in Oka began.

How did this series of events influence the perceptions of Native Indians expressed by our subjects at the University of Waterloo? Most students at the University of Waterloo were certainly not personally involved in the crisis, but the situation did result in Native affairs, most notably the issues of land claims and Native self-government, temporarily entering the media spotlight.

As indicated in Table VIII, during the winter study (Zanna et al., 1990) Native Indians received a moderately favorable mean overall evaluation and examination of the correlation coefficients and the unstandardized regression coefficients suggests that, at this time, emotions were most predictive of subjects attitudes, with symbolic beliefs not playing a significant predictive role. Although subjects' mean overall evaluation of Native Indians did not change significantly during the summer when the crisis at Oka was occurring, the pattern of prediction of these attitudes shifted (see Table VIII; Haddock et al., 1991). Symbolic beliefs now proved to be most predictive of subjects' attitudes, with emotions showing reduced predictive power. The fact that symbolic beliefs did not show similar changes in their ability to predict attitudes toward the four other target groups suggests that the effect obtained for Native Indians did not generalize.[14]

This finding is reminiscent of evidence of symbolic racism toward blacks in the United States following their demands for social change. It seems that

[14]In fact, aside from the change in the pattern of prediction of attitudes toward Native Indians, the summer study yields results that replicate those of the winter study.

TABLE VIII
Change in Prediction of Attitudes toward Native Indian People in
Response to the Oka Uprising[a]

	Mean attitude	St-Att[b]	SB-Att[b]	E-Att[b]
Before Oka uprising	66.20	.24*[b]	.17	.44***
During Oka uprising	62.35	.22	.33**	.29*

	Variable	Unstandardized regression coefficient (b)
Before Oka uprising	Stereotypes	−0.03
	Symbolic Beliefs	1.54
	Emotions	12.21**
	Multiple $r = .45$, $p < .01$	
During Oka uprising	Stereotypes	2.08
	Symbolic Beliefs	7.74*
	Emotions	6.18
	Multiple $r = .39$, $p < .05$	

[a]Before Oka uprising, $N = 71$; during Oka uprising, $N = 65$.
[b]St, stereotypes; SB, symbolic beliefs; E, emotions; Att, attitudes.
*, $p < .05$; **, $p < .01$; ***, $p < .001$ (two-tailed tests).

making salient Native Indians' demands for social change in Canada likewise led to symbolic beliefs dominating our subjects' attitudes toward the group. We should note that this effect seems to be an exception to our hypothesis that symbolic beliefs may best predict attitudes toward groups that are perceived in a relatively unfavorable light. Even though subjects' attitudes did not generally become less favorable toward Native Indians during the Oka crisis, media presentations seem to have primed symbolic beliefs so that they were given additional weight in determining these attitudes.

Summary

The findings obtained to date suggest that the prediction of attitudes toward social groups benefits from the assessment of both affect and cognition. In particular, emotions and symbolic beliefs both uniquely contribute to attitudes toward other groups, with stereotypes seeming to play more of an indirect role.[15] The evidence is clear, then, that there is more to prejudice

[15]It is not our intent to minimize the role of stereotypes in intergroup relations. It has been amply documented elsewhere that stereotypes have numerous consequences for our perceptions of groups and the individual members of the groups (e.g., Hamilton, 1979, 1981).

than merely the attribution of stereotypes to groups. Overall, for attitudes toward target groups to which subjects did not belong, the additional variance explained by taking emotions and symbolic beliefs into account ranges from 15 to 31%.

In focusing on the relative roles of affect and cognition in predicting attitudes toward social groups, our research suggests that broad generalizations would be misguided. Rather, their relative contributions depend variously on the target group in question, the type of individual whose attitude we are trying to predict, and salient situational forces. Based on our limited range of target groups, we have some preliminary evidence to suggest that, overall, symbolic beliefs may play a greater unique role in predicting attitudes toward groups that are perceived in an unfavorable light and that emotions may play a greater unique role in predicting attitudes toward various other groups. We also have determined that the relatively negative attitudes toward other groups held by individuals who are high in right-wing authoritarianism seem to be most uniquely predicted by symbolic beliefs. In contrast, the more positive attitudes toward other groups held by individuals who are low in right-wing authoritarianism seem to be most uniquely predicted by emotions.

These findings suggest that symbolic beliefs may play their greatest role in intergroup attitudes when they refer to the *blocking* of our cherished values. It may be that when our values seem to be threatened, they are especially likely to become salient and to influence our attitudes toward other groups. High right-wing authoritarians are especially sensitive to this type of threat because they have a strong commitment to traditional social norms coupled with low tolerance for deviance (Altemeyer, 1982). In the absence of a perceived threat to our values, emotions (which may partially stem from the characteristics we initially attribute to groups) dominate in determining attitudes toward other groups. In addition to the above processes, situational forces may, at times, override our usual proclivities by priming specific components of our attitudes.

Our findings also demonstrate that our initial decision to divide cognitions into characteristics attributed to a group and symbolic beliefs about the group was justified. Adopting the most broad definition of a stereotype available, that it is "a cognitive structure containing the perceiver's knowledge, beliefs, and expectancies about a social group" (Hamilton & Trolier, 1986, p. 142), would have led us to lump characteristics and symbolic beliefs together. However, we have found that not only are they often uncorrelated, but of perhaps greater importance, they are differentially predictive of intergroup attitudes. Thus, empirically as well as operationally, symbolic beliefs are relatively independent of characteristics attributed to a group. This suggests that symbolic beliefs and attributed characteristics may play very different roles in the development of intergroup attitudes. Keeping them separate may thus help us to further understand the nature of prejudice. For our purposes, then, it is worth-

while to distinguish between symbolic beliefs and characteristics attributed
to a group, just as our subjects seem to do.

Future Research Directions

A number of future research directions are implicated. First, it would be
interesting to determine whether different findings are systematically obtained for different types of social groups. For example, attitudes toward
groups that are publicly advocating social change may be especially likely to
be based on symbolic beliefs (especially for high right-wing authoritarians)
because these groups are likely to be perceived as threatening our values. In
contrast, attitudes toward various disabled groups may be especially likely
to be based on emotions (Esses, Beaufoy, & Philipp 1992) because of our
apparent "gut reaction" to disabilities and the individuals who possess
them. It would also be of interest to examine additional individual difference variables that may moderate our findings. For example, we are currently developing a Feeling–Belief Measure to assess the extent to which
individuals believe that they generally base their attitudes and behavior on
cognitive or affective information (Haddock & Zanna, 1992a). Results obtained using a preliminary version of the scale (which includes items such as
"Making a proper decision requires a long period of thought" and "My
emotions often dictate my behavior") suggest that individual differences on
this measure moderate the primary predictors of intergroup attitudes.

It is also obvious that there is still considerable variance in intergroup
attitudes left to be explained. One refinement that may be required is improved measurement techniques. Although we have attempted to develop
assessment devices that are tailored to the individual, there may still be a
considerable gap between the conceptual variables of interest and our measurement tools. For example, at the level of our criterion variable, attitudes,
the one-item evaluation thermometer might benefit from being expanded
into several related dimensions (e.g., bad–good).

Of course, what we have been attempting to measure may not be sufficient. As mentioned early on, there is a third component to attitudes in addition to affect and cognitions, namely, information concerning past
behavior. As suggested by Bem (1972), our attitudes may be partially in-
ferred from our past behaviors and the conditions under which these behaviors occurred. In the context of intergroup attitudes, this component
may be conceptualized as how we have behaved toward, or, at least, believe
that we have behaved toward members of a social group in the past. Thus,
our interpretations of how we have behaved toward group members in the
past may contribute to our current intergroup attitudes. We are presently
developing a measure of perceived past behaviors in order to determine
whether it holds significant predictive power. We suspect that it will play its

greatest role in contributing to the prediction of attitudes toward groups with which we frequently interact. Not only may our behavior patterns become rather automatic, but they may dominate our attitudes.

In a related vein, we have recently developed a measure of past experiences with target groups that is similar to our other open-ended measures. That is, subjects are asked to list their recent experiences with members of a group, to rate the valence of each experience, and to indicate the percentage of the group to which each experience applies. In a preliminary study (Haddock & Zanna, 1992b), experiences as measured using this procedure contributed significantly to attitudes toward feminists. In addition, when subjects were divided on the basis of an independent contact scale into those who had experienced frequent and infrequent contact with feminists, the type of experiences elicited in the open-ended measure contributed significantly only to attitudes held by subjects who had experienced frequent contact.

Although we have occasionally used the terms determinants or bases in referring to the components of intergroup attitudes, we must emphasize that our findings, to date, are strictly correlational in nature. That is, our research has not examined the causal connections between intergroup attitudes and their affective, cognitive, and behavioral components. In order to begin to examine the relative contribution of each component to the formation of intergroup attitudes, we are currently conducting a study in which we are manipulating the valence of different types of information provided about fictitious immigrant groups in order to examine the effects on attitudes that are subsequently formed (Maio, Esses, & Bell, 1992). The main shortcoming of such a procedure is that it cannot take into account the interdependence or reciprocal relations between components of intergroup attitudes that probably occur in the real world (as suggested by the correlations we obtain between stereotypes and emotions). In order to more fully examine causal pathways, a longitudinal approach examining the formation of new attitudes may be called for. In addition to the more traditional approach of examining in children the development of attitudes toward established groups, it may be possible to examine in adults the formation of attitudes toward new groups, such as recently arrived immigrant groups in a community.

The multicomponent view of intergroup attitudes also has important implications that may provide direction for future research. First, this view suggests another way of thinking about ambivalence in the intergroup context, namely, in terms of inconsistency between the components of an attitude. This inconsistency may involve positive feelings and negative symbolic beliefs, positive past behaviors and negative feelings, or various other combinations of positive and negative components. As suggested by Katz and his colleagues (Hass, Katz, Rizzo, Bailey, & Eisenstadt, 1991; Katz *et al.*, 1986), ambivalence may, at times, lead to response amplification.

Situational forces or experiences that reinforce or support one component may not only lead to the salience of that component, but may also discredit the inconsistent component. As a result, the inconsistency may become salient, thus initiating efforts to eliminate it. One way of eliminating the observed inconsistency may be to deny the influence of the discredited component on one's attitude toward the group. In order to do so, one may give the supported component unusual weight in determining one's attitude and overcompensate by polarizing one's attitude in the direction of the supported component. For example, if one initially holds a moderate attitude toward a group based on positive feelings and negative symbolic beliefs, support for the negative symbolic beliefs may lead to a denial of the positive feelings through additional weighting of the negative symbolic beliefs and the expression of an extreme negative attitude. Thus, intergroup attitudes that are based on inconsistent sources of information may be especially unstable and may also lead to highly variable outcomes.

Second, the component on which an intergroup attitude is most heavily based may determine the behavioral consequences of the attitude. That is, the same attitude may have different behavioral consequences depending on its primary source. For example, negative intergroup attitudes that are primarily based on symbolic beliefs may be especially likely to lead to aggression (Struch & Schwartz, 1989) and to influence voting on public policy issues (Sears, 1988).

Finally, knowledge of the crucial components of intergroup attitudes may contribute to efforts to change these attitudes. We may find that attempts to modify intergroup attitudes may usefully be targeted at the critical components of these attitudes. We may also discover that certain components of intergroup attitudes are easier to change than others. For example, overall, cognitions may be more susceptible to influence than are feelings or perceived past behaviors. This would suggest that in attempting to modify intergroup attitudes, the most susceptible and relevant components should be targeted first. In addition, as suggested by Zanna and Rempel (1988), different strategies may prove most fruitful in changing attitudes based on different components.

Conclusions

In this chapter, we have attempted to provide a framework for conceptualizing attitudes toward social groups. We believe that this framework not only helps to organize previous findings in the area, but also suggests a means of unifying current research efforts. We have also presented a new, individualized approach to the measurement of intergroup stereotypes, feelings, and symbolic beliefs. We believe that this approach is an improvement over previous measures in that it more realistically captures individuals' spontaneous reactions and can be applied to attitudes toward any social group. Our initial research findings demonstrate that our framework and methodology are fruitful in providing new insight into prejudice, and suggest numerous directions for future research. We hope that this will have convinced the reader that, despite its long history, there are many interesting and important issues still to be addressed in the area of intergroup attitudes.

Acknowledgments

Preparation of this chapter was facilitated by a Canada Research Fellowship from the Social Sciences and Humanities Research Council of Canada to V. M. Esses. The research on which this chapter is based was supported, in part, by a research grant from the Social Sciences and Humanities Research Council of Canada to V. M. Esses and M. P. Zanna.

We thank Diane Mackie, David Hamilton, and Robert Gardner for their helpful comments on an earlier draft of this chapter.

References

Adorno, T. W., Frenkel-Brunswik, E., Levinson, D. J., & Sanford, R. N. (1950). *The authoritarian personality*. New York: Harper.

Ajzen, I. (1984). Attitudes. In R. J. Corsini (Ed.), *Wiley encyclopedia of psychology* (Vol. 1, pp. 100–102). New York: Wiley.

Allport, G. W. (1954). *The nature of prejudice*. Reading, MA: Addison-Wesley.

Altemeyer, B. (1982). *Right-wing authoritarianism*. Winnipeg, Canada: University of Manitoba Press.

Altemeyer, B. (1988). *Enemies of freedom: Understanding right-wing authoritarianism*. San Francisco: Jossey-Bass.

Altemeyer, B. (1993). Reducing prejudice in right-wing authoritarians. In M. P. Zanna & J. M. Olson (Eds.), *The psychology of prejudice: The Ontario symposium* (Vol. 7). Hillsdale, NJ: Erlbaum.

Anderson, N. H. (1981). *Foundations of information integration theory*. New York: Academic Press.

Bem, D. J. (1972). Self-perception theory. In L. Berkowitz (Ed.), *Advances in experimental social psychology* (Vol. 6, pp. 1–62). New York: Academic Press.

Brigham, J. C. (1971a). Ethnic stereotypes. *Psychological Bulletin, 76*, 15–38.

Brigham, J. C. (1971b). Racial stereotypes, attitudes, and evaluations of and behavioral intentions toward Negroes and Whites. *Sociometry, 34*, 360–380.

Brigham, J. C. (1972). Racial stereotypes: Measurement variables and the stereotype-attitude relationship. *Journal of Applied Social Psychology, 2*, 63–76.

Cacioppo, J. T., & Petty, R. E. (1982). The need for cognition. *Journal of Personality and Social Psychology, 42*, 116–131.

Campbell, A. (1971). *White attitudes toward Black people*. Ann Arbor, MI: Institute for Social Research.

"Chronology of main events in Oka dispute." (1990, September 3). *The Globe and Mail*, p. A3.

Crosby, F., Bromley, S., & Saxe, L. (1980). Recent unobtrusive studies of Black and White discrimination and prejudice: A literature review. *Psychological Bulletin,* **87,** 546–563.

Dijker, A. J. M. (1987). Emotional reactions to ethnic minorities. *European Journal of Social Psychology,* **17,** 305–325.

Dijker, A. J., & Frijda, N. H. (1988). *Towards a model of stereotype-based emotions.* Paper presented at the annual meeting of the American Psychological Association, Atlanta, GA.

Dollard, J., Doob, L., Miller, N., Mowrer, O., & Sears, R. (1939). *Frustration and aggression.* New Haven, CT: Yale University Press.

Eagly, A. H., & Mladinic, A. (1989). Gender stereotypes and attitudes toward women and men. *Personality and Social Psychology Bulletin,* **15,** 543–558.

Ehrlich, H. J. (1973). *The social psychology of prejudice.* New York: Wiley.

Esses, V. M., Haddock, G., & Zanna, M. P. (1993). The role of mood in the expression of intergroup stereotypes. In M. P. Zanna & J. M. Olson (Eds.), *The psychology of prejudice: The Ontario symposium* (Vol. 7). Hillsdale, NJ: Erlbaum.

Esses, V. M., Beaufoy, S. L., & Philipp, F. H. (1992). *Determinants of attitudes toward stigmatized groups.* Paper presented at the annual meeting of the Society for Experimental Social Psychology, San Antonio, TX.

Esses, V. M., & Zanna, M. P. (1989). *Mood and the expression of ethnic stereotypes.* Paper presented at the annual meeting of the American Psychological Association, New Orleans, LA.

Esses, V. M., & Zanna, M. P. (1990). *The relation between stereotypes and prejudice.* Unpublished manuscript, University of Toronto.

Evans, M. G. (1991). The problem of analyzing multiplicative composites. *American Psychologist,* **46,** 6–15.

Gaertner, S. L. (1976). Nonreactive measures in racial attitude research: A focus on "Liberals." In P. A. Katz (Ed.), *Toward the elimination of racism* (pp. 183–211). New York: Pergamon.

Gaertner, S. L., & Dovidio, J. F. (1986). The aversive form of racism. In J. F. Dovidio & S. L. Gaertner (Eds.), *Prejudice, discrimination, and racism* (pp. 61–89). Orlando, FL: Academic Press.

Gardner, R. C. (1993). Stereotypes as consensual beliefs. In M. P. Zanna & J. M. Olson (Eds.), *The psychology of prejudice: The Ontario symposium* (Vol. 7). Hillsdale, NJ: Erlbaum.

Gardner, R. C. (1973). Ethnic stereotypes: The traditional approach, a new look. *Canadian Psychologist,* **14**(2), 133–148.

Gardner, R. C., Wonnacott, E. J., & Taylor, D. M. (1968). Ethnic stereotypes: A factor analytic investigation. *Canadian Journal of Psychology,* **22,** 35–44.

Gardner, R. C., Lalonde, R. N., Nero, A. M., & Young, M. Y. (1988). Ethnic stereotypes: Implications of measurement strategy. *Social Cognition,* **6,** 40–60.

Haddock, G., & Zanna, M. P. (1992a). An individual difference approach to the relative impact of affect and cognition on attitudes. Unpublished raw data.

Haddock, G., & Zanna, M. P. (1992b). Perceptions of the advocation of social change and determinants of intergroup attitudes. Unpublished raw data.

Haddock, G., Zanna, M. P., & Esses, V. M. (1991). *The influence of Oka on the determinants of prejudice toward Native Indians.* Paper presented at the annual meeting of the Canadian Psychological Association, Calgary, Canada.

Hamilton, D. L. (1979). A cognitive-attributional analysis of stereotyping. In L. Berkowitz (Ed.), *Advances in experimental social psychology* (Vol. 12, pp. 53–84). New York: Academic Press.

Hamilton, D. L. (Ed.). (1981). *Cognitive processes in stereotyping and intergroup behavior.* Hillsdale, NJ: Erlbaum.

Hamilton, D. L., & Trolier, T. K. (1986). Stereotypes and stereotyping: An overview of the cognitive approach. In J. F. Dovidio & S. L. Gaertner (Eds.), *Prejudice, discrimination, and racism* (pp. 127–163). Orlando, FL: Academic Press.

Hass, R. G., Katz, I., Rizzo, N., Bailey, J., & Eisenstadt, D. (1991). Cross-racial appraisal as related to attitude ambivalence and cognitive complexity. *Personality and Social Psychology Bulletin,* **17,** 83–92.

Insko, C. A., Nacoste, R. W., & Moe, J. L. (1983). Belief congruence and racial discrimination: review of the evidence and critical evaluation. *European Journal of Social Psychology,* **13,** 153–174.

Kaplan, K. J. (1972). On the ambivalence-indifference problem in attitude theory and measurement: A suggested modification of the semantic differential technique. *Psychological Bulletin,* **77,** 361–372.

Karlins, M., Coffman, T. L., & Walters, G. (1969). On the fading of social stereotypes: Studies in three generations of college students. *Journal of Personality and Social Psychology,* **13,** 1–16.

Katz, D., & Braly, K. (1933). Racial stereotypes of one hundred college students. *Journal of Abnormal and Social Psychology,* **28,** 280–290.

Katz, D., & Stotland, E. (1959). A preliminary statement of a theory of attitude structure and change. In S. Koch (Ed.), *Psychology: A study of a science* (Vol. 3, pp. 423–475). New York: McGraw-Hill.

Katz, I. (1970). Experimental studies of Negro-white relationships. In L. Berkowitz (Ed.), *Advances in Experimental Social Psychology* (Vol. 5, pp. 71–117). New York: Academic Press.

Katz, I. (1981). *Stigma: A social psychological analysis.* Hillsdale, NJ: Erlbaum.

Katz, I., & Hass, R. G. (1988). Racial ambivalence and American value conflict: Correlational and priming studies of dual cognitive structures. *Journal of Personality and Social Psychology,* **55,** 893–905.

Katz, I., Glass, D. C., & Cohen, S. (1973). Ambivalence, guilt, and the scapegoating of minority group victims. *Journal of Experimental Social Psychology,* **9,** 423–436.

Katz, I., Wackenhut, J., & Hass, R. G. (1986). Racial ambivalence, value duality, and behavior. In J. F. Dovidio & S. L. Gaertner (Eds.), *Prejudice, discrimination, and racism* (pp. 35–59). Orlando, FL: Academic Press.

Kinder, D. R. (1986). The continuing American dilemma: White resistance to racial change 40 years after Myrdal. *Journal of Social Issues,* **42,** 151–171.

Kovel, J. (1970). *White racism: A psychohistory.* New York: Pantheon.

Lalonde, R. N., & Gardner, R. C. (1989). An intergroup perspective on stereotype organization and processing. *British Journal of Social Psychology,* **28,** 289–303.

Maio, G. R. , Esses, V. M. & Bell, D. W. (1992). The role of emotions, characteristics, and values in the formation of intergroup attitudes. Manuscript submitted for publication.

McConahay, J. B. (1986). Modern racism, ambivalence, and the modern racism scale. In J. F. Dovidio & S. L. Gaertner (Eds.), *Prejudice, discrimination, and racism* (pp. 91–125). Orlando, FL: Academic Press.

McConahay, J. B., & Hough, J. C., Jr. (1976). Symbolic racism. *Journal of Social Issues,* **32,** 23–45.

Ostrom, T. M. (1984). Attitude theory. In R. J. Corsini (Ed.), *Wiley encyclopedia of psychology* (Vol. 1, pp. 102–103). New York: Wiley.

Peabody, D. (1968). Group judgments in the Philippines: Evaluative and descriptive aspects. *Journal of Personality and Social Psychology,* **10,** 290–300.

Picard, A., & Platiel, R. (1990, September 1). "Factions fuel confusion." *The Globe and Mail,* pp. A1, A3.

Rokeach, M. (1968). *Beliefs, attitudes, and values: A theory of organization and change.* San Francisco: Jossey-Bass.

Rokeach, M., & Mezei, L. (1966). Race and shared belief as factors in social choice. *Science,* **151,** 167–172.

Rokeach, M., Smith, P. W., & Evans, R. I. (1960). Two kinds of prejudice or one? In M. Rokeach (Ed.), *The open and closed mind* (pp. 132–168). New York: Basic Books.

Rosenberg, M. (1979). *Conceiving the self.* New York: Basic Books.

Saenger, G., & Flowerman, S. (1954). Stereotypes and prejudicial attitudes. *Human Relations,* 7, 217–238.

Schwartz, S. H., & Struch, N. (1989). Values, stereotypes, and intergroup antagonism. In D. Bar-Tal, C. F. Graumann, A. W. Kruglanski, & W. Stroebe (Eds.), *Stereotyping and prejudice: Changing conceptions* (pp. 151–167). New York: Springer-Verlag.

Schwarz, N., & Clore, G. L. (1988). How do I feel about it? The informative function of affective states. In K. Fiedler & J. Forgas (Eds.), *Affect, cognition and social behavior* (pp. 44–62). Toronto, Canada: Hogrefe.

Sears, D. O. (1988). Symbolic racism. In P. A. Katz & D. A. Taylor (Eds.), *Eliminating racism* (pp. 53–84). New York: Plenum.

Sears, D. O., & Kinder, D. R. (1971). Racial tensions and voting in Los Angeles. In W. Z. Hirsch (Ed.), *Los Angeles: Viability and prospects for metropolitan leadership* (pp. 51–88). New York: Praeger.

Sears, D. O., & Kosterman, R. (1991). Is it really racism? The origins and dynamics of symbolic racism. In C. Judd (Chair), *Political psychology.* Symposium conducted at the annual meeting of the Society for Experimental Social Psychology, Columbus, OH.

Smith, A. J., & Clark, R. D. (1973). The relationship between attitudes and beliefs. *Journal of Personality and Social Psychology,* 26, 321–326.

Stangor, C., Sullivan, L. A., & Ford, T. E. (1991). Affective and cognitive determinants of prejudice. *Social Cognition,* 9, 359–380.

Stephan, W. G. (1985). Intergroup relations. In G. Lindzey & E. Aronson (Eds.), *The handbook of social psychology* (Vol. 2, pp. 599–658). Hillsdale, NJ: Erlbaum.

Struch, N., & Schwartz, S. H. (1989). Intergroup aggression: Its predictors and distinctness from in-group bias. *Journal of Personality and Social Psychology,* 56, 364–373.

Tajfel, H., & Turner, J. (1979). An integrative theory of intergroup conflict. In W. G. Austin & S. Worchel (Eds.), *The social psychology of intergroup relations* (pp. 33–47). Monterey, CA: Brooks/Cole.

Tajfel, H., & Turner, J. (1985). The social identity theory of intergroup behavior. In S. Worchel & W. G. Austin (Eds.), *Psychology of intergroup relations* (pp. 7–24). Chicago, IL: Nelson-Hall.

Zanna, M. P., Haddock, G., & Esses, V. M. (1990). *On the nature of prejudice.* Paper presented at the Nags Head Conference on Stereotypes and Intergroup Relations, Nags Head Conference Center, Kill Devil Hills, NC.

Zanna, M. P., & Rempel, J. K. (1988). Attitudes: A new look at an old concept. In D. Bar-Tal & A. Kruglanski (Eds.), *The social psychology of knowledge* (pp. 315–334). New York: Cambridge University Press.

Zawadzki, B. (1948). Limitations on the scapegoat theory of prejudice. *Journal of Abnormal and Social Psychology,* 43, 127–141.

Chapter 8

Stereotypes and Evaluative
Intergroup Bias

JOHN F. DOVIDIO
Department of Psychology
Colgate University
Hamilton, New York

SAMUEL L. GAERTNER
Department of Psychology
University of Delaware
Newark, Delaware

Introduction

Research on impression formation has historically followed two seem-ingly separate tracks (Hamilton, 1991). There has been a long tradition of research on how people form impressions of individuals (e.g., Anderson, 1981; Asch, 1946). Studies and theories in this area have generally focused on how information is integrated and weighted to form a unified, coherent representation of the individual. There is also deep social psychological tra-dition in the conceptions of social groups and on how group membership influences impressions formed of individual members (e.g., Allport, 1954; Katz & Braly, 1933; Tajfel, 1970). This work has mainly considered how social groups are perceived and evaluated. Although some theorists have fo-cused on the similarities in the processes that govern these phenomena (see Hamilton, 1991), others have emphasized that different modes of process-ing are involved. These different modes critically influence cognitive repre-sentations and affective, or evaluative, responses.

Brewer (1988), for example, has proposed "a dual process model of impression formation." The primary distinction in this model is between two types of processing: person based and category based. Following the traditional theories of forming impressions of individuals, processing that is person based is bottom up. This process is data driven, involving the piecemeal acquisition and integration of information that begins "at the most concrete level and stops at the lowest level of abstraction required by the prevailing processing objectives" (Brewer, 1988, p. 6). Category-based processing, in contrast, proceeds from global to specific; it is top down. In top-down processing, how the external reality is perceived and experienced is influenced by category-based, subjective expectations. According to Brewer, category-based processing is more likely to occur than person-based processing, because social information is typically organized around social categories.

Fiske and Neuberg (1990) have presented an alternative model concerning "a continuum of impression formation, from category-based to individuating processes." According to this model, "people form impressions of others through a variety of processes that lie on a continuum reflecting the extent to which the perceiver utilizes a target's particular attributes" (Fiske & Neuberg, 1990, p. 2). At one end of the continuum are category-based processes, in which category membership determines impressions with minimal attention to individual attributes. At the other end of the continuum are individuating processes, in which individual characteristics, but not group membership, influence impressions. Among other differences (see Fiske, 1982, 1988), this model places greater emphasis on evaluative judgments and affective reactions than does Brewer's model, which focuses on cognitive representations. Nevertheless, like Brewer, Fiske and Neuberg posit the precedence of category-based processes over individual-based processes.

We take Brewer's and Fiske and Neuberg's shared assumptions as our starting point in this chapter. First, we assume that category-based processes typify impression formation. Theoretically, categorization is seen as adaptive (Anderson, 1991) in that category-based expectations act as a filter and allow the perceiver to screen out irrelevant or, sometimes, inconsistent information. This selective process is based upon a major assumption of cognitive psychology: The amount of attention available to experience the world is of finite quantity. To expend this finite amount of attention on details that have no apparent implications for the perceiver's well-being is inefficient and may, in fact, be detrimental by diverting attention away from perceiving what is essential for survival. Empirically, category-based processing has been shown to be faster (Brewer, 1988), more efficient for demanding tasks (Rothbart, Fulero, Jensen, Howard, & Birrell, 1978), and more common (Pryor & Ostrom, 1981) than attribute-based processing.

Second, we agree that categorization may occur spontaneously and automatically, at least for some well-developed schemas. According to Brewer's (1988) position, which is somewhat controversial given the limited empirical evidence available, the identification of a person as a member of a social category is automatic, unconscious, without intention, and stimulus controlled rather than attentionally mediated (Bower & Karlin, 1974; Bruner, 1957; McArthur & Baron, 1983). In addition, categorization may occur spontaneously on the basis of physical similarity, proximity, or shared fate (Campbell, 1958).

Third, we acknowledge that categorizing a person as a member of a social group immediately increases the accessibility of category-based responses (Fiske & Neuberg, 1990). Thus, social categorization influences impressions of others in systematic and significant ways. Once categorized, individuals are seen as group members who are relatively homogeneous in characteristics (Mullen & Hu, 1989) and who possess category-appropriate attributes (Secord, 1959). Category-based influences occur very early in the perceptual process (Devine, 1989; Klatzky, Martin, & Kane, 1982) and shape the interpretations of the behavior of others (e.g., Sagar & Schofield, 1980).

In this chapter, we attempt to build on previous work by examining some of the consequences of category-based processing. We are not presenting a new or alternative model, but we are instead considering the implications of other work on impression formation and intergroup relations for understanding category-based responses. This chapter focuses on three questions: (1) Is ingroup–outgroup categorization sufficient to activate category-based affect? (2) Can cognitive and affective (i.e., evaluative) components in category-based impression formation be independent? (3) Do deliberative considerations modify the spontaneous expressions of impressions? In the final section, we consider the implications of the answers to these questions and briefly suggest ways in which cognitive factors related to the processing of social categories can alter affective responses to outgroup members.

Is Ingroup–Outgroup Categorization Sufficient to Activate Category-Based Affect?

Models of category-based processing, such as those of Brewer (1988; see also Brewer & Miller, 1984) and Fiske and Neuberg (1990), assume that "the mere presentation of a stimulus person activates certain classification processes that occur automatically and without conscious intent. . . . The process is one of 'placing' the individual social object along well-established stimulus dimensions such as age, gender, and skin color" (Brewer, 1988, pp. 5–6). Although the activation of category-based schemas may arise almost immediately upon classification, at least for well-established and hedonically relevant categories, we speculate that a primitive type of categorization may also have a high probability of spontaneously occurring, perhaps in parallel process. This is the categorization of individuals as members of one's ingroup or not. Because of the centrality of the self in all perception (Higgins & Bargh, 1987; Kihlstrom *et al.*, 1988), we propose that social categorization involves most fundamentally a distinction between the group containing the self, the ingroup, and other groups, the outgroups—between the "we"s and the "they"s. In the next section, we briefly review some of the well-documented consequences of ingroup and outgroup categorization.

Impressions of Members of the Ingroup and Outgroups

The significance of classification of individuals as members of the ingroup or of the outgroup is demonstrated by the broad and substantial effects of the establishment of groups that are functionally meaningless and not previously established, as in the minimal intergroup paradigm (Brewer, 1979; Tajfel, Flament, Billig, & Bundy, 1971). For example, once people are categorized as members of groups, those in the outgroups are seen as more similar to and more interchangeable with one another (the outgroup homogeneity effect; Mullen & Hu, 1989) and as generally more *dis*similar to the ingroup (McGarty & Penny, 1988; Tajfel *et al.*, 1971; Wilder, 1981). These results can be obtained even if assignment to the group is arbitrary (e.g., random) and the group label is socially meaningless (e.g., the blue group; see Rabbie, 1982). Categorization of others as members of the ingroup, in contrast, increases perceptions of similarity to the self (Stein, Hardyck, & Smith, 1965). Increases in the salience of the ingroup boundary increases ingroup members' perceived similarity to the self, particularly on dimensions central to group membership (Hogg & Turner, 1987).

The mere categorization of people into groups is sufficient to increase attraction to ingroup members and may, at times, lead to a devaluation of people identified as outgroup members (Brewer, 1979; Rosenbaum & Holtz, 1985). People behave more positively and helpfully toward ingroup than toward outgroup members (e.g., Billig & Tajfel, 1973; Piliavin, Dovidio, Gaertner, & Clark, 1981); they also evaluate ingroup members more favorably and associate more desirable personal and physical characteristics to ingroup than to outgroup members (e.g., Doise *et al.*, 1972).

In addition, people process and retain information about ingroup and outgroup members differentially. They process information in a more detailed fashion for ingroup members than for outgroup members (Park & Rothbart, 1982), have better memory for information about ways ingroup members are similar and outgroup members are dissimilar to the self

(Wilder, 1981), and remember less positive information about outgroup members (Howard & Rothbart, 1980). Increasing the accessibility or salience of the outgroup facilitates processing of stereotype-consistent traits (Smith & Branscombe, 1986) and of prototypic physical characteristics (Klatzky *et al.*, 1982).

Different explanations are also made about the behaviors of ingroup and outgroup members. Positive behaviors and successful outcomes are more likely to be attributed to internal, stable characteristics (the personality) of ingroup than outgroup members (Hewstone, Jaspers, & Lalljee, 1982; Taylor & Jaggi, 1974). Blame for an accident and other negative outcomes are more likely to be ascribed to the personality of outgroup members than that of ingroup members (Hewstone, Bond, & Wan, 1983; Wang & McKillip, 1978). In general, behavior that disconfirms expectancies tends to be attributed to situational, rather than internal, causes (Crocker, Hannah, & Weber, 1983; Kulik, 1983).

The robustness and breadth of the consequences of the categorization of people into ingroups and outgroups argue for the importance of the ingroup/outgroup distinction in impression formation. This, however, is not sufficient evidence to indicate the automaticity of these effects that would occur if the ingroup/outgroup distinction were a fundamental aspect of category-based responding. In the next section, we investigate the automaticity of evaluative responses to stimuli indicating ingroup and outgroup membership. To eliminate the effects of the activation of category-based attributes associated with well-established schemas (such as men, women), these experiments examined the effects of general ingroup and outgroup designators, such as "we" and "they."

Automatic Activation and Ingroup–Outgroup Designation

We propose that words designating ingroup and outgroup status (such as the pronouns "we" and "they") activate fundamental category-based processing and may automatically introduce evaluative biases into the perception of new and unfamiliar people. In automatic processing, the mere presence of a stimulus activates a concept or response, even if the person attempts to ignore the stimulus (Shiffrin & Dumais, 1981). Thus, simply using an ingroup designator (e.g., "we") in thought or speech to refer to a person may automatically establish a positive predisposition toward that person, whereas the use of an outgroup designator (e.g., "they") may elicit a less positive or even a negative predisposition.

In this section, we summarize four experiments that investigated how ingroup and outgroup designators could systematically affect the way information is processed and how new evaluative associations are formed. One study examined the evaluative associations to nonsense syllables that were formed through repeated pairings with ingroup and outgroup pronouns.

The second experiment explored the priming effects of ingroup and out-group primes presented out of awareness on positive and negative traits. The third experiment investigated the facilitation effects of ingroup, out-group, and control primes on recognition of positive and negative charac-teristics. The fourth study considered how the use of pronouns to refer to others can influence interpersonal interaction.

Ingroup and Outgroup Associations

The question addressed in the first of this series of experiments (Perdue, Dovidio, Gurtman, & Tyler, 1990, Experiment 1) was whether, through classical conditioning, ingroup and outgroup designators (e.g., we and they) could function to establish evaluative responses to novel, unfamiliar targets. The principles of higher-order conditioning predict that if a word with emo-tional meaning "is paired a number of times with a neutral stimulus, like a nonsense syllable, the meaningless word will in the process come to elicit the meaning response" (Staats, 1968, p. 25). Words such as "us" or "them" used consistently and contiguously with names for novel groups or target persons may therefore produce classically conditioned affective responses to those names (and, by extension, to those persons). For example, Staats and Staats (1957) found that a meaningless syllable (e.g., xeh) was rated as more pleasant if it had been consistently paired with real words having pos-itive connotations; pairings with real words having negative connotations eventually produced an unpleasant rating of the nonsense syllable. In addi-tion, in a related study, Staats and Staats (1958) conditioned evaluative re-sponses to national labels (Swedish, Dutch) by pairing them with either positive words (sacred, happy) or negative words (ugly, failure). Ratings of the nationalities were more evaluatively positive when they had been paired with more evaluatively positive words. Thus, merely encountering the word "us" in association with a group label or with the name of an individual may, with repetition, condition a positive predisposition to that group or person, even if the person or group is novel or previously evaluatively neu-tral. The word "them" cooccurring with the name of a group or a person could establish less positive associations, or perhaps even some negative as-sociations (Holtz, 1989; Rosenbaum & Holtz, 1985).

To evaluate this hypothesis, subjects were repeatedly exposed to pair-ings of collective pronouns and neutral (nonsense) syllables embedded in a lexical decision task, in which subjects were asked to indicate which letter string in a pair was an actual word. Among the 108 trials were 20 in which a nonsense syllable (e.g., xeh) was paired with ingroup-designating pro-nouns (us, we, or ours) and 20 in which another nonsense syllable was paired with outgroup-designating pronouns (them, they, or theirs). After the lexical decision task, subjects rated the pleasantness of the nonsense syl-

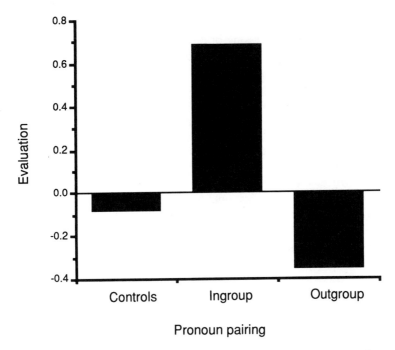

Figure 1 Ratings of target syllables as a function of pronoun pairing. From Perdue *et al.* (1990). Reprinted by permission of the American Psychological Association.

lable associated with the ingroup pronouns, the nonsense syllable associated with outgroup pronouns, and four control nonsense syllables.

As predicted (see Figure 1), nonsense syllables paired with ingroup pronouns were rated more positively than the syllables paired with outgroup pronouns and the control syllables ($ps < .001$). The syllables paired with outgroup pronouns were rated somewhat, but not significantly less positively than the control pronouns. Furthermore, when debriefed, subjects showed no awareness of the actual contingency between the selected nonsense syllables and the group-designating pronouns paired with them. Thus, ingroup and outgroup designation, even without reference to specific groups, elicited spontaneously different evaluative associations and conveyed these evaluations to new stimuli despite the fact that subjects could not articulate the contingencies between them.

Semantic Priming

Whereas the previous experiment investigated classical conditioning of evaluative responses, a second experiment (Perdue *et al.*, 1990, Experiment

2) examined the hypothesis that exposure to ingroup and outgroup designators could bias the processing of any subsequently encountered information because of the effects of semantic priming (Meyer & Schvaneveldt, 1971). Specifically, ingroup and outgroup designators (e.g., we and they) were presented briefly (55 msec) on a computer screen and then masked by positive or negative trait adjectives in such a way that subjects had no conscious awareness of the designators (see Perdue & Gurtman, 1990). Previous research has demonstrated that words presented outside of awareness can temporarily increase the accessibility of semantically (Fowler, Wolford, Slade, & Tassinary, 1981) and evaluatively (Perdue & Gurtman, 1990) related constructs for the perceiver (see Greenwald, 1992). Subjects in this study were asked to decide as quickly as possible whether each trait adjective was positive or negative, with decision latencies as the dependent measures. Shorter latencies are assumed to reflect greater association.

It was hypothesized that priming with ingroup and outgroup designators would automatically activate other highly associated constructs in memory. For example, Fazio, Sanbonmatsu, Powell, and Kardes (1986) found that attitude objects with strong evaluative associations automatically facilitated responses to similarly valenced (positive or negative) trait adjectives. If ingroup-referent terms elicit more evaluatively positive associates, then the effect of such prior activation should be to prime subsequently encountered positive constructs, facilitating response times to positive trait information (e.g., helpful) in relation to those for negative trait information (e.g., clumsy). Response times to negative traits might also be facilitated following the presentation of an outgroup prime (Holtz, 1989).

Consistent with the predictions, the results of this study indicated that ingroup and outgroup pronouns at least transiently influence social information processing by altering the relative accessibility of constructs with similar evaluative connotations. In particular, subjects were able to make decisions concerning positive traits more quickly after exposure to the masked words "us," "we," "ours," than after being primed by the words "them," "they," and "theirs" ($p < .03$). Conversely, traits with negative connotations were processed more quickly when preceded by outgroup designators than when primed by ingroup designators ($p < .02$). The conceptions of an individual as a "we" or a "they" may thus automatically and unconsciously bias the constructs used to construe that person.

Priming: Favoritism or Derogation?

Although the previous priming experiment demonstrated that ingroup- and outgroup-designating terms influenced the *relative* accessibility of positive and negative constructs, it remains unclear whether ingroup designators facilitate positive associations or inhibit negative associations, whether outgroup designators facilitate negative associations or inhibit positive associations, or whether some combination of these effects occurs. Thus, another experiment (Perdue *et al.*, 1990, Experiment 3) was designed to examine the automatic effects of an ingroup designator and an outgroup designator in relation to a no-prime baseline condition in which the target trait words were preceded by a semantically meaningless control string (xxx) (see Fazio *et al.*, 1986).

As in the previous priming study, subjects were asked to make decisions concerning positive and negative adjectives after the presentation of a masked priming stimulus. The subject's task was quite different in this case, however. In this study, two group-related primes were selected (we and they) as well as a neutral control string. Following the procedure of Bargh and Pietromonaco (1982), the primes were presented for 75 msec and then immediately masked by a letter string, which also cued subjects to think about a specific category of targets—either people (cued by PPPPP), the category of interest, or houses (cued by HHHHHH), a type of control category. Then, after a 250-msec delay, a test word appeared. The subject's task was to decide if this word could ever describe a person. The test words of interest were positive and negative person-descriptive words (e.g., kind and cruel). The house primes and the use of test words that could describe houses but not people (e.g., drafty) were used to ensure that the correct answer was not always "yes." The dependent measure was again response latency.

The results, which are illustrated in Figure 2, revealed the anticipated Prime (we, they, xxx) × Trait (positive, negative) interaction ($p < .02$). Comparing just the "we" and the "they" primes, positive traits were responded to faster following "we" than following "they" ($p < .02$); negative traits were responded to somewhat, but not significantly ($p < .16$) faster following "they" than following "we." Thus, as seen in the previous priming study, an ingroup-designating word (we) presented outside the perceiver's conscious awareness facilitated access to positive constructs in semantic memory in relation to the effects of an outgroup-designating word (they). In addition, as seen in Figure 2, response latencies following the control (xxx) prime closely tracked the latencies following the "they" prime. This finding suggests that the outgroup prime was not actively promoting negative construct accessibility but instead that it was more neutral in priming consequences than was the ingroup designator. This interpretation is consistent with Brewer's (1979) conclusion that intergroup biases, at least in the minimal intergroup situation, are more a product of ingroup favoritism than of outgroup derogation. In a later section, we consider whether these effects that we see for nonspecific ingroup and outgroup designators apply to well-established and meaningful social categories, namely racial categories. In the next study, we examined whether a person's use of ingroup pronouns when referring to other people systematically influences expectations of those others.

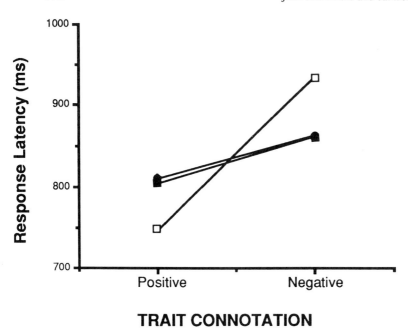

Figure 2 Response latencies to positive and negative traits as a function of prime type: we (□), they (●), or xxx (■). From Perdue *et al.* (1990). Reprinted by permission of the American Psychological Association.

Priming Expectations

The first three experiments that we presented in this section have been highly cognitive and microscopic in nature. Ratings of nonsense syllables and response latencies were the dependent measures. In addition, the experimental contexts have been nonsocial; subjects participated individually, often interacting primarily with a computer. The question we next asked, then, was whether the priming effects we observed have any implications for actual social interaction.

This study concerned the expectations that people form of others, with whom they expect to interact, on the basis of the ingroup and outgroup references (Dovidio, Tobriner, Rioux, & Gaertner, 1991). From our previous experiments, we hypothesized that referring to others in ingroup terms (i.e., using we, us, and ours) compared to outgroup terms (i.e., using they, them, and theirs) would elicit more positive expectations. Furthermore, in this study we explicitly evaluated the explanation that these more positive expectations would be due, at least in part, to the belief that these others are or are not members of one's own group.

Subjects in this study initially participated individually but were led to believe that they would be interacting with two other participants on a problem-solving task. After the subject completed some background information, the experimenter mentioned that the problem-solving session would be audio recorded and that one person would be asked to briefly identify the session number and the task instructions so that the experimenter could "keep track of the conditions." Subjects were informed that they were "randomly" selected to identify the session and then asked to memorize a brief script and to repeat it into a microphone. The key manipulation was the pronouns used to describe the participants. In half of the cases, ingroup designators were consistently used. The script read: "Subjects are participating in a study involving problem solving. *We* have been asked to evaluate a given situation. *Our* task is to make decisions how *we* would respond in this situation." In the other half of the cases, ingroup pronouns were replaced by outgroup pronouns (e.g., "they" for "we"). Subjects were next asked to rate what they thought their interaction would be like on two 7-point ("not at all" to "very much") scales ("feeling like one group" and feeling like "separate individuals") and to evaluate what they expected the "other two participants" to be like on 7-point scales representing the positive (e.g., good) and negative (e.g., bad) dimensions used in the priming studies and on a "similar to self" scale. Separate analyses examining how the use of pronouns influences feelings toward others were performed for positive and negative evaluative ratings.

Mediation analysis was performed to evaluate the extent to which conceptions of group boundaries influenced, first, expectations of other participants prior to interaction and then, second, evaluations of others' behaviors during interaction (see Baron & Kenny, 1986). Mediation analysis, which is a form of path analysis, requires that a series of regression equations be estimated. Initially, the dependent variable (e.g., positive evaluations of others prior to interaction) is regressed on the independent variable (e.g., use of pronouns) to establish a significant relationship. Then, in other equations, each of the potential mediators (e.g., one-group representation, similarity to self) are regressed upon the hypothesized antecedent effect to demonstrate significant paths. Finally, in the last equation, the dependent variable is again regressed upon the independent variable, but this time considering the effects of the mediating variables. In this equation, the effect of the independent variable should be weaker than in the original equation because if there were perfect mediation, the independent variable would have no effect beyond the association between the mediators and the dependent variable.

The results of the mediation analysis for positive evaluations of other participants prior to interaction are summarized in Figure 3 (bold arrows indicate significant paths, $p < .05$). In the initial regression equation, which did not consider the effects of the hypothesized mediators, use of pronouns

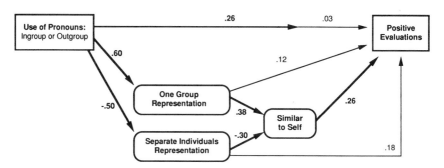

Figure 3 The direct and indirect effects of the use of ingroup and outgroup pronouns on interpersonal expectations.

was significantly related to positive evaluations (β = .26; see the first segment of the uppermost pathway). Consistent with the priming research, even though they were unaware of the manipulation, subjects who used ingroup pronouns had more positive expectations of the other participants than did subjects who used outgroup pronouns. Subsequent regression equations, which were performed to examine the potential mediating influences, revealed the expected pathways: subjects using ingroup pronouns reported that the interaction would feel more like one group and less like separate individuals than did subjects who used outgroup pronouns; these ratings, in turn, influenced feeling of closeness. The more the interaction was expected to feel like one group and the less like separate individuals, the more they felt that the others would be similar to them. These feelings of similarity to the self then directly related to positive evaluations. Demonstrating the importance of the proposed mediating mechanisms, the direct path from pronoun use to evaluation was nonsignificant when the mediating variables were considered in the final regression equation. As illustrated in the uppermost path of Figure 3, whereas the path from pronoun use to positive evaluations prior to interaction was significant *before* the mediators were considered (β = .26; first segment), the path was nonsignificant *after* the mediators were considered (β = .03; second segment). This result provides strong evidence of mediation of positive expectations of others. The analyses performed on the negative evaluative items, in contrast, were nonsignificant. In general, at least in terms of positive feelings, the overall pattern of the results suggests that the use of ingroup designating pronouns in thought and speech may be sufficient to generate different conceptions of group boundaries, which in turn lead to differentially positive expectations of others.

The importance of group conceptions of boundaries was also evidenced after subjects had the opportunity to interact. Ratings of being like one group directly predicted positive evaluations (β = .46) and indirectly predicted positive evaluation through perceived similarity to the self (βs for those two paths were .52 and .37).

In summary, many current theories of schema-based responding propose that the identification and classification of individuals as members of groups activates schema-relevant cognitions and evaluations. The results of the four studies we have presented in this section suggest that ingroup–outgroup categorization may have a basic, general effect. That is, the fundamental categorization of an individual as a member of one's own group or not, in itself, can give rise to differential affect and evaluation, regardless of the specific group to which the person belongs. These evaluative responses occur spontaneously and without conscious awareness, and, even without category-specific (i.e., stereotypic) cognitive representations, they can bias the nature of subsequent interactions. In the next section of this chapter, we examine the joint role of category-based cognitive representations (stereotypes) and affect in impression formation.

Can Cognitive and Affective Components in Category-Based Impression Formation Be Independent?

Existing models of category-based processes imply that categorization can influence both cognitive representations (Brewer, 1988) and evaluative responses (Fiske, 1982). We propose that category-based processes can independently, but parallelly, influence cognitive representations and evaluative reactions. In terms of impression formation, Wyer and Gordon (1984) postulated that people engage in "dual coding of information." Wyer and Gordon (1984) state: "First, they may attempt to encode and classify behaviors in terms of the traits they exemplify, thus forming trait-behavior clusters. . . . In addition, subjects with a general impression set may extract the evaluative implications of the information presented" (p. 130). Thus, consistent with our position concerning separate cognitive and affective responses, behaviors of a person may be represented twice in memory, independently in a trait-behavior cluster (based on its descriptive implications) and in an evaluation-based representation (based on its evaluative implications) (Wyer & Srull, 1989). In terms of group representations, Stephan and Stephan (Chapter 6, this volume) propose that cognition and affect are parallel systems. In their model (see Figure 2 in their chapter), as we hypothesize, activation of a group representation may initially independently activate trait and evaluative associations.

The independence of cognitive and affective category-based responses fits well with recent approaches to intergroup attitudes, specifically the attitudes of whites toward blacks. For example, according to aversive (Gaertner & Dovidio, 1986), symbolic (Sears, 1988), and modern (McConahay,

1986) racism theories, societal pressures toward egalitarianism may differentially influence cognitive and affective components of racial attitudes. Although the cognitive aspects of racial attitudes (i.e., racial beliefs) have changed relatively rapidly, anti-black affect is not necessarily changing at the same rate. Instead, anti-black sentiment is lingering and is changing much more slowly (McConahay & Hough, 1976). Negative feelings toward blacks that whites acquire early in life persist into adulthood but are expressed symbolically (Sears, 1988) or in subtle, rationalizable ways that do not challenge the person's nonprejudiced self-image (Gaertner & Dovidio, 1986). Thus, intergroup beliefs and affect may be dissociated.

It should be noted that the findings of our ingroup/outgroup priming studies in and of themselves also imply an answer to the second major question we pose in this section, "Can affective and cognitive components of category-based responses be independent?" To the extent that affective reactions occur in the absence of specific category-based cognitive representations, such as stereotypes, the answer is yes. In the remainder of the section, we extend our consideration of this question to responses to well-established and specific cognitive categories: racial groups.

Racial Categories and Information Processing

Social research has traditionally focused on the content of racial stereotypes and on how they are acquired and transmitted (e.g., Karlins, Coffman, & Walters, 1969; Katz & Braly, 1933). Contemporary research, however, considers stereotypes to be more than mere descriptions; they are cognitive structures that importantly influence perception, attention, and memory (Hamilton, 1981). They may also influence affect (Fiske, 1982).

In terms of racial stereotyping, Gaertner and McLaughlin (1983), using a lexical decision task patterned after that used by Meyer and Schvaneveldt (1971), demonstrated how racial biases affect information processing. In this lexical decision task, the subject was presented simultaneously with two strings of letters and asked to decide (yes or no) if both strings were words. Meyer and Schvaneveldt's (1971) results suggested that the associative strength between words could be gauged by the speed of responding in this task. Gaertner and McLaughlin found that both high- and low-prejudice scoring white subjects responded faster when "smart," "ambitious," and "clean" were paired with "whites" than when they were paired with "blacks" or "Negroes." White subjects, however, responded no more quickly to "stupid," "lazy," and "welfare" when they were paired with "blacks" and "Negroes" than when they were paired with "whites." In addition, a rating-scale procedure (Gaertner & McLaughlin, 1983, Study 3) demonstrated that whites did not rate blacks as more "stupid," "lazy," and "dirty" than whites, but they did rate whites as more "smart," "ambitious," and "clean" than blacks. Gaertner and McLaughlin concluded that whites no longer associate negative characteristics more strongly with blacks than with whites, but that whites continue to associate positive characteristics more strongly with whites than with blacks.

Cognitive Representations and Evaluative Associations

There are two possible theoretical explanations that could account for the Gaertner and McLaughlin (1983) results. One explanation involves the cognitively represented descriptive content of racial stereotypes. This explanation assumes that the stronger a feature's stereotypic association is, the more information processing is facilitated. Gaertner and McLaughlin suggested that "smart," "ambitious," and "clean" were part of the contemporary stereotype of whites but that "lazy," "stupid," and "welfare" were no longer part of the stereotype of blacks. There was, however, no independent assessment of stereotypes in their study. Another explanation focuses on affective associations. This interpretation suggests that Gaertner and McLaughlin's response latency results may indicate that current feelings of whites may be relatively positive toward whites but not relatively negative toward blacks. Because stereotypic association and evaluation may be confounded in the stimuli that Gaertner and McLaughlin used, their study does not differentiate between cognitively based and affectively based influences. Follow-up research, however, attempted to evaluate these two potential influences.

Disentangling Cognitive and Affective Contributions

Dovidio, Evans, and Tyler (1986) conducted a priming study to examine separately cognitive and affective responses to blacks and whites. In their priming methodology, white subjects were first presented for 2 sec with the primes "black" and "white," explicitly indicating the racial groups, or the control prime "house." After a 500-msec interval, a test word appeared. The subject's task was to decide if this word could ever describe a person. To independently assess cognitive and affective associations, the test-word stimuli represented the four combinations of stereotypic association (white and black stereotypic) and evaluation (positive and negative). Included among the 8 person-descriptive test adjectives in this study were four characteristics that, based on adjective checklist responses, were related to the black stereotype and four words that were related to the white stereotype. Half of these traits represented favorable characteristics and half represented relatively unfavorable characteristics. The four types of person-descriptive test words were, specifically, positive white stereotypic (ambitious, practical), positive black stereotypic (musical, sensitive), negative white stereotypic (conventional, stubborn), and negative black stereotypic (lazy, imitative).

It was hypothesized that, to the extent that category-based semantic (i.e., cognitive) associations influence processing, then stereotypicality would influence response latencies. Specifically, it was predicted that response times would be faster to white stereotypic words following "white" primes than following "black" primes, and, conversely, response times to black stereotypic words would be faster following "black" primes than "white" primes. To the extent that evaluative reactions are linked to representations (Wyer & Srull, 1989) and categorization (Fiske, 1982), it would be expected that, because positive characteristics have been associated more with whites than with blacks (Karlins *et al.*, 1969), faster response times would be expected to positive traits after the "white" prime than after the "black" prime; faster response times to negative traits might also be expected following "black" primes than following "white" primes.

Consistent with the idea that cognitive and affective category-based responses may be independent, separate Prime × Stereotypic Trait and Prime × Evaluative Trait interactions were obtained ($ps < .03$). These interactions are illustrated in Figure 4. With respect to the influence of cognitive representations, the primes of "black" and "white" most facilitated responses to characteristics stereotypically associated to these social groups ($ps < .001$). With respect to evaluative influences, positive traits tended to be responded more quickly following "white" primes than "black" primes, and negative traits were responded to faster following "black" primes than "white" primes ($p < .02$). It should be noted that this last effect is not entirely consistent with the results of Gaertner and McLaughlin (1983), which revealed differences for positive but not negative characteristics. Consistent with the notion that cognitive and affective components of social schemata may be independent, the 3-way, Prime × Stereotypic Trait × Evaluative Trait interaction did not approach significance.

The generalizability of the effects of semantically primed racial categories is demonstrated by experiments using photographs as primes. Baker and Devine (1988) found that subjects responded faster to black stereotypic words following faces of blacks than of whites; they also responded faster to white stereotypic words following photographs of whites than of blacks. Zarate and Smith (1990) showed that individuals who show stronger tendencies to categorize photographs on the basis of race hold stronger stereotypic beliefs. These studies provide evidence that the effects of semantic activation in the Dovidio *et al.* (1986) and Gaertner and McLaughlin (1983) experiments are in fact due to racial categorization and not simply based on spontaneous associations with the colors black and white. In addition, we pursued the question of generalizability of our results across a wider range of characteristics.

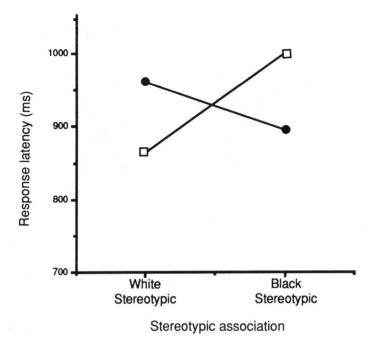

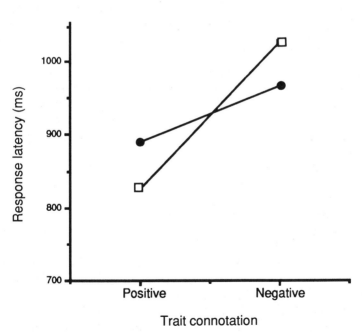

Figure 4 The independence stereotypic and evaluative activation: Response latencies to white and black stereotypic characteristics and to positive and negative traits as a function of "black" and "white" primes. (□), white; (●), black. From Dovidio *et al.* (1986). Reprinted by permission of Academic Press, Inc.

Extending the Evaluative and Cognitive Range

Because the stimuli used in the Dovidio *et al.* (1986) experiment were matched for both stereotypic association and favorability, the sample of characteristics was relatively small and the range of favorability was limited. Thus, within this paradigm itself, there may be some question about the generality of the conclusions. We therefore conducted another priming study with white subjects that used the same procedure but included a larger sample (n = 30) of characteristics that represented a broader range of favorability (Dovidio, Evans, & Tyler, 1988). Among these stimuli were test words ranging from characteristics strongly associated with whites (e.g., materialistic; see Dovidio & Gaertner, 1986) to characteristics strongly associated with blacks (e.g., musical). Other test words reflected positive and negative characteristics not traditionally differentially associated with blacks and whites (e.g., kind and cruel).

Regression analyses were performed at the aggregate level to identify the independent effects of stereotypicality and evaluation. Specifically, the mean response latency difference as a function of racial category prime for each of the 30 person-descriptive characteristics was the dependent measure. The independent variables, entered simultaneously in the equation, were stereotypicality (difference in the percentage of subjects in an independent sample selecting a trait as typical of blacks or whites) and evaluation (based on item favorableness ratings of an independent sample of subjects), and the interaction of stereotypicality and evaluation.

The effect of stereotypicality was significant (β = −.38, p < .03); the greater the stereotypic association of a trait to a particular racial group, the greater the relative facilitation of responses following that prime. The effect for evaluation was marginal (β = −.26, p < .14), but in the expected direction: the more positive the characteristic, the greater the response time advantage following the "white" prime than following the "black" prime. Further inspection of the data, however, also revealed a quadratic trend for evaluation (β = .30, p < .085). When the 30 characteristics were divided into five groups based on their evaluative values (very positive, somewhat positive, neutral, somewhat negative, and very negative), the nature of this trend is apparent. The response time advantage of the "white" prime over the "black" prime is greatest for very positive characteristics (82 msec) and diminishes for the somewhat positive (64 msec) and neutral (9 msec) characteristics. For somewhat negative characteristics, response times are slower following "white" than "black" primes (-50 msec). The trend, however, reverses for very negative traits: subjects again respond faster following the "white" prime (43 msec). Consistent with the hypothesized independence of stereotypicality and evaluation, the interaction term was not significant.

These results, which at first glance may appear surprising and contradictory, actually help to reconcile the results of Gaertner and McLaughlin (1983) and Dovidio *et al.* (1986) for negative characteristics. Recall, Gaertner and McLaughlin found no difference in response times to negative traits for blacks and whites; Dovidio *et al.* demonstrated that response times for negative traits were faster following "black" than "white" primes. One difference in these studies, though, involves the degree of unfavorability of the negative traits used in these two experiments. In Gaertner and McLaughlin's study, these traits were in the very negative range, whereas in the experiment by Dovidio *et al.* the traits were in the somewhat unfavorable range. Thus, across three studies we see no differences for very negative characteristics but greater evaluative association with blacks than with whites for somewhat negative traits. Perhaps, as some researchers have proposed (McConahay, 1986; Sears, 1988), whites may currently harbor more subtle and milder forms of prejudice, which may be rooted in a fundamental ingroup/outgroup bias (Gaertner & Dovidio, 1986), and reject the blatant anti-black feelings that have characterized traditional forms of prejudice. This evidence and explanation was suggestive, and so another study was conducted to verify the curvilinear relationship between evaluation and response time.

This study (Dovidio, 1988) used the same priming procedure as the previous study, but systematically varied the test words. In particular, the 8 person-descriptive test words were selected to range in favorability from very positive (brilliant, honest), to somewhat positive (sophisticated, methodical), to somewhat negative (impulsive, suggestible), to very negative (cowardly, deceitful). These characteristics were also not strongly stereotypically associated with either blacks or whites, at least based on previous adjective checklist studies and our pretesting.

The results of this study conformed to the curvilinear pattern suggested by the previous study. White subjects responded substantially faster to very positive words following the "white" than the "black" prime ($p < .001$) and considerably faster to somewhat positive words following the "white" than the "black" prime ($p < .028$). For somewhat negative traits, subjects responded significantly faster after the "black" prime than after the "white" prime ($p < .05$) but not for very negative traits ($F < 1$).

Despite the rather consistent curvilinear evidence for category-based evaluative responses across a number of experiments, the meaning of this pattern should be interpreted cautiously. On one hand, as we suggested earlier, it might reflect a genuine shift, which is indicated in nationwide polls (see Dovidio & Gaertner, 1986), among whites away from strongly negative feelings toward blacks. Nevertheless, it may also reflect a conscious inhibition of the expression of one's spontaneous feelings toward blacks (see Dovidio & Fazio, 1992). This leads us to the third major question in this chapter.

Do Deliberative Considerations Modify
Spontaneous Expressions of Impressions?

The expression of racial feelings and beliefs poses a particular problem for studying category-based responses. Because of prevailing norms of egalitarianism, people are guarded about making responses that can be interpreted by others or oneself as reflecting bias (Gaertner & Dovidio, 1986). Of course, these norms extend to other types of bias and issues, as well (see Dovidio & Fazio, 1992). Thus, it is important to note that although the latency methods involved in these particular priming studies helped to avoid contamination from the gross impression management strategies commonly associated with self-report measures, relatively long stimulus onset asynchronies in these studies of racial representations and evaluation do not preclude the influence of some fundamental controlled processes (see Messick & Mackie, 1989). Furthermore, the mere knowledge that these studies involve judgments of blacks may prime the conscious, egalitarian aspects of subjects' self-images and reduce racial bias, particularly for negative attributes (Gaertner & Dovidio, 1986). Given these concerns, we conducted additional research to investigate *nonconscious and automatic* processes.

Automatic Evaluative Influences

This study (Dovidio, 1990) used the same stimuli, representing four different levels of evaluation, that were used in the previous study. However, it involved the masked prime methodology that was adapted from the procedure of Bargh and Pietromonaco (1982) and employed in one of the ingroup priming studies (Perdue *et al.*, 1990, Experiment 3). Briefly, subjects were presented with instructions similar to the instructions used in the previous priming study. They were told that they would see a string of letters, Ps or Hs, on the left or right side of a computer screen. When they saw Ps, they were asked to think of a typical person; when they saw Hs, they were instructed to think of a typical house. Subjects were then presented with various characteristics, including the positive and negative traits used in the previous priming study, and asked to decide if each trait could ever describe the designated category (i.e., person or house). What subjects were not informed about was that the word "black" or "white" was presented for 75 msec before the Ps (representing the person category). Thus, the purpose of this study was to examine the correspondence between nonconscious racial associations and the potentially conscious associations demonstrated in the earlier experiment.

The results for very positive characteristics were similar to the results for the priming study that involved conscious, controlled processes. Subjects responded to very positive characteristics more quickly following the "white" subliminal prime than following the "black" subliminal prime ($p < .05$). Even nonconsciously, then, very positive characteristics are associated more with whites than with blacks. No significant effects due to prime were obtained for the somewhat positive and the somewhat negative traits. For the very negative traits, however, there was a clear discrepancy between nonconscious and conscious responding. Specifically, negative characteristics were responded to significantly faster following a "black" prime than following a "white" prime. Thus, even though at a conscious level whites may reject very negative feelings toward Blacks, at a nonconscious level these feelings may exist and shape their responses. This study therefore suggests that at least some people who consciously and genuinely embrace egalitarian personal ideals may, *outside of their awareness,* still harbor negative feelings toward blacks that may be spontaneously available.

Additional research supports this conclusion and again indicates that these effects are due to racial categorization and not simply based on spontaneous associations with the colors black and white. Devine (1989), without using the specific label "black," found automatic activation of negative racial stereotypes of blacks, regardless of whether white subjects scored high or low in prejudice on a self-report measure [McConahay's (1986) Modern Racism Scale]. Given the opportunity for deliberation, however, low-prejudice-scoring subjects inhibited these spontaneous reactions and replaced them with more egalitarian thoughts (see Devine & Monteith, Chapter 14, this volume).

Summary and Implications

We began this chapter by asserting that we were not developing new theory but instead were asking three questions that we believed were important to the study of category-based responding. The first question was whether ingroup–outgroup categorization is sufficient to activate category-based affect. Across four studies, the answer was consistently yes. Priming with an ingroup designator produced, automatically and without consciousness, more positive evaluative associations than did priming with an outgroup designator. In these cases in which ingroup and outgroup membership was primed without reference to a specific outgroup (e.g., Iraqis), the category-based response was primarily one of ingroup favoritism rather than outgroup devaluation, as Brewer's (1979) analysis suggested. The differential evaluative associations spontaneously generated by ingroup and outgroup primes can bias initial expectations of others; perceptions of ingroup membership can then exert a continuous influence on the nature of interactions and create a self-fulfilling prophecy.

The second question posed was, "Can cognitive and affective (i.e., evaluative) components in category-based impression formation be independent?" The answer is again yes. In the studies of ingroup/outgroup priming, differential evaluative associations were elicited even though there was no specifically delineated ingroup or outgroup. Thus, independent of well-established social schemata in which specific category-based attributes may be activated, different evaluative responses occur. Furthermore, even when specific social categories are involved (for, example, blacks and whites in this chapter), cognitive attribute-based responses and affective (evaluative) responses appear to be independent.

The third question we raised concerned whether deliberative considerations can modify the spontaneous expressions of impressions. With respect to socially sensitive issues, such as race, people may inhibit or deny negative feelings toward and beliefs about social categories in order to appear non-prejudiced to others or to themselves (Devine, 1989; Dovidio & Gaertner, 1991; Gaertner & Dovidio, 1986; Sears, 1988). This process involves more than simply methodological issues; it has theoretical and practical implications. As Gaertner and Dovidio (1986) outlined, the simultaneous existence of conscious egalitarian beliefs and nonconscious negative affect can produce the ambivalence that characterizes a modern, subtle form of racial prejudice, aversive racism. Devine and her colleagues (Devine, Monteith, Zuwerink, & Elliot, 1991; see also Devine & Monteith, Chapter 14, this volume) suggest that a discrepancy between automatic negative reactions to stigmatized groups and nonprejudiced beliefs and standards produces feelings of compunction that can motivate people to behave in ways that will reaffirm their self-image and help establish a pattern of nonprejudiced responding.

One important implication of the potential independence of affective responses and stereotypical beliefs is that traditional ways of reducing prejudice may not be completely effective. For example, even if successful, attempts at changing stereotypical beliefs may not be sufficient to eliminate affective bias; cognitions are just one aspect of category-based responding. If cognitive representations and evaluations are independent, negative affect toward outgroups or differentially positive affect toward ingroups may linger and continue to influence perceptions, expectations, personal interactions, and, consequently, social policy (Feagin, 1991).

Attempts to change evaluative responses directly may thus provide an important complementary strategy for eliminating bias. Within the intergroup literature, there has been some convergence of opinion that partially degrading the salience of the ingroup/outgroup boundary reduces evaluative intergroup biases. While decategorization has been the common goal, various strategies have been used with different objectives. For example, individuating members of an outgroup by revealing variability in their opinions (Wilder, 1981) or creating more personalized interactions on the basis of personal or intimate information (Brewer & Miller, 1984) may blur or alter the prior categorization scheme and reduce reliance on category-based processes.

Alternatively, rather than focusing on *de*categorizing outgroup members, strategies aimed at the *re*categorization of former outgroup members as members of a common, superordinate ingroup may also be effective (Gaertner & Dovidio, Anastasio, Bachman, & Rust, 1993; Gaertner, Mann, Dovidio, Murrell, & Pomare, 1990; Gaertner, Mann, Murrell, & Dovidio, 1989). In recategorization, ingroup favoritism is not eliminated; instead it is redirected in ways that produce more positive evaluations of former outgroup members. The objective is to encourage new perceptions of former outgroup members as members of a common ingroup. Once recategorized as members of the ingroup, favoritism biases should extend to these former outgroup members. With enhanced evaluations of these individuals, evaluative bias based on original group membership is thereby reduced. Gaertner and Dovidio (1991) propose that a common ingroup identity initially increases positive attitudes toward former outgroup members heuristically and in an undifferentiated manner. Nevertheless, more elaborated, differentiated, and personalized impressions, which can change stereotypes, are likely to soon develop because the newly formed positivity bias may encourage more open communication and self-disclosing interaction with former outgroup members. In practice, recategorization from two groups to one group can be achieved by increasing the salience of existing common superordinate group memberships or by introducing new factors (e.g., common tasks or fate) that are perceived to be shared by the memberships.

In conclusion, we have proposed that, at least in terms of social cognition, category-based responses inherently involve an evaluative, or affective, component. These affective responses may be based on two factors. First, identification of a person as a member of one's own group or another group is sufficient to automatically activate differential evaluations or affective reactions. Second, through dual coding (evaluation and semantic) of the same information or through independent experiences and sources of information, affect may be triggered by the activation of a specific group schema (e.g., of blacks). Category-based responding may also involve a cognitive component, a stereotype. In cases of well-established categories, the activation of cognitive and affective components may be automatic and nonconscious. More generally, Fazio (1986) proposes that the likelihood of automatic activation is a function of the strength of the association in memory between the attitude object and the cognitive representation and evaluation of the object. We recognize that because affective and cognitive category-based responses *can* be independent, it does not always mean that they are always independent (as the title of this volume suggests). Nevertheless, we believe that an understanding of the potential dissociation between affective and cognitive components of category-based responses argues for the need for diverse, multifaceted strategies for the elimination of social biases such as racism.

Acknowledgments

Preparation of this chapter was supported by NIMH Grant #MH48721-01.

References

Allport, G. W. (1954). *The nature of prejudice.* Reading, MA: Addison-Wesley.

Anderson, J. R. (1991). The adaptive nature of human categorization. *Psychological Review,* **98,** 409–429.

Anderson, N. H. (1981). *Foundations of impression integration theory.* New York: Academic Press.

Asch, S. E. (1946). Forming impressions of personality. *Journal of Abnormal and Social Psychology,* **41,** 258–290.

Baker, S. M., & Devine, P. G. (1988). *Faces as primes for stereotype activation.* Paper presented at the 60th annual meeting of the Midwestern Psychological Association, Chicago.

Bargh, J. A., & Pietromonaco, P. (1982). Automatic information processing and social perception: The influence of trait information presented outside of conscious awareness on impression formation. *Journal of Personality and Social Psychology,* **43,** 437–449.

Baron, R. M., & Kenny, D. A. (1986). The moderator-mediator variable distinction in social psychological research: Conceptual, strategic and statistical considerations. *Journal of Personality and Social Psychology,* **51,** 1173–1182.

Billig, M., & Tajfel, H. (1973). Social categorization and similarity in intergroup behavior. *European Journal of Social Psychology,* **3,** 27–52.

Bower, G. H., & Karlin, M. B. (1974). Depth of processing pictures of faces and recognition memory. *Journal of Experimental Psychology,* **103,** 751–757.

Brewer, M. B. (1979). In-group bias in the minimal intergroup situation: A cognitive-motivational analysis. *Psychological Bulletin,* **86,** 307–324.

Brewer, M. B. (1988). A dual process model of impression formation. In T. S. Srull & R. S. Wyer, Jr. (Eds.), *Advances in social cognition: Vol. I: A dual process model of impression formation* (pp. 1–36). Hillsdale, NJ: Erlbaum.

Brewer, M. B., & Miller, N. (1984). Beyond the contact hypothesis: Theoretical perspectives on desegregation. In N. Miller & M. B. Brewer (Eds.), *Groups in contact: The psychology of desegregation* (pp. 281–302). Orlando, FL: Academic Press.

Bruner, J. S. (1957). On perceptual readiness. *Psychological Review,* **64,** 123–152.

Campbell, D. T. (1958). Common fate, similarity, and other indices of the status of aggregates of persons as social entities. *Behavioral Science,* **3,** 14–25.

Crocker, J., Hannah, D. B., & Weber, R. (1983). Person memory and causal attributions. *Journal of Personality and Social Psychology,* **44,** 55–66.

Devine, P. G. (1989). Stereotypes and prejudice: Their automatic and controlled components. *Journal of Personality and Social Psychology,* **56,** 5–18.

Devine, P. G., Monteith, M. J., Zuwerink, J. R., & Elliot, A. J. (1991). Prejudice with and without compunction. *Journal of Personality and Social Psychology,* **60,** 817–830.

Doise, W., Csepeli, G., Dann, H., Gouge, C., Larsen, K., & Ostell, A. (1972). An experimental investigation into the formation of intergroup relations. *European Journal of Social Psychology,* **2,** 202–204.

Dovidio, J. F. (1988). *Evaluative responses to racial primes.* Unpublished manuscript, Department of Psychology, Colgate University, Hamilton, NY.

Dovidio, J. F. (1990). *Evaluative responses to racial primes: Automatic activation.* Unpublished manuscript, Department of Psychology, Colgate University, Hamilton, NY.

Dovidio, J. F., & Fazio, R. H. (1992). New technologies for the direct and indirect assessment of attitudes. In J. Tanur (Ed.), *Questions about survey questions: Meaning, memory, attitudes, and social interaction.* (pp. 204–237). New York: Russell Sage Foundation.

Dovidio, J. F., & Gaertner, S. L. (1986). Prejudice, discrimination, and racism: Historical trends and contemporary approaches. In J. F. Dovidio & S. L. Gaertner (Eds.), *Prejudice, discrimination, and racism* (pp. 1–34). Orlando, FL: Academic Press.

Dovidio, J. F., & Gaertner, S. L. (1991). Changes in the nature and expression of racial prejudice. In H. Knopke, J. Norrell, & R. Rogers (Eds.), *Opening doors: An appraisal of race relations in contemporary America* (pp. 201–241). Tuscaloosa, AL: University of Alabama Press.

Dovidio, J. F., Evans, N., & Tyler, R. G. (1986). Racial stereotypes: The contents of their cognitive representations. *Journal of Experimental Social Psychology, 22,* 22–37.

Dovidio, J. F., Evans, N., & Tyler, R. B. (1988). *Cognitive and Evaluative responses to racial primes: Extending the range.* Unpublished manuscript, Department of Psychology, Colgate University, Hamilton, NY.

Dovidio, J. F., Tobriner, M., Rioux, S., & Gaertner, S. L. (1991). *Say "we": Priming interpersonal expectations.* Unpublished manuscript, Department of Psychology, Colgate University, Hamilton, NY.

Fazio, R. H. (1986). How do attitudes guide behavior? In R. M. Sorrentino & E. T. Higgins (Eds.), *The handbook of motivation and cognition: Foundations of social behavior* (pp. 204–243). New York: Guilford Press.

Fazio, R. H., Sanbonmatsu, D. M., Powell, M. C., & Kardes, F. R. (1986). On the automatic activation of attitudes. *Journal of Personality and Social Psychology, 50,* 229–238.

Feagin, J. R. (1991, August). *The continuing significance of race: The Black middle-class experience.* Paper presented at the annual meeting of the American Sociological Association. Cincinnati, Ohio.

Fiske, S. T. (1982). Schema-triggered affect: Applications to social perception. In M. S. Clark & S. T. Fiske (Eds.), *The seventeenth annual Carnegie symposium on cognition* (pp. 55–78). Hillsdale, NJ: Erlbaum.

Fiske, S. T. (1988). Compare and contrast: Brewer's Dual Process Model and Fiske *et al.'s* Continuum Model. In T. S. Srull & R. S. Wyer, Jr. (Eds.), *Advances in social cognition: Vol. I: A dual process model of impression formation* (pp. 65–76). Hillsdale, NJ: Erlbaum.

Fiske, S. T., & Neuberg, S. L. (1990). A continuum of impression formation, from category-based to individuating processes: Influences of information and motivation on attention and interpretation. In M. Zanna (Ed.), *Advances in experimental social psychology* (Vol. 23, pp. 1–74). Orlando, FL: Academic Press.

Fowler, C. A., Wolford, G., Slade, R., & Tassinary, L. (1981). Lexical access with and without awareness. *Journal of Experimental Psychology: General, 110,* 341–362.

Gaertner, S. L., & Dovidio, J. F. (1986). The aversive form of racism. In J. F. Dovidio & S. L. Gaertner (Eds.), *Prejudice, discrimination, and racism* (pp. 61–89). Orlando, FL: Academic Press.

Gaertner, S. L., Dovidio, J. F., Anastasio, P. A., Bachman, B. A., & Rust, M. C. (1993). The common ingroup identity model: Recategorization and the reduction of intergroup bias. In W. Stroebe & M. Hewstone (Eds.), *European Review of Social Psychology, 4.*

Gaertner, S. L., & McLaughlin, J. P. (1983). Racial stereotypes: Associations and ascriptions of positive and negative characteristics. *Social Psychology Quarterly, 46,* 23–30.

Gaertner, S. L., Mann, J. Murrell, A., & Dovidio, J. F. (1989). Reduction of intergroup bias: The benefits of recategorization. *Journal of Personality and Social Psychology, 57,* 239–249.

Gaertner, S. L., Mann, J., Dovidio, J. F., Murrell, A., & Pomare, M. (1990). How does cooperation reduce intergroup bias? *Journal of Personality and Social Psychology, 59,* 692–704.

Greenwald, A. G. (1992). New look 3: Unconscious cognition reclaimed. *American Psychologist, 47,* 766–779.

Hamilton, D. L. (Ed.). (1981). *Cognitive processes in stereotyping and intergroup behavior.* Hillsdale, NJ: Erlbaum.

Hamilton, D. L. (1991). *Perceiving persons and groups: A social cognitive perspective.* Invited address presented at the American Psychological Convention, San Francisco, California.

Hewstone, M., Jaspers, J., & Lalljee, M. (1982). Social representations, social attribution, and social identity: The intergroup images of "public" and "comprehensive" schoolboys. *European Journal of Social Psychology, 12,* 241–269.

Hewstone, M., Bond, M. H., & Wan, K. (1983). Social facts and social attributions: The explanation of intergroup differences in Hong Kong. *Social Cognition, 2,* 142–157.

Higgins, E. T., & Bargh, J. A. (1987). Social cognition and social perception. *Annual Review of Psychology, 38,* 369–425.

Hogg, M. A., & Turner, J. C. (1987). Intergroup behaviour, self-stereotyping, and the salience of social categories. *British Journal of Social Psychology, 26,* 325–340.

Holtz, R. (1989). *New and old group members and the locus of intergroup bias: Evidence for in-group favoritism and out-group derogation.* Paper presented at the 61st Annual Meeting of the Midwestern Psychological Association, Chicago.

Howard, J. M., & Rothbart, M. (1980). Social categorization for in-group and out-group behavior. *Journal of Personality and Social Psychology, 38,* 301–310.

Karlins, M., Coffman, T. L., & Walters, G. (1969). On the fading of social stereotypes: Studies in three generations of college students. *Journal of Personality and Social Psychology, 13,* 1–16.

Katz, D., & Braly, K. W. (1933). Racial stereotypes of 100 college students. *Journal of Abnormal and Social Psychology, 28,* 280–290.

Kihlstrom, J. F., Cantor, N., Albright, J. S., Chew, B. R., Klein, S. B., & Niedenthal, P. M. (1988). Information processing and the study of the self. In L. Berkowitz (Ed.), *Advances in experimental social psychology* (pp. 145–180). Orlando, FL: Academic Press.

Klatzky, R. L., Martin, G. L., & Kane, R. A. (1982). Increase in social-category activation on processing of visual information. *Social Cognition, 1,* 95–109.

Kulik, J. (1983). Confirmatory attribution and the perpetuation of social beliefs. *Journal of Personality and Social Psychology, 44,* 1171–1181.

McArthur, L. Z., & Baron, R. M. (1983). Toward an ecological theory of social perception. *Psychological Review, 90,* 215–238.

McConahay, J. B. (1986). Modern racism, ambivalence, and the Modern Racism Scale. In J. F. Dovidio & S. L. Gaertner (Eds.), *Prejudice, discrimination, and racism* (pp. 91–125). Orlando, FL: Academic Press.

McConahay, J. B., & Hough, J. C., Jr. (1976). Symbolic racism. *Journal of Social Issues, 32,* 23–45.

McGarty, C., & Penny, R. (1988). Categorization, accentuation, and social judgment. *British Journal of Social Psychology, 27,* 147–157.

Messick, D. M., & Mackie, D. M. (1989). Intergroup relations. In M. R. Rosenweig & L. W. Porter (Eds.), *Annual Review of Psychology, 40,* 45–82.

Meyer, D. E., & Schvaneveldt, R. W. (1971). Facilitation in recognizing pairs of words: Evidence of dependence between retrieval operations. *Journal of Experimental Psychology, 90,* 227–234.

Miller, N., Brewer, M. B., & Edwards, K. (1985). Cooperative interaction in desegregated settings: A laboratory analog. *Journal of Social Issues, 41,* 63–75.

Mullen, B., & Hu, L. T. (1989). Perceptions of ingroup and outgroup variability: A meta-analytic integration. *Basic and Applied Social Psychology, 10,* 233–252.

Park, B., & Rothbart, M. (1982). Perception of outgroup homogeneity and levels of social categorization: Memory for the subordinate attributes of ingroup and outgroup members. *Journal of Personality and Social Psychology, 42,* 1050–1068.

Perdue, C. W., & Gurtman, M. B. (1990). Evidence for the automaticity of ageism. *Journal of Experimental Social Psychology, 26,* 199–216.

Perdue, C. W., Dovidio, J. F., Gurtman, M. B., & Tyler, R. B. (1990). "Us" and "Them": Social categorization and the process of intergroup bias. *Journal of Personality and Social Psychology, 59,* 475–486.

Piliavin, J. A., Dovidio, J. F., Gaertner, S. L., & Clark, R. D., III (1981). *Emergency intervention.* New York: Academic Press.

Pryor, J. B., & Ostrom, T. M. (1981). The cognitive organization of social information: A converging operations approach. *Journal of Personality and Social Psychology, 41,* 628–641.

Rabbie, J. M. (1982). The effects of intergroup competition and cooperation on intragroup and intergroup relationships. In V. J. Derlega & J. Grzelak (Eds.), *Cooperation and helping behavior: Theories and research* (pp. 123–149). New York: Academic Press.

Rosenbaum, M. E., & Holtz, R. (1985). *The minimal intergroup discrimination effect: Outgroup derogation, not in-group favoritism.* Paper presented at the 93rd Annual Convention of the American Psychological Association, Los Angeles.

Rothbart, M., Fulero, S., Jensen, C., Howard, J., & Birrell, P. (1978). From individuating to group impressions: Availability heuristics in stereotype formation. *Journal of Experimental Social Psychology, 14,* 237–255.

Sagar, H. A., & Schofield, J. W. (1980). Racial and behavioral cues in black and white children's perceptions of ambiguously aggressive acts. *Journal of Personality and Social Psychology, 39,* 590–598.

Sears, D. O. (1988). Symbolic racism. In P. Katz & D. Taylor (Eds.), *Towards the elimination of racism: Profiles in controversy* (pp. 53–84). New York: Plenum.

Secord, P. F. (1959). Stereotyping and favorableness in the perception of Negro faces. *Journal of Abnormal and Social Psychology, 59,* 309–321.

Shiffrin, R. M., & Dumais, S. T. (1981). The development of automatism. In J. R. Anderson (Ed.), *Cognitive skills and their acquisition.* Hillsdale, NJ: Erlbaum.

Smith, E. R., & Branscombe, N. R. (1986). *Stereotypes can be processed automatically.* Unpublished manuscript, Purdue University, Lafayette, Indiana.

Staats, A. W. (1968). *Language, learning, and cognition.* NY: Holt, Rinehart & Winston.

Staats, A. W., & Staats, C. K. (1958). Attitudes established by conditioning. *Journal of Abnormal and Social Psychology, 57,* 74–80.

Staats, C. K., & Staats, A. W. (1975). Meaning established by classical condition. *Journal of Experimental Psychology, 54,* 496–501.

Stein, D. D., Hardyck, J. A., & Smith, M. B. (1965). Race *and* belief: An open and shut case. *Journal of Personality and Social Psychology, 1,* 281–299.

Tajfel, H. (1970). Experiments in intergroup discrimination. *Scientific American, 233,* 96–102.

Tajfel, H., Flament, C., Billig, M. G., & Bundy, R. F. (1971). Social categorisation: An intergroup phenomenon. *European Journal of Social Psychology, 1,* 149–177.

Taylor, D. M., & Jaggi, V. (1974). Ethnocentrism and causal attribution in a South Indian context. *Journal of Cross-Cultural Psychology, 5,* 162–171.

Wang, H., & McKillip, J. (1978). Ethnic identification and judgements of an accident. *Personality and Social Psychology Bulletin, 4,* 296–299.

Wilder, D. A. (1981). Perceiving persons as a group: Categorization and intergroup relations. In D. L. Hamilton (Ed.), *Cognitive processes in stereotyping and intergroup behavior* (pp. 213–257). Hillsdale, NJ: Erlbaum.

Wyer, R. S., Jr., & Gordon, S. E. (1984). The cognitive representation of social information. In R. S. Wyer, Jr. & T. K. Srull (Eds.), *The handbook of social cognition* (Vol. 2, pp. 73–150). Hillsdale, NJ: Erlbaum.

Wyer, R. S., Jr., & Srull, T. K. (1989). *Memory and cognition in its social context.* Hillsdale, NJ: Erlbaum.

Zarate, M. A., & Smith, E. E. (1990). Person categorization and stereotyping. *Social Cognition, 8,* 161–185.

Chapter 9

Mere Exposure Effects with Outgroup Stimuli

ROBERT F. BORNSTEIN
Department of Psychology
Gettysburg College
Gettysburg, Pennsylvania

Introduction

On occasion, people find themselves in situations wherein they are repeatedly exposed to another person yet—for any of a variety of reasons—they do not have the opportunity to interact directly with that person. Anyone who has commuted to work via public transportation has probably had this type of experience. Each morning, as the commuter arrives at the bus or train stop, she encounters many of the same people. At first, the commuter probably has few feelings—either positive or negative—regarding her fellow travelers. However, over time, the commuter may find that she views her fellow commuters more favorably than she did initially. They are a predictable part of her commuting experience. They are familiar, and may even come to be regarded as "friends." A fellow commuter's presence at the bus or train stop comes to be expected and anticipated, and oddly enough, they may even be missed if they fail to appear one morning. Strangest of all, as anyone who has had this experience knows, this complex affective and attitudinal shift often takes place without any direct interaction whatsoever between the commuters.

Common experiences such as the one just described led Zajonc (1968) to hypothesize that repeated, unreinforced exposure is sufficient to enhance one's attitude toward a stimulus, object, or person (see Zajonc, 1968 for a detailed discussion of anecdotal evidence bearing on the exposure-affect relationship). This phenomenon has come to be known as the "mere exposure effect." Since the publication of Zajonc's seminal paper, there have been more than 200 published experiments examining parameters of the mere exposure effect. Furthermore, as Stang (1974) noted, numerous studies conducted before Zajonc formalized (and named) the exposure effect also evaluated the hypothesis that repeated exposure to a stimulus is sufficient to enhance one's attitude toward it. Thus, there now exists a large body of published research testing directly Zajonc's exposure effect hypothesis (see Bornstein, 1989; Harrison, 1977; Stang, 1974 for reviews). The exposure effect has proven to be a robust and reliable phenomenon; a variety of stimuli, exposure conditions, and rating procedures produce strong mere exposure effects.

Of course, Zajonc's (1968) hypotheses regarding the exposure effect were not based entirely on anecdotal evidence. In fact, his hypotheses were derived in part from earlier research on the effects of exposure on interracial attitudes (e.g., Cook & Selltiz, 1952; Deutsch & Collins, 1951; MacKenzie, 1948; Wilner, Walkley & Cook, 1952). In many of these early studies, researchers found that increased contact with members of other ethnic groups enhanced individuals' attitudes toward those groups. Although there are several viable explanations for these results (e.g., attitude enhancement in these studies might have been due to reinforcement derived from pleasant social interaction rather than from "mere" exposure), it is not surprising that early studies in this area led researchers to hypothesize that exposure effects have potential value as a tool for the reduction of prejudice against members of outgroups.

Although Zajonc's (1968) paper on the "attitudinal effects of mere exposure" created a great deal of interest in the mere exposure effect, not all researchers accepted uncritically Zajonc's notion that mere exposure, in and of itself, was sufficient to enhance attitudes toward members of other racial and ethnic groups. When Amir (1969) examined the empirical literature on the effects of intergroup contact on ethnic relations, his conclusions regarding the potential value of "mere exposure" as a tool for prejudice and stereotype reduction were quite different from those drawn by Zajonc. Amir argued that exposure to members of other ethnic groups enhanced attitudes toward those ethnic groups only under certain conditions.

Specifically, Amir (1969) suggested that intergroup contact was likely to result in more favorable attitudes toward members of the outgroup when intergroup contact (1) involved individuals of comparable social status, or when the minority group members were of higher status than the majority group members; (2) was voluntary, socially sanctioned, and encouraged or reinforced by group leaders; (3) was intimate rather than casual, and involved cooperation rather than competition; and (4) was pleasant and constructive rather than tension laden or uncomfortable. Thus, Amir concluded that intergroup exposure under favorable conditions enhances the attitudes of individuals toward members of other ethnic groups, while intergroup contact under unfavorable conditions produces more negative intergroup attitudes.

There have been relatively few studies of exposure effects involving stimuli that are presented under unfavorable conditions. However, the results of these studies tend to support the hypotheses of Zajonc (1968) more strongly than they support those of Amir (1969). For example, there have been several studies of exposure effects involving simple (i.e., nonsocial) stimuli that are disliked (e.g., Brickman, Redfield, Harrison & Crandall, 1972; Imamoglu, 1974), or even feared (Litvak, 1969). These studies suggest that exposure under unfavorable conditions can produce significant attitude enhancement. Moreover, there have been several studies of exposure effects involving social stimuli (Brickman, Meyer & Fredd, 1975; Brockner & Swap, 1976; Pheterson & Horai, 1976; Saegert, Swap, & Zajonc, 1973; Shuntich, 1976; Swap, 1977) which also suggest that attitude enhancement can occur under less than optimal conditions (e.g., when contact occurs between individuals of unequal status, when contact involves competition rather than cooperation, or when contact takes place in an unpleasant context).

The (1973) study by Saegert *et al.* illustrates the robustness of mere exposure effects for social stimuli even under unpleasant conditions. In two separate experiments, Saegert *et al.* exposed undergraduate women to varying numbers of encounters with unfamiliar women who served as "stimulus persons." Exposure took place in the guise of a taste preference study, which afforded the experimenters a cover story for the "pleasant" and "unpleasant" context conditions in which stimulus persons were encountered. For each subject, half the stimulus persons were encountered under "pleasant" conditions, in which the subject was asked to taste and rate solutions of Kool-Aid. Half the stimulus persons were encountered under "unpleasant" conditions, in which the subject tasted and rated weak solutions of vinegar, quinine, and citric acid. Following each experiment, subjects completed a General Information Questionnaire which asked—among other things—for the subject's rating of each stimulus person on a 7-point like–dislike scale. Saegert *et al.* found that the context in which stimulus persons were encountered had no effect on liking ratings. Under both "pleasant" and "unpleasant" conditions, liking ratings of stimulus persons increased with increasing exposure frequency.

The findings reported by Saegert *et al.* (1973) and others suggest that mere exposure effects may have value as a tool for enhancing people's attitudes toward members of outgroups. After all, if repeated, unreinforced exposure to an unfamiliar person under unpleasant conditions enhances subjects' attitudes toward that person, the exposure effect for social stimuli must be robust indeed (cf. Amir, 1969). Moreover, if mere exposure effects enhance subjects' attitudes toward social stimuli that are initially disliked (e.g., Brickman *et al.*, 1975; Swap, 1977), it is possible that exposure effects can enhance subjects' attitudes toward members of outgroups, who tend to be evaluated negatively by ingroup members on a variety of rating dimensions (see Snyder, 1980; Tajfel, 1969, 1970; Wilder, 1981).

The purpose of this paper is to evaluate the potential of the mere exposure effect as a tool for stereotype and prejudice reduction. Specifically, I review research that tests—directly or indirectly—the hypothesis that repeated, unreinforced exposure to members of an outgroup is sufficient to enhance subjects' attitudes toward that outgroup. The review proceeds in several steps. First, I briefly discuss the processes underlying the mere exposure effect, in order to place the ensuing review of the empirical literature in context. I then review research on mere exposure effects with outgroup stimuli and report some meta-analytic findings wherein the relative magnitudes of the mere exposure effect produced by ingroup and outgroup stimuli are compared. Next, I use the results of research on exposure effects with outgroup stimuli to draw some tentative conclusions regarding the potential of mere exposure effects as a tool for stereotype and prejudice reduction. Finally, I offer some suggestions for future research on mere exposure effects with outgroup stimuli.

Processes Underlying the Mere Exposure Effect

Zajonc (1980, 1984) hypothesized that mere exposure effects represent an example of a "pure" affective response to an external stimulus—"pure" in the sense that, in Zajonc's view, mere exposure effects occur with little or no intervening cognitive activity. In support of this hypothesis, Zajonc reviewed research on affective responses to repeated, unreinforced stimulus exposures, focusing primarily on two sets of findings. First, Zajonc argued that experiments demonstrating the existence of subliminal mere exposure effects (e.g., Kunst-Wilson & Zajonc, 1980) offered strong support for the hypothesis that higher-level cognitive processes are not involved in the production of the exposure effect (see Zajonc, 1984, for a detailed discussion of this position). Second, Zajonc discussed neuroanatomical evidence which suggested that affective responding to familiarized stimuli may be mediated by a direct pathway from reticular formation to hypothalamus, a pathway which bypassed completely those areas of the cerebral cortex that mediate conscious cognitive activity.

Zajonc's (1980, 1984) speculations regarding the neuroanatomical pathways that are involved in producing the mere exposure effect remain just that, speculations. There have been no direct tests of Zajonc's formulations in this area. However, a great deal of research has been conducted which addresses Zajonc's hypotheses regarding the role of affective and cognitive processes in the mere exposure effect. The results of this research do not support Zajonc's hypothesis that the mere exposure effect represents a purely affective response to an external stimulus. Rather, studies in this area demonstrate that—contrary to Zajonc's assertions—cognitive processes are critical in the production of mere exposure effects.

A detailed review of studies which demonstrate that extensive cognitive processing of a stimulus is required for the production of the mere exposure effect is beyond the scope of this chapter. Bornstein (1989, 1992) has discussed these experiments and their implications in some detail. However, in the present context, three implications of these studies warrant mention. First, findings from studies of subliminal mere exposure effects confirm that although conscious awareness of stimulus content is not required for the production of the exposure effect (Bornstein, Leone & Galley, 1987), considerable cognitive activity nonetheless mediates the exposure effect (see Harrison, 1977; Lazarus, 1984). Second, the results of several experiments demonstrate that implicit learning mediates the exposure effect (see Bornstein, 1989; Gordon & Holyoak, 1983). Third, studies indicate that an attribution process is involved in generating affect ratings of merely exposed stimuli under a variety of experimental conditions (see Bornstein, 1992; Mandler, Nakamura & Van Zandt, 1987).

Taken together, findings from studies of the affective and cognitive processes involved in generating the mere exposure effect suggest that the exposure effect results from a reduction in "response competition" which follows repeated, unreinforced stimulus exposures. The mechanism by which a reduction in response competition produces increased liking for a merely exposed stimulus is as follows. First, an unfamiliar stimulus evokes a large number of competing responses (e.g., curiosity, surprise, interest, apprehension). This results in an unpleasant state of arousal, as the individual attempts to select the most appropriate response to the stimulus from among a large number of competing responses. As a subject is repeatedly exposed to a stimulus, however, certain responses become strengthened while others weaken. Specifically, as the stimulus proves to be nonthreatening, negative responses to the stimulus (e.g., fear) weaken, while more positive responses (e.g., interest) are strengthened, at least temporarily (Bornstein, Kale, & Cornell, 1990). Consequently, the subject comes to like the stimulus better. Thus, although the end result of repeated, unreinforced stimulus exposures is, as Zajonc (1968, 1980, 1984) hypothesized, a more positive affective response to the stimulus, considerable cognitive activity is involved in generating this affective response.

Implicit in the response competition model of the mere exposure effect is a second, related notion: The reduction of response competition that accompanies repeated, unreinforced exposure to a stimulus involves disconfirmation of negative expectancies regarding that stimulus. Consider, for example, a subject in a typical laboratory mere exposure experiment. Despite the experimenter's reassurances, the subject is unsure as to the "real" purpose of the experiment, and is a bit worried about what will happen to her during the course of the study. Thus, as stimulus exposures begin, many competing responses are elicited in the subject, and some of these responses are quite negative (e.g., fear). However, as stimulus exposures continue, it becomes apparent that the stimulus is harmless. The subject's negative expectancies regarding the stimulus are disconfirmed, negative responses to the stimulus weaken, and the subject's attitude toward the now familiar stimulus becomes more positive.

A similar process occurs in mere exposure effect experiments involving social stimuli, even when these experiments take place in field settings. In these situations, initial exposure to an unfamiliar person elicits a large number of competing responses, some of which are positive (e.g., interest), and some of which are negative (e.g., anxiety and apprehension). As the subject is repeatedly exposed to that person and the person turns out to be harmless (or even pleasant), negative expectancies are disconfirmed, and the subject comes to like the person better. The mere exposure effect has occurred.

The fact that disconfirmation of negative expectancies plays an important role in the exposure effect has implications for research on exposure effects with outgroup stimuli. Because outgroup stimuli initially tend to evoke more negative responses from subjects than do ingroup stimuli (see Brewer, 1979; Snyder, 1981), the expectancy disconfirmation model predicts that repeated, unreinforced exposure to outgroup stimuli will actually have stronger effects on attitudes and affective responses than will repeated, unreinforced exposure to ingroup stimuli. Thus, the expectancy disconfirmation model of the exposure effect predicts that exposure effects should be stronger for outgroup stimuli than for ingroup stimuli.

On the other hand, numerous studies have demonstrated that negative perceptions of outgroup members are particularly resistant to the effects of disconfirming evidence (see Hamilton, 1981; Rothbart, 1981). Consequently, negative attitudes regarding outgroup members can be very difficult to extinguish. These findings suggest that exposure effects should be stronger for ingroup stimuli than for outgroup stimuli.

Thus, the expectancy disconfirmation model of the mere exposure effect and studies of the persistence of negative perceptions of outgroup members lead to opposite predictions regarding the effectiveness of mere exposure as a tool for prejudice reduction. Fortunately, it is possible to test these two hypotheses against one another. This requires only that one compare the magnitude of the mere exposure effect produced by ingroup stimuli to the magnitude of the exposure effect produced by outgroup stimuli. In the following sections, I (1) briefly review the studies conducted to date that have examined the exposure effect for outgroup stimuli; and (2) report the results of a meta-analytic comparison of the magnitude of the exposure effect produced by outgroup stimuli versus the magnitude of the exposure effect produced by ingroup stimuli. Following the review and meta-analysis, I discuss the theoretical and practical implications of these findings.

Exposure Effects Involving Outgroup Stimuli

Given researchers' long-standing interest in the potential of exposure effects as a tool for prejudice and stereotype reduction (Harrison, 1977; Stang, 1974), one might expect that numerous experiments examining exposure effects for outgroup stimuli would have been conducted during the past two decades. In fact, researchers have paid surprisingly little attention to this issue. To date, there have been only six published studies investigating exposure effects with outgroup stimuli. Two general strategies have been used in these studies. Harrison (1969) used a correlational approach and several researchers (Ball & Cantor, 1974; Cantor, 1972; Hamm, Baum & Nikels, 1975; Perlman & Oskamp, 1971; Zajonc, Markus & Wilson, 1974) used experimental designs. Correlational and experimental data bearing on the exposure-affect relationship for outgroup stimuli will be considered separately.

Correlational Findings

Harrison (1969) examined the relationship between frequency of exposure to the names of various religious, political, ethnic, and occupational groups, and subjects' attitudes toward members of those groups. Within each category, Harrison found a positive correlation between exposure frequency and rated likability for members of that social group. Exposure-likability correlations ranged from .20 (for ethnic group names) to .56 (for names of political groups), with the mean exposure-likability correlation being .28. Harrison interpreted his findings to suggest that frequency of exposure may play a significant role in enhancing subjects' attitudes regarding different social groups.

Unfortunately, there is at least one serious problem with Harrison's (1969) interpretation of these results: Harrison's correlational data provided no information regarding possible causal relationships between exposure and rated likability. It is possible, as Harrison suggests, that exposure leads to increased liking for members of different groups. However, an equally tenable interpretation of these data is that subjects become familiar with members of groups about which they already have positive attitudes. Stronger conclusions regarding the exposure-affect relationship for outgroup stimuli may be drawn from the results of experimental studies of this issue.

Experimental Findings

Two experiments examined exposure effects for outgroup stimuli using children as subjects. These experiments used similar procedures and produced highly consistent results. Both Cantor (1972), and Ball and Cantor (1974) assessed the effects of stimulus exposure frequency on white children's evaluative ratings of photographs of black and white children. The child subjects in both experiments came from midwestern public schools with very few black students. In the first of these experiments, Cantor exposed a mixed-sex sample of white elementary school children to ten brief presentations of each of six photographs. Three photographs depicted black children, and three photographs depicted white children. Following exposure to all the photographs, the subjects were asked to rate each black child—as well as three unfamiliar black children—for the "degree to which they'd like to bring the child home."

Cantor (1972) found that familiarized black children were rated significantly more positively than were nonfamiliarized black children. In fact, there was a 12% increase in favorability ratings of the black children following less than two minutes of exposure to each photograph. A comparable increase in ratings was not found for photographs of white children. Ball and Cantor (1974) subsequently replicated and extended this finding using a new subject sample. Consistent with Cantor's earlier findings, Ball and Cantor found that familiarized photograph stimuli received significantly more positive ratings than nonfamiliarized stimuli only when the child depicted in the photograph was black. Again, mere exposure produced a 12% increase in evaluative ratings of outgroup stimuli. However, consistent with Cantor's results, Ball and Cantor found that ratings of white children were unrelated to exposure frequency.

Hamm et al. (1975) took a different approach to examining exposure effects with outgroup stimuli. Two experiments comprised this study. In their first experiment, Hamm et al. asked a mixed-sex sample of white college students to rate yearbook photographs of black and white college graduates for the degree to which they viewed the person pictured in the photograph "favorably." Following the initial ratings, half the subjects were exposed to ten repetitions of each photograph, while the remaining subjects performed an unrelated filler task. All subjects then provided follow-up ratings of the photographs. Hamm et al. found that—regardless of the race of the person pictured in the photograph—repeated exposures enhanced favorability ratings; subjects in the "exposure" condition showed a significant increase in favorability ratings of both black and white stimuli from pretest to posttest, while control subjects (who engaged in the filler task) showed no increase in ratings for either type of stimulus.

To extend their initial results, Hamm et al. (1975, Experiment 2) conducted a follow-up experiment in which initial favorability ratings of the photograph stimuli was treated as an independent variable. In this experiment, only photographs of black men were used, and each photograph was classified into either a "high favorability" or "low favorability" group based on pilot subjects' ratings. Consistent with the results of their first experiment, Hamm *et al.* found a significant increase in favorability ratings from pretest to posttest only for subjects in the "exposure" condition; subjects who engaged in an unrelated distractor task showed no change in favorability ratings of the photographs from pretest to posttest. Furthermore, repeated exposure enhanced favorability ratings of both the high- and low-favorability photographs. Not only does mere exposure enhance evaluative ratings of outgroup stimuli in college student subjects, but the initial favorability of the outgroup stimulus appears to not affect the magnitude of the change in these evaluative ratings that follows repeated, unreinforced exposure.

Along slightly different lines, Perlman and Oskamp (1971) examined the influence of context on the exposure effect with outgroup stimuli. In this study, white college students were shown a series of photographs of black and white men, with different photographs presented at different exposure frequencies. Photographs depicted the stimulus persons in one of three contexts: (1) positive (e.g., posing as an executive or a clergyman); (2) neutral (i.e., with no clues regarding social status or profession); or (3) negative (e.g., posing as a janitor or a prison inmate). Following stimulus exposures, subjects rated each stimulus person on a series of 7-point scales, with each scale indicating the degree to which the stimulus person was perceived as having a particular trait. Five categories of trait ratings were included in Perlman and Oskamp's experiment: (1) general evaluative traits (e.g., likable); (2) "positive" racial stereotypes (e.g., musical); (3) negative racial stereotypes (e.g., lazy); (4) positive nonstereotypes (e.g., forgiving); and (5) negative nonstereotypes (e.g., faultfinding).

Perlman and Oskamp (1971) found that—for both black and white stimulus persons—repeated exposure enhanced subjects' evaluative ratings across all rating categories only when the stimulus person was depicted in a positive or neutral context. Furthermore, the exposure effect was stronger when the stimulus person was depicted in a positive context than when the stimulus person was depicted in a neutral context. For both black and white stimulus persons, a slight decrease in evaluative ratings with increasing exposure frequency was found when the stimulus person was depicted in a negative context. There were no main effects or interactions involving race of stimulus person in Perlman and Oskamp's experiment.

Although Zajonc *et al.* (1974) used different stimuli and rating procedures than those of Perlman and Oskamp (1971), they obtained results that were similar to those found in the earlier study in one important respect: stronger exposure effects were obtained in a "positive context" condition than were obtained in a "negative context" condition. In the experiments by Zajonc *et al.* groups of white college students viewed photographs of Chinese men presented at different exposure frequencies, following which the subjects were asked to rate each stimulus person on a series of evaluative dimensions (e.g., like–dislike, honest–dishonest). In each experiment, half the subjects were told that the photographs depicted "famous scientists and scholars" (the "positive context" condition), and the remaining subjects were told that the photographs depicted "men who have committed serious crimes" (the "negative context" condition).

Because the different evaluative dimensions used in these experiments produced similar patterns of results, Zajonc *et al.* (1974) combined these dimensions into a single composite rating. In both experiments, subjects gave more positive ratings overall to stimulus persons in the "positive context" condition than to stimulus persons in the "negative context" condition. In addition, evaluative ratings of stimulus persons in the "positive context" condition showed a more rapid increase with increasing exposure frequency than did evaluative ratings of stimulus persons in the "negative context" condition. Thus, consistent with the findings of Perlman and Oskamp (1971), Zajonc *et al.*'s results suggest that the context in which an outgroup member is encountered may influence the degree to which exposure effects can enhance attitudes toward that person.

The Relative Magnitudes of Ingroup and Outgroup Mere Exposure Effects

As noted earlier, the expectancy disconfirmation model predicts that outgroup stimuli should produce stronger mere exposure effects than ingroup stimuli, while research on the persistence of negative attitudes toward outgroup members leads to the opposite prediction. In this section, I report the results of a meta-analytic comparison of the magnitude of the exposure effect produced by outgroup stimuli versus the magnitude of the exposure effect produced by ingroup stimuli.

Bornstein (1989) conducted a meta-analysis assessing the magnitude of the mere exposure effect in all published experiments examining the exposure-affect relationship. He found that—across all 208 published mere exposure experiments—the mean correlation between frequency of exposure and subjects' affect or attitude ratings of a stimulus was .26. Using the procedures described by Rosenthal (1984), it was possible to derive an overall effect size for studies of the mere exposure effect that employed outgroup stimuli, again using the effect size estimate r to represent the magnitude of the exposure-affect relationship. This effect size was computed by first converting whatever outcome statistic was used in a particular study (F, t, etc.) into a correlation coefficient. A combined (average) effect size was then calculated by transforming each r into a Fisher's Z coefficient, obtaining the sum of the Fisher's Zs, dividing the sum by the number of effect sizes that was used to obtain it, and converting the resulting Z back into an r (see Bornstein, 1989, for a detailed discussion of the procedures used to derive effect size estimates in mere exposure experiments).

The six studies of exposure effects for outgroup stimuli that were described in the previous section yielded a total of eight separate effect sizes [the Hamm *et al.* (1975) and Zajonc *et al.* (1974) studies each reported two experiments]. These eight effect sizes produced a mean exposure-affect correlation of .36 (which, parenthetically, is nearly 40% larger than the average effect size for all mere exposure experiments).

To compare directly the relative magnitudes of ingroup versus outgroup mere exposure effects, I derived an overall effect size estimate for all mere exposure experiments that used ingroup stimuli, employing the same procedures that were used to calculate the overall effect size for exposure effect studies that used outgroup stimuli. There are 24 such experiments in the published literature. These experiments are described in detail by Bornstein (1989). Although the majority of these experiments used photographs of ingroup members as stimuli, a few studies used actual persons (i.e., experimental confederates) as stimuli. The mean exposure-affect correlation obtained in the 24 mere exposure studies that used ingroup stimuli was .23. Thus, exposure effects for outgroup stimuli (where, as noted earlier, the mean r was .36) are more than 50% larger than are the exposure effects produced by ingroup stimuli. A focused comparison of the effect sizes produced by mere exposure effect studies that used ingroup stimuli versus mere exposure effect studies that used outgroup stimuli (see Rosenthal, 1984, pp. 83–84) confirmed that the latter set of experiments produced a significantly larger mere exposure effect, $Z = 3.61$, $p = .0002$.

Exposure Effects with Outgroup Stimuli: Theoretical and Practical Implications

The experiments and meta-analytic results just described allow two general conclusions to be drawn regarding exposure effects with outgroup stimuli. First, the results of individual mere exposure experiments that used outgroup stimuli confirm that repeated, unreinforced exposure to an outgroup stimulus enhances attitudes toward that stimulus, at least in the short term. Second, consistent with the "disconfirmation of negative expectancies" model discussed earlier, the meta-analytic results just described indicate that mere exposure effects for outgroup stimuli are significantly larger than are mere exposure effects produced by ingroup stimuli.

The aforementioned experiments and meta-analytic results also allow three more narrow conclusions to be drawn regarding the exposure effect obtained with outgroup stimuli. First, it is clear that relatively little exposure to an outgroup stimulus is required to produce a robust exposure effect; typically, 1–2 minutes of exposure to an outgroup stimulus has proved sufficient to enhance evaluative ratings of that stimulus. Second, robust exposure effects for outgroup stimuli may be obtained with both child and adult subjects, and for both child and adult stimulus persons. Third, it appears that exposure effects produce changes in a wide variety of evaluative ratings of outgroup stimuli, including affect judgments (Zajonc *et al.*, 1974), reports of desire for future contact (Ball & Cantor, 1974), and trait ratings (Perlman & Oskamp, 1971).

Although the experimental and meta-analytic results described in the previous section confirm that repeated, unreinforced exposure to outgroup stimuli produces particularly strong exposure effects, this conclusion must be qualified in one important respect: the context in which outgroup stimuli are presented clearly influences the likelihood that mere exposure effects will be obtained. Both Perlman and Oskamp (1971) and Zajonc *et al.* (1974) found stronger exposure effects for outgroup stimuli presented in positive or neutral contexts than for outgroup stimuli presented in a negative context. Interestingly, the findings obtained by Perlman and Oskamp and Zajonc *et al.* support Amir's (1969) contention that contact with members of outgroups will produce more positive attitudes toward the outgroup members only when contact takes place in a positive (or at the very least, neutral) context. Contrary to Zajonc's (1968) hypothesis [and in contrast to the results obtained with simple stimuli that are initially disliked (see Bornstein, 1989; Harrison, 1977)] these results suggest that the context in which exposure takes place may significantly affect the likelihood of obtaining mere exposure effects with outgroup stimuli.

Of course, in interpreting the results of these investigations and applying these findings to broader questions regarding the role of exposure effects in stereotype and prejudice reduction, it is important to keep in mind the limitations of the experiments conducted thus far. For example, all experiments assessing the exposure effect with outgroup stimuli used photographs of outgroup members during both the familiarization and rating procedures. The extent to which findings from these studies generalize to actual persons is open to question. Similarly, the degree to which repeated exposure to one or several members of an outgroup produces attitude change toward other outgroup members (i.e., the extent to which exposure effects for individual outgroup stimuli generalize to other members of the outgroup) is an empirical question that has not been addressed. The extent to which outgroup mere exposure effects generalize from laboratory to field and from individual to group is, of course, a critical issue. If these findings do not generalize in both domains, the degree to which mere exposure effects have practical value as a tool for prejudice and stereotype reduction is, to say the least, limited.

One other methodological limitation of these experiments warrants mention: all studies conducted to date have collected attitude ratings immediately following exposure to the outgroup stimuli. Although exposure effects for simple, abstract stimuli can remain strong for periods of several weeks or more (Bornstein, 1989; Harrison, 1977), the extent to which exposure effects for outgroup stimuli may be obtained following a period of delay between stimulus exposures and ratings warrants further study. Again, this is a critical issue which must be addressed before strong conclusions may be drawn regarding the practical value of outgroup mere exposure effects.

Unfortunately, there have been no field experiments examining exposure effects with outgroup stimuli that would allow the interpretive limitations that characterize laboratory mere exposure experiments to be overcome. However, Hamilton and Bishop's (1976) well-known study of the effects of neighborhood integration on white residents' attitudes toward minority groups suggests that mere exposure effects may have some potential as a tool for prejudice reduction in naturalistic settings. Although Hamilton and Bishop's investigation does not meet the most stringent criteria for a mere exposure experiment (e.g., subjects in this study had the opportunity to interact directly with the families that moved into their neighborhoods; affect or attitude ratings of the new residents were not collected in this study), the results of this investigation nonetheless have important implications for understanding the role of "mere exposure" in prejudice and stereotype reduction in real settings.

Hamilton and Bishop (1976) interviewed white residents in 18 unintegrated neighborhoods into which new families were about to move. In eight of the neighborhoods, a black family was about to move in; in the other 10 neighborhoods, a white family was about to move in. Interviews were designed to obtain information regarding racial attitudes and attitudes toward social issues, and this information was used to derive a "symbolic racism" score for each family. Interviews were conducted four times with each family: (1) before the new residents arrived; (2) one month after the new residents moved in; (3) two months later; and (4) one year after the arrival of the new residents.

Numerous findings were obtained in this study, but in the present context, two results are particularly noteworthy. First, one year after the new families had moved in, individuals in integrated neighborhoods showed significantly lower "symbolic racism" scores than did residents of unintegrated neighborhoods. Second, "symbolic racism" scores were unrelated to the amount of contact that a resident had with the newly arrived family. Apparently, while exposure to new black residents in a formerly unintegrated neighborhood results in diminished racism among the white residents, the amount of face-to-face contact with the new black neighbors does not predict racism scores one year after neighborhood integration takes place. Just as the commuter may come to like her fellow travelers better over time, despite having had no real contact with the other commuters, residents of previously unintegrated neighborhoods can develop more positive attitudes regarding black neighbors (and minority group members in general) despite having had little or no direct contact with their new black neighbors.

In light of the fact that the amount of contact between white residents and their new black neighbors did not predict changes in prejudicial attitudes in Hamilton and Bishop's (1976) study, the source of prejudice reduction in this investigation must lie elsewhere. It seems likely that disconfirmation of white residents' negative expectancies regarding the effects of black families on the neighborhood's atmosphere and property values, for example, might in fact have been the most important factor underlying the white residents' attitudinal shift (see Hamilton & Bishop, 1976, p. 66, for a detailed discussion of this issue).

Conclusions

Researchers have described a number of strategies that are potentially useful in reducing prejudice toward members of outgroups. For example, Wilder (1981, 1986) argued that individuation of outgroup members will allow members of the ingroup to overcome stereotype-based perceptions by providing trait and behavioral information that supplants more global stereotype-based perceptions of outgroup persons. Along different lines, Sherif, Harvey, White, Hood and Sherif's (1961) classic work on the effects of cooperation on intergroup attitudes and behavior suggests that prejudice against outgroup members can be alleviated by forcing the ingroup and outgroup members to work together toward a common goal, thereby creating a new, inclusive ingroup (see also Allport, 1954). Devine (1989) has taken a different approach to this issue, suggesting that while long-held stereotypic beliefs regarding outgroup members may never be completely overcome, deliberate (i.e., effortful) inhibition of stereotype-based attitudes and behaviors is possible.

Research on mere exposure effects with outgroup stimuli suggests that repeated, unreinforced exposure to outgroup members might also prove useful as a tool for prejudice and stereotype reduction. Initial studies in this area, though few in number, are promising. In addition to suggesting that exposure effects may be useful in reducing prejudice toward outgroup members, these studies point to several important issues that remain unaddressed.

The most pressing issue in this area involves moving from highly artificial laboratory studies of exposure effects with outgroup stimuli to more naturalistic studies of this phenomenon. In a sense, this shift entails moving from basic to applied mere exposure research. Naturalistic studies would have the advantage of examining subjects' attitudes and/or behaviors toward familiar versus nonfamiliar outgroup persons in the setting where social contact between members of different ethnic and racial groups typically takes place. To the extent that actual behaviors can be assessed directly rather than relying on subjects' evaluative ratings of outgroup members, problems with self-report and self-presentation bias are likely to diminish (Crosby, Bromley & Saxe, 1980) and the ecological validity of mere exposure effect studies will increase.

It would also be useful to conduct mere exposure effect studies using artificially created outgroups, in order to examine the degree to which exposure effects are useful in enhancing attitudes toward members of long-standing cultural outgroups versus outgroups that have no cultural or historical basis (see, e.g., Tajfel & Billig, 1974; Tajfel, Billig, Bundy & Flament, 1971). Systematic manipulation of various parameters related to the origin and characteristics of outgroups would be possible within this context, and might prove useful in elucidating which characteristics of outgroups enhance or undermine the mere exposure effect.

Clearly, mere exposure in and of itself is not sufficient to reduce prejudice toward outgroup members in every situation. The 1971 results of Perlman and Oskamp and the 1974 Zajonc *et al.* findings demonstrate that negative context is a limiting condition on the exposure effect with outgroup stimuli. Beyond that, numerous real-world situations involving repeated exposure to members of other ethnic groups confirm that—although intergroup contact can sometimes lead to more positive attitudes toward members of the outgroup—this does not always happen. Contact between Israelis and Palestinians has hardly enhanced the attitudes of members of these groups toward each other. Similarly, as black and Asian residents in New York City increasingly come into contact, intergroup attitudes appear to grow more negative rather than more positive.

Thus, although Zajonc (1968) was correct in his assertion that, in general, mere exposure leads to more positive attitudes toward a stimulus, object, or person, Amir (1969) was also correct in his contention that there are numerous parameters that can interfere with such exposure effects when outgroup stimuli are involved. Despite the potential problems involved in applying exposure effects research in real-world settings, and the paucity of laboratory data examining exposure effects with outgroup stimuli, researchers should continue to explore this issue. As noted elsewhere (Bornstein, 1989), the possibility of using principles derived from mere exposure research to enhance the attitudes of different ethnic, religious, and cultural groups toward one another is too intriguing and potentially beneficial to ignore.

References

Allport, G. W. (1954). *The nature of prejudice*. Reading, MA: Addison-Wesley.

Amir, Y. (1969). Contact hypothesis in ethnic relations. *Psychological Bulletin, 71*, 319–342.

Ball, P. M., & Cantor, G. N. (1974). White boys' ratings of pictures of whites and blacks as related to amount of familiarization. *Perceptual and Motor Skills, 39*, 883–890.

Bornstein, R. F. (1989). Exposure and affect: Overview and meta-analysis of research, 1969–1987. *Psychological Bulletin, 106*, 265–289.

Bornstein, R. F. (1992). Subliminal mere exposure effects. In R. F. Bornstein and T. S. Pittman (Eds.) Perception without awareness: Cognitive, Clinical, and Social Perspectives. (pp. 191–210). New York, NY: Guilford Press.

Bornstein, R. F., Leone, D. R., & Galley, D. J. (1987). The generalizability of subliminal mere exposure effects: Influence of stimuli perceived without awareness on social behavior. *Journal of Personality and Social Psychology, 53*, 1070–1079.

Bornstein, R. F., Kale, A. R., & Cornell, K. R. (1990). Bordeom as a limiting condition on the mere exposure effect. *Journal of Personality and Social Psychology, 58*, 791–800.

Brewer, M. B. (1979). In-group bias in the minimal intergroup situation: A cognitive-motivational analysis. *Psychological Bulletin, 86*, 307–324.

Brickman, P., Redfield, J., Harrison, A., & Crandall, R. (1972). Drive and predisposition as factors in the attitudinal effects of mere exposure. *Journal of Experimental Social Psychology, 8*, 31–44.

Brickman, P., Meyer, P., & Fredd, S. (1975). Effects of varying exposure to another person with familiar or unfamiliar thought processes. *Journal of Experimental Social Psychology, 11*, 261–270.

Brockner, J., & Swap, W. C. (1976). Effects of repeated exposure and attitudinal similarity on self-disclosure and interpersonal attraction. *Journal of Personality and Social Psychology, 33*, 531–540.

Cantor, G. N. (1972). Effects of familiarization on childrens' ratings of pictures of blacks and whites. *Child Development, 43*, 1219–1229.

Cook, S. W., & Selltiz, C. (1952). *Contact and intergroup attitudes: Some theoretical considerations*. New York: Research Center for Human Relations.

Crosby, F., Bromley, S., & Saxe, L. (1980). Recent unobtrusive studies of black and white discrimination and prejudice: A literature review. *Psychological Bulletin, 87*, 546–563.

Deutsch, M., & Collins, M. E. (1951). *Interracial housing: A psychological evaluation of a social experiment*. Minneapolis: University of Minnesota Press.

Devine, P. G. (1989). Stereotypes and prejudice: Their automatic and controlled components. *Journal of Personality and Social Psychology, 56*, 5–18.

Gordon, P. C., & Holyoak, K. J. (1983). Implicit learning and generalization of the mere exposure effect. *Journal of Personality and Social Psychology, 45*, 492–500.

Hamilton, D. L. (1981). Illusory correlation as a basis for stereotyping. In D. L. Hamilton (Ed.), *Cognitive processes in stereotyping and intergroup behavior* (pp. 115–144). Hillsdale, NJ: Erlbaum.

Hamilton, D. L., & Bishop, G. D. (1976). Attitudinal and behavioral effects of initial integration of white suburban neighborhoods. *Journal of Social Issues, 32*, 47–67.

Hamm, N. H., Baum, M. R., & Nikels, K. W. (1975). Effects of race and exposure on judgments of interpersonal favorability. *Journal of Experimental Social Psychology, 11*, 14–24.

Harrison, A. A. (1969). Exposure and popularity. *Journal of Personality, 37*, 359–377.

Harrison, A. A. (1977). Mere exposure. In L. Berkowitz (Ed.), *Advances in experimental social psychology* (Vol. 10, pp. 39–83). New York: Academic Press.

Imamoglu, E. O. (19774). Initial evaluation of stimuli as another limiting condition of the exposure effect. *British Journal of Social and Clinical Psychology, 13*, 157–159.

Kunst-Wilson, W. R., & Zajonc, R. B. (1980). Affective discrimination of stimuli that cannot be recognized. *Science*, 207, 557–558.

Lazarus, R. L. (1984). On the primacy of cognition. *American Psychologist*, 39, 124–129.

Litvak, S. B. (1969). Attitude change by stimulus exposure. *Psychological Reports*, 25, 391–396.

MacKenzie, B. K. (1948). The importance of contact in determining attitudes toward negroes. *Journal of Abnormal and Social Psychology*, 43, 4.

Mandler, G., Nakamura, Y., & Van Zandt, B. J. (1987). Nonspecific effects of exposure to stimuli that cannot be recognized. *Journal of Experimental Psychology: Learning, Memory and Cognition*, 13, 646–648.

Perlman, D., & Oskamp, S. (1971). The effects of picture content and exposure frequency on evaluations of negroes and whites. *Journal of Experimental Social Psychology*, 7, 503–514.

Pheterson, M., & Horai, J. (1976). The effects of sensation seeking, physical attractiveness of stimuli and exposure frequency on liking. *Social Behavior and Personality*, 4, 241–247.

Rosenthal, R. (1984). *Meta-analytic procedures for social research*. Beverly Hills, CA: Sage.

Rothbart, M. (1981). Memory processes and social beliefs. In D. L. Hamilton (Ed.), *Cognitive processes in stereotyping and intergroup behavior* (pp. 145–182). Hillsdale, NJ: Erlbaum.

Saegert, S., Swap, W., & Zajonc, R. B. (1973). Exposure, context and interpersonal attraction. *Journal of Personality and Social Psychology*, 25, 234–242.

Sherif, M., Harvey, O. J., White, B. J., Hood, W. R., & Sherif, C. W. (1961). *Intergroup conflict and cooperation: The Robbers Cave experiment*. Norman, OK: University Book Exchange.

Shuntich, R. J. (1976). Some effects of attitudinal similarity and exposure on attraction and aggression. *Journal of Research in Personality*, 10, 155–165.

Snyder, M. (1981). On the self-perpetuating nature of social stereotypes. In D. L. Hamilton (Ed.), *Cognitive processes in stereotyping and intergroup behavior* (pp. 183–212). Hillsdale, NJ: Erlbaum.

Stang, D. J. (1974). Methodological factors in mere exposure research. *Psychological Bulletin*, 81, 1014–1025.

Swap, W. C. (1977). Interpersonal attraction and repeated exposure to rewarders and punishers. *Personality and Social Psychology Bulletin*, 3, 248–251.

Tajfel, H. (1969). Cognitive aspects of prejudice. *Journal of Social Issues*, 25, 79–94.

Tajfel, H. (1970). Experiments in intergroup discrimination. *Scientific American*, 223, 96–102.

Tajfel, H., & Billig, M. (1974). Familiarity and categorization in intergroup behavior. *Journal of Experimental Social Psychology*, 10, 159–170.

Tajfel, H., Billig, M., Bundy, R. P., & Flament, R. C. (1971). Social categorization and intergroup behavior. *European Journal of Social Psychology*, 1, 149–178.

Wilder, D. A. (1981). Perceiving persons as a group: Categorization and intergroup relations. In D. L. Hamilton (Ed.), *Cognitive processes in stereotyping and intergroup behavior* (pp. 213–258). Hillsdale, NJ: Erlbaum.

Wilder, D. A. (1986). Social categorization. In L. Berkowitz (Ed.), *Advances in experimental social psychology* (Vol. 19, pp. 291–355). New York: Academic Press.

Wilner, D. M., Walkley, R. P., & Cook, S. W. (1952). Residential proximity and intergroup relations in public housing projects. *Journal of Social Issues*, 8, 1.

Zajonc, R. B. (1968). Attitudinal effects of mere exposure. *Journal of Personality and Social Psychology Monograph*, 9 (2, Pt. 2), 1–27.

Zajonc, R. B. (1980). Feeling and thinking: Preferences need no inferences. *American Psychologist*, 35, 151–175.

Zajonc, R. B. (1984). On the primacy of affect. *American Psychologist*, 39, 117–123.

Zajonc, R. B., Markus, H., & Wilson, W. R. (1974). Exposure effects and associative learning. *Journal of Experimental Social Psychology*, 10, 248–263.

Chapter 10

Applications of Emotion Theory and Research to Stereotyping and Intergroup Relations

ERIC J. VANMAN and NORMAN MILLER
Department of Psychology
University of Southern California
Los Angeles, California

*Mind rarely, probably never, perceives any object with absolute in-
difference, that is, without feeling.*
　　　　　　　　—Sherrington, 1900, cited in Blumenthal, 1977

*Our judgments concerning the worth of things, big or little, depend
on the* feelings *the things arouse in us. Where we judge a thing to
be precious in consequence of the* idea *we frame of it, this is only
because the idea is itself associated already with a feeling.*
　　　　　　　　　　　　　　　　　　—James, 1915

Introduction

These statements by Sherrington and James have special relevance to
the field of intergroup relations. As Hamilton (1981) wrote, "if there is any
domain of human interaction that history tells us is laden with strong, even
passionate, feelings, it is in the area of intergroup relations" (p. 347). Gordon Allport (1954) described prejudice as "an antipathy based upon a
faulty and inflexible generalization. It may be felt or expressed" (p. 10).
Allport went on to speculate about distinct emotions that constitute this

213

antipathy: frustration, hatred, fear, anxiety, and jealousy. Yet little subsequent research in intergroup relations has focused on either affect or specific emotional components. The rise of the cognitive approach and its focus on information processing has certainly contributed to this vacuum. Tajfel (1969), at an early point, even argued that a cognitive approach was the only practical one: "a consideration of prejudice as a phenomenon in the minds rather than in the guts of men should take precedence over views which are, on the whole, not only untestable but also useless in the planning of any form of relevant social change" (p. 190).[1]

In contrast, like the other contributors to this volume, we believe that is is useful to consider the role of emotion and affect in stereotyping and intergroup relations. When we speak of *emotion*, we specifically refer to the differentiated states of positive and negative affect such as happiness, joy, anger, and fear. Although emotion theorists tend to disagree about a precise definition, most would describe emotions as "including appraisals or appreciations, patterned physiological processes, action tendencies, subjective feelings, expressions, and instrumental behaviors" (Fischer, Shaver, & Carnochan, 1990, p. 85). Thus, we consider emotion as more complex than *affect*, which we refer to as an overall positive/negative subjective feeling. For some, the latter defines attitude. Zanna and Rempel (1988) defined *attitude* as "the categorization of a stimulus object along an evaluative dimension" (p. 319). They proposed that cognition, past behavior, and emotion can each serve as independent sources of information for object evaluation. We thus consider emotions as a potential source of information upon which attitudes can be generated, rather than as a component of attitudes, as some attitude theorists have proposed (e.g., Rosenberg & Hovland, 1960).

Given the advances in social psychology made by concentrating on the cognitive bases of intergroup attitudes, how might the study of emotions enhance our understanding of intergroup relations and stereotyping? Specific emotions are associated with a limited number of general antecedents and related behaviors and are shared generally across situations and cultures. For example, fear is usually preceded by a stimulus that is considered dangerous and is typically followed by an escape behavior. This scriptlike nature of emotions (Russell, 1991) may reflect a set of emotion-specific circuits in the brain (see Panksepp, 1989, for a review). The identification of specific emotions that characterize aspects of intergroup relations may point to particular features of the situation that elicit those emotions. In addition, because the prediction of *behavior* toward others in intergroup settings is a core problem for this area of research, the study of emotions in

---

[1]Although Tajfel later incorporated motivational processes in his Social Identity Theory (e.g., Tajfel, 1978, 1981; Tajfel & Turner, 1979), we distinguish those processes (e.g., the need to maintain a positive social identity) from the emotional/affective processes that are the focus of this chapter.

such settings should improve behavioral prediction.

In support of this view, some theorists, when discussing the attitude-behavior relationship (e.g., Breckler & Wiggins, 1989; Zanna & Rempel, 1988), have proposed that emotions predict some behaviors better than more cognitive-based measures of attitudes. For instance, emotional responses elicited by a political candidate predict subjects' voting behavior better than do cognitions or beliefs about the candidate (Abelson, Kinder, Peters, & Fiske, 1982). As Millar and Tesser (1986) have suggested, behaviors for more instrumental purposes may be more cognitively driven (e.g., solving a puzzle to improve one's analytic ability), whereas behaviors performed for more noninstrumental purposes may be more emotionally driven (e.g., solving a puzzle simply to please oneself). Emotionally driven behaviors may therefore be better predicted by the specific emotions that are associated with them than by any related cognitions.[2] When subjects who solve puzzles for instrumental purposes focus on the cognitive basis of their attitude and those who solve puzzles for noninstrumental purposes focus on the emotional basis of theirs, the correlation between the evaluations of the puzzles and the time later spent in free-play with the puzzles is much higher than it is for those in which the emotional/cognitive focus is reversed (Millar & Tesser, 1986).

Exclusive consideration of the cognitive basis of intergroup attitudes also neglects the potential benefit of tailoring attempts to change attitudes to features of their initial source. Newer attitudes that primarily have emotional origins are more impervious to influence by persuasive appeals that rely on rational argumentation than those that are more affectively based (Edwards, 1990). By contrast, for well-established attitudes, those that are more cognitively based are more influenced by emotional appeals, whereas those that are more affectively based are more susceptible to rational appeals (Millar & Millar, 1990).

Clearly, a consideration of stereotyping and prejudice as "a phenomenon in the mind rather than in the guts" has its limits. In this chapter we urge that research on stereotyping and intergroup relations go beyond those limits by considering recent advances in theory, methodology, and research concerned with emotion. Doing so will increase and enrich our understanding of intergroup relations. After first briefly reviewing current emotion theory and methodology, we present a framework in which emotion research and theory can be integrated with phenomena associated with stereotyping and intergroup relations. Finally, we conclude with suggestions for expanding intergroup theory and research.

---

[2]We use the term *cognition* in this chapter generally to include appraisals, causal attributions, stereotypes, inferences, and categorizations, as well as other common usages of the word in psychology.

Emotion Theory and Methodology: A Brief Primer

Before addressing the specific role of emotions in intergroup relations, we review briefly general emotion theory and methodology.

Current Emotion Theory

During the past decade or so, reviewers of the emotion literature (e.g., Izard, 1989; Zajonc & Markus, 1984) have grouped the large number of emotion theories into two categories: (1) *appraisal* or *constructivist* theories, and (2) *biosocial* theories. These two broad categories differ mainly in the role they assign to cognition.

Appraisal theories generally propose that an emotion requires cognition in the form of appraisals (e.g., Frijda, 1986; Lazarus, 1991; Lazarus, Kanner, & Folkman, 1980; Mandler, 1984; Ortony, Clore, & Collins, 1988; Schachter, 1964). Appraisals are interpretations one makes of the significance of changes in the environment. Two people responding to the same stimulus will experience different emotions if they make different appraisals of it. For example, the presentation of a rare snake may elicit joy from a zoologist interested in reptiles, but may elicit great fear from one scared of snakes. Appraisal theories differ from one another mainly in terms of the specific dimensions they define as relevant for emotional appraisals. According to Lazarus (1991), the emotion that will be elicited by a situation is determined primarily by how the person appraises the event in terms of (1) goal relevance, (2) goal congruence, and (3) type of ego involvement. For example, anger is predicted to occur when there is goal relevance, goal incongruence, and when ego involvement is engaged to protect self- or social esteem. In addition, to be angry at another person, Lazarus proposes that one must make an appraisal of blame, based on the knowledge that the other person is accountable for the harmful actions. By comparison, Ortony *et al.* (1988) also specify three primary dimensions upon which an anger appraisal is made about an agent's actions: (1) whether the agent is self or other; (2) whether the action is approved or disapproved; and (3) whether the action affects personal well-being. Thus, according to Ortony *et al.*, anger will occur when the agent is other, the action is negatively evaluated, and the action affects personal well-being. Finally, some appraisal theorists (e.g., Schachter, 1964; Mandler, 1984; and Ortony *et al.*, 1988) propose that, for emotion to occur, physiological arousal must coexist with a cognition. The idea that arousal (operationalized as autonomic activation) is necessary has been present for at least 70 years (e.g., Marañon, 1924), and gained recent prominence with the 1964 publication of Schachter's theoretical formulation of the relationship between physiological arousal and the cognitive labeling of that arousal.

In contrast, biosocial theories generally propose that although cognition is sometimes sufficient, minimal processing of stimulus information can elicit emotion without cognitive mediation (e.g., Campos, Barrett, Lamb, Goldsmith, & Stenberg, 1983; Ekman, 1984; Izard, 1977, 1989; Tomkins, 1962, 1963; Zajonc, 1980, 1984). Also in contrast to appraisal theorists, biosocial theorists generally rely more on biological processes in their explanation of emotions, reflecting their emphasis on the evolutionary function and innateness of emotions. Central to most biosocial theories is the role of the face in the generation, regulation, and expression of the emotion. Several studies (e.g., Ekman, 1973; Ekman, Friesen & Ellsworth, 1982; Izard, 1971) have found agreement across a wide variety of cultures (including preliterate cultures in New Guinea and Iran) in the recognition of distinct emotional meanings in a small set of facial expressions. This universality has led some (e.g., Ekman & Oster, 1979) to hypothesize that expressions of anger, disgust, happiness, sadness, fear, and surprise are hardwired, a notion consistent with Darwin's (1872/1965) ideas about the evolutionary importance of facial movement in emotional expression.[3] These same universal expressions are offered by biosocial theorists as evidence for a set of "basic" or primary emotions, although these theorists disagree about exactly which emotions comprise this set and what is the precise role of the face in generating them. (See Ortony & Turner, 1990, however, for an argument against the concept of basic emotions.)

As we have noted, the debate about whether cognition is necessary for emotion to occur is the primary source of the distinction between appraisal and biosocial theories. Rather than advocating one position over the other, in this chapter we will make use of both sets of theories. That is, we will mainly focus on both proposed causal relationships and the theories of emotion relevant to each: cognition causing emotion (primarily the interest of appraisal theorists) and emotion causing cognition (primarily the interest of biosocial theorists).

Emotion Methodology

Although many emotion theories can be applied to intergroup relations, none will be very useful if issues pertaining to the measurement of emotion constructs are not considered. Indeed, the ability to measure emotion sets limits on the theoretical questions that can be addressed.

Despite their differences, there is some agreement between appraisal and biosocial theorists about the measurement of emotion. Nearly all agree that to measure the emotional *experience* properly, one must incorporate

---

[3]It is important to note that the existing cross-cultural research does not necessarily show that emotional expressions are hardwired. Other lines of research (e.g., developmental, comparative, genetic) will likely provide stronger tests of Darwin's ideas.

verbal measures that go beyond simple valence and intensity dimensions and access the quality of distinct emotions (e.g., "fear," "anger").

In addition, as we mentioned earlier, many emotion theorists emphasize that the role of the face in emotional expression makes it an important source of data about emotion and affect, whether through coding systems of overt facial activity (e.g., Ekman & Friesen, 1978; Izard, 1979) or the measurement of covert facial muscle activity via electromyographic (EMG) recording. Several researchers (e.g., Fridlund, Schwartz, & Fowler, 1984; McHugo, Smith, & Lanzetta, 1982; Schwartz, Fair, Salt, & Mandel, 1976) have found that the *zygomaticus major* (the muscle in the cheek that pulls up the lip corner) and the *corrugator supercilii* (the muscle above the eye that pushes the brows together) typically exhibit increased activity during times at which the subject later reports having experienced positive or negative affect, respectively, even though the face showed no expression overtly at the time. Facial EMG activity recorded from the cheek and brow regions distinguishes between mild and moderate positively and negatively valenced stimuli, respectively (Cacioppo, Petty, Losch, & Kim, 1986). Thus, facial EMG activity can differentiate the valence and intensity of affective reactions, and is less susceptible to some of the problems associated with traditional self-report measures, such as demand characteristics and concerns about socially desirable responding (cf. McHugo & Lanzetta, 1983). Specific waveforms of the EMG response can also index momentary changes in affect while a subject engages in conversation during an interview, even though a trained observer cannot detect such changes in the overt facial expressions (Cacioppo, Martzke, Petty, & Tassinary, 1988).

The use of facial EMG does have limitations, however. For example, increased facial EMG activity at the cheek site does not necessarily mean that the subject consciously is experiencing an increase in positive affect. Subjects will show more cheek EMG activity to positive stimuli when either an implied or actual audience is present compared to times when one is not, but do not report more enjoyment of the stimulus in the audience conditions (Fridlund, 1991). And, whether recording facial EMG will enable one to differentiate distinct emotions is still unclear. Some research suggests the possibility of differentiating at least four distinct emotions (anger, happiness, fear, and disgust) by recording at muscle sites that are involved in the generation of those emotional expressions, however such differentiation may only be possible when the emotions are expressed at intense levels (Geen, 1989; Schwartz *et al.*, 1976).

The role of the autonomic nervous system (ANS) in the generation of emotions is more controversial, as is its measurement (cf. Stemmler, 1989; Rimé, Philippot, & Cisamolo, 1990). Although, as noted above, some theorists (e.g., Mandler, 1984; Schachter, 1964) consider ANS arousal necessary for emotional experience, it is difficult to specify definitively what constitutes ANS arousal; is it increased heart rate, blood pressure, palmar sweating, finger temperature, respiratory activity, or an increase in all of these? In fact, ANS measures have small correlations with each other across a variety of settings that are said to be "arousing" (Lacey, 1967; Neiss, 1988). This lack of correlation between psychophysiological measures does not necessarily mean that the ANS plays a small role in emotions. Ekman, Levenson, and Friesen (1983) found that skin temperature and heart rate patterns could distinguish between some emotions. Conditions in which subjects reported feeling anger were associated with increased heart rate and increased skin temperature, whereas fear and sadness were associated with increased heart rate and decreased skin temperature. This ANS differentiation of emotion has been reported in subsequent studies as well (e.g., Geen, 1989; Levenson, Carstensen, Friesen, & Ekman, 1991; Levenson, Ekman, & Friesen, 1990), although the specific pattern of ANS activity has differed from study to study.

Despite the conceptual and methodological problems with ANS arousal, a number of early researchers in intergroup relations (e.g., Cooper, 1959; Porier & Lott, 1967; Rankin & Campbell, 1955; Tognacci & Cook, 1975; Vidulich & Krevanick, 1966) looked for a relationship between arousal and ethnic prejudice by measuring electrodermal activity (EDA). These studies used photographs of targets, written descriptions of groups, or the presence of confederates whose ethnicity was either the same as or different from the subject's. Some subjects in these studies indeed showed "increased arousal" to members of the outgroup in comparison to targets from the ingroup (e.g., Rankin & Campbell, 1955). Most of this research, however, either failed to show a relationship between the valence of the subject's reported racial attitudes and EDA or suffered from other methodological concerns. Instead, the most consistent finding was that attitude intensity, whether favorable or unfavorable toward the outgroup target, was sometimes accompanied with increased EDA. The problem with these studies should be evident from our earlier discussion of physiological arousal as a construct. Certainly the reliance on a single ANS measure (i.e., EDA) has only compounded the problem. And, although increased positive *or* negative feelings may be accompanied by increased arousal, it is unclear whether it is necessary for these feelings to occur. A number of other current emotion theories have in fact abandoned the concept of arousal altogether, viewing it as neither necessary nor sufficient for emotions to occur. It is evident, then, that investigations of ANS activity in emotion should use *multiple* psychophysiological measures, but, also, rather than using them to measure the global level of ANS activation, attempt to differentiate among emotions on the basis of ANS patterning (see also Blascovich & Kelsey, 1990, for a discussion of these issues).

Psychophysiological measures of emotion are, of course, more difficult to incorporate into studies of naturalistic intergroup interactions than are traditional self-report measures: movement is limited, the psychophysiological laboratory setting can appear artificial, analyses are often more complicated, and the cost of data collection from more than one subject at a time is high. However, recent advances in psychophysiological methodology (cf. Cacioppo & Tassinary, 1990) perhaps make this kind of research more attractive than it might have been in the past. For example, the use of radiotelemetry (i.e., the subject carries a remote device that sends physiological data such as heart rate via a radio transmitter to the recording equipment) allows the researcher to study subjects outside the laboratory in natural interaction. In addition, new developments in time series analysis have allowed some to study psychophysiological processes during dyadic interactions (e.g., Levenson & Gottman, 1985). Further, as the use of these methods becomes more widespread and technological advances continue, the price of equipment, set-up time, and training in psychophysiology appears to be not nearly as high as it once was.

Having briefly reviewed emotion theory and methodology, we now turn to the main concern of this chapter: how the psychology of emotions and affect can be integrated with the psychology of stereotyping and intergroup relations. We approach this problem by considering the ways in which the two causal relationships mentioned earlier (viz., cognition causing emotion and emotion causing cognition) enter into intergroup phenomena. Finally, we consider the consequences of cognition and emotion on intergroup behavior.

Cognition Causing Emotions

As we see it, there are at least four components of intergroup relations that influence how cognition generates emotions: (1) social categorization; (2) the actions of others; (3) the features of the contact setting; and (4) stereotype activation. In the discussion below we will address only the first three components. Other contributors to this volume (e.g., Esses, Haddock, & Zanna, Chapter 7; Fiske & Ruscher, Chapter 11; Devine and Monteith, Chapter 14) discuss the affective consequences of stereotype activation.

Social Categorization

One cognition that readily occurs in intergroup settings is a determination of the group affiliation of others in relation to one's own group membership(s)—a social categorization. Whereas the categorization itself can be considered primarily a cognitive process, its consequences (e.g., increasing the salience of a social identity) probably include emotional, motivational, and other cognitive components. Given the robustness of intergroup bias (cf. Brewer, 1979; Hinkle & Schopler, 1986), one would expect that people (cf. Brewer, 1979; Hinkle & Schopler, 1986), one would expect that people experience more positive affect when focusing on ingroup members and more negative affect when focusing on outgroup members. In addition to this distinction in affect, are there specific emotions elicited on the basis of category differentiation? Of course, the answer to this question will vary as a function of, for example, features of the setting and the history of the groups involved. Some studies, however, have identified specific emotions that seem to vary simply as a function of the ingroup/outgroup categorization and perhaps social identity processes.

For instance, Dijker (1987) identified the emotions of native Dutch adults elicited by three outgroups living in their country: Surinamers, Turks, and Moroccans. In a factor analysis of respondents' ratings of 18 emotions possibly felt toward each of the target groups, emotions primarily loaded on four factors: positive mood, irritation, anxiety, and concern (or worry). Subjects' reported feelings differed, however, in terms of which outgroup was the target: anxiety was felt toward all three outgroups, but irritation was especially associated with the Turkish and Moroccan targets. Dijker noted that Surinamers, in contrast to most Turks and Moroccans, speak Dutch and share more similar cultural customs. Thus, the particular "strangeness" of the Turks and Moroccans probably contributed to the greater irritation subjects reported. If one views the ingroup/outgroup distinction as continuous, then it seems reasonable to characterize the Surinamers as closer to the ingroup than Turks and Moroccans. This suggests that the greater the perceived differences between ingroup and outgroup, the more intense are the negative emotions elicited by the outgroup.

In our own research involving imagined interracial settings, such as having a casual conversation with someone of a different race or, for comparison, someone of the same race, we asked subjects ($n = 213$) to indicate all emotions that they might feel from a set of 48 emotion terms. For the interracial scenario, the most frequently chosen emotions were irritation (54.9%), dislike (46.9%), apprehension (45.5%), and anxiety (41.3%). Positive emotions such as happiness (89.2%) and enjoyment (80.3%) were most frequently chosen for the same race encounter. Thus, the emotions chosen by our sample of Southern California college students are quite similar to those that differentiated Dutch feelings toward other racial groups in Dijker's (1987) study.

In a study using an entirely different intergroup distinction (Jackson & Sullivan, 1989), factor analyses of self-report ratings revealed four dimensions of emotion expressed by heterosexual male subjects while evaluating either a heterosexual or homosexual applicant: negative affect (e.g., angry, disgusted), positive affect (e.g., happy, cheerful), tension (e.g., nervous, uncomfortable), and self-righteousness (e.g., superior, proud). Two of these dimensions, negative affect and tension, predicted evaluations of homosexual targets. The contents of the latter factor (viz, nervous and uncomfortable), although labeled tension by Jackson and Sullivan, appear to correspond substantively to the irritation dimension found in the two preceding studies.

Whereas the studies described above appear to show the emotional consequences of increasing the salience of one's social identity in an intergroup setting, in our research we have also examined the affective consequences of manipulating the categorization process itself by using EMG to record covert facial muscle activity of subjects in a study of the crossed categorization effect. The studies mentioned thus far have focused on single ingroup/outgroup dimensions for category differentiation. In most real world instances a person belongs to many groups. Sometimes several may be salient simultaneously (e.g., while discussing abortion with Sue, Joe thinks about her as both a Republican *and* a Catholic). What happens when some salient memberships are shared by people but others are not? Such situations, those in which more than one category is salient and two people share one category membership but do not share *another*, have been defined as instances of "crossed categorization" (e.g., Deschamps & Doise, 1978). When compared to instances where groups have no common category memberships, they generally result in reduced intergroup bias, as operationalized by reward allocations and expressions of liking (see Vanbeselaere, 1991, for a review).

In our research (Vanman, Kaplan, & Miller, 1991), college women viewed slides of individuals each of whom were described as belonging to two groups. The two dimensions that defined group membership (i.e., university and sorority/fraternity affiliation) allowed the subject to share membership with the target on either both dimensions, neither dimension, or one dimension but not the other; the latter constituted the crossed categorization condition. Brow EMG activity was highest and cheek EMG activity was lowest for targets who were outgroup members on both category dimensions. However targets whose category memberships crossed with those of the subject elicited EMG patterns that were more positive (i.e., increased cheek and decreased brow activity). Further, the EMG patterns for crossed category targets were equal to those elicited by targets who shared group membership on both dimensions with the subject. Verbal ratings of liking paralleled the EMG results. We interpret these findings as supportive of Vanbeselaere's (1991) explanation of the crossed categorization effect: when two categorizations are crossed, the accentuation of the perceived similarities on the shared membership are counteracted by the accentuation of the perceived differences on the opposing membership. Thus, the negative affect generated by the presence of outgroup others can be diminished simply by making crossed category memberships salient.

Actions of Others

In addition to cognitions regarding social categorization, attributions about the behavior of another will also influence the generation of specific emotions. For our purposes, we distinguish between the behaviors of others that are primarily emotional from those that are primarily nonemotional.

Emotional Behaviors

A consideration of emotional behaviors includes the impact of the facial expressions of those in an intergroup setting on each other. Facial expressions of emotions can elicit facial mimicry in others, as seen, for example, in the effects of the facial expressions of a president on those of his audience (McHugo, Lanzetta, Sullivan, Masters, & Englis, 1985). In other research covert EMG activity at the cheek region increased in response to pictures of smiling faces and activity at the brow region increased in response to pictures of angry faces (Dimberg, 1982). Furthermore, this facial mimicry can affect one's own emotional experience. Subjects smile more and report more enjoyment when watching videos of stand-up comedy that contain visual dubs of audience members laughing at the comedian than do subjects who watch the same videos without the dubs (Bush, Barr, McHugo, & Lanzetta, 1989).

Although there is considerable debate about the extent to which the face actually is responsible for the entire generation of emotion, it does appear, as some theorists have proposed (e.g., Tomkins, 1962, 1984), that the movement of the face contributes to the experience of emotion (cf. Izard, 1989), either by enhancing or diminishing it, as during moments of pain (Lanzetta, Cartwright-Smith, Kleck, 1976), or when smelling pleasant or disgusting odors (Kraut, 1982). Thus, the facial expressions of outgroup members in an intergroup contact setting might determine how ingroup members will feel about the contact. In particular, research by Hansen and Hansen (1988) has shown that people may be predisposed to detecting angry expressions in a crowd more readily than other expressions. Consequently, even if the majority of outgroup members are expressing smiling faces (and perhaps masking antipathy), one angry expression by an outgroup member may be more influential on ingroup members' emotions than the remaining friendly ones. Indeed, this is consistent with the finding that positive feedback from a dominant outgroup is often discounted (Crocker, Voelkl, Testa, & Major, 1991; see also Major & Crocker, Chapter 15, this volume). We know of no research that has actually focused on facial expressions in intergroup settings, but one would expect that the expression of negative emotions is a frequent occurrence in more hostile contact situations.

Nonemotional Behaviors

Turning now to a consideration of the nonemotional behaviors of others, some appraisal theories of emotion have included attributional processes in the generation of emotions (e.g., Ortony et al., 1988; Weiner, 1985). With increased interest in intergroup attributions (e.g., Taylor & Jaggi, 1974; Hewstone & Jaspars, 1984; Stephan, 1977), this area may be particularly fruitful for the study of emotions in intergroup relations. If one considers the ingroup as an extension of "self," and the outgroup as an extension of "other," then it is fairly easy to adapt emotion theories to intergroup settings.

For example, Ortony *et al.* (1988) proposed a class of emotions, called "attribution emotions," which depend on attributions made about the actions of agents. According to this theory, one frequently makes valenced evaluations of such actions (i.e., approval, disapproval) that elicit particular emotions depending on who is the actor, what is the outcome, and the outcome's relevance to self concerns. If the agent is self, one can feel either pride or shame about the action. If the agent is other, one can feel admiration or reproach. Further, if one's own well-being is affected by the action of the agent, one can feel gratification or remorse toward self, and gratitude or anger toward another. Thus, extending this reasoning to intergroup settings, attributing the actions of outgroup members that are detrimental to the ingroup should result in felt anger toward the outgroup. In contrast, ingroup members' actions considered detrimental to the ingroup should lead more to a feeling like remorse rather than anger. Furthermore, the finding that subjects show a biased tendency to attribute positive outcomes to the ingroup and negative outcomes to the outgroup (see Hewstone, 1989, for a recent review) would mean that feelings of reproach and anger toward outgroup members should be more common.

Features of the Contact Setting

Finally, another important aspect of intergroup situations that will influence the way cognitions generate emotions is the nature of the contact setting. We consider some relevant features below.

Amount of Contact

Contrary to the original contact hypothesis, in his study of Dutch natives' emotions about immigrant populations now residing in their country, Dijker (1987) found that negative emotions such as irritation, anxiety, and concern increased with an increase in the frequency of casual contacts. Moreover, although personalized interaction is often included as a feature that promotes intergroup acceptance (Allport, 1954), more personal forms of contact with the target groups did not always lead to positive effects. For example, when these natives visited Surinamers in their homes, positive emotions occurred more frequently, whereas when they visited Turks, *irritation* was more common.

In contrast, Stephan and Stephan (1989) found that high levels of intergroup anxiety characterized the interactions of Asian Americans and whites in Hawaii, and those of Hispanics and whites in New Mexico, when these interactions were *less* personal. One should note, however, that Stephan and Stephan's measure of "intergroup anxiety" was a composite index of 15 terms that included a variety of emotional experiences other than anxiety, such as frustration, irritation, awkwardness, impatience, and shame. Consequently, their composite score occludes distinct qualities of the emotions. Despite their results on the composite measure, it is possible that the items that tapped the specific emotions which corresponded to those studied by Dijker yielded effects that paralleled his. Whatever the case, Stephan and Stephan propose that the relation between emotion and amount of contact is largely mediated by the amount of knowledge gained by such contact. According to their thinking, more contact leads to greater knowledge about the outgroup which, in turn, leads to a reduction of intergroup anxiety. In contrast, Dijker's data suggest that, if the knowledge gained from contact reveals that the outgroup is unpredictable or "strange," then ingroup members may experience an *increase* in anxiety or irritation. This prediction fits in well with the thinking of several appraisal theorists who propose that anxiety is elicited when people feel they have little control over an unknown fate (e.g., Lazarus *et al.*, 1980; Roseman, Spindel, & Jose, 1990).

Structure of the Task

When two groups work in proximity to each other, the nature of the task interdependence should also influence the cognition–emotion relationship. For instance, in desegregated school settings, teachers frequently direct students from different ethnic groups to work together on various tasks. Generally, it is believed that tasks that involve outcome interdependence (i.e., participants share a common outcome) will be more conducive to the reduction of intergroup bias than those with no interdependence (e.g., Johnson & Johnson, 1989).

In a study using facial EMG (Vanman, Paul, Kaplan, & Miller, 1990), we tested this interdependence assumption by examining the affective reactions of white students in imagined interracial settings in which their partners were described as being deficient in the skills required to perform a task. Subjects viewed 28 slides of students (half of them black) and, for each, imagined working with that person in a cooperative situation. In half of these trials the described situation led to a joint or shared outcome; in the other half it led to independent outcomes. EMG was recorded from the cheek, brow, and lip (*orbicularis oris*) regions. Lip EMG activity has not typically been found to vary as a function of the affective significance of a stimulus (Petty & Cacioppo, 1983). Analyses revealed that EMG activity over the brow region was lowest for white targets, and highest for blacks, whereas activity over the cheek region was highest for white targets, and lowest for blacks. Moreover, brow activity was greatest during conditions that described joint outcomes, and lowest for independent ones. Lip activity did not vary across conditions. In contrast, self-report ratings of liking for the target showed greater liking for partners in the independent outcome conditions, which paralleled the brow findings, but also showed more liking for black targets. For this latter race factor, the discrepancy between the EMG activity and the self-report data is consistent with other recent reports documenting a form of dissembling in the self-reports of racial attitudes: for example, symbolic racism (Sears, 1988), modern racism (McConahay, Hardee, & Batts, 1981), and aversive racism (Gaertner & Dovidio, 1981). In today's society, norms dictate that one should not express negative attitudes about another based on race, even though one might actually harbor contrary inclinations. Whether subjects were in fact aware of the negative affective responses suggested by our data, or believed that they actually held positive feelings toward blacks, cannot be answered by this study[4] (however, see Devine, 1989, for a recent discussion of these issues).

Thus far in our research we have only used facial EMG to differentiate positive and negative affect, but have not used it to distinguish distinct emotional states. On the basis of some appraisal theories, however, one can speculate about specific emotions that occur in cooperative settings like the ones imagined by the subjects in Vanman et al. (1990). When the outcome is interdependent and one's partner is perceived as an impediment to success, several theories of emotion (e.g., Frijda, 1986; Ortony et al., 1988) predict that anger or frustration is likely. By removing this perceived impediment, as in the independent outcomes, happiness is more likely. Competitive interactions, in which the outgroup, by competing with the ingroup, becomes a source of goal frustration should also produce more negative emotions like anger (Berkowitz, 1989). In their study of boys at summer camp, Sherif and his colleagues found that such anger was easily elicited by placing groups in competitive situations (Sherif, Harvey, White, Hood, & Sherif, 1961). Indeed, the increased ingroup bias that occurs in competitive reward structures (e.g., Johnson, Johnson, & Maruyama, 1984) may be mediated by such emotion.

Findings about emotions generated in interdependent situations at the interpersonal level may not always generalize to such situations at the intergroup level. For example, Tesser and his colleagues (cf. Tesser, 1991) have found that when a close other performs better than self on a task dimension that is considered relevant to self identity, one will feel jealousy about the other's accomplishment. However, if the other outperforms self on a task

[4]One could speculate that these responses are consistent with a distinction Izard (1989) has made between unconscious and conscious emotion action tendencies, where facial EMG activity could represent unconscious action tendencies and self-report data represent conscious ones that are under voluntary control. Or, as Zajonc (1984) has argued, the stimulus "black student" might immediately elicit stored negative affect about such targets with minimal processing. However, making a conscious verbal response likely invokes cognitive mediation involving norms and self-presentational concerns that could "mask" the negative affect elicited by the target.

that is considered irrelevant to self identity, one will feel pride about the other person's accomplishments, especially when the other is considered similar to self. Now consider this situation at the intergroup level. Although a friend may outperform self and become the starting pitcher for a baseball game, when that friend now plays superbly causing the team to win, self should feel happiness, not jealousy. Social identity theory argues that groups seek positive distinctiveness from other groups. When this need for positive distinctiveness is especially enhanced, the well-documented positive relation between similarity and liking at the interpersonal level may not be upheld at the intergroup level. The more similar two groups are to each other on various dimensions, the more likely the need for positive distinctiveness will produce evaluative bias (Brown, 1988). This suggests that Tesser's hypothesis about the relation between pride and similarity may not extend to intergroup settings.

Finally, cooperative and competitive reward structures may also differentially affect the empathy felt for the other participants (Lanzetta & Englis, 1989). In cooperative situations, subjects show greater empathy (reflected in ANS and facial EMG activity) for a coactor (e.g., when the coactor smiles, the subject smiles). By contrast, subjects show greater counterempathy (e.g., more smiling when the coactor grimaces) in competitive situations. Thus, empathy may lead to greater liking and unity with others in cooperative situations, whereas counterempathy may promote dislike and anger toward competitive others.

Numerousness

Another feature that characterizes the setting is the ratio of outgroup to ingroup members. When the ratio is high, ingroup members may feel emotions such as fear or anxiety. Group identities become more salient in such situations (McGuire, McGuire, & Winton, 1979), and thus minority members may perceive that there is immediate danger to self in the form of some sort of discrimination based on previous experiences in similar circumstances (Konrad & Gutek, 1987). How a majority group intends to treat the minority members may also be unclear, thus creating anxiety because one's fate is uncertain (Lazarus et al., 1980). Finally, as the outgroup/ingroup ratio increases, so does self-focus (Mullen, 1983), perhaps causing individuals to feel self-conscious and anxious. Clearly, being in the minority will likely lead to some sort of negative affect.

Relative Status

As Brewer and Miller (1984) have noted, equal status between members of different groups at the structural level may not correspond to equal status at the psychological level. These perceptions of inequity in status should have consequences on the emotions generated. In inequitable close relationships, anger not only is frequently experienced by those who are underbenefiting, but also (along with some guilt) by those who are overbene-fiting (Sprecher, 1986). Likewise in intergroup situations, high-status groups may feel resentment about having to work with low-status others, or, as suggested by Stephan and Stephan (1985), they may feel guilt about their advantaged position. Low-status groups may be more likely to experi-ence anger like the underbenefiting subjects in Sprecher's (1986) study, or they may feel fear or anxiety for the same reasons that groups might feel those emotions when they are the minority (i.e., high-status groups might actively discriminate against the low-status group). Whereas the anger ex-pressed by black Americans during the civil rights movement of the 1960s supports this thinking, the effects of intergroup status on anger have not been studied empirically. However, increased anxiety has been found to be associated with lower status in such situations (Stephan & Stephan, 1989).

Emotion Causing Cognitions

Earlier, we noted that biosocial theorists posit that emotion can also occur independently of cognitive processing. In this section we will ignore the role of emotion as a modifier of cognitive processes (e.g., the effects of mood on learning) and refer the reader to other chapters in this volume that address this and related issues (Bodenhausen, Chapter 2; Stroessner & Mackie, Chapter 4; Hamilton, Stroessner, & Mackie, Chapter 3; Stephan & Stephan, Chapter 6). Instead, we briefly consider emotion as a mediator or antecedent of specific cognitions. This discussion is particularly relevant to the formation of stereotypes and the cognitive representation of affect.

The Formation of Stereotypes

The content of stereotypes, as we noted earlier, can determine the emo-tional reactions to outgroup members. On the other hand, some intergroup theorists (e.g., Campbell, 1967; Dijker, 1989) have suggested that stereo-types may reflect a justification or rationalization for emotions felt when around the outgroup. If so, an analysis of the content of stereotypes may also indicate which emotions may have contributed to their creation. For example, if one feels some irritation in a particular setting that has little to do with the outgroup member (e.g., a mutual task is difficult, the room is too noisy), the irritation might mistakenly be attributed to the outgroup member along with an appraisal/belief that the ingroup member creates in order to rationalize the emotion (e.g., "members of that group do annoying things"). Besides the association of incidental affect with the stereotype, it is also likely that this occurs with more "integral" affect. For example, if whites feel fear in the presence of blacks, they may develop the stereotype that blacks are particularly aggressive to rationalize the emotion. In addition to negative emotions, positive affect may also contribute to stereo-typing. This effect is addressed more fully by other contributors to this volume (Bodenhausen, Chapter 2; Hamilton, Stroessner, & Mackie, Chapter 3; Stroessner & Mackie, Chapter 4).

Storage of Affect

Leventhal (1980) and others have proposed that emotions are represented in an independent memory mechanism apart from more cognitive-based memories. The existence of separate emotion memories suggests that stereotypes not only consist of cognitions or beliefs about the target group, but also include separate representations of felt emotions about the group. Leventhal proposed that emotion memories may be more difficult to change than cognitive memories. One might infer then that specific knowledge or beliefs about outgroup members should be easier to change than the associated emotion memory. If so, then the presentation of disconfirming information about the stereotyped group should not be as effective in changing intergroup bias as might attempts to change affective reactions to the group. And, for those beliefs based on primarily affective information, presentation of information counter to the stereotype should be ineffective in changing those beliefs. Indeed, the relative resiliency of stereotypes may reflect the fact that most stereotypes are primarily emotion based.

Consequences for Behavior

In the introduction to this chapter we argued that a reason to study emotions in intergroup situations was that emotions generally have a limited set of subsequent behaviors that they can elicit. When someone feels happy, one would not expect that the person normally will aggress against others. In fact, the emotion-behavior relationship is one area about which emotion theorists tend to have some consensus. In this section we not only discuss the consequences of emotion on one's own behavior, but on the behaviors of others as well.

Own Behavior

As we have said, a limited number of stereotyped behaviors or action tendencies are associated with each emotion. Frijda (1986) in particular has emphasized the role of behavior in emotion. In his theory the appraisal *and* an accompanying action tendency constitute the emotion. Thus, Frijda defines several emotions in terms of their action tendencies, such as desire (the tendency to approach), fear (the tendency to avoid), disgust (the tendency to reject), anger (the tendency to aggress), and anxiety (the tendency to inhibit). Therefore, according to Frijda's theory, identification of the emotions in intergroup settings should by definition enable one to predict the behaviors that will occur in such settings.

In support of these ideas, in Dijker's (1987) study of feelings toward outgroup members, Dutch subjects showed a tendency for physical and verbal aggression that was associated with feelings of irritation toward the target group; a tendency to "keep one's distance" was associated with feelings of anxiety. We have already noted that anxiety or fear frequently characterizes intergroup situations. Therefore the tendency to avoid should be also quite frequent. In fact, ingroup members more frequently avoid than aggress against outgroup members in unobtrusive studies of white–black interactions (Crosby, Bromley, & Saxe, 1980). And, in situations where subjects cannot avoid the outgroup, as in some experimental investigations of intergroup contact, subjects are visibly tense and anxious in their interactions (Ickes, 1984; Word, Zanna, & Cooper, 1974).

Acts of aggression have also frequently characterized intergroup relations, and we would expect in those instances that anger or frustration, rather than fear or anxiety, would be the emotional antecedents of such behaviors. For instance, we hypothesized earlier that underbenefiting low-status groups should frequently experience feelings of anger or frustration. Thus, low-status groups should also exhibit more aggression against outgroup targets because those targets are appraised as the instigators of the angry feelings. In fact, Wilson and Rogers (1975) found that black subjects directed more physical and verbal aggression toward white victims than toward black victims, whereas white subjects directed less aggression toward black victims compared to whites. However, when a black confederate provokes white subjects with an insult, they show greater aggression toward the black than they do toward a white confederate (Rogers & Prentice-Dunn, 1981). It appears that the anger created by a provocating insult induces stronger retaliatory aggression when an outgroup member has been the provocateur. Of course, aggressive behaviors are not always displayed when one is angry. Concerns about retaliation, the effectiveness of the aggression, and personality variables, for example, can inhibit aggressive behaviors. Meta-analysis, however, shows that the aggressive inducing effect of the sight of aggression cues (e.g., a weapon) is further increased when the target is clearly of low status or an outgroup members (Carlson *et al.*, 1990).

One should also consider the behaviors that are likely to occur as a result of positive emotions such as happiness or pride. Smiling frequently accompanies feelings of happiness and may in itself be an instigator for happiness and feelings of good will in intergroup situations. Positive emotions also often lead to more helping behavior, friendliness, risk taking (e.g., getting to know strangers), and cooperativeness (Isen, 1987). Naturally, such behaviors will be more conducive to fostering good intergroup relations and perhaps the weakening of negative stereotypes.[5]

Cues for Others' Behavior

Finally, it is important to remember that the emotional behaviors one displays in an intergroup setting can become cues for the feelings that others will have in that situation. As we have noted, the face provides a readout of someone's feelings. Elicited facial expressions, which can be readily identified by others, then serve as information about one's internal state, or how one appraises the situation. This information can play a role in others' appraisals (e.g., "If she is afraid of me, then I am in control"). As previously noted, it can also create mimicry in others, especially if one is the leader of a group. This mimicry can then follow the same process we outlined earlier in affecting the emotional experience of others by either enhancing or diminishing their feelings. Anger expressed by one participant elicits anger in another, which in turn may escalate feelings that lead to aggressive behaviors. Again, we know of no research that has tracked such emotional interchange in intergroup situations, but these predictions appear reasonable based on our own intergroup experiences.

Conclusions

In this chapter we have argued that a consideration of recent advances in emotion theory and methodology will greatly enrich current thinking about stereotyping and intergroup relations. The many emotion theories we have only briefly presented here have yet to make any significant impact on either the prevailing theories of intergroup relations or on the methods used in this research.

Much of current intergroup theory, as we have stated, has been dominated by the cognitive approach. For instance, though Social Identity Theory (Tajfel, 1981; Tajfel & Turner, 1979) originally posited motivational processes, it has said little about emotion. Moreover, in a recent extension of it, Turner's Self-Categorization Theory is almost exclusively concerned with cognitive processes (cf. Turner, Hogg, Oakes, Reicher, & Wetherell, 1987). Most often emotions are viewed as ephemeral phenomena that have little to do with the core mediators of intergroup behaviors and cognitions. When emotion, or more precisely, affect, has been incorporated in intergroup theory, it has been posited as the motivator that drives particular

---

[5]Although help giving often elicits hostility toward the helper (e.g., Nadler, 1991), in a cooperative intergroup setting such negative effects do not invariably occur (Cook & Pelfrey, 1985).

behaviors [one has various sorts of negative affect about some outgroup which causes one to derogate them or show prejudicial behaviors against them (e.g., Symbolic Racism Theory; Sears, 1988)]. In such theories, however, the distant or immediate origins of this negative affect have largely been ignored. This chapter suggests places where one might investigate these origins.

Of course, the reason why intergroup theories have not attempted to account for emotional processes probably reflects the paucity of research that has attempted to measure specific emotions in stereotyping and intergroup relations. Measurement of intergroup emotions has been difficult and its conclusions unclear. Advances in psychophysiology promise better methods to measure physiological processes that accompany emotions, although their use probably requires more sophistication in design and inference than that seen in earlier attempts to use these procedures. Furthermore, whether such measures will provide the needed differentiation among emotional states is unclear. In addition to recent developments in psychophysiological methods, measures of verbal reports of emotions and observations of facial expressions and other emotional behaviors in intergroup situations have also advanced (e.g., Tickle-Degnen & Rosenthal, 1987). However, the veracity of verbal reports in more emotionally volatile settings (e.g., interracial situations) may be questionable.

Clearly, an approach to intergroup relations that addresses cognitive processes will be enhanced when emotional processes are incorporated. The rate at which such integration occurs will be determined by advances in research and theory in *both* intergroup relations and emotions.

Acknowledgments

We wish to thank Patricia A. Brennan, Brian P. Cotton, Tiffany A. Ito, and Thomas R. Geen for their helpful comments on early drafts of this chapter. Preparation of this chapter was facilitated by a grant from the National Science Foundation (BNS-8719439) to N. Miller and a Haynes Doctoral Dissertation Fellowship to E. Vanman.

References

Abelson, R. P., Kinder, D. R., Peters, M. P., & Fiske, S. T. (1982). Affective and semantic components in political person perception. *Journal of Personality and Social Psychology, 42,* 619–630.

Allport, G. W. (1954). *The nature of prejudice.* Reading, MA: Addison-Wesley.

Berkowitz, L. (1989). Frustration-aggression hypothesis: Examination and reformulation. *Psychological Bulletin, 106,* 59–73.

Blascovich, J., & Kelsey, R. M. (1990). Using electrodermal and cardiovascular measures of arousal in social psychological research. In C. Hendrick & M. S. Clark (Eds.), *Research methods in personality and social psychology* (pp. 45–73). Newbury Park, CA: Sage.

Blumenthal, A. L. (1977). *The process of cognition.* Englewood Cliffs, NJ: Prentice-Hall.

Breckler, S. J., & Wiggins, E. C. (1989). On defining attitude and attitude theory: Once more with feeling. In A. R. Pratkanis, S. J. Breckler, & A. G. Greenwald (Eds.), *Attitude structure and function* (pp. 407–427). Hillsdale, NJ: Erlbaum.

Brewer, M. B. (1979). Ingroup bias in the minimal group situation: A cognitive-motivational analysis. *Psychological Bulletin, 86,* 307–324.

Brewer, M. B., & Miller, N. (1984). Beyond the contact hypothesis: Theoretical perspectives on desegregation. In N. Miller & M. B. Brewer (Eds.), *Groups in contact: The psychology of desegregation* (pp. 281–302). Orlando, FL: Academic Press.

Brown, R. (1988). *Group processes: Dynamics within and between groups.* Oxford: Basil Blackwell.

Bush, L. K., Barr, C. L., McHugo, G. J., & Lanzetta, J. T. (1989). The effects of facial control and facial mimicry on subjective reactions to comedy routines. *Motivation and Emotion, 13,* 31–52.

Cacioppo, J. T., & Tassinary, L. G. (Eds.). (1990). *Principles of psychophysiology: Physical, social, and inferential elements.* Cambridge: Cambridge University Press.

Cacioppo, J. T., Petty, R. E., Losch, M. E., & Kim, H. S. (1986). Electromyographic activity over facial muscle regions can differentiate the valence and intensity of affective reactions. *Journal of Personality and Social Psychology, 50,* 260–268.

Cacioppo, J. T., Martzke, J. S., Petty, R. E., & Tassinary, L. G. (1988). Specific forms of facial EMG response index emotions during an interview: From Darwin to the continuous flow hypothesis of affect-laden information processing. *Journal of Personality and Social Psychology, 54,* 592–604.

Campbell, D. T. (1967). Stereotypes and the perception of group differences. *American Psychologist, 22,* 817–829.

Campos, J., Barrett, K., Lamb, M., Goldsmith, H., & Stenberg, C. (1983). Socioemotional development. In M. Haith & J. Campos (Eds.), *Infancy and developmental psychology.* New York: Wiley.

Carlson, M., Marcus-Newhall, A., & Miller, N. (1990). Effects of situational aggression cues: A qualitative review. *Journal of Personality and Social Psychology, 58,* 622–633.

Cook, S. W., & Pelfrey, M. (1985). Reactions to being helped in cooperating interracial groups: A context effect. *Journal of Personality and Social Psychology, 49,* 1231–1245.

Cooper, J. B. (1959). Emotion in prejudice. *Science, 130,* 314–318.

Crocker, J., Voelkl, K., Testa, M., & Major, B. (1991). Social stigma: The affective consequences of attributional ambiguity. *Journal of Personality and Social Psychology, 60,* 218–228.

Crosby, F., Bromley, S., & Saxe, L. (1980). Recent unobtrusive studies of black and white discrimination and prejudice: A literature review. *Psychological Bulletin, 87,* 546–563.

Darwin, C. (1965). *The expression of emotions in man and animals.* Chicago: University of Chicago Press (originally published in 1872).

Deschamps, J.-C., & Doise, W. (1978). Crossed category memberships in intergroup relations. In H. Tajfel (Ed.), *Differentiation between social groups* (pp. 141–158). Cambridge: Cambridge University Press.

Devine, P. (1989). Automatic and controlled processes in prejudice: The role of stereotypes and personal beliefs. In A. R. Pratkanis, S. J. Breckler, & A. G. Greenwald (Eds.), *Attitude, Structure, and Function* (pp. 181–212). Hillsdale, NJ: Erlbaum.

Dijker, A. J. M. (1987). Emotional reactions to ethnic minorities. *European Journal of Social Psychology, 17,* 305–325.

Dijker, A. J. M. (1989). Ethnic attitudes and emotions. In J. P. van Oudenhoven & T. M. Willemsen (Eds.), *Ethnic minorities: Social psychological perspectives* (pp. 77–93). Amsterdam: Swets & Zeitlinger.

Dimberg, U. (1982). Facial reactions to facial expressions. *Psychophysiology, 19*, 643–647.

Edwards, K. (1990). The interplay of affect and cognition in attitude formation and change. *Journal of Personality and Social Psychology, 59*, 202–216.

Ekman, P. (1973). Cross-cultural studies of facial expression. In P. Ekman (Ed.), *Darwin and facial expression: A century of research in review*. New York: Academic Press.

Ekman, P. (1984). Expression and the nature of emotion. In K. R. Scherer & P. Ekman (Eds.), *Approaches to emotion* (pp. 319–343). Hillsdale, NJ: Erlbaum.

Ekman, P., & Friesen, W. V. (1978). *The facial action coding system (FACS): A technique for the measurement of facial action*. Palo Alto, CA: Consulting Psychologists Press.

Ekman, P., & Oster, H. (1979). Facial expressions of emotion. *Annual Review of Psychology, 30*, 527–554.

Ekman, P., Friesen, W. V., & Ellsworth, P. (1982). What are the similarities and differences in facial behavior across cultures? In P. Ekman (Ed.), *Emotion in the human face* (pp. 128–143). Cambridge: Cambridge University Press.

Ekman, P., Levenson, R. W., & Friesen, W. V. (1983). Autonomic nervous system activity distinguishes among emotions. *Science, 221*, 1208–1210.

Fischer, K. W., Shaver, P. R., & Carnochan, P. (1990). How emotions develop and how they organise development. *Cognition and Emotion, 4*, 81–127.

Fridlund, A. J. (1991). Sociality of solitary smiling: Potentiation by an implicit audience. *Journal of Personality and Social Psychology, 60*, 229–240.

Fridlund, A. J., Schwartz, G. E., & Fowler, S. C. (1984). Pattern recognition of self-reported emotional state from multiple-site facial EMG activity during affective imagery. *Psychophysiology, 21*, 567–589.

Frijda, N. H. (1986). *The emotions*. Cambridge: Cambridge University Press.

Gaertner, S. L., & Dovidio, J. F. (1981). Racism among the well-intentioned. In E. Clausen & J. Bermingham (Eds.), *Pluralism, racism, and policy: The search for equality* (pp. 208–222). Boston: Hall.

Geen, T. R. (1989). *Emotional imagery and the recruitment of patterned somatovisceral activity*. Unpublished doctoral dissertation, University of Iowa, Iowa City.

Hamilton, D. L. (1981). Stereotyping and intergroup behavior: Some thoughts on the cognitive approach. In D. L. Hamilton (Ed.), *Cognitive processes in stereotyping and intergroup behavior* (pp. 333–353). Hillsdale, NJ: Erlbaum.

Hansen, C. H., & Hansen, R. D. (1988). Finding the face in the crowd: An anger superiority effect. *Journal of Personality and Social Psychology, 54*, 917–924.

Hewstone, M. (1989). *Causal attribution: From cognitive processes to collective beliefs*. Oxford: Blackwell.

Hewstone, M., & Jaspars, J. M. F. (1984). Social dimensions of attribution. In H. Tajfel (Ed.), *The social dimension: European developments in social psychology*. Cambridge:Cambridge University Press.

Hinkle, S., & Schopler, J. (1986). Bias in the evaluation of ingroup and outgroup performance. In S. Worchel & W. G. Austin (Eds.), *Psychology of intergroup relations*. Chicago: Nelson-Hall.

Ickes, W. (1984). Compositions in black and white: Determinants of interaction in interracial dyads. *Journal of Personality and Social Psychology, 47*, 330–341.

Isen, A. M. (1987). Positive affect, cognitive processes, and social behavior. In L. Berkowitz, (Ed.), *Advances in experimental social psychology, Vol. 20* (pp. 203–253). San Diego: Academic Press.

Izard, C. E. (1971). *The face of emotion*. New York: Appleton-Century-Crofts.

Izard, C. E. (1977). *Human emotions*. New York: Plenum.

Izard, C. E. (1979). *The maximally discriminative facial movement coding system (Max)*. Newark, DE: University of Delaware, Instructional Resources Center.

Izard, C. E. (1989). The structure and function of emotions: Implications for cognition. motivation, and personality. In I. S. Cohen (Ed.), *The G. Stanley Hall Lecture Series, Vol. 9* (pp. 39–73). Washington, DC: American Psychological Association.

Jackson, L. A., & Sullivan, L. A. (1989). Cognition and affect in evaluations of stereotyped group members. *The Journal of Social Psychology, 129,* 659–672.

James, W. (1915). *Talks to teachers on psychology: And to students on some of life's ideals.* New York: Henry Holt Co.

Johnson, D. W., & Johnson, R. T. (1989). *Cooperation and competition: Theory and research.* Edina, MN: Interaction Book Company.

Johnson, D. W., Johnson, R. T., & Maruyama, G. (1984). Goal interdependence and interpersonal attraction in heterogeneous classrooms: A meta-analysis. In N. Miller & M. B. Brewer (Eds.), *Groups in contact: The psychology of desegregation* (pp. 187–212). Orlando: Academic Press.

Konrad, A. M., & Gutek, B. A. (1987). Theory and research on group composition: Applications to the status of women and ethnic minorities. In S. Oskamp & S. Spacapan (Eds.), *Interpersonal processes* (pp. 85–119). Newbury Park, CA: Sage.

Kraut, R. E. (1982). Social presence, facial feedback, and emotion. *Journal of Personality and Social Psychology, 42,* 853–863.

Lacey, J. I. (1967). Somatic response patterning and stress: Some revisions of activation theory. In M. H. Appley & R. Trumbull (Eds.), *Psychological stress: Issues in research* (pp. 14–42). New York: Appleton-Century-Crofts.

Lanzetta, J. T., & Englis, B. G. (1989). Expectations of cooperation and competition and their effects on observers' vicarious emotional responses. *Journal of Personality and Social Psychology, 56,* 543–554.

Lanzetta, J. T., Cartwright-Smith, J., & Kleck, R. E. (1976). Effects of nonverbal dissimulation on emotional experience and autonomic arousal. *Journal of Personality and Social Psychology, 33,* 354–370.

Lazarus, R. S. (1991). *Emotion and adaption.* New York: Oxford University Press.

Lazarus, R. S., Kanner, A. D., & Folkman, S. (1980). Emotions: A cognitive phenomenological analysis. In R. Plutchik & H. Kellerman (Eds.), *Emotion: Theory, research, and experience, Volume 1: Theories of emotion* (pp. 189–217). New York: Academic Press.

Levenson, R. W., & Gottman, J. M. (1985). Physiological and affective predictors of change in relationship satisfaction. *Journal of Personality and Social Psychology, 49,* 85–94.

Levenson, R. W., Ekman, P., & Friesen, W. V. (1990). Voluntary facial action generates emotion-specific autonomic nervous system activity. *Psychophysiology, 27,* 363–384.

Levenson, R. W., Carstensen, L. L., Friesen, W. V., & Ekman, P. (1991). Emotion, physiology, and expression in old age. *Psychology and Aging, 6,* 28–35.

Leventhal, H. (1980). Toward a comprehensive theory of emotion. In L. Berkowitz (Eds.), *Advances in experimental social psychology* (Vol. 13, pp. 140–207). Orlando: Academic Press.

Mandler, G. (1984). *Mind and body: Psychology of emotion and stress.* New York: Norton.

Marañon, G. (1924). Contribution à l'étude de l'action émotive de l'adrenaline. *Revue Française d'Endocrinologie, 2,* 301–325.

McConahay, J. B., Hardee, B. B., & Batts, V. (1981). Has racism declined in America? It depends on who is asking and what is asked. *Journal of Conflict Resolution, 25,* 563–579.

McGuire, W. J., McGuire, C. V., & Winton, W. (1979). Effects of household sex composition on the salience of one's gender in the spontaneous self-concept. *Journal of Experimental Social Psychology, 15,* 77–90.

McHugo, G. J., & Lanzetta, J. T. (1983). Methodological decision in social psychophysiology. In J. T. Cacioppo & R. E. Petty (Eds.), *Social psychophysiology: A sourcebook* (pp. 630–665). New York: Guilford Press.

McHugo, G. J., Smith, C. A., & Lanzetta, J. T. (1982). The structure of self-reports of emotional response to film segments. *Motivation and Emotion, 6*, 365–385.

McHugo, G. J., Lanzetta, J. T., Sullivan, D. G., Masters, R. D., & Englis, B. G. (1985). Emotional reactions to a political leader's expressive displays. *Journal of Personality and Social Psychology, 49*, 1513–1529.

Millar, M. G., & Millar, K. U. (1990). Attitude change as a function of attitude type and argument type. *Journal of Personality and Social Psychology, 59*, 217–228.

Millar, M. G., & Tesser, A. (1986). Effects of affective and cognitive focus on the attitude-behavior relation. *Journal of Personality and Social Psychology, 51*, 270–276.

Mullen, B. (1983). Operationalizing the effect of the outgroup on the individual: A self-attention perspective. *Journal of Experimental Social Psychology, 19*, 295–322.

Nadler, A. (1991). Help-seeking behavior: Psychological costs and instrumental benefits. In M. S. Clark (Ed.), *Prosocial behavior* (pp. 290–311). Newbury Park, CA: Sage.

Neiss, R. (1988). Reconceptualizing arousal: Psychobiological states in motor performance. *Psychological Bulletin, 103*, 345–366.

Ortony, A., & Turner, T. J. (1990). What's basic about basic emotions? *Psychological Review, 97*, 315–331.

Ortony, A., Clore, G. L., & Collins, A. (1988). *The cognitive structure of emotions.* Cambridge: Cambridge University Press.

Panksepp, J. (1989). The neurobiology of emotions: Of animal brains and human feelings. In H. L. Wagner & A. S. R. Manstead (Eds.), *Handbook of social psychophysiology* (pp. 5–26). Chichester, England: Wiley.

Petty, R. E., & Cacioppo, J. T. (1983). The role of bodily responses in attitude measurement and change. In J. T. Cacioppo & R. E. Petty (Eds.), *Social psychophysiology: A sourcebook* (pp. 51–101). New York: Guilford.

Porier, G. W., & Lott, A. J. (1967). Galvanic skin responses and prejudice. *Journal of Personality and Social Psychology, 5*, 253–259.

Rankin, R. E., & Campbell, D. T. (1955). Galvanic skin response to Negro and white experimenters. *Journal of Abnormal and Social Psychology, 51*, 30–33.

Rimé, B., Philippot, P., & Cisamolo, D. (1990). Social schemata of peripheral changes in emotion. *Journal of Personality and Social Psychology, 59*, 38–49.

Rogers, R. W., & Prentice-Dunn, S. (1981). Deindividuation and anger-mediated interracial aggression: Unmasking regressive racism. *Journal of Personality and Social Psychology, 41*, 63–73.

Roseman, I. J. (1984). Cognitive determinants of emotions: A structural theory. In P. Shaver (Ed.), *Review of personality and social psychology* (Vol. 5, pp. 11–36). Beverly Hills, CA: Sage.

Roseman, I. J., Spindel, M. S., & Jose, P. E. (1990). Appraisals of emotion-eliciting events: Testing a theory of discrete emotions. *Journal of Personality and Social Psychology, 59*, 899–915.

Rosenberg, M. J., & Hovland, C. I. (1960). Cognitive, affective, and behavioral components of attitude. In M. J. Rosenberg, C. I. Hovland, W. J. McGuire, R. P. Abelson, & J. W. Brehm (Eds.), *Attitude organization and change: An analysis of consistency among attitude components* (pp. 1–14). New Haven, CT: Yale University Press.

Russell, J. A. (1991). In defense of a prototype approach to emotion concepts. *Journal of Personality and Social Psychology, 60*, 37–47.

Schachter, S. (1964). The interaction of cognitive and physiological determinants of emotional states. In L. Berkowitz (Ed.), *Advances in experimental social psychology, Vol. 1* (pp. 49–80). New York: Academic Press.

Schwartz, G. E., Fair, P. L., Salt, P., Mandel, M. R., & Klerman, G. L. (1976). Facial muscle patterning to affective imagery in depressed and nondepressed subjects. *Science, 192*, 489–491.

Sears, D. O. (1988). Symbolic racism. In P. A. Katz and D. A. Taylor (Eds.), *Eliminating racism: Profiles in controversy*. New York: Plenum.

Sherif, M., Harvey, O. J., White, B. J., Hood, W. R., & Sherif, C. W. (1961). *Intergroup conflict and cooperation: The robber's cave experiment*. Norman: Oklahoma University Press, Institute of Group Relations.

Sprecher, S. (1986). The relation between inequity and emotions in close relationships. *Social Psychology Quarterly, 49*, 309–321.

Stemmler, G. (1989). The autonomic differentiation of emotions revisited: Convergent and discriminant validation. *Psychophysiology, 26*, 617–632.

Stephan, W. G. (1977). Stereotyping: Role of ingroup-outgroup differences in causal attribution of behavior. *Journal of Social Psychology, 101*, 255–266.

Stephan, W. G., & Stephan, C. W. (1985). Intergroup anxiety. *Journal of Social Issues, 41*, 157–175.

Stephan, W. G., & Stephan, C. W. (1989). Antecedents of intergroup anxiety in Asian-Americans and Hispanic-Americans. *International Journal of Intercultural Relations, 13*, 203–219.

Tajfel, H. (1969). Cognitive aspects of prejudice. *Journal of Biosocial Science, 1*, 173–191.

Tajfel, H. (1978). *Differentiation between social groups*. London: Academic Press.

Tajfel, H. (1981). *Human groups and social categories: Studies in social psychology*. Cambridge: Cambridge University Press.

Tajfel, H., & Turner, J. C. (1979). An integrative theory of intergroup conflict. In S. Worchel & W. G. Austin (Eds.), *The social psychology of intergroup relations*. Monterey, CA: Brooks-Cole.

Taylor, D. M., & Jaggi, V. (1974). Ethnocentrism and causal attribution in a South Indian context. *Journal of Cross-Cultural Psychology, 5*, 162–171.

Tesser, A. (1991). Emotion in social comparison and reflection processes. In J. Suls & T. A. Wills (Eds.), *Group comparison: Contemporary theory and research* (pp. 117–145). Hillsdale, NJ: Erlbaum.

Tickle-Degnen, L., & Rosenthal, R. (1987). Group rapport and nonverbal behavior. In C. Hendrick (Ed.), *Group processes and intergroup relations* (pp. 113–166). Newbury Park, CA: Sage.

Tognacci, L. N., & Cook, S. W. (1975). Conditioned autonomic responses as bidirectional indicators of racial attitude. *Journal of Personality and Social Psychology, 31*, 137–144.

Tomkins, S. S. (1962). *Affect, imagery, and consciousness (Vol. 1. The positive affects)*. New York: Springer.

Tomkins, S. S. (1963). *Affect, imagery, and consciousness (Vol. 2. The negative affects)*. New York: Springer.

Tomkins, S. S. (1984). Affect theory. In K. R. Scherer & P. Ekman (Eds.), *Approaches to emotion* (pp. 163–195). Hillsdale, NJ: Erlbaum.

Turner, J. C., Hogg, M. A., Oakes, P. J., Reicher, S. D., & Wetherell, M. S. (1987). *Rediscovering the social group: A self-categorization theory*. Oxford: Blackwell.

Vanbeselaere, N. (1991). The different effects of simple and crossed categorizations: A result of the category differentiation process or of differential category salience? In W. Stroebe & M. Hewstone (Eds.), *European review of social psychology, Vol. 2.* (pp. 247–278). Chichester, England: Wiley.

Vanman, E. J., Paul, B. Y., Kaplan, D. L., & Miller, N. (1990). Facial electromyography differentiates racial bias in imagined cooperative settings [Meeting Abstract]. *Psychophysiology, 27*, S63.

Vanman, E. J., Kaplan, D. L., & Miller, N. (1991). Facial EMG activity and bias between social groups: A replication and extension [Meeting Abstract]. *Psychophysiology, 28*, S59.

Vidulich, R. N., & Krevanick, F. W. (1966). Racial attitudes and emotional response to visual representations of the negro. *Journal of Social Psychology, 68*, 85–93.

Weiner, B. (1985). An attributional theory of achievement motivation and emotion. *Psychological Review, 92*, 548–573.

Wilson, L., & Rogers, R. W. (1975). The fire this time: Effects of race of target, insult, and potential retaliation on black aggression. *Journal of Personality and Social Psychology, 32*, 857–864.

Word, C. O., Zanna, M. P., & Cooper, J. (1974). The nonverbal mediation of self-fulfilling prophecies in interracial interaction. *Journal of Experimental Social Psychology, 10*, 109–120.

Zajonc, R. B. (1980). Feeling and thinking: Preferences need no inferences. *American Psychologist, 35*, 151–175.

Zajonc, R. B. (1984). On primacy of affect. In K. R. Scherer & P. Ekman (Eds.), *Approaches to Emotion* (pp. 259–270). Hillsdale, NJ: Erlbaum.

Zajonc, R. B., & Markus, H. (1984). Affect and cognition: The hard interface. In C. E. Izard, J. Kagan, & R. B. Zajonc (Eds.), *Emotions, cognition, & behavior* (pp. 73–102). Cambridge: Cambridge University Press.

Zanna, M. P., & Rempel, J. K. (1988). Attitudes: A new look at an old concept. In D. Bar-Tal & A. W. Kruglanski (Eds.), *The social psychology of knowledge* (pp. 315–334). Cambridge: Cambridge University Press.

Chapter 11

Negative Interdependence and Prejudice: Whence the Affect?

SUSAN T. FISKE

Department of Psychology
University of Massachusetts at Amherst
Amherst, Massachusetts

JANET B. RUSCHER

Department of Psychology
Tulane University
New Orleans, Louisiana

The initial fact, therefore, is that human groups tend to stay apart. . . . The fact is adequately explained by the principles of ease, least effort, congeniality, and pride in one's own culture. . . . And perhaps most important of all, the separateness may lead to genuine conflicts of interests, as well as to many imaginary conflicts.
—Allport, 1954

Introduction

A woman joins a previously all-male police force and is subjected to such constant verbal and physical harassment that she files a lawsuit. An African American manager joins an all European American corporation, only to find that his "office" consists of a pile of boxes walling off a corner of a storage room. Children shun other children with physical stigmas. Ethnic strife routinely plagues emerging nations in Eastern Europe and Africa.

Why do people persist in disliking and mistrusting people from outgroups? This fundamental issue motivates virtually all research on prejudice but, despite this massive effort, something is missing from our attempts to account for the origins of negative affect toward outgroup members. Why do people react to outgroup members as irritating or dangerous instead of merely interesting or unique? Why is human difference seen as disadvantage or threat instead of asset? Whence the negative affect in response to the Other?

This chapter will highlight some previous attempts to answer this question, and then it will develop a new perspective based on negative interdependence between groups, as it influences social cognition. In effect, we will examine both Allport's "genuine conflicts of interest, as well as many imaginary conflicts." We will discuss the mechanisms that underlie negative affect toward outgroup members and describe some supporting evidence from both our own research and some of the hallmark works in stereotyping, affect, and prejudice. Finally, we will reconsider two major techniques of negative affect reduction (avoidance and contact) in light of our current perspective.

A Theoretical Gap

Numerous researchers have attempted to account for the prejudice associated with outgroup members. Some approaches to this problem start at the level of the individual and largely confine their analysis to processes that occur within the individual. Other approaches start at the level of society, examining the interactions of groups as groups, that is, concentrating their analyses on several people interacting with several other people.

Within the individualistic approaches, some are explicitly intrapsychic in tone. The Authoritarian Personality research group (Adorno, Frenkel-Brunswik, Levinson, & Sanford, 1950) posited that anti-Semitic bigots project their own unacceptable sexual and aggressive impulses onto ethnic outgroups. Hence, in this view, hostility would result from one's own repressed hostility; for example, disgust or envy toward the outgroup's alleged sexual practices would result from one's own repressed sexual urges. The character of prejudice, in this view, stems from intrapsychic conflict externalized onto a convenient external object (for reviews, see Allport, 1954; Brown, 1965).

A more recent intrapsychic perspective appears in the work of Katz and his colleagues on the ambivalence of American whites toward blacks (e.g., Katz, 1981; Katz, Glass, & Cohen, 1973; Katz, Wackenhut, & Hass, 1986). European Americans view African Americans with ambivalence essentially because the latter create a perceived value conflict between egalitarianism and individualism. According to egalitarian values, Americans honor the democratic and humanitarian precept that all people are created equal and should have an equal chance in life. According to individualistic values, personal freedom and self-reliance determine an individual's worth through hard work, sacrifice, and achievement. African Americans are seen as deserving support and sympathy for their status as fellow human beings who have been mistreated in the past. But at the same time they are seen as deserving contempt and anger for their perceived violation of work-ethic norms. Higher rates of illegitimacy, welfare dependence, school failure, crime, and drug addition are blamed on personal traits of the African Americans themselves. Thus, like the Authoritarian Personality work, the Katz explanation of ambivalence relies on psychological processes (specifically, conflicts) within the individual to account for the origins of feelings that result from stereotypes.

Another explanation posits intraindividual conflict even more directly related to the object of one's prejudice. From the aversive racism perspective (Gaertner, 1976; Gaertner & Dovidio, 1986), European Americans find their own prejudice objectionable, and they are concerned about promoting a nonracist self-image. Hence, aversive racists avoid acting in recognizably unfavorable or inappropriate ways, but they will act on their prejudice given alternative excuses for their behavior. The conflict here occurs between egalitarian values and the perceiver's own unacknowledged negative feelings. This theory accounts for ambivalent feelings, and it describes a motivation for superficially expressed positive feelings, but it does not actually posit the origins of the negative feelings. (For a related account, see Devine, 1989.)

A fourth example of this type of intraindividual analysis could be extrapolated from work conducted for another purpose. Eagly and Mladinic (1989) have identified stereotypes of women that the authors interpret as conveying positive attitudes toward women. We would reinterpret their well-documented content of the stereotype as conveying ambivalence instead. People seem to view women as simultaneously likable (consistent with Eagly's interpretation) but also as not worthy of much respect (our interpretation). For example, women are seen as warm and gentle but also as servile and fussy. This suggests that people feel simultaneously affectionate toward women and slightly scornful of them. If this ambivalent interpretation is tenable, then one could characterize affective reactions toward women as resulting from the conflict between valuing women as traditionally nurturing caretakers and derogating them as traditionally noncompetitive in the workplace.[1] Of course, this interpretation is entirely our own and in no way places the Eagly work in an intrapsychic theoretical camp. Nevertheless, it seems possible that ambivalent attitudes toward

---

[1]Stereotypes of men, on the other hand, consistently imply respect, if not always liking (e.g., independent and active but also cynical and arrogant).

women might result from the conflicting values they represent. Several theories, thus, can be interpreted as describing prejudice that results from intraindividual conflict.

Quite a different type of individualistic analysis relies on learning theory. In contrast to the implicitly or explicitly conflict-based individualistic explanations are those individualistic explanations that rely on conditioned affective reactions. The idea that prejudice could be a conditioned response came up in stimulus-response theories within social psychology (e.g., Staats & Staats, 1963), and one-trial, traumatic conditioning has also been proposed as an account for some forms of prejudice (Allport, 1954, p. 313). Conditioning was similarly proposed as one possible origin for instantaneous schema-triggered or category-based affective responses (Fiske, 1982; Fiske & Pavelchak, 1986). Of all the range of affective reactions to outgroups, conditioning accounts best for phobic types of affective responses.

What is wrong with these individualistic (intrapsychic conflict and learning) theories of prejudice? Nothing, except that they neglect the explicitly social origins of prejudice. We are interested in the reactions of an individual actually interacting with another individual perceived to be from an outgroup, in what might be called mixed-group dyads, so we need to look at a broader level of analysis.

Of course, there are approaches that do address a more macro, intergroup level of analysis, but this level is more macro than the one we have in mind. For example, one early theory can be construed as addressing the societal origins of intergroup affect. Realistic group conflict theory holds that groups competing for scarce resources derogate each other in order to justify their goal of gaining at the expense of the other. The winners derogate the losers in order to justify the status quo as the supposed natural order of things. And the losers may derogate the winners in order to explain the allegedly unfair methods by which the winners came out on top. The greater the value of the outcomes under dispute, the greater the hostility. And the less the overlap in economic interests, the less the hostility. Intergroup hostility is, in this view, an expression of the group's struggle for power, income, and prestige (e.g., Allport, 1954; Blau, 1977; LeVine & Campbell, 1972; Sherif, 1948; Sumner, 1906; see Simpson & Yinger, 1986, for a review). Hence, prejudice can be viewed as a group's weapon in macro-level conflict.[2] Our own interest, however, lies in individual, face-to-face relationships and less in the interactions of groups qua groups.

This distinction between group and individual relationships becomes clearer in considering social identity theory (Tajfel, 1972, 1981; Tajfel &

---

[2]A related perspective holds that intergroup hostility results from a group-level link between frustration and aggression (Myrdal, 1944). There is less documentation on this point, however.

Turner, 1979; for reviews, see Brewer & Kramer, 1985; Messick & Mackie, 1989; Tajfel, 1982; Turner, 1981). This theory posits that people categorize people into ingroup and outgroup on the basis of ethnicity, nationality, gender, age, occupation, or the like. They identify with the ingroup and derogate the outgroup in order to maintain their self-esteem as a function of membership in the apparently superior ingroup. Although evidence is mixed on the actual self-esteem functions of outgroup stereotyping and prejudice (see Fiske & Taylor, 1991), this analysis does capture an important origin of intergroup affective reactions. Moreover, this analysis also suggests an origin for the negative views of (i.e., prejudice against) outgroup members, although evidence is strongest for ingroup favoritism and weaker on outgroup derogation (also see self-categorization theory, e.g., Turner, 1987). More to the point here, this theory does not address the personal, one-on-one relationships within a mixed-group dyad. It may be useful to frame this distinction in terms of Tajfel's continuum of interaction from interpersonal to intergroup, which depends on the salience of group membership. Research on social identity theory falls at the intergroup extreme of this continuum, especially when several members of each group are simultaneously present and interacting as group members. Our own interest lies in interactions just short of this extreme, namely situations in which two people have a relationship and group membership is one factor influencing that relationship.

Thus, between the individual-level analyses of psychodynamic and learning theories on one hand, and the group-level analyses of group conflict and social identity theories on the other hand lies an intermediate level of analysis. We propose to examine the structure of interdependence between individuals who are cognizant of their status as members of different groups; interdependence structures offer a mid-level view of some sources of prejudice.

Interdependence as a Source of Emotion

In our view, it is difficult to overestimate the importance of interdependence to the psychology of social life. Interdependence is a, if not the, fundamental feature of human social life. At work and at play, our happiness largely depends on the behavior of other people, as well as on our own behavior toward them. Moreover, interdependence is a core theoretical concept in social psychology, stemming from the earliest theoretical frameworks of Lewinian field theory (Kelley, 1990). Kelley's personal relationships theory (1979; Kelley *et al.*, 1983; Kelley & Thibaut, 1978; Thibaut & Kelley, 1959) defines interdependence as a situation in which each person's outcomes depend both on one's own behavior and that of the other person.

Interdependence as a Source of Emotion in Close Relationships

For present purposes, interdependence can tell us something about the origins of emotion in prejudice against outgroups. An interdependence analysis of emotion in close personal relationships has already proved extremely profitable, and we would venture a similar analysis in the emotions of mixed-group dyads. Hence, it is helpful to describe first the role of interdependence in emotion within close relationships.

The basic idea is that emotions result in part from the interruption of complex goal sequences (Mandler, 1975). Interruptions lead to arousal, which at least intensifies emotions, and in the strong form of this argument, is a necessary component of all emotion, in combination with cognitive analyses of the perceived causes of one's arousal (cf. Schachter & Singer, 1962).

The application to close relationships is elegant in its simplicity: when two people are intimate, they have enmeshed goal sequences, and thus the ability to interrupt each other's complex goal-directed behavior; such interruptions provoke emotion (Berscheid, 1983). For example, when one person depends on the other for a ride to work (enmeshed goal sequence), if the latter is late, the former person will be late too and presumably interrupted as well as irritated. More important goals (e.g., career, family) may also depend on the partners' cooperation, leaving each person vulnerable to interruption by the other. When intermeshed sequences run off smoothly, with no surprises, there is little emotion, as in a well-established and coordinated relationship that is companionable but not exciting. Interruptions can be positive, due to unexpected facilitation, or negative, due to unexpected hindrance. The greater the interdependence, the greater the distress upon dissolution of the relationship (Simpson, 1987) and the longer the relationship generally lasts (Berscheid, Snyder, & Omoto, 1989). While acknowledging the preliminary nature of the research on this framework and noting that not all intimate emotions have this origin, we would still suggest that this view provides a straightforward key to the role of interdependence in emotions within other contexts as well.

Negative Interdependence and Prejudice

To the extent that two people are interdependent (willingly or not), they have the ability to interrupt or facilitate each other's goals. In any relationship, whether intimate or not, two people depend on each other, so each by definition influences the other's goals. This interruptive potential equally applies to interdependence that is imposed from outside, as might well occur when a person has to depend on an outgrouper. Hence, any interdependent relationship would be a candidate for the experience of strong emotional reactions. We propose to apply this framework to a mixed-group dyad, in which each person's outcome depends on the other.

Our basic hypothesis is that an outgroup member is spontaneously presumed to hinder one's goals. Hence, the outgrouper is intrinsically interruptive and provokes negative affective reactions. Thus, it is an inevitable feature of outgroup members that they will be mistrusted (at least initially) because they are expected to get in the way, either passively or actively, of the perceiver's long-term goals and short-term daily functioning.

This proposal follows in a straightforward manner from the definition of a group as a social category. A group may be defined in Gestalt terms as being an entity, that is, having "entitativity" (Campbell, 1958). The individuals are seen as having a common fate, similarity, and proximity. It is not a big step to conclude that group members are seen as having shared goals, given their similarity and common fate. Indeed, basic textbook definitions note "The sharing of common goals is one of the strongest unifying factors within groups, and shared goals also motivate group members to behave in ways that result in the group's successful goal completion" (Forsyth, 1983, p. 10). Moreover, cognitive theories of stereotyping posit that categorizing people into groups minimizes perceived within-group differences and maximizes perceived between-group differences (Tajfel, 1972; Taylor, 1981). Thus, group members endorse the slogan of the Three Musketeers, "all for one and one for all."

By contrast, outgroup members are seen as pitted against the ingroup. They have their own shared goals which, by virtue of being in the outgroup category, are seen as intrinsically different from the perceiver's and the ingroup's goals. Therefore, people from other groups are perceived as having goals that may disrupt the perceiver's own goals. This is not the same thing as saying that the ingroup and outgroup necessarily are in direct competition. It is a broader point, for an outgroup member can interfere merely by pursuing outgroup goals without any explicit intention of harming the ingroup. For example, one group's goal of having a decent party with a "reasonable" volume for music may interfere with an outgroup member's goal of sleeping at a "reasonable" hour. In fact, evidence from the minimal intergroup paradigm indicates that ingroup favoritism is the clearcut phenomenon, while disadvantaging the outgroup is a far less reliable occurrence (Brewer, 1979). Thus, merely by existing as a member of a group not one's own, the outgroup individual is seen as having different and potentially interfering goals. Indeed, one may perceive the outgrouper's difference as a potential threat to the entire social order.

This is not to say that perceived interdependence occurs inevitably, whenever one encounters a member of the outgroup. However, given potential or even minimal interdependence, an outgrouper will be seen as a probable threat to one's interests. It is revealing that, even in the absence of interaction, mere outgroup membership elicits category-based responses (e.g., Allport, 1954; Fiske, Neuberg, Beattie, & Milberg, 1987), many of which are negative. No doubt some of these negative responses are based on previous interdependence and not strictly tied to current interdependence and potential interruption. Moreover, people may dislike members of groups whom they have never met (Allport, 1954). For example, people disliked Turks in the original Katz and Braly (1933) study, even though subjects actually had never met a Turk. Negative responses can even occur when outgroups are entirely fictitious. And evidence obtained using the minimal group paradigm indicates that mere categorization into an outgroup results in that group being perceived less favorably than the ingroup (Brewer & Kramer, 1985). How do such results fit with the idea that negative reactions result from interruptive interdependence? From our perspective, people assume that, if encountered under at least minimal interdependence, an outgroup member would somehow interfere with (or at least not facilitate) their own goals (cf. Hoyle, Pinkley, & Insko, 1989).

Merely by interrupting in any fashion, the outgrouper elicits negative affect, a point that follows from Berscheid's and Mandler's emotion theories. One might argue that this analysis also follows from the frustration-aggression hypothesis (Allport, 1954). However, in our analysis, it is not a matter of irrelevant interruptions causing displaced hostility, but of negative affect directed at the source of the interruption or potential interruption.

There are two basic forms of interference to be expected from an outgroup member, and each elicits affect, as the following section will elaborate. To anticipate, first, *mere membership* threatens the ingroup member's basic assumptions about daily functioning, fundamental interaction rules, and the most trivial of habitual behaviors (for interracial examples, see Jones, 1986; Kochman, 1981). For example, what is interpreted as respectful eye contact (direct or averted gaze when listening to a superior) may differ from one group to another (Feldman & Saletsky, 1986). Due to such violations of basic assumptions about interaction, one's nonverbal behavior may then reflect discomfort (e.g., Weitz, 1974; Word, Zanna, & Cooper, 1974). Perceptions that the other will "get in the way" or "doesn't fit in" express this concern in verbal terms. Note that there must be some minimal interdependence for the outgrouper's differences to matter enough to be interruptive and thus to cause discomfort and stronger emotions.

In addition to mere membership, outgroup members are potentially interfering because of *presumed blockage* of ingroup goals. To the extent that the outgroup is assumed to possess goals dissimilar to those of the ingroup, some of those goals will inevitably be seen as mutually exclusive with the perceiver's goals. This may, in fact, be a veridical perception, to the extent that realistic group conflict theory is correct and to the extent that ingroup favoritism happens to operate in a zero-sum game, where the ingroup's gain is the outgroup's loss. Otherwise, outgroup goals—merely because they are different—may interfere with the ingroup; even if the interference is inadvertent, the blocking may be experienced as intentional. As an aside, it is worth noting that some ingroup–outgroup goals are relatively symbiotic; that is, conceivably, the pursuit of different goals could sometimes be mutually facilitative. In such cases, blockage alone would be unlikely to account for prejudice, any more than blocking accounts for prejudice when ingroup–outgroup goals are relatively nondependent (cf. LeVine & Campbell, 1972).

In the two sections immediately following, we discuss in greater detail these two forms of interference, mere membership and presumed blockage, presenting evidence from the existing empirical literature.

Mere Membership

Given at least minimal interdependence, an outgroup member can interfere and elicit negative affect simply because the person is a member of the outgroup. That is, the mere attributes (or presumed attributes) of the outgroup member are disruptive to the ingroup member's current goals. First, disruption can occur if the outgroup is novel (i.e., rarely encountered by the ingroup). Second, outgroup members are assumed to have a "different way of doing things." Whether real or imagined, whether novel or familiar, this differentness "gets in the way" of currently pursued goals. An outgroup member's very traits and behaviors are thus a second potential source of interruption.

Mere Membership and Novelty

Extreme novelty is, quite simply, disruptive to smooth interaction. An outgroup member's novel appearance, behavior, and attitudes are distracting, diverting perceivers from their own current goals; this has apparent affective consequences. For example, when people expect to interact with an outgroup member from an unfamiliar category (e.g., a schizophrenic), there is marked change in nonverbal behavior (Neuberg & Fiske, 1987), suggesting affective disturbance. Similarly, nonverbal signs of discomfort are found when people believe they are interacting with a mental patient (Farina and Ring, 1965) or a physically disabled person (Kleck, 1968; Kleck, Ono, & Hastorf, 1966).

During interaction with novel others, attention is directed to the microlevel of interaction management because the habitual forms of interaction are suddenly called into question. Entertaining a visitor with an unfamiliar accent, for example, redirects attention to understanding her specific words, rather than deeply considering the conversation content; this consequently inhibits the social flow. For an able-bodied person, an initial conversation with someone confined to a wheelchair focuses attention on eye contact (e.g., trying not to stare at the person's physical differences) and other non-verbals (e.g., determining how close to stand, how to synchronize movements). Again, this involves micro-management of behavior, to the detriment of normal interaction goals (Goffman, 1963; Jones *et al.*, 1984). People then perceive their performance to be disrupted, even when it may be objectively superior (Farina & Ring, 1965). As the habitual assumptions become problematic, attention is directed increasingly downward toward more micro-analysis of activity; this inevitably distracts from monitoring progress toward broader goals (cf. Vallacher & Wegner, 1987). Novelty due to mere membership thus not only disrupts the current interaction per se; it can hinder perceivers' progress toward their more major goals. Novelty thus has pervasive effects.

Novelty varies in degree and impact. Too much novelty is apparently aversive (Fiske & Maddi, 1961; Mandler, 1975). That is, moderate novelty is interesting, and, once assimilated, the variation is a pleasant change; the work to assimilate it is just enough to be stimulating but not so much as to be disruptive to current goals. In contrast, extreme novelty cannot be assimilated easily, and it is disruptive. Thus, the more novel the outgroup members, the more disruptive the person is likely to be perceived as being, and thus the more intense the affect.

To the extent that the novelty of some outgroup members is disruptive, then prior exposure should lessen potential for disruption and emotion in an impending interaction. For example, people feel uncomfortable when their need to stare at stigma-bearing persons, at least those who are visually novel, conflicts with social sanctions against staring; this approach–avoidance conflict itself disrupts smooth interactions. However, the discomfort can be alleviated when perceivers have opportunities unobtrusively to view a novel person before actually interacting. Langer *et al.* found that subjects sat farther from and oriented their chairs more away from a novel person (pregnant or wearing a leg brace) than from a "normal" person. This indicates disruption of normal scripted interaction patterns. With prior exposure, however, nonverbal behavior more resembled normal interaction patterns. Prior exposure, then, seems to reduce the disruptiveness created by novelty.

Mere Membership and Differentness (Real or Imagined)

Yet even after novelty "wears off" (through prior or repeated exposure), mere membership in the outgroup remains potentially disruptive. The outgrouper does things differently (or presumably does), even if the outgrouper's appearance, behavior, and attitudes are predictable based on previous experience with the individual or group. As long as the other is not an ingroup member, a certain amount of lower-level monitoring is necessary, simply because the outgroup person will always be unfamiliar relative to the ingroup. This lower-level monitoring again interferes with metaprogress toward basic goals.

Some sources of continued disruptiveness are in the eye of the beholder. Outgroup members are presumed to possess stereotypical traits, which distinguish them from the ingroup (Allen & Wilder, 1979; Wilder, 1981) in often negative ways (Allport, 1954). The assumed negativity of outgroup attributes influences judgment speed (Dovidio, Evans, & Tyler, 1986), recognition speed (Gaertner & McLaughlin, 1983), and encoding (Duncan, 1976; Sagar & Schofield, 1980). Hence, people's information-processing abilities are tied up by the presumed differentness and negativity of the outgrouper. Ironically, being "cognitively busy" (e.g., Gilbert, Pelham, & Krull, 1988) with the outgrouper's difference probably means the person's actions will be attributed even more to dispositional causes such as outgroup membership, rather than situational constraints, and thus exacerbates prejudice (see also Pettigrew, 1979, on the Ultimate Attribution Error).

Perceivers do expect the presumed negative attributes to be disruptive. For example, compared to partners believed to be "normal," partners believed to be mentally ill are rated less able to get along with others, less able to understand others, less able to understand themselves, and more unpredictable (Farina & Ring, 1965). Moreover, although subjects themselves did not reportedly differ in their own liking ratings, subjects reported that others would dislike the ill partner more than the normal partner. This is reminiscent of the argument against hiring someone from an outgroup, supposedly not because the employers object, but because they imagine their clients will object. This argument is usually made without any relevant data, which leads one to suspect it is easier to admit the assumed prejudice of others than one's own prejudice.

The expected disruption and discomfort then change actual interaction but, interestingly, not always in the expected ways. When each member of the pair thought the other was mentally ill, objective performance (at Labyrintspel, a joint hand-eye coordination game) was actually better than if each member thought the other was "normal." Nevertheless, subjects who believed their partners ill also believed that the partner hindered performance, even though people with "ill" partners did better than people with normal partners. Ironically, subjects with "ill" partners indicated that they would have preferred to perform the task alone rather than with the partner (see also Farina, Holland, & Ring, 1966).

Apparently, the greater the potential for disruption, the greater the difference in affect. For example, Neuberg and Fiske's (1987) subjects who anticipated interaction with a schizophrenic evaluated him differently, depending on the magnitude of potential disruption. In one of these experiments, subjects attending to uniformly positive (and stereotype-inconsistent) information about the schizophrenic (e.g., friendly) evaluated him more favorably than subjects who read only neutral information. Presumably, the subjects reading positive information expected a relatively smooth interaction with the outgroup member. Moreover, from the subjects' perspective, the positively described target's true membership in the category could seem less certain. The schizophrenic had been presented as a "former patient," who was reintegrating into society; maybe he was not a schizophrenic any more. Or, even if he remained a schizophrenic, evidence unequivocally suggested that he was relatively normal at the moment and should not be very disruptive. In contrast, perceivers attending to relatively neutral information obtained no evidence that the target was "cured" or "in control" and were left expecting the disruptions predicted by the outgroup membership. Thus, as with prior exposure to a physical stigma, negative anticipatory emotions can be attenuated when people have evidence that the individual outgroup member is somewhat less disruptive than mere membership predicts.

These ingroup–outgroup differences (real or imagined) are themselves sources of perceived conflict. Like realistic conflict theory (Allport, 1954; Blau, 1977; LeVine & Campbell, 1972; Sherif, 1948; Sumner, 1906), the current perspective maintains that people assume outgroup members are hostile and will behave in an adversarial fashion (a.k.a. presumed blockage). We add here, however, that in dyadic encounters, real and imagined outgroup differences (e.g., novelty, nonverbal behavior, speech patterns, language, and behavioral scripts) themselves create conflict and disruption. These differences are likely to maintain the conflict and, even though they are not directed at the ingroup, may even be seen as sources of hostility. Jones (1986) suggests, for example, that African American culture operates under a different notion of time than does mainstream European American culture. To the extent that arriving at a particular time may have a different meaning for each group, there is potential conflict and possible interruptions in goals. Even if the different pattern of behavior is not perceived as intentionally hostile or passively aggressive, negative affect stemming from interruption will continue to feed prejudice.

Such intrinsic sources of conflict were noticeably missing in the Robber's Cave study of realistic group conflict (Sherif, Harvey, White, Hood, & Sherif, 1961), wherein a homogeneous group of boys was randomly divided into two groups. Although there were presumed differences when the two groups first interacted, these eventually faded once superordinate goals were created (and explicit competition ceased).[3] In the absence of goal blockage, the subjects' similarity in race, sex, religious background, and socioeconomic background left few sources of disruption from mere member-

---

[3]The authors do not report any additional games between the boys, and certainly not games with prizes at stake.

ship. This allowed successful and continued cooperative interaction and presumably the attenuation of negative emotions. Unfortunately, intergroup interactions in the real world (where many mere membership issues remain) are probably more difficult to resolve.

Mere Membership: An Old Controversy Revisited

Admittedly, the idea that prejudice stems from mere membership is hardly new (Allport, 1954); our extension, though, is that prejudice and negative affect arise from the potential for disruption. This brings to mind the old controversy over whether prejudice stemmed from mere membership in race (e.g., Triandis, 1961) or from disparate beliefs and values (e.g., Rokeach, 1960, 1961). Eventually, Triandis and Davis (1965) proposed that certain prejudiced behaviors stemmed from race whereas others stemmed from beliefs. Specifically, they demonstrated that race was most closely involved with relatively intimate behaviors (e.g., marriage, close friendship) whereas values and beliefs were mostly related to less intimate behaviors (e.g., working on a campaign with the outgroup member; admiring the work of the outgroup member).

These classes of behaviors can be reconsidered in terms of their potential for disruption. First, with less intimate behaviors (often not requiring contact), race is less likely to be disruptive than with more intimate behaviors. Relative to intimate behaviors, nonintimate behaviors are, by definition, those in which one can keep the other at a distance. A European American, for example, can admire an African American actor with no actual interaction taking place. Keeping outgroup members at a distance reduces their capacity to distract, to interfere by virtue of their allegedly or actually different habits, and so on. Mere membership in such cases has less potential for disruption in nonintimate than intimate situations. This is not to say that mere membership has no disruptive capacity in nonintimate situations, but that there are proportionate decreases in disruptiveness with decreases in intimacy.

In contrast, intimate behaviors by definition require contact and heightened, enmeshed interdependence. The potential for disruption is therefore higher in such situations. Mere membership in another race, or some other outgroup, carries with it all the disruptiveness discussed earlier. Moreover, ingroups often sanction against intimate behaviors with outgroup members or exert social pressure in some other fashion (Insko, Nacoste, & Moe, 1983). An ingroup member's exogenous, interdependent relationships may be disrupted by engaging in intimate behaviors with an outgroup member. For example, a mixed-group roommate pair could exist peacefully, with little negative affect ensuing, until a visiting family member becomes disconcerted by novelty or differentness.

Conclusion

It is our position, then, that mere membership alone is sufficient to produce negative affect in mixed-dyad encounters. The magnitude of the affect will be commensurate with the magnitude of potential disruption. With respect to mere membership, potential sources of disruption are the level of novelty, the extent to which the outgroup possesses (or is believed to possess) negative attributes, the extent to which the outgroup has intrinsically different attributes, and the degree of intimacy (and thus type of interdependence) of the encounter. The next section considers the role of interdependence in greater detail, because of its obvious relevance to goal blockage.

Presumed Blockage by Outgroup Members

As noted earlier, the capacity for blocking by an outgroup member, stemming from the outgroup's different goals, is a second source of negative affect. The outgroup's different or conflicting goals, as well as implicit or explicit competition, are nonfacilitative of (and often interfering to) the ingroup's goals. Of course, blocking of all these types (e.g., competition, conflicting goals, uncooperativeness) no doubt can evoke negative affect, irrespective of group membership. Our point here is that, all things being equal, outgroup blocking potentially produces more affect than equivalent ingroup blocking because an adversarial relationship is already assumed (cf. Insko, Schopler, Hoyle, Dardis, & Graetz, 1990).[4] In effect, the assumption of outgroup blockage creates a negative interdependence in the mind of the perceivers. People begin with an adversarial assumption and are chronically primed to interpret an outgroup member's behavior as adversarial. Furthermore, the salience of group membership, either the physical presence of the groups (Insko et al., 1987; McCallum et al., 1985; cf. Rehm et al., 1987) or being explicitly labeled as a representative of an outgroup (Insko et al., 1987) increases competitiveness. With naturally existing ingroup–outgroup dyads, group membership is often evident and should enhance the presumption of blocking.

Competition

We suggested that blocking by an outgroup member in competitive interdependence may produce more negative affect than comparable blocking

---

[4]In the vein proposed by Katz (e.g., Katz et al., 1986) reactions toward outgroups may polarize such that goal facilitation from an outgroup member (e.g., receiving help) might elicit more affect than a similar gesture from an ingroup member.

by an ingroup member. Competition may be explicit and acknowledged. Or, to the extent that competitive interdependence is represented by situations in which one person's gains necessitate the other person's losses, competition may be implicit as well.

Even an outgroup member who is merely minding his or her own business may be construed as unfairly competitive if the perceiver and the other are to be compared and evaluated by third parties. For example, a particularly productive outgrouper may be perceived as rate busting (raising expectations for other people by virtue of producing more than average). An ingrouper who does the same thing may be perceived negatively as well, but the rate-busting ingrouper should be less threatening for several reasons (the potential for pride in an ingrouper's accomplishments, the presumed possibility of influencing the person to slow down, the likelihood of shared benefits, and other cooperative side effects of same-group membership; for an analogue within close relationships, see Tesser's (1988) model of self-evaluation maintenance). Thus, even an individualistically oriented outgrouper may be perceived as implicitly competitive, by virtue of not adhering to prior norms established by the ingroup.

Competitions, whether implicit or explicit, between already interdependent persons can have negative affective consequences. For example, being outshined by a friend (social interdependence) on a self-relevant task is unpleasant (Tesser, Millar, & Moore, 1988). According to Tesser's (1988) model, the psychological closeness of a friend invites comparative evaluation whereas outperformance by a stranger is not particularly threatening and is relatively less aversive. In effect, the comparative evaluation disrupts the individual's goal of maintaining a particular self-image. This is consistent with Berscheid's (1983) analysis that intimate, positive interdependence increases potential for emotion.

Extending Tesser's results to our analysis, preexisting negative interdependence may also intensify affect. Being outperformed (i.e., blocked) by an adversary should evoke more social comparison than being blocked by a stranger, with whom there is no preexisting interdependence. To the extent that group membership is salient, being outdone by "one of them" on a self-relevant dimension should be quite threatening indeed. Indeed, our own previous work finds little evidence of negative affect in competing, same-sex, ingroup dyads (Ruscher & Fiske, 1990). It is plausible that competing outgroup dyads would show more negative affect.

Conflicting Goals

Conflicting, but not competitive goals, are also sufficient to produce affect in mixed dyads. Outgroup members' pursuit of their individualistic goals may be manifested or interpreted as uncooperativeness. Perhaps the most pertinent research is a questionnaire study by Dijker (1987) that measured emotional responses to ethnic outgroups; positive feelings, anxiety, irritation, and concern were all reported responses, each related to relevant action tendencies (Frijda, 1986). For example, positive feelings were associated with impulses to seek contact, irritation with impulses to aggression, anxiety with impulses to keep apart, concern with anticipating negative consequences of contact and the desire to prevent future contact (also see Dijker, 1991).

Dijker's analysis focuses on the relationship between emotions and action tendencies during contact. In contrast, our current analysis focuses on the role of interdependence per se in creating affective responses. Nevertheless, his results are consistent with the current analysis in terms of the interruptive potential of outgroup members. Positive feelings express a lack of anticipated interruption or the expectation of being able to manage it; irritation may express frustration with disruption; anxiety and concern express the fear of interruption.

Preliminary data suggest an integration of these two approaches: an outgroup member who refuses to cooperate in an interdependent task elicits particularly strong emotional responses (Dijker & Fiske, 1991). Thus, anticipated interaction with an uncooperative outgroup member produces more negative feelings than does an interaction with a similarly uncooperative ingroup partner. People may infer that obtaining the cooperation of an ingroup member remains a possibility. An explicitly uncooperative outgroup member, however, is simply abandoned as a lost cause.

As with mere membership, it seems that the greater the potential for disruption via blocking, the greater the affect. In a companion study to one study discussed earlier, Neuberg and Fiske (1987) crossed cooperative interdependence with the presence or absence of a schizophrenic label; subjects all read negative information about the schizophrenic. Interacting with a schizophrenic would be potentially disruptive (owing to mere membership) regardless of interdependence, as would cooperating with a partner who had uniformly negative characteristics that would indicate uncooperativeness (i.e., blocking). Therefore, these three conditions should yield the lowest evaluations. In contrast, the least potential disruption was for individuals expecting to meet, but not work with, an unlabeled target. And it is precisely here that the evaluations were most favorable. In sum, there is scattered evidence for the affective consequences of conflicting goals in mixed-group dyads.

Conflicting Goals in Asymmetrical Interdependence

Many real-world mixed dyads do not comprise two homogeneous equal-status parties. Interdependencies are often asymmetrical, in which one party has more power to block the other's goals and hence more power over outcomes. From the current perspective, the low-power participant would experience negative emotions as a result of goal blocking. Some evidence for this is found in Word, Zanna, and Cooper's (1974, Experiment 2) study in which European American interviewees were treated as if they were African American or European American, by varying the interviewers' goal-facilitating behaviors (e.g., nonverbal displays of interest, time allowed for the interview). The interviewees tended to report more negative moods (results were in expected direction, but not statistically significant), which would be expected when people's goals are thwarted. Consistent with the current perspective, goals were thwarted by using techniques frequently adopted against the outgroup. That is, being cut short, not attended to, or not directly faced prevents the low-power person from presenting the self in a favorable (and stereotype-disconfirming) light. The powerless persons apparently were frustrated.

Powerful persons in asymmetrical interdependence also experience negative affect, although this is less obvious, because their goals would seem relatively shielded from blocking. If one is in power, how could one's subordinate possibly interfere? From our perspective, low-power persons can interfere particularly when they are outgroup members. First, their mere membership qualities (novelty, differentness) block the ability of the high-power person to complete current goals.

More to the point, the high-power person's goals may not be conducive to the low-power person's goals *and* vice versa. For example, the subordinate may wish to finish work by 4:55, in order to catch a 5:00 bus; the high-power person may want one (or two) more things done immediately. This places the high-power person in the position to experience interruptions and negative affect. As we suggested earlier, this may be exacerbated in mixed-group encounters, because of adversarial or mixed-goal assumptions. For example, in Word *et al.*'s first investigation (1974, Experiment 1), the behavior of subject interviewers (i.e., the powerful) toward confederate job candidates (i.e., the powerless) was markedly different depending on the confederate's race. Some behaviors (e.g., increased speech error rate) indicate goal interruption, and perhaps negative emotion as well. The majority of the interviewers' behaviors, however, can be construed also as strategies for minimizing interruptions (e.g., shorter interviews, reduced eye contact, increased personal distance). By reducing their exposure to an aversive stimulus (i.e., the outgroup member), interviewers were perhaps attempting to minimize interruption and attenuate additional negative emotions.

In asymmetrical relationships, the relations among negative affect, prejudice, interdependence, and stereotyping are thus particularly insidious. The goal of the powerful person seems less to conduct a sound, accurate interview (cf. Neuberg, 1989) than to avoid interruptions from an aversive outgroup member. This negative affect (or the defense against negative affect) on the part of the powerful person minimizes the less powerful person's chance to provide positive, individuating, or stereotype-discon-firming information. And if less powerful persons do try to provide such information (e.g., by giving a more informative answer, by disagreeing with the more powerful person, etc.) or by behaving in ways intending to counteract potential stereotyping and prejudice (e.g., Hilton & Darley, 1985), those interruptions may evoke additional negative emotion.[5] For example, gender role-incongruent (i.e., counterstereotypic) behavior evokes negative reactions (e.g., Brown & Geis, 1984; Costrich, Feinstein, Kidder, Maracek, & Pascale, 1975). In many respects, low-power outgroup members may often find themselves in no-win situations.

Reducing Negative Affect: Avoidance versus Contact?

Given the inherent potential for disruption and affect in mixed-group dyadic encounters, there are at least two alternative recourses: avoid contact or use contact to try to overcome negative affect. In this final section, we consider the implications of these solutions (or quasi-solutions) in light of our current perspective.

Avoidance

Avoiding aversive circumstances is of course a basic fact of existence. From our perspective, perceivers anticipate outgroup members to be disruptive and thus evoke negative emotions; avoiding outgroup members circumvents these aversive consequences.

Avoiding outgroup members averts real or perceived risk to physical health as well as the risk of contaminating one's social reputation (Jones *et al.*, 1984); high-level goals are thus protected from potential disruption. For example, Goffman (1963) discusses avoidance due to the "peril" of "courtesy stigma." The risk of associating with an outgroup member carries the implication that there is something wrong with the ingroup member (e.g., why is the person so desperate for friends that the person must associate with an outgroup member?). And in the case of more concealable outgroup membership, one may be deemed guilty by association (e.g., perhaps that person is an X, too). Avoidance of outgroupers averts all that unpleasantness.

Moreover, intimate connections with the outgroup can disrupt exogenous relationships, as noted earlier. Research by Stafford and Petway (1977), for example, showed that the spouses of alcoholics were considered

---

[5]Indeed, to the extent that those behaviors are viewed in an affectively congruent or stereotype-consistent manner (e.g., the outgroup member is aggressive), those behaviors might be used as "reasons" for discrimination.

less worthwhile as friends. As another example, one woman we know finds that if people know her only as the mother of a handicapped child, they avoid her, but if they know her only as the mother of her other child, not handicapped, they seek her advice and friendship. In effect, she has a courtesy stigma in half of her maternal identity. Avoidance of the stigmatized and even their close associates protects the higher-order goals of maintaining one's broader social network and social self-esteem while simultaneously circumventing the negative effect evoked when these goals are in jeopardy. Again, avoidance of the outgrouper avoids certain kinds of interruption and negative emotion.

At an even higher level of abstraction, the need to believe in a just world (Lerner, 1980) is also threatened by contact with certain outgroup members. The elderly, the physically disabled, the homeless, and powerless outgroups interfere with this defensive need. Not only this, but these groups are also blatant reminders of myriad negative circumstances of fate that might interfere with life goals. Avoidance defends one against such unpleasant and interruptive reminders.

Avoidance can also protect egalitarian self-perceptions. Paradoxically, although disruption itself is aversive, it is also aversive to acknowledge avoiding someone because the person might be disruptive. For example, Jones *et al.* (1984, p. 184) note that the fear of "behaving in a way that will contradict their images of themselves as sympathetic, nonprejudiced people . . . [can lead normals to] simply refrain from interacting with the stigmatized." Various researchers have documented that a sizable number of European Americans espouse egalitarian values regarding race (e.g., Gaertner & Dovidio, 1986; Katz, Wackenhut, & Hass, 1986; McConahay, 1986), and this probably extends to other outgroups. Avoidance protects these beliefs, because it is easy to see oneself as nonprejudiced against outgroups when one never actually interacts with outgroup members.

Ironically, prolonged noninteraction probably makes the outgroup appear all the more different, however, once interaction occurs. Mere membership's capacity to be disruptive is therefore enhanced by avoidance, self-perpetuating the cycle. Of course, deliberate avoidance would certainly not sustain egalitarian self-perceptions. People can be actively avoidant or passively allow the social system to prevent interaction. Segregated schools, special education schools, mental institutions, and nursing homes simultaneously define outgroups and minimize interaction with them. Indeed, institutional racism can be seen as more than the European American majority's way of maintaining hegemony (Sidanius, 1989). Such institutions can be construed as large-scale avoidance and emotion management.

Quasi-Contact: Avoiding the Issue of Difference

Pure avoidance is not always practical or possible, of course. In such events, people may attempt to reduce potential disruptions by controlling the nature of the interaction. Thus, preferring to see themselves as nonprej-udiced, people may interact with outgroup members on a regular basis. This may, however, be primarily in situations in which the ingroup has the upper hand or situations in which the outgroup member must behave like an ingroup member in order to "fit in." Not only does this reduce the chance for the outgroup member to be disruptive, but the outgroup member probably does not have a history of disrupting. Consider the following ob-servations made by an African American Princeton student (quoted in Jones *et al.*, 1984, p. 94–95):

> A great many white students here are perfectly willing to be friends with blacks, and thus are confused and frustrated about the lack of interaction. The problem is that many of these individuals are only willing to interact on their own terms. . . . A friend of mine never really noticed that whenever we did things together it was al-ways in her predominantly white environment, at mostly white dinner tables or par-ties, listening to her music. . . .

Also avoiding the dilemma of difference, people of low or minority sta-tus may attempt to reduce their potential disruption as outgroupers by try-ing to fit in. This minimizes disruption for both ingroup and outgroup members alike. One strategy is to "pass" as an ingroup member, by adopt-ing behaviors inconsistent with their own group membership or at least consistent with the ingroup:

> When jokes were made about "queers" I had to laugh with the rest, and when talk was about women I had to invent conquests of my own. I hated such moments, but there seemed to be nothing else that I could do. (Goffman, 1963, 87)

If successful, "passing" as an ingroup member virtually obliterates dis-ruption inherent in mixed-group dyads. Successful passing indicates that evidence of mere membership is absent, and the presumption of blockage is removed. In a sense, passing is a kind of avoidance in that it keeps groups apart, at least consciously. It has other costs in that, although tem-porary passing allows prior interaction patterns to be established, discov-ery of group membership may be interpreted as a deceitful betrayal and reduce liking (Jones & Gordon, 1972; Ruscher, 1991), except perhaps by intimates (Kleck, 1968). And of course, there are substantial personal costs to passing.

Not all group membership is sufficiently concealable to permit passing. Nor do all outgroupers even wish to pass, assuming they could. But some sources of disruption inherent in mere membership can be covered to some extent, if the person wishes to endeavor this. An outgroup member can adopt at least some of the ingroup's stereotypic behaviors, appearance (e.g., clothing and hairstyle, plastic surgery), and speech patterns. For instance, a woman on a daytime fishing trip who wants to be treated as "one of the guys" refrains from painting her fingernails that morning, curses on occasion, and baits her hook without squirming. Learning to be bicultural, and move within and between two worlds, is a way of minimizing sources of disruption. But it is not easy, as the requirements of the two worlds are often conflicting (see Jones, 1986).

Contact

Given the proper conditions, intergroup contact can undercut prejudice. Cooperation, equal status, and stereotype-disconfirming outgroup members have all been identified as necessary factors for reducing prejudice and discrimination (e.g., Allport, 1954; Amir, 1976; Cook, 1984). Our current perspective helps explain why contact sometimes backfires, despite these conditions and the best intentions.

Cooperative Goal Structures

For example, cooperative goal structures are known to foster beneficial contact and reduce prejudice. This is not surprising because, insofar as cooperating outgroup members share the perceiver's goals, they are unlikely to intentionally block the perceiver's goal. Nor should perceivers generally believe that cooperating outgroup members are intentionally blocking.

Yet, interdependence with an outgroup member increases the chances for interruption. Both the assumed and actual differentness of outgroup members may make cooperation difficult or frustrating for the perceiver. For example, goals may be identical, but cooperating partners can easily disagree about how those goals should be achieved. As we noted earlier, outgroup members are presumed to have a "different way" of doing things. Moreover, outgroup members can interfere with goals unintentionally, simply through aspects of mere membership. Thus while cooperative goal structures may be better than competitive ones, cooperation need not always facilitate goals nor reduce negative affect.

Equal Status

Like cooperative interdependence, equal status has implications for interruptions and prejudice. As discussed earlier, higher-status persons may engage in behaviors designed to reduce potential interruptions and negative affect. For persons accustomed to higher status (i.e., in most of their real-world interactions), an equal status condition increases the likelihood of interruption. Thus, although equal status allows individuating information to be presented and absorbed, it simultaneously increases the possibility for negative emotion, to the extent that outgroup members' differentness is perceived as aversive or is disruptive. On the other hand, to the extent that persons accustomed to high status find the newly created equality aversive, they may subtly assert higher status in other ways as a sophisticated strategy of emotion management.

Stereotype Disconfirmation

Another requirement for successful contact involves exposure to stereotype-disconfirming outgroup members. Our own research over the past decade specifically addresses this requirement by demonstrating that attention to stereotype-inconsistent information can lead to more individuated impression formation processes which, in turn, can attenuate negative affect. At least under cooperation, more individuated impressions should generally reduce expectations of disruption because the outgroup member is perceived as an individual rather than merely as outgroup member. The assumed negative characteristics are disconfirmed or at least diluted by the stereotype-disconfirming information. This results in affective responses that are less category based and more attribute based (Fiske *et al.*, 1987; Neuberg & Fiske, 1987). Pure individuation means, in effect, that category membership is only one attribute of the person.

Unfortunately, much as we would like it to be, individuation is not social cognition's cure-all for prejudice. Attribute-based affect is likely advantageous when the evaluative sum of the individual's attributes is more favorable than the evaluation of the category. To the extent that most stereotypes are negative, and to the extent that individuation involves incorporating stereotype-inconsistent attributes (which is therefore usually positive information), individuation should usually reduce prejudice.

What is "stereotype disconfirming" in these instances, however, is often "ingroup similar." For example, attributes inconsistent with European Americans' stereotypes of African or Hispanic Americans are often attributes presumably possessed by the European Americans (Dijker & Fiske, 1991; Goodwin & Fiske, 1991). Stereotype-disconfirming outgroup members may simply possess fewer attributes with the capacity to interrupt ingroup members (or they have learned to pass or cover those attributes). It is therefore no wonder that ingroup members would be less prejudiced against outgroup members with these qualities than against outgroup members in general. This is consistent with European Americans' seeming preference for outgroups to assimilate into the mainstream culture by abandoning their ethnicity.

When stereotype-inconsistent information is predominantly negative, however, individuation may actually increase negative affect. For example, stereotypes associated with certain physical stigmas (e.g., paraplegia) are often positive, with stereotype-*inconsistent* features being negative. Individuating processes will thus direct attention to negative attributes, themselves potential sources of disruption, and reduce liking (Fiske & Von Hendy, 1992). On one hand, the resulting affect does not seem to be prejudice, given that the resulting affect is attribute based. On the other hand, outgroup members with negative, stereotype-inconsistent characteristics may be seen as failing to live up to their stereotypes. The paraplegic who is not cheerful, the woman who is not sweet, and the Asian American with no competence in mathematics, for example, may upset members of the dominant culture. Indeed, stereotype disconfirmation can have affective consequences, as sometimes people more favorably evaluate those who are typical of their groups (Wilder, 1984). Stereotype disconfirmation in these cases can have behavioral consequences (see Fiske *et al.*, 1991, and accompanying Brief for Amicus Curiae, 1988).

Conclusions

We have argued that outgroup members are inherently disruptive by virtue of mere membership in a different group and by virtue of presumed blockage of ingroup goals. Disruption is a sufficient cause for emotion and therefore prejudice. These ideas raise a number of remaining issues.

Who Is Motivated to Smooth the Interaction?

In a mixed-group dyad, each person is an outgroup member to the other. Given the interruption-emotion dynamics of such dyads, who is more likely to be motivated to smooth the disruption and minimize negative affect? It is most likely a question of power. For example, "passing" would be done by the less powerful member of the dyad. In this case, power may be determined by sheer numbers in the current situation (e.g., a solo in an otherwise homogenous group) or in society more generally (e.g., the stigmatized). Or power may be determined by who has more at stake in the interaction (asymmetrical interdependence).

Certainly, low-power outgroupers are in a bind about whether to try to disconfirm ingroup members' stereotypes; doing so could produce negative emotions, as Jones *et al.* note (1984, p. 181):

> Markables themselves often hold stereotypes of what others think and feel about them, and these stereotypes guide their relationship with nonmarkables (Scott, 1969). . . . To disabuse another or his or her false beliefs can produce costs as well as rewards for the marked person. Markers will often be displeased when their beliefs are revealed to be invalid. . . . At the very least, the discovery of a false belief may produce embarrassment.

Goffman (1963) advises the stigmatized that it is their job to ease situational stress, perhaps because they have more at stake. For example, he suggests that stigmatized persons should ignore "slights, snubs, and untactful remarks." Or stigmatized persons can "make an effort at sympathetic re-education of the normal, showing him, point for point, quietly, and with delicacy that in spite of appearances the stigmatized individual is, underneath it all, a fully-human being" (p. 116). Moreover, when "normals have difficulty ignoring the [stigmatized person's] failing, [the person] should try to help them and the social situation by conscious effort to reduce tensions." One example cited by Goffman (1963) includes ice breaking through levity. A man with hooks in lieu of hands lights a cigarette saying "There's one thing I never have to worry about. That's burning my fingers" (p. 117). Alternatively, outgroup members may use the principle of prior exposure (Langer *et al.*, 1976) to attenuate novelty, interruption, and negative affect. A disfigured man notes "When I have an appointment with a new contact, I try to manage to be standing at a distance and facing the door, so the person will have more time to see me and get adjusted to my appearance before we start talking" (p. 118).

But all these "solutions" place the burden on the low-power outgrouper. In any given context, one group may be more numerous or powerful than another, regardless of whether or not the group is stigmatized by society at large. It is the stigmatized and the isolated outgroup member who presumably has more at stake than the normal and the majority ingroup member, so they probably will be more motivated to smooth the interaction. Whether this is fair or not is another question. Moreover, if one is chronically an outgrouper (e.g., because of frequently being in a minority or being culturally low in power), then one has more practice at dealing with the awkwardness ensuing from one's status. Hence, regardless of who "should" smooth the interaction, the more habitual object of prejudice has more motivation and likely more knowledge about how to do so. Acting on this may be difficult, of course, given that the person is also in a low-power position.

Is This Whole Argument Circular?

We have said that outgroup membership leads to presumed or actual disruption of the ingrouper's goals and that this leads to emotion. One might imagine that this is a circular argument, in that prejudice leads one to declare another an adversary in the first place, which then leads to disruptions and prejudice. However, we are not claiming that prejudice leads to the perception of outgroup membership and disruption. Rather, categorization leads to perceived outgroup membership and affective responses. Hence, we are placing cognitive factors in a squarely causal role, in combination with the motivations that transpire when people's goals are blocked.

Is This a Group-Level or Individual-Level Phenomenon?

Our analysis has focused on dyadic interactions between people who are members of what at least one perceives to be different groups. Hence, the individuals are embedded in an intergroup context, but they are not interacting as groups. Group-level interdependence differs in some important ways from individual-level interdependence (e.g., McCallum *et al.*, 1985; Ruscher, Fiske, Miki, & Van Manen, 1991). Hence, we would expect the issues of mere membership and presumed blockage to change somewhat at the level of group interactions. Our hunch is that group-level disruption and prejudice is a more intense version of the phenomena identified here, assuming there is ingroup consensus on goals and their disruption.

Last Few Words

Our interest in this topic is partly motivated by a naive dismay at the inability of human beings to feel immediately good about and to deal easily and constructively with people who are different from themselves. Despite the best intentions, prejudice is rampant and perennial. Others who have worried about this issue are countless and have offered just as many explanations. Our particular explanation is couched in terms of social cognition and interdependence structures as origins of prejudiced affective responses.

In coming to this perspective, we have also been informed by the difficulties of conducting our own research. We have often wondered, whatever happened to all the positive stereotypes? Our research typically employs a strategy of counterbalancing positive and negative expectancies or stereotypes, in order to examine people's responses to stereotype-inconsistent (and therefore potentially individuating) information without confounding inconsistency with valence. In conducting this research, we have been plagued by the dearth of positive stereotypes. It is not too hard to find stereotypes characterized by simultaneous respect and dislike. Many groups are envied by various other groups: Jews, Japanese, Germans, rich people, even college professors. But admiring a group's ability, perseverance, or achievement is not the same thing as liking them. Indeed, many of these groups are seen as threatening by the same people who view them as highly competent. In contrast, groups who are seen as likable (grandmothers, daycare workers, perhaps women in general) are not especially respected. Hence, there appear to be few if any uniformly positive stereotypes, except that of one's ingroup, which may be seen as both likable and competent, to the extent it is stereotyped at all.

What are the implications of the preponderance of negative stereotypes? What conclusions can we draw, then, about the role of interdependence in mixed-group affective reactions, that is, prejudice? Given that most stereotypes are negative, individuating information is likely to be relatively more positive. People attend more to individuating information when they are interdependent, and thus interdependence opens the door to nonstereotyped reactions. But we have also said that interdependence allows interruptions and negative affect. Hence, ironically, interdependence is potentially both a cause and a cure for prejudice.

Acknowledgments

We want to thank the editors for their extremely helpful comments on an earlier version. The writing of this chapter was supported by NIMH Grant 41801 to S. T. Fiske. J. B. Ruscher was supported by a University Fellowship from the University of Massachusetts at Amherst.

References

Adorno, T. W., Frenkel-Brunswik, E., Levinson, D. J., & Sanford, R. N. (1950). *The authoritarian personality*. New York: Harper.

Allen, V. L., & Wilder, D. A. (1979). Group categorization and attribution of belief similarity. *Small Group Behavior, 10*, 73–80.

Allport, G. (1954). *The nature of prejudice*. Reading, MA: Addison-Wesley.

Amir, Y. (1976). The role of intergroup contact in change of prejudice and ethnic relations. In P. A. Katz (Ed.), *Toward the elimination of racism* (pp. 245–308). New York: Pergamon Press.

Berscheid, E., (1983). Emotion. In H. H. Kelley, E. Berscheid, A. Christensen, J. H. Harvey, T. L. Huston, G. Levinger, E. McClintock, L. A. Peplau, & D. R. Peterson (Eds.), *Close relationships*. New York: Freeman.

Berscheid, E. Snyder, M., & Omoto, A. M. (1989). The relationship closeness inventory: Assessing the closeness of interpersonal relationships. *Journal of Personality and Social Psychology, 57*, 792–807.

Blau, P. (1977). A macrosociological theory of social structure. *American Journal of Sociology, 83*, 26–54.

Brewer, M. B. (1979). In-group bias in the minimal intergroup situation: A cognitive-motivational analysis. *Psychological Bulletin, 86*, 307–324.

Brewer, M. B., & Kramer, R. M. (1985). The psychology of intergroup attitudes and behavior. *Annual Review of Psychology, 36*, 219–243.

Brief for Amicus Curiae American Psychological Association in Support of Respondent, *Price Waterhouse v. Hopkins*, 109 S. CT. 1775 (1988).

Brown, R. (1965). *Social psychology*. New York: Free Press.

Brown, V., & Geis, F. L. (1984). Turning lead into gold: Evaluations of men and women leaders and the alchemy of social consensus. *Journal of Personality and Social Psychology, 46*, 811–824.

Campbell, D. T. (1958). Common fate, similarity, and other indices of the status of aggregates of persons as social entities. *Behavioral Science, 3*, 14–25.

Cook, S. W. (1984). Cooperative interaction in multiethnic contexts. In N. Miller & M. B. Brewer (Eds.), *Groups in contact: The psychology of desegregation*. Orlando, Fl: Academic Press.

Costrich, N., Feinstein, J., Kidder, L., Marecek, J., & Pascale, L. (1975). When stereotypes hurt: Three studies of penalties for sex-role reversals. *Journal of Experimental and Social Psychology, 11*, 520–530.

Devine, P. G. (1989). Stereotypes and prejudice: Their automatic and controlled components. *Journal of Personality and Social Psychology, 56*, 5–18.

Dijker, A. J. M. (1987). Emotional reactions to ethnic minorities. *European Journal of Social Psychology, 17*, 305–325.

Dijker, A. J. M. (1991). *Cognitive and emotional aspects of stereotypes.* Unpublished doctoral dissertation, Universiteit van Amsterdam, Amsterdam.

Dijker, A. J. M., & Fiske, S. T. (1991). *Emotional responses to an uncooperative outgroup member.* Unpublished data.

Dovidio, J. F., Evans, N., & Tyler, R. B. (1986). Racial stereotypes: The contents of their cognitive representations. *Journal of Experimental Social Psychology, 22*, 22–37.

Duncan, S. L. (1976). Differential social perception and attribution of intergroup violence: Testing the lower limits of stereotyping of blacks. *Journal of Personality and Social Psychology, 34*, 590–598.

Eagly, A. H., & Mladinic, A. (1989). Gender stereotypes and attitudes toward women and men. *Personality and Social Psychology Bulletin, 15*, 543–558.

Farina, A., & Ring, K. (1965). The influence of perceived mental illness on interpersonal relations. *Journal of Abnormal Psychology, 70*, 47–51.

Farina, A., Holland, C. H., & Ring, K. (1966). Role of stigma and set in interpersonal interaction. *Journal of Abnormal Psychology, 71*, 421–428.

Feldman, R. S., & Saletsky, R. D. (1986). Nonverbal communication in interracial teacher–student interaction. In R. S. Feldman (Ed.), *The social psychology of education* (pp. 115–131). Cambridge: Cambridge University Press.

Fiske, D. W., & Maddi, S. R. (1961). *Functions of varied experience.* Homewood, IL: Dorsey.

Fiske, S. T. (1982). Schema-triggered affect: Applications to social perception. In M. S. Clark & S. T. Fiske (Eds.), *Affect and cognition: The 17th Annual Carnegie Symposium on Cognition* (pp. 55–78). Hillsdale, NJ: Erlbaum.

Fiske, S. T., & Pavelchak, M. A. (1986). Category-based versus piecemeal-based affective responses: Developments in schema-triggered affect. In R. M. Sorrentino & E. T. Higgins (Eds.), *Handbook of motivation and cognition: Foundations of social behavior* (pp. 167–203). New York: Guilford Press.

Fiske, S. T., & Taylor, S. E. (1991). *Social Cognition.* (2nd Ed.) New York: McGraw-Hill.

Fiske, S. T., & Von Hendy, H. M. (1992). Personality feedback and situational norms can control stereotyping processes. *Journal of Personality and Social Psychology, 62*, 577–596.

Fiske, S. T., Neuberg, S. L., Beattie, A. E., & Milberg, S. J. (1987). Category-based and attribute-based reactions to others: Some informational conditions of stereotyping and individuating processes. *Journal of Experimental Social psychology, 23*, 399–427.

Fiske, S. T., Bersoff, D. N., Borgida, E., Deaux, K., & Heilman, M. E. (1991). Social science research on trial: The use of sex stereotyping research in *Price Waterhouse v. Hopkins. American Psychologist, 46*, 1049–1060.

Forsyth, D. R. (1983). *A introduction to group dynamics.* Monterey, CA: Brooks/Cole.

Frijda, N. H. (1986). *The emotions.* New York: Cambridge University Press.

Gaertner, S. L. (1976). Nonreactive measures in racial attitude research: A focus on "Liberals." In P. Katz (Ed.), *Toward the elimination of racism* (pp. 183–211). New York: Pergamon Press.

Gaertner, S. L., & Dovidio, J. F. (1986). The aversive form of racism. In J. F. Dovidio & S. L. Gaertner (Eds.), *Prejudice, discrimination, and racism,* (pp. 61–90). Orlando, FL: Academic Press.

Gaertner, S. L., & McLaughlin, J. P. (1983). Racial stereotypes: Associations and ascriptions of positive and negative characteristics. *Social Psychology Quarterly, 46*, 23–40.

Gilbert, D. T., Pelham, B. W., & Krull, D. S. (1988). On cognitive busyness: When person perceivers meet persons perceived. *Journal of Personality and Social Psychology, 54*, 733–739.

Goffman, E. (1963). *Stigma: Notes on the management of spoiled identity.* New York: Simon & Schuster.

Goodwin, S. A., & Fiske, S. T. (1991). *Power, responsibility, and stereotyping.* Unpublished data.

Hilton, J. L., & Darley, J. M. (1985). Constructing other persons: A limit on the effect. *Journal of Experimental Social Psychology, 21,* 1–18.

Hoyle, R. H., Pinkley, R. L., & Insko, C. A. (1989). Perceptions of social behavior: Evidence of differing expectations for interpersonal and intergroup interaction. *Personality and Social Psychology Bulletin, 15,* 365–376.

Insko, C. A., Nacoste, R. W., & Moe, J. L. (1983). Belief congruence and racial discrimination: Review of the evidence and critical evaluation. *European Journal of Social Psychology, 13,* 153–174.

Insko, C. A., Pinkley, R. L., Hoyle, R. H., Dalton, B., Hong, G., Slim, R., Landry, P., Holton, B., Ruffin, P. F., & Thibaut, J. (1987). Individual-group discontinuity: The role of intergroup contact. *Journal of Experimental Social Psychology, 23,* 250–267.

Insko, C. A., Schopler, J., Hoyle, R. H., Dardis, G. J., & Graetz, K. A. (1990). Individual–group discontinuity as a function of fear and greed. *Journal of Personality and Social Psychology, 58,* 68–79.

Jones, E. E., & Gordon, E. (1972). The timing of self-disclosure and its effects on personal attraction. *Journal of Personality and Social Psychology, 24,* 358–365.

Jones, E. E., Farina, A., Hastorf, A. H., Markus, H., Miller, D. T., & Scott, R. A. (1984). *Social stigma: The psychology of marked relationships.* New York: Freeman.

Jones, J. M. (1986). Racism: A cultural analysis of the problem. In J. F. Dovidio & S. L. Gaertner (Eds.), *Prejudice, discrimination, and racism* (pp. 279–314). Orlando, FL: Academic Press.

Katz, D., & Braly, K. (1933). Racial stereotypes in one hundred college students. *Journal of Abnormal and Social Psychology, 28,* 280–290.

Katz, I. (1981). *Stigma: A social psychological analysis.* Hillsdale, NJ: Erlbaum.

Katz, I., Glass, D. C., & Cohen, S. (1973). Ambivalence, guilt, and the scapegoating of minority group victims. *Journal of Experimental Social Psychology, 9,* 423–436.

Katz, I., Wackenhut, J., & Hass, R. G. (1986). Racial ambivalence, value duality, and behavior. In J. F. Dovidio & S. L. Gaertner (Eds.), *Prejudice, discrimination, and racism* (pp. 35–60). Orlando, FL: Academic Press.

Kelley, H. H. (1979). *Personal relationships: Their structures and processes.* Hillsdale, NJ: Erlbaum.

Kelley, H. H. (1990). *Lewin, situations, and interdependence.* Kurt Lewin Award invited address at the meeting of the American Psychological Association, Boston, Massachusetts.

Kelley, H. H., & Thibaut, J. W. (1978). *Interpersonal relations: A theory of interdependence.* New York: Wiley-Interscience.

Kelley, H. H., Berscheid, E., Christensen, A., Harvey, J. H., Huston, T. L., Levinger, G., McClintock, E., Peplau, L. A., & Peterson, D. R. (1983). Analyzing close relationships. In H. H. Kelley, E. Berscheid, A., Christensen, J. H. Harvey, T. L. Huston, G. Levinger, E. McClintock, L. A. Peplau, & D. R. Peterson (Eds.), *Close relationships* (pp. 20–67). New York: Freeman.

Kleck, R. (1968). Physical stigma and nonverbal cues emitted in face-to-face interaction. *Human Relations, 21,* 19–28.

Kleck, R., Ono, H., & Hastorf, A. (1966). The effects of physical deviance on face to face interaction. *Human Relations, 19,* 425–436.

Kochman, T. (1981). *Black and white styles in conflict.* Chicago: University of Chicago Press.

Langer, E. J., Taylor, S. E., Fiske, S. T., & Chanowitz, B. (1976). Stigma, staring, and discomfort: A novel stimulus hypothesis. *Journal of Experimental Social Psychology, 12,* 451–463.

Lerner, M. J. (1980). *The belief in a just world: A fundamental delusion.* New York: Plenum.

LeVine, R. A., & Campbell, D. T. (1972). *Ethnocentrism: Theories of conflict, ethnic attitudes and group behavior*. New York: Wiley.

Mandler, G. (1975). *Mind and emotion*. New York: Wiley.

McCallum, D. M., Harring, K., Gilmore, R., Drenan, S., Chase, J. P., Insko, C. A., & Thibaut, J. (1985). Competition and cooperation between groups and between individuals. *Journal of Experimental Social Psychology*, **21**, 301–320.

McConahay, J. B. (1986). Modern racism, ambivalence, and the modern racism scale. In J. F. Dovidio & S. L. Gaertner (Eds.), *Prejudice, discrimination, and racism*. Orlando, FL: Academic Press.

Messick, D. M., & Mackie, D. M. (1989). Intergroup relations. In M. R. Rosenzweig & L. W. Porter (Eds.), *Annual review of psychology* (Vol. 40, pp. 45–81). Palo Alto, CA: Annual Reviews.

Myrdal, G. (1944). *An American dilemma: The Negro problem and modern democracy*. New York: Harper.

Neuberg, S. L. (1989). The goal of forming accurate impressions during social interactions: Attenuating the impact of negative expectancies. *Journal of Personality and Social Psychology*, **56**, 374–386.

Neuberg, S. L., & Fiske, S. T. (1987). Motivational influences on impression formation: Outcome dependency, accuracy-driven attention, and individuating processes. *Journal of Personality and Social Psychology*, **53**, 431–444.

Pettigrew, T. F. (1979). The ultimate attribution error: Extending Allport's cognitive analysis of prejudice. *Personality and Social Psychology Bulletin*, **5**, 461–476.

Rehm, J., Steinleitner, M., & Lilli, W. (1987). Wearing uniforms and aggression—A field experiment. *European Journal of Social Psychology*, **17**, 357–360.

Rokeach, M. (1960). *The open and closed mind*. New York: Basic Books.

Rokeach, M. (1961). Belief vs. race as determinants of social distance: Comment on Triandis' paper, *Journal of Abnormal and Social Psychology*, **62**, 187–188.

Ruscher, J. B. (1991). *Skeleton out of the closet: How previously-concealed stigma affects ongoing impressions*. Unpublished doctoral dissertation, University of Massachusetts at Amherst.

Ruscher, J. B., & Fiske, S. T. (1990). Interpersonal competition can cause individuating processes. *Journal of Personality and Social Psychology*, **58**, 832–843.

Ruscher, J. B., Fiske, S. T., Miki, H., & Van Manen, S. (1991). Individuating processes in competition: Interpersonal versus intergroup. *Personality and Social Psychology Bulletin*, **17**, 595–605.

Sagar, H. A., & Schofield, J. W. (1980). Racial and behavioral cues in black and white children's perception of ambiguously aggressive acts. *Journal of Personality and Social Psychology*, **39**, 590–598.

Schachter, S., & Singer, J. E. (1962). Cognitive, social and physiological determinants of emotional state. *Psychological Review*, **69**, 379–399.

Scott, R. A. (1969). *The making of blind men*. New York: Russell Sage Foundation.

Sherif, M. (1948). *An outline of social psychology*. New York: Harper & Row.

Sherif, M., Harvey, O. J., White, B. J., Hood, W. R., & Sherif, C. W. (1961). *Intergroup conflict and cooperation: The Robber's Cave experiment*. University of Oklahoma: Institute of Group Relations.

Sidanius, J. (1989). *Symbolic racism and Social Dominance Theory: A comparative application to the case of American race relations*. Paper delivered at the annual meetings of the Society of Experimental Social Psychology, Los Angeles.

Simpson, G. E., & Yinger, J. M. (1986). *Racial and cultural minorities* (5th Ed.). New York: Plenum.

Simpson, J. A. (1987). The dissolution of romantic relationships: Factors involved in relationship stability and emotional distress. *Journal of Personality and Social Psychology*, **53**, 683–692.

Staats, A. W., & Staats, C. K. (1963). *Complex human behavior: a systematic extension of learning principles.* New York: Holt, Rinehart, and Winston.

Stafford, R. A., & Petway, J. M. (1977). Stigmatization of men and women problem drinkers and their spouses: Differential perception and leveling of sex differences. *Journal of Studies on Alcohol,* **38,** 2109–2121.

Sumner, W. G. (1906). *Folkways.* Lexington, MA: Ginn.

Tajfel, H. (1972). Social categorization [English ms. of La categorization sociale]. In S. Moscovici (Ed.), *Introduction à la psychologie sociale* (Vol. 1, pp. 272–302). Paris: Larousse.

Tajfel, H. (1981). *Human groups and social categories: Studies in social psychology.* Cambridge, England: Cambridge University Press.

Tajfel, H. (1982). *Social psychology of intergroup relations.* In M. R. Rosenzweig & L. W. Porter (Eds.), *Annual review of psychology* (Vol. 33, pp. 1–39). Palo Alto, CA: Annual Reviews.

Tajfel, H., & Turner, J. C. (1979). An integrative theory of intergroup conflict. In W. G. Austin & S. Worchel (Eds.), *The social psychology of intergroup relations.* Monterey, CA: Brooks/Cole.

Taylor, S. E. (1981). A categorization approach to stereotyping. In D. L. Hamilton (Ed.), *Cognitive processes in stereotyping and intergroup behavior.* (pp. 88–114). Hillsdale, NJ: Erlbaum.

Tesser, A. (1988). Toward a self-evaluation maintenance model of social behavior. In L. Berkowitz (Ed.), *Advances in experimental social psychology* (Vol. 21, pp. 181–227) New York: Academic Press.

Tesser, A., Millar, M., & Moore, J. (1988). Some affective consequences of social comparison and reflection processes: The pain and pleasure of being close. *Journal of Personality and Social Psychology,* **54,** 49–61.

Thibaut, J. W., & Kelley, H. H. (1959). *The social psychology of groups.* New York: Wiley.

Triandis, H. C. (1961). A note on Rokeach's theory of prejudice. *Journal of Abnormal and Social Psychology,* **62,** 184–186.

Triandis, H. C., & Davis, E. E. (1965). Race and belief as determinants of behavioral intentions. *Journal of Personality and Social Psychology,* **2,** 715–725.

Turner, J. C. (1981). The experimental social psychology of intergroup behaviour. In J. C. Turner & H. Giles (Eds.), *Intergroup behavior* (pp. 66–101). Chicago: The University of Chicago Press.

Turner, J. C. (1987). *Rediscovering the social group: A self-categorization theory.* New York: Basil-Blackwell.

Vallacher, R. R., & Wegner, D. M. (1987). What do people think they're doing? Action identification and human behavior. *Psychological Review,* **94,** 3–15.

Weitz, S. (Ed.). (1974). *Nonverbal communication.* New York: Oxford University Press.

Wilder, D. A. (1981). Perceiving persons as a group: Categorization and intergroup relations. In D. L. Hamilton (Ed.), *Cognitive processes in stereotyping and intergroup behavior* (pp. 213–258). Hillsdale, NJ: Erlbaum.

Wilder, D. A. (1984). Predictions of belief homogeneity and similarity following social categorization. *British Journal of Social Psychology,* **23,** 323–333.

Word, C. O., Zanna, M. P., & Cooper, J. (1974). The nonverbal mediation of self-fulfilling prophecies in interracial interaction. *Journal of Experimental Social Psychology,* **10,** 109–120.

Chapter 12

Stereotyping and Affect in Discourse: Interpreting the Meaning of Elderly, Painful Self-Disclosure

KAREN HENWOOD
Department of Human Sciences
Brunel University
Uxbridge, United Kingdom

HOWARD GILES
Department of Communication
University of California, Santa Barbara
Santa Barbara, California

JUSTINE COUPLAND and NIKOLAS COUPLAND
School of English Studies, Journalism, and Philosophy
University of Wales, College of Cardiff
Cardiff, Wales, United Kingdom

Introduction

The term stereotype is derived from the Greek words "stereos," meaning form or solid, and "typos," meaning the making of an impression or model. It referred, originally, to a metal plate, cast from a mold taken from a body of movable type, which was used in printing (Miller, 1982). In its social scientific usage, the term was first introduced by Walter Lippmann in 1922. He described stereotypes as "pictures in our heads," or phenomenological simplifying devices which play an important role in enabling people to make sense of an otherwise "too busy, too complex, and too fleeting" (p. 16) external world as it impinges on our senses. This latter meaning of the term persists in social psychology today, together with general acceptance of the idea that stereotypes represent the cognitive component of attitudes held toward human groups or social categories (see, e.g., Lippa, 1990). At one level, therefore, one may say that a quiet confidence exists among social psychologists regarding the way stereotypes should be conceptualized in order to orient researchers to the kinds of questions and problems they wish to study. In brief, they are viewed as the mental structures, images, or beliefs which facilitate action toward liked or disliked social groups.

On the other hand, a fascinating feature of the history of research on the stereotype concept is its variable, and sometimes contested, definition. This occurs because research on stereotypes has been located within different paradigms of social psychological enquiry, and is of particular relevance to the issue of affective processes in stereotyping. It is always possible, of course, to subsume research on stereotyping within a general attitude-behavior framework, where attitudes are held to comprise an affective as well as conative and cognitive dimensions. However, neither of the key orienting assumptions in stereotype research mentioned thus far—namely, that stereotypes are simplified mental images or the cognitive components of attitudes—focuses specifically on what has been described as the evaluative, emotional, affective, or motivational significance of stereotypical beliefs themselves.

In this chapter, we argue that a concern with affective issues is an important means of enhancing contemporary stereotype research, because it represents one way of bringing stereotypes in touch with practical, everyday understanding. Our own adopted perspective, however, is to further broaden the focus of enquiry by studying affect and cognition in stereotyping as aspects of meaning, as this becomes manifest in discourse and social text. The utility of this approach is illustrated with reference to some of our own empirical research in the field of communication and aging. We report on one study which points to the way stereotypes can function in a practical, discursive way to render discomfort in situated interaction sequences socially meaningful.

Stereotype Research: Past and Present Perspectives

During the early years of research, a good deal of attention was focused on identifying the defining properties of stereotypes. In a manner reminiscent of the original etymological meaning of the term stereotype, they were defined as "rigid," "inflexible," or "persistent"[1] beliefs, images, or representations (e.g., Adorno *et al.*, 1950; Katz & Braly, 1933; Meenes, 1943; Richter, 1956; Simpson & Yinger, 1965). Similarly, they were defined as "overgeneralizations" (e.g., Allport, 1954) which were either wholly factually inaccurate or which have only a "kernel of truth" (e.g., Harding *et al.*, 1969; Katz & Braly, 1933; Klineberg, 1951; Prothro & Melikian, 1955; cf. Mackie, 1973).

These properties marked the special relationship held to exist between stereotypes and prejudice. The research of Katz and Braly (1933) is considered seminal for introducing the technology of the adjective checklist as a way of measuring social stereotypes, defined as "consensual" beliefs or beliefs with a widespread existence. However, this research also provided the first empirical demonstration of a link between stereotypes and prejudice, since the adjectives assigned to particular groups by raters using the checklist did not appear as evaluatively neutral. Rather, the evaluative connotations of traits were found to match rankings of those groups in society at large, both in terms of their perceived objective social position and attempts by majority group members to seek social distance from them (Katz & Braly, 1935, 1947).

Probably the most significant theoretical contribution to stereotype research during the early period was made when Adorno *et al.* (1950) identified stereotyping as a characteristic mode of thinking of people with authoritarian or prefascist personalities. Adorno *et al.* adopted a psychodynamic approach to stereotyping and prejudice, arguing that feelings of racial hatred occur as a result of ambivalent feelings of love and hate for powerful parental, and later other authority, figures. Repression of the hostile feelings is said to result in a build-up of psychic tension which is then redirected or displaced onto targets chosen for their relative weakness and lack of ability to retaliate; hence the approach is also sometimes known as the theory of "scapegoating" (e.g., Zawadski, 1948).

The role played by affective and motivational processes in stereotyping is clear within this psychodynamic or scapegoating formulation. The various properties of stereotypes as aberrant cognitions—their negativity, extremity, rigidity, persistence, and factual inaccuracy—are seen as explicable in terms of the functioning of the deep-seated personality structure and dynamics of prejudiced individuals. Stereotypes are also held to play a powerful role as rationalizations, or attempts to justify and explain away feelings

---

[1]Fishman (1956) points up the confusions that have existed in the literature over the notion of "persistence." He argues that a belief can only be cast in derogatory light for its persistence if it remains unchanged in the face of contradictory evidence. He distinguishes between persistence and rigidity, where the latter is a property of a person's cognitive functioning.

and expressions of hostility which are seen as essentially irrational and un-warranted because they have no basis in reality.

Over the last twenty years or so, we have witnessed a cognitive revolution in social psychology, such that concern has shifted away from motivational issues. From the perspective of what tends to be called cognitive social psychology or social cognition (see, e.g., Carroll & Payne, 1976; Eiser, 1980; Fiske & Taylor, 1984), human beings are viewed as organisms, somewhat akin to computers, which perceive, encode, transform, and generally process information. The methodology of research in this tradition is mainly experimental, being borrowed from the paradigms of cognitive psychology (Sherman, Judd, & Park, 1989). Stereotypes are construed as ordinary cognitions which play a role in the active interpretation of information derived from the senses (see, e.g., Ashmore & Del Boca, 1981; Jones, 1982), rather than as the irrational beliefs of people with distorted personalities. The social cognitive view of the stereotype has existed since the earliest days of research (Lippmann, 1922; Vinacke, 1949, 1956), with Allport (1954) making the case most clearly that stereotypes are the normal products of natural and universal cognitive processes. However, research undertaken within contemporary social cognition has advanced Allport's position further, providing a detailed account of the structure and functioning of stereotypes as part of an integrated symbol-manipulating and information-processing system.

Stereotypes have been variously characterized from the social cognitive perspective as categories (e.g., Park & Hastie, 1987), person or role schemata (e.g., Linville & Jones, 1980; Taylor & Crocker, 1981), implicit personality theories (Ashmore, 1981) and, following intense interest in the work of Eleanor Rosch and others (see, e.g., Rosch & Mervis, 1975), as category prototypes (e.g., Brewer, Dull, & Lui, 1981; Deaux *et al.*, 1985; see also Clifton, McGrath & Wick, 1976). A somewhat different approach to the conceptualization of stereotypes within social cognition has been proposed by McCauley and Stitt (1978; see also McCauley, Stitt, & Segal, 1980) in response to the question of how best to measure them. Known, most precisely, as the "diagnostic ratio" approach, a stereotype is said to exist when a person believes that the percentage of people in a group possessing a certain trait differs significantly from the percentage of people thought to possess that trait in the population generally; from this perspective, then, stereotypes are defined as probabilistic beliefs about the relationship between category membership and the possession of certain traits.

The Rationality Debate in Stereotyping: "Cold" versus "Hot" Cognition

There is a view that human information processing activity commonly does, or should, follow fairly formal statistical and logical procedures and rules. Such a view is associated with the idea that people function as lay scientists who attempt to deal with incoming information logically, consistently, and exhaustively. Forgas (1981, 1983) has called this the overly "rational" and Fiske and Taylor (1984), among others, the "cold" view of human cognition.

One illustration of research in the area of social information processing that is underpinned by such a cold, rational view is the 1982 research by Locksley, Hepburn, & Ortiz on stereotypical beliefs as "base rates." Base rates are prior probabilities regarding the frequency within an overall population of traits associated with certain categories. The view of these authors is that use of stereotypical base rate information should follow the axioms of Bayes' Theorem. That is to say, stereotypical information in the form of base rates should be combined in a statistically optimal way with individuating information that is diagnostic of some relevant criterion.

Locksley *et al.*'s (1982) research has, however, been thoroughly criticized on methodological (Rasinski *et al.*, 1985), empirical (Krueger & Rothbart, 1988), and theoretical (Bodenhausen & Lichtenstein, 1987; see also Freund, Kruglanski, & Shpitzajzen, 1985; Kruglanski & Ajzen, 1983) grounds. Accordingly, it is useful in revealing how much dissatisfaction exists within contemporary social cognition with such an overly formal and rational view of social information processing activity. Locksley *et al.*'s own findings are that stereotypical base rate information is often *neglected* in favor of more salient or available individuating information, leading to the persistence of stereotypical beliefs. Such findings may, therefore, be taken to support the rather different theoretical view of people as limited information processors (Simon, 1957), who use a variety of shortcuts or judgmental heuristics (Tversky & Kahneman, 1974), which can often lead to errors and biases in human judgment and decision making (Nisbett & Ross, 1980).

The idea that human information processing is an inherently limited, biased, and error-prone activity is a central tenet of the majority of research in contemporary social cognition. Empirical studies of stereotyping have burgeoned from this perspective, premised on the understanding that the processes and outcomes of stereotyping are underpinned by a whole range of perceptual and cognitive heuristics or biases. Part of the attraction of this research is its ability to account for many of the traditional characteristics of stereotypes as prejudicial beliefs, without making reference to the psychodynamic origins of individual personality differences. Hamilton and colleagues, for example, have established a cognitive basis for stereotypes in the phenomenon of illusory correlation. Illusory correlation is the tendency to perceive a relationship of covariation between infrequent behaviors or traits and infrequent classes of people where none exists. It is said to provide an explanation for the *extremity* and *negativity* of stereotypical beliefs (see, e.g., Hamilton, 1981; Hamilton & Gifford, 1976). Rothbart and colleagues have demonstrated the tendency of stereotypical beliefs to lead to expectancy confirmation and a lack of responsiveness to disconfirming information (see, e.g., Rothbart, 1981; Rothbart, Evans, & Fulero, 1979; Rothbart & Lewis, 1988). Here, a possible explanation is provided for the persistence of stereotypical beliefs.[2] More recently, it has been ascertained that category labels and attributes can be identified more quickly when the links between them are stereotype consistent (Dovidio, Evans, & Tyler, 1986; Gaertner & McLaughlin, 1983). This could be read as evidence for some form of categorization bias, which could, again, play a part in reinforcing stereotypical beliefs and in contributing to their factual inaccuracy.

In 1981, Pettigrew described the approach of social cognition as "primarily interested in seeing how far it can push a purely cognitive analysis" (p. 311). According to Pettigrew, this strategy constituted the approach's greatest strength, but also its greatest weakness. Its strength was identified as shifting the focus away from a concern with individual differences and the easy assumption that bigotry is peculiar to a relatively small number of individuals. Its major weakness, on the other hand, was diagnosed as a preoccupation with purely cognitive heuristics and biases, to the neglect of possible motivational or "hot" cognitive influences.

This weakness has not proved to be a long-term impediment to research in social cognition, which has subsequently incorporated a concern with affective, motivational, or hot cognitive biases into its theoretical and empirical program. Showers and Cantor (1985) have described the shift toward motivated cognition as one which views social cognition in more complex, personally involving contexts, and which looks at the way motivation becomes translated into strategic cognitive activity. Motivational elements, including goals, moods, and expertise, are held to convey incentives for behavior and as guiding interpretations and plans.

Two basic questions have guided empirical research on the relationship between affect (particularly mood states) and knowledge structures such as prototypes and stereotypes. First, What is the cognitive basis of affect? It has been found that more complex (Linville, 1982) and less consistent or tightly organized (Tesser, 1978) schemata lead to more moderate evaluations, and that schemata (such as stereotypes) which are themselves affect laden lead to the triggering of affective reactions to the extent that stimuli fit prior knowledge stored about them (Fiske, 1982). The second question is, What is the affective basis of cognition? Here, a good deal has been writ-

---

[2]Lately, however, far more attention has been paid in social cognition research to elaborating the way stereotypical beliefs may be involved in more flexible information processing. For example, Rothbart and colleagues have attached considerable importance to the way observations of disconfirming behavior by individual group members may generalize, leading to the revision of preexisting beliefs, where disconfirming behavior is engaged in by typical category members (Rothbart & Lewis, 1988; see also Wilder, 1984).

ten about the pervasive effects of mood, defined as low-level feeling states about nonspecific targets, on judgment and memory (e.g., Clark & Isen, 1982). Positive moods are said to prime or activate more positive thoughts and more readily available positive memories, and vice versa for negative moods, due to the linkage of similarly toned material in memory. This development in research has been extended by Bower and colleagues' network model of emotion (see, e.g., Bower, 1981; Bower & Cohen, 1982), which offers a more detailed account of the mechanisms and processes underpinning the effects of mood on memory. Emotion is said to be represented in nodes embedded in an elaborate associative network and connected to other nodes representing expressive behavior, autonomic activity, verbal labels, and eliciting stimuli and events. Emotion is, therefore, said to function as a retrieval cue, such that reinstating any particular mood will help people to remember mood-congruent material linked to it in memory.

Residual doubts have been expressed about aspects of the social cognitive enterprise; for example, for reducing such essentially independent phenomena as affect and emotion to the realm of cognition (Leventhal & Tomarken, 1986; Zajonc, 1980, 1984). Also noteworthy is the observation that to talk in terms of errors and biases in performance implies the implicit acceptance of some rational, normative standard against which such deviations can be measured (Gigerenzer & Murray, 1987; Jungermann, 1986; Lopes, 1991). Nevertheless, major benefits have accrued to social cognition's overt disclaimers of the rational character of human judgment and decision making. As Forgas (1981, 1983) has argued, the view of human social actors as complex information-processing machines is limited as a basis for understanding the social dimension of thought, particularly as it functions in everyday life. From the latter perspective, one must consider the role of affect and emotions, the values attached to objects and their hedonic relevance, and the frequently normative, shared, and public character of beliefs. The view of human beings as limited, biased, and error-prone processors of information is important because, by severely eroding the previously clear distinction between rational cognitive and irrational motivational approaches to human activity, it has opened the door for a renewed interest in the role of affect and motivation in human thought and understanding. By so doing, it has effectively reconnected human cognition with one key aspect of human social functioning in everyday life.

Our starting point in this chapter, therefore, is the general theoretical proposition that knowledge cannot exist in some pure, disinterested realm abstracted away from the particular, situated contexts of its use (Bowers, 1990). Rather, we would agree with Coulter (1986) that affect and rationality are more closely related than has hitherto often been thought to be the case. Coulter comes to this conclusion by drawing a distinction between feelings, as a category of sensations, and emotions. His point is that whereas feelings are determined by inner experiences, the warranted[3] as-cription of emotions is bound up with performed actions, cognitive ap-praisals, and specific arrays of meaningful circumstances. This parallels, of course, the early realization in social psychology (see, e.g., Schachter & Singer, 1962) that physiological state of arousal does not account for the specificity and diversity of emotional states which are attributed in line with features of social context.

Coulter (1986) goes on to argue that it is possible to investigate what he calls the "social logic" of emotions, based on the way public expres-sions of emotion are intimately related to people's awareness of tasks, problems, social conventions, and other sociocultural dimensions. In other words, he is drawing attention to the need to locate the meaning of emo-tion in the domain of practical, discursive human activity situated in spe-cific social contexts.

In this chapter, we seek to convert Coulter's philosophically oriented treatise into a programmatic statement for social psychology, and thereby to build on Schachter and Singer's (1962) original insight regarding the con-text specificity of the labeling of emotions. We do this by assuming that im-portant social psychological phenomena such as emotions, beliefs, values, identities, and stereotypes can be usefully studied as they are enacted in so-cial interaction and made manifest in discourse or talk. Rather than view such phenomena as having a fixed, intrinsic reality as part of a material world which is simply reflected in language, our view is that they can, alter-natively, be studied as meanings constituted and reconstituted in specific discourses and social texts. We would, therefore, summarize our approach as interpretive or constructionist in orientation, drawing on the traditions of ethnomethodology, hermeneutics, and discourse analysis to analyze and understand the shifting meanings of specific sequences of interaction and talk.

The Management and Meaning of Sequences of Elderly, Painful Self-Disclosure: Introduction to an Interpretive Analysis of Some Discourse Data

The background to the interpretive or constructionist movement in modern social psychology has been mapped out by Gergen (1985; see also Gergen & Davis, 1985; Gergen & Shotter, 1989; Parker & Shotter, 1990). Drawing on developments in the sociology of knowledge which undermine the absolute status of the foundations of human knowledge, it is argued that what passes as the brute facts of social psychological knowledge should

---

[3]Note that use of the term "warranted" ascription is intended to convey the idea that the basis for emotion assignment has to be accepted as secure or legitimate.

be reexamined as renderings, accomplishments, or meanings established in social life. These ideas are encapsulated in the dominant metaphor in social constructionism of social life as a set of socially, and hence historically, specific discourses or texts. Evidently, one consequence of such a position is a commitment, shared with a variety of other traditions in the human sciences, to emphasizing the importance of language and other symbolic systems when studying the relationships between persons, nature, and society. Where the perspective of social constructionism does tend to be distinctive, however, is in its rejection of a realm of knowable phenomenal or material realities beyond the linguistic or symbolic domain. Rather than view language as a medium for interpreting some underlying reality, research is conducted into the very social and symbolic practices which render experiences or events intelligible or socially meaningful.

The practical research implications of conducting research from a constructionist perspective are illustrated in the following section. We consider an interpretive analysis of some discussion or discourse data which reveals the role of stereotypes in making sense of situations that appear to involve negative affect or discomfort. These data were collected as part of an integrated program of empirical work concerned with the management and meaning of sequences of elderly, painful self-disclosure (PSD), where painful self-disclosure is taken to refer to talk falling within the five topic subcategories of bereavement, ill-health, immobility, disengagement and loneliness, and other (an assortment of family, financial, and social troubles). It is this program, therefore, to which we first turn.

The center piece of the empirical program was a study of 40 dyadic interactions involving 20 younger (aged 30–45 years) and 20 elderly (aged 70–87 years) women. The younger women were recruited through a newspaper advertisement; most were married with families. The elderly women were members of one of two local day centers; most lived alone and were widowed. A proportion of the elderly participants were known to one another prior to the study; however, the dyads were arranged to ensure that all the observed interactions were between strangers. Each woman interacted with one peer and one woman of a different generation for 10 minutes in a comfortable video studio, leading to a data corpus of 20 intergenerational, 10 peer-young, and 10 peer-elderly interactions. Analysis of these video- and audio-taped interactions gave rise to the need for a second study, the outcome of which is the main focus of attention in this chapter.

The first study identified sequences of painful self-disclosure (PSD) as a significant feature of intergenerational disclosure in the data corpus. More specifically, PSD was found to be primarily a feature of elderly discourse, with the younger people therefore tending to occupy the role of recipient. A taxonomy was devised to account, exhaustively, for the strategies disclosers and recipients variably used during sequences of PSD and their sequential possibilities (J. Coupland, Coupland, Giles, & Wiemann, 1988), and detailed distributional analyses were conducted to illustrate who, among the participants, used which strategies most frequently (N. Coupland, Coupland, Giles, Henwood, & Wiemann, 1988).

The distributional analyses confirmed that PSD was considerably more characteristic of the elderly than the young participants. Elderly PSD was found in 18 out of 20 intergenerational encounters (accounting for 15.6% of speaking time) but young PSD was found in only 2 out of 20 of such encounters (4% of speaking time). The relevant figures for peer-generational talk were 9 out of 10 peer-elderly (16.5% of speaking time) and 5 out of 10 peer-young (6.3% of speaking time).

A second finding was that elderly people often provided their own pretext (called a discloser-determined precontext) for making a painful self-disclosure, rather than being led into such talk by the remarks of their interlocutors (recipient-determined precontext) or other noncontrived developments in the conversation (textually determined precontext). Specifically, elderly people were found to determine 53% of their own PSDs as opposed to 20% being textually and 26% recipient determined. These results further strengthen a global characterization of the elderly participants as disclosing more than the young in this study.

The distributional analyses also revealed, however, the full extent of the *young* women's involvement in engendering and maintaining elderly PSD. Young interactants were found to elicit disclosure from their elderly partners far more than did elderly participants, on 34% of the occasions compared to 12%, respectively. Moreover, the young interactants often adopted interrogatory rights with their elderly partners which they did not do with peer partners. This meant that elderly recipients frequently had little option other than to disclose, irrespective of any personal wishes they might have had. Also, in their follow-up responses to PSD, younger interlocutors tended to further disclosure by making requests for clarification, expressing surprise, and providing sympathy (N. Coupland *et al.*, 1990; see also J. Coupland *et al.*, 1988).

These sequences of elderly, painful self-disclosure were further analyzed using Brown and Levinson's (1987) approach to interaction management. This approach is based on considerations of facework and politeness. The analyses led us to describe the encounters as highly problematical, and to believe that they involved feelings of negative affect or discomfort. The discloser exposes her own positive face (the desire to be well thought of) by divulging negatively valenced personal information to a relative stranger or by engaging in behavior which, in Berger and Bradac's (1982) terms, is counternormative. The recipient has her negative face (the right to unviolated personal space) threatened as she is left with the task of dealing appropriately with information about the personal trauma of someone she barely knows. The recipient's positive and/or negative face can also, then, be threatened repeatedly, as she tries to find a response among what could be described as a series of dispreferable options (J. Coupland *et al.*, 1988). If she attempts to shift or change topic away from the topic of disclosure, she might be thought to be dismissive of her partner's conversational needs and emotional concerns or to lack the resources to cope with this depth of exchange, and her positive face is thus threatened. Alternatively, if she chooses the option of encouraging (e.g., by asking for elaboration) or at least not discouraging (e.g., by giving a sympathetic or neutral/minimal response), then she risks having her negative face threatened again.

In describing the management of sequences of elderly PSD as discomforting or difficult in this way, the researchers had no privileged access, of course, to interlocuters' own perceptions and interpretations of the encounters. A second study was conducted, therefore, to gain some further insight into this issue of discomfort in the management of interaction involving sequences of elderly PSD.

A total of 16 snippets or extracts were selected by the researchers from the original corpus of data on young and elderly interactions for use in the second study. They were chosen to cover as many of the permutations of elderly PSD discourse found in the previous study as possible. Four made references to ill health, three involved talk of bereavement, and two, the experience of loneliness. The remaining seven were non-PSD items chosen to illustrate the variety of other kinds of sequence found in the original study. Each extract was of approximately 30 seconds duration. An illustrative example of an ill-health transcript may be seen in Extract 1.

Women were then recruited to take part in the research who were similar in age, background, and family circumstances to the younger women in the original study. They were asked to listen to snippets of the recorded sequences of elderly PSD in groups of between 3 and 6 women, while imagining that they were, themselves, the recipients or younger women on the tape. All together there were 11 sessions with a total of 43 women taking part. The snippets of conversation ended immediately after a disclosure had been made and respondents were asked to explore how they felt "as the snippet came to an end."

Since the researches were interested in participants' own perceptions and views of the tape-recorded encounters involving elderly PSD, but the snippets had been preselected by the researchers, it was considered important that participants should be fully informed about the nature of the original study and subsequent operations. Therefore, volunteers were given information on the general characteristics of the original volunteers, where the research took place, and what the study was understood to be about. The researchers also made known their awareness that any subsequent data analysis would have to be seen in the light of the process of prior selection of extracts. Presentation of the snippets was followed by a semistructured interview, where a number of planned questions were raised by the female

Extract 1

Ruby (shown as 'R') is an elderly woman and Judith ('J') is a younger woman.

```
 1   R:  I think you see when you're getting older at this age
 2        you (2.0) there's lots of things can make us a bit
 3        miserable but (.) we have to look on the bright side
                       [                              ]
 4   J:                         oh yes mm
 5   J:  yes
 6   R:  nobody wants you when you're miserable and moaning
                          [       ]                   [      ]
 7   J:                      mm                         mm
 8   R:  and groaning
 9   J:  no that's (laughs) quite true
                            [                    ]
10   R:                       they don't you know?
11   J:  and it doesn't matter if you're elderly or if you're
12        younger I mean=
13   R:  =no=
14   J:  =it's they don't want you=
15   R:  =no it applies
            [
16   J:       the younger moaner either=
17   R:  =it applies all ages really doesn't it you know=
                        [   ] [   ]
18   J:                   yes    yes
19   J:  =certainly=
20   R:  =because I can't breathe I've got (.) emphysema and I'm
                       [   ]      [ ][       ]
21:  J:                 mm        mm   mm
22   R:  full of (.) osteoarthritis and what have you but erm
                    [   ]               [      ]
23   J:              mm                  mm
24:  R:  thank goodness the old brain-box is still going
```

interviewer/facilitator. These were: How difficult or easy was it for you to imagine yourselves in the role of the younger woman?; What was it about the snippets of conversation that influenced you most?; and What was it about the snippets of conversation that you found most problematic, if anything? It was also made clear to volunteers that they should raise any issues they felt were pertinent. In order to further minimize the possibility of unwittingly forcing respondents to comment only within a framework imposed by the researchers, every attempt was made to encourage respondents to dissent from and broaden out the debate. For example, it was routinely asked whether the respondents thought that the investigation had at any time involved leading questions.

The Invoking of Stereotypes and Other Themes in Accounts of Elderly, Painful Self-Disclosure

The audio-taped discussions of people's responses with respect to the sequences of elderly PSD were analyzed using interpretive, discourse analytic procedures (Potter & Wetherell, 1987; Van Dijk, 1987), with basic thematic categories evolving out of the use of more standard approaches to qualitative data analysis (see, e.g., Bulmer, 1979; Glaser & Strauss, 1967). In practical terms, all instances in the data corpus were isolated, which bore some relation to the issue of discomfort or difficulty as made manifest in the group discussions. These were then organized around a number of emergent categories or themes. Instances in the data which illustrated aspects of the emerging analysis particularly well were retained for more detailed discursive analysis, where special attention was paid to the detailed structuring and sequencing of illustrative extracts of spoken text. In the manner of qualitative research, no numerical criteria were used in guiding these operations. Rather, the two guiding principles were the use of categories and themes which both *fit* the data well and are *relevant* to the problem at hand. However, these principles do not amount to binding and formal rules of method. Interpretive discourse work is far more about using any analytic resources researchers have at their disposal to make sense of their data. In this sense, it is a far more open-ended exercise than research aimed at falsifying hypotheses deduced from strong a priori theory.

Inspection of the data revealed some instances in the group discussions where respondents' comments seemed to match the researchers' original concern with discomfort and difficulty in interaction management. For example, a strong statement of negative affect in dealing with sequences of elderly PSD is made by LJ[4] in a remark from group discussion 4 (GD4) when she states *if they're feeling lonely and depressed then that hurts me very strongly.* KM's (GD10) comment *the girl didn't know what to say back to her* and PV's (GD4) remark that *your mind is on one thing . . . and it could be difficult to suddenly (breaths in) switch to find something to say to follow up* conveys clear recognition of a classic problem in interaction management of finding a subsequently appropriate verbal response to elderly

---

[4]Respondents are referenced by fictitious initials.

PSD. As a threat to the smooth running of interaction, this is a potentially potent source of embarrassment and also, perhaps, frustration. Finally, DG's (GD3) statement that *you're trying to be tactful . . . you want to show sympathy (.) and yet you want to put the other side of the case as well* is suggestive of dissatisfaction due to the demands of competing response requirements. The requirements of positive face seem to suggest that an expression of sympathy is necessary. However, for DG, this simultaneously competes with her negative face rights by acting against her desire to put across the other point of view.

Overall, however, the interpretive analysis indicated how people's attempts to make sense of what they heard, and to respond to questioning about problems with respect to elderly painful self-disclosure, were conducted far less at the level of talk about immediate interactional experiences, and far more at the general level of ideas about elderly people, their personal and social characteristics, and their position as an underprivileged or "undesirable" social group. Four broadly distinguishable themes or discourses were isolated bearing some relationship with the issue of how elderly people are described and categorized and the attendant problem of social stigmatization. These are discourses of: sadness and empathy for elderly people; stereotyping; individualization/exceptions (concerned with elderly people held to constitute exceptions to the rule); and anti- or counterstereotyping. The interpretive analysis became mainly devoted, therefore, to describing and illustrating these four themes, together with the way they function either to affirm or deny the experience of discomfort with respect to elderly PSD and in relationships with elderly people generally. In this chapter, we discuss these four themes, placing a special emphasis on the relationship between stereotyping and other discourses. Identification of the discourse of stereotyping brings into sharp relief the question of what makes a particular verbal utterance count as an instance of stereotyping. This, from a social constructionist perspective, would be called the problem of stereotype constitution (see Potter & Wetherell, 1987). We conclude that the invoking and challenging of stereotypes in discourse plays a significant part in the process of making sense of discomfort in social interaction, by placing it within a framework of social meanings.

The Discourse of Sadness and Empathy for Elderly People

An important theme to emerge was that of sadness and empathy for elderly people, which took the form of a global response to the condition of being elderly. Central to this discourse is a recognition of the difficult lives of elderly people and the affective response it inspires. For example, LJ (GD2) describes how *if they're feeling lonely and depressed then that oh hurts me very strongly . . . the very lonely people . . . I felt sorry for those because you think of people who are in that situation um there must be thousands of people like that all over the world.*

At one level, this utterance supports the view that discomfort may be experienced in relation to intergenerational encounters. However, in the more specific sense of dealing with sequences of elderly PSD, the experience of discomfort is effectively denied. In response to a question about what she found problematic, PE (GD2) replies *the general situation of old age.* MS in the same discussion follows up, however, by denying that she found the conversation difficult, a response which PE seems to need to match, back-tracking somewhat on her previous remark.[5] The discussion then developed in ways which repudiated entirely the idea that dealing with elderly PSD is a problematical affair, with MS asserting that elderly people *like to talk about their husband who passed away seven years ago.* Later, NS also comments *I mean you don't have to say anything,* implying that there is no threat to her positive face in this. Once again, the outcome of this response is to deny any experience of discomfort and difficulty, this time on the grounds that such conversations require no significant degree of recipient involvement.

The Discourse of Stereotyping

Another recurrent theme in the data is that of young people stereotyping the elderly. Analyzing the invoking and use of social stereotypes in discourse and in relation to specific situated sequences of interaction vividly highlights difficulties in deciding when a particular remark, statement, or ascription counts as stereotypical. In our data, no explicit and totally uncompromising statements were made to the effect that all elderly people (or more elderly people than in the population at large) are characterized by a particular trait or set of traits. Generalized or relatively inclusive statements were made, but these tended to be accompanied by what Hewitt and Stokes (1975; see also Holmes, 1984) call disclaimers or hedges. For example, the qualifying remarks *I think, tend to,* and *sort of* would all seem to be functioning as hedges in the following comments: *I think that older people tend to sort of ramble on* (EK, GD5) and *I think that's true of older people . . . they do tend to ramble on a bit* (KM, GD10). Respondents also made less inclusive suggestions about some elderly people and stereotypical ascriptions, where traits are assigned to particular category members as opposed

---

[5]PE may have felt obliged to modify her earlier remark in the light of comments by other group members. Normative influences may, therefore, have been at work in this situation. We would suggest that the operation of such influences is pervasive in social encounters where people are seeking to make sense of their own behavior by comparing it with the actions of others.

to the category generally. For example, DG (GD3) comments, respectively, that *some elderly people are very much like young children they want to be the center of attention for as long as possible and you know full well that this person is a cantankerous old so and so.*

In counting the above examples as instances of stereotyping, we are implicitly recognizing that, when analyzing the discursive manifestation of stereotypes, it is necessary to go beyond the idea of stereotypes as abstract cognitions or beliefs. A truism in the social study of language is the idea that the meaning of utterances is negotiable in interaction and reconstructed in relation to the contexts of their use. It is therefore possible to argue, following Van Dijk (1987), that the use of hedges or disclaimers in conjunction with generalized statements about elderly people can constitute a subtle form of prejudicial stereotyping. Seem in these terms, the disclaimer serves as a potential face-saving device, should accusations of prejudice be made, rather than as a simple statement of lack of certainty about the veracity of one's remark.

In the previously cited example of less inclusive stereotyping, respondent DG arguably uses a number of particularly trite and cliched descriptive terms (viz., *like young children, playing for sympathy,* and *wanting to be the center of attention*). We would suggest that these descriptors are themselves socially meaningful, in terms of their ability to carry a specific and especially pejorative connotation when associated with old age. Moreover, we would substantiate the claim that people are able to orient themselves to such publically available meanings by referring to the way DG acted to restrict the generalizability of her own observations about elderly people. Her sequence of remarks began in highly generalized terms, simply stating that *they* (elderly people) *play for sympathy.* An all-inclusive introduction to her next sentence (*they're very much like*) was quickly replaced, however, with the more guarded *some elderly people . . .,* as if DG recognized the problems inherent in her first, more global, remark. By this time, however, the unflattering view of elderly people as emotionally dependent and demanding has already been introduced into the public domain as some kind of social fact (Berger & Luckman, 1967) where it is available to others to be drawn upon and used. To avoid the charge of stereotyping in these circumstances would require the respondent to engage in considerable reparative and explanatory work. In our judgment, more reparatory work would be needed, in order to avoid the charge of negative stereotyping, than is apparent in the mere shift of reference from they to *some* in the example here.

The decision to count or discount particular remarks as stereotypical is particularly difficult when considering examples of stereotypical ascriptions, where an association is made between an attribute and a person or person's activity, such as a conversation. Two examples of stereotypical ascriptions from the data corpus are DG's (GD3) claim that *you know full well that this person is a·cantankerous old so and so* and HP's (GD3) comment about *moaning type conversations*. Decisions, here, are always a matter of fine judgment. One has to deal with questions about the meaningfulness and mode of expression of attributes, to what extent the ascription appears to have been grounded in observations of individual behavior as opposed to the target's status as category member, and the even more complex question of an utterance's potential, actual, intended, or unintended social consequences. The decision about the description of an elderly person as "a cantankerous old so and so" rested mainly on the nature of the particular adjective and form of expression used. Rather less important was the evidence pointing to the individualized/categorical basis of the judgment. With regard to the "moaning type conversations" ascription, the decision was made mainly on the basis of an examination of the structural interrelationship between themes (see next section). From the perspective of analyzing stereotypes as they are made manifest in discourse, and in relation to practical judgments of sequences of situated interaction, therefore, it must be recognized that all such decisions are active interpretations of the available evidence including the social implications of an utterance. As such, the meaning of purportedly stereotypical statements must be accepted as inherently ambiguous and open to challenge and negotiation.

If decisions about stereotyping in discourse are always matters of judgment which have to be defended on the basis of reasoned evidence and argument, evidence of social stereotyping becomes clearer the more a remark is phrased in generalized as opposed to specific terms. Extract 2 is particularly instructive here. It illustrates an aspect of the process of stereotyping which only becomes apparent through its study as an aspect of practical judgment and decision making in relation to situated interactions. By this is meant the discursive processes by which people arrive at progressively more clear-cut categorical statements. These relatively clear-cut categorical statements follow the making of initially more restricted observations about individuals or a small number of people.

In Extract 2, shifts of reference from talking about particular individuals to discussion of more generalized tendencies are to be found in comments about both young and elderly. Most of the early remarks in the extract refer to individual people heard on the stimulus tapes. Third person references to *the girl* (line 11) and *the young girl* (line 32), given the design of the study, uncertainly identify either the young recipient on the stimulus tapes or the young evaluators. Aware of this, R (the researcher) repeatedly addresses her questions to the evaluators themselves (referenced as *you*) between lines 14 and 17 to check that they, themselves, acknowledge having experienced feelings of embarrassment in the conversations in question. At least one young evaluator then shows that she is sensitive to this issue of ambiguous reference by shifting her mode of response to R to indicate her own personal thoughts (*I think it was just . . .*) on line 20. Turning now to references to elderly people, between lines 18 and 36 all of RT's negative

Extract 2

```
 1    RT:  I think a lot of them were embarrassed
 2    *R:  the elderly woman or the younger woman?=
 3    RT:  the younger women=
 4     R:  the younger women were more embarrassed you think
 5         and is that how you were feeling as well? for some
 6         some of them?
 7    RT:  some of them yeah I was feeling embarrassed (4 or
 8         5 syllables)
 9     R:  can you think of any in particular I know it's
10         difficult to think back where you felt embarrassed

             .
             .
             .

11    KM:  the girl who didn't know what to say
12     R:  right
13    KM:  back to her

             .
             .
             .

14     R:  =why did you think that was? why do you feel why
15         do you think what was it particularly about that
16         conversation that made you feel as if you wanted to
17         cringe so much=
18    RT:  well probably because she wasn't because getting
19         enough she had some relatives (.) but nobody really
20         well no it wasn't so much that I think it was just
21         her attitude towards it
                                  [               ]
22     R:                          right which was
                                  [
23    RT:                                  that was embarrassing
24         that she said that she didn't know whether they
25         cared or not she supposed they did (.) but
                                                  [   ]
26     R:                                          yeah
27    RT:  she just came across as though she
28         wanted to moan about it to somebody and I
                                          [     ]
29     R:                                  right
30    RT:  just thought that was really embarrassing
31     R:  right
```

32	RT:	and you know the the young girl was saying
33		that they do care cause they were ringing her
34		but she she was just going on about how lonely
35		she was even though they rang her every day
36		(some incomprehensible syllables)
37		there's a few there is a few others like
38		that as well where (.) I think they were trying to
39		make the other uncomfortable embarrassed
40	R:	what the elderly people yeah you think they're
41		actually <u>try</u>ing to do it
42	KM:	yeah trying to m make you feel sorry for them
43		in some way

* 'R' indicates the researcher

(and often stereotypical-sounding) remarks focus on individual elderly people referenced as *she* and *her* (e.g., *she just came across as if she wanted to moan about it to somebody* (lines 27–28) and *her attitude towards it* (line 21). By line 37, however, RT begins to widen the generalizability of her remarks by pointing out that *there is a few others like that as well*. In the next sentence, reference to a *few others* is replaced by the plural third person reference *they*, something which R repeats when she asks RT to confirm her understanding of what had been said: *you think they're actually trying to do it* (lines 40–41).

There is an individual ascription early on in the extract (viz., 27–28) that, arguably, can be classified as age stereotypical. Evidence of stereotyping would seem to become more easily interpretable as such, however, as the reference shifts to third person plural and more apparently categorical references. When RT says *they were trying to make the other uncomfortable embarrassed* (lines 38–39), it is still ambiguous whether the intended reference is just a few particular elderly people on the stimulus tapes or elderly people more generally. But by line 42, when KM intervenes to show her agreement with the developing sentiments by saying *yeah trying to make you feel sorry for them in some way,* it becomes less easy to avoid interpreting her reference to *them* (that is elderly people) in anything other than intergroup and stereotypical terms. This is because the reference is now three times removed from the original, more guarded, remark implicating just a few elderly people. The stereotypical appearance is also further strengthened by the fact that the reference to *you* on line 42 is quite clearly intended to carry the sense of one, or people in general. In other words, both sets of people involved appear to have become referenced in global, categorical, or intergroup terms.

Clearly, arriving at negative age stereotypical judgments affirms an experience of dissatisfaction in intergenerational exchanges involving sequences of elderly PSD. This point is often illustrated in the data when volunteers offer a stereotypical remark as a reason or explanation for their discomfort or difficulty with respect to elderly PSD. DG's aforementioned comment about an old person as a cantankerous old so and so falls into this category. As with talk about the sadness and empathy one feels for elderly people with difficult lives, however, the discourse of stereotyping is not always invoked in the act of affirming an experience of discomfort or difficulty. Talk of undesirable elderly behavior can also function to downgrade estimates of the problems caused. This is illustrated in GD3 when both EB and RHW maintain that conversations involving sequences of elderly PSD are not difficult for listeners because they are *routine* or *because one has come across those before*. The logic behind such a statement is not altogether clear until RHW states how *in some respects you have to take it with a pinch of salt*. One then comes to realize that the discomfort or difficulty is being denied because the respondents do not believe the discloser's claim (about loneliness) to be genuine. This is one of the most striking and disturbing instances of stereotyping to be found in the study. It is compounded by DG's final comment confirming the classical inverted-U stereotype of the old as children (see, e.g., Coupland and Coupland, 1990).

The Discourse of Individualization–Exceptions

A pattern emerges in the data where positive remarks, pointing up the valued qualities of elderly exceptions to the rule, alternate with negative, stereotypical remarks. This pattern is particularly well illustrated in exchanges between NL and HP in GD3.

Some particularly unfavorable ascriptions are made in GD3 to people and conversations with people who are old. For example, NL describes how *it can be rather boring to be with an old person for any length of time and a bit frustrating and you feel a bit resentful of the time that you have to spend perhaps you know its the sort of duty things (breathes in) and its a comparative rarity when you have you really want to see an old person and spend time with them.* Prior to making the above comment, NL had made many cuts, pauses, and inhalations, suggestive of feelings of discomfort as she embarked on a discourse of stereotyping. However, other aspects of the discourse surrounding such remarks suggest that their verbalization may be facilitated because they are embedded within comments of a more positive nature.

Directly following her negative remarks, NL introduces the rather different idea that there are exceptional old people whose company she enjoys and this theme of individualization/exceptions is then developed further by HP who emphasizes how some elderly people's conversations are indeed *buoyant* and *elated*. It is almost as if the downswing embodied by the discourse of stereotyping obliged respondents to offer some counterbalancing and temporizing thoughts. The upswing represented by the introduction of a theme of individualization/exceptions is, however, followed once again by verbal stereotyping: *some were very very downcasting . . . sort of moaning conversations*. Evocation of the idea that not all elderly people can be described by negative age-stereotypical characteristics brings temporary respite from the discourse of stereotyping. Nevertheless, maybe one cannot afford to be too sanguine about the impact of these ideas whose main functional role could be, at the end of the day, to further facilitate and legitimize the expression of negative, stereotypical remarks.

This pattern of what could be called the structural interrelationship between themes is similar to one which has been noted by Hewitt and Stokes (1975) and by Potter and Wetherell (1987). One could characterize the preparatory and contrasting remarks as a form of "credentialling." The classic form of credentialling according to Hewitt and Stokes is to preface a prejudicial remark with a statement such as "some of my best friends are but. . . ." Use of statements indicating positive empathy and recognition of the fact that there are exceptions to the rule in our data may, therefore, constitute attempts to provide people with credentials that permit them to commit a prejudicial act without becoming typified, in consequence, as age prejudiced.

Counterstereotyping or Antistereotyping

Elderly stereotyping is an important and recurrent theme in the data. However, as we have seen, people did often appear to have misgivings about uttering stereotypical remarks and the frequency and severity of stereotyping in the data corpus should not, therefore, be overstated.

Typically, by stereotyping is meant the idea that people actively engage in or personally endorse (Henwood, 1987) stereotypical ascriptions made on the basis of verbal, written, or nonexistent data. There are other ways of invoking stereotypes, however, and at least two of these are found in the discussion data. For example, people can observe others engaging in what they perceive to be stereotypical behavior, even while they, themselves, remain aloof and distance themselves from it. This occurs in the data where participants observe the young women in the tape-recorded extracts *patronizing* (CT/GD5, JC/GD8) the elderly in their talk. Some respondents also acted on their observations to challenge stereotypical behavior on the part of their fellow volunteers. Extract 3 is an illustration of this, showing CT's repeated attempts to interject (lines 5 and 10–14) after categorical statements have been made by other members of the group, as if she does not want to be seen to be agreeing with the kind of sentiment they are expressing. In a previous context this kind of challenging behavior has been

Extract 3

```
1    EK:                        yeah but its instinctive
2          to let the older person talk isn't it? (.) it's
3          instinctive to let them just talk away (.)
4          and feed (.) them openings
                  [      ]
5    CT:       I just
          .
          .
          .
6    EK:  it seemed a very lopsided conversation I think
7          that's partly natural because I think as I said I
8          think older people tend to sort of
9          ramble on          but I think the
          .
          .
          .
10   CT:  um yeh I I felt that that it just depended on who
11         was talking sometimes I felt as if I could you
12         know see it from their put myself in their
13         position and sometimes I didn't it depended on what
14         sort of things they were saying=
```

called counter- or antistereotyping (Henwood, Giles, Coupland and Coupland, 1987).

Another form of counterstereotyping occurs when respondents identify the cycle, *spiral,* or *script* of stereotyping itself as the problem. This is seen in GD5 when CT progresses from the observation that she did not very much like the way the young women on the tapes were behaving to the diagnosis that *talking in (.) sort of stereotypes was the problem.* The complaint is made that people all too easily get into these classic (JC, GD8) patterns of intergenerational communication. Also, particularly in discussions involving CT (GD5) and JC (GD8), the frustration volunteers can feel at watching this kind of cycle is made explicit. At one level, there is a similarity between the discourses of individualization/exceptions and antistereotyping: both involve the idea of elderly people who do not conform to expectations for the category. These two categories of themes were distinguished because of differences in their functional role in discourse. In the former, the idea of exceptional elderly people was seen to play a significant role in bolstering the theme of negative, elderly stereotyping. In the latter, invoking the idea of elderly exceptions served mainly to challenge the legitimacy and/or presumed accuracy of stereotypical ideas.

Concluding Remarks

The history of research on the social psychology of stereotypes has been characterized by a debate over the rationality of stereotypical beliefs. Until recently, the irrationality of stereotypes was understood solely in terms of the distorted emotional dynamics of prejudiced individuals. This could be contrasted with a minority view of stereotypes as cognitive constructs, the operation of which is guided by cold or rational computational principles. The contemporary characterization of social cognition as an inherently biased and error-prone activity has eroded the previously clear distinction between rational cognitive and irrational motivational influences on human functioning. Today, therefore, stereotypes are simultaneously construed as the ordinary cognitive products of biased information-processing activity, *and* as affect-laden schemata, motivated or hot cognitions.

An increased concern with emotion or affect in social cognition is to be welcomed since it represents one way of bringing cognition into touch with practical, social activity and everyday life. Another possible way of overcoming the previously unhelpful dichotomy between cognition and affect, however, is to construe them as aspects of meaning constituted within historically specific discourses and social texts. This suggestion follows from the thesis of social constructionism which advocates that social psychological phenomena can be usefully studied as they are constituted or rendered meaningful within the social and linguistic practices of a culture.

Some aspects of the interpretive analysis of the discussion data reported in this chapter supported the idea that the interactional management of elderly PSD is discomforting and difficult. However, overall, respondents seemed to prefer to articulate their concerns at a more generalized level, by talking about the difficulties encountered by elderly people in their day-to-day lives and the personal and social characteristics of elderly people as members of a stigmatized or relatively disliked social group. This finding could be attributable, in part, to methodological aspects of the study. Volunteers did not always find it easy to imagine themselves in the role of the younger women on the tapes, and the group discussion methodology could also have predisposed people to exchange beliefs at a general social level if this is what people typically do in such circumstances. Nevertheless, we take it as significant that the four emergent themes served to affirm and/or deny the experience of discomfort and difficulty in encounters involving elderly PSD, and in relationships with elderly people generally. For this reason, we would argue that the discourse of stereotyping, together with the other themes with which it is closely related, can serve the important function of rendering any discomfort or difficulty experienced in encounters with members of different social groups socially meaningful.

Identification of the way stereotypes can function in this way suggests that affect or emotion in face-to-face encounters can be involved in the production, reproduction, and challenging of stereotypical representations themselves. In past research on the social psychology of stereotypes, where the emphasis has been either on cataloguing the overarching content of stereotypes or the intraindividual or cognitive process of stereotyping, stereotypes have taken on the appearance of relatively abstract ideations, representations, or beliefs. In the research documented here, however, it becomes apparent that the use of at least some stereotypes of old age is very much grounded in the practical realities and conversational routines of everyday life.

A number of other novel aspects of the relationship between cognition and affect in stereotypes emerge from the exercise of studying stereotypes as they become manifest in discourse; that is as discourse acts (see, e.g., Condor & Henwood, 1986; Henwood, 1992; also Austin, 1962). For example, analysis of the discussion data revealed that verbal stereotyping can be bolstered by the credentialling function of other discourses, such as those of exceptions/individualization and sadness and empathy, and by the face-saving use of linguistic devices such as hedges which make possible a subtle form of prejudice. It also became apparent, on the other hand, that it is possible for stereotypes to be challenged discursively, through the invoking of criticism of the role of disclosers and recipients in following conventional scripts (the discourse of counterstereotyping). It proved possible to trace the discursive processes by which generalized statements about elderly people as a social category can evolve out of the more limited exercise of observing encounters involving single, or small groups of, elderly people. And, it was recognized that decisions about what counts as an act of stereotyping are inherently ambiguous and subject to negotiation. Such decisions necessitate taking into account the interactional pragmatics of encounters, including their consequences at a broader social and ideological level.

To conclude, then, we hope that this chapter has demonstrated the value of studying stereotypes as they are made manifest in discourse, in relation to practical dimensions of human judgment and socially situated activity. Historical debates on the rationality issue in stereotyping can begin to be resolved if it is accepted that neither affective nor cognitive processes should be focused on in research to the exclusion of the other. The theoretical and methodological approach advocated here represents one way of examining the close interrelationship between affect and cognition in stereotyping.

Acknowledgment

The authors are extremely grateful to the editors for their patience, encouragement, and comprehensively helpful comments on previous drafts of this chapter.

References

Adorno, T. M., Frenkel-Brunswik, E., Levinson, D. J., & Sanford, R. N. (1950). *The authoritarian personality.* New York: Harper and Row.

Allport, G. (1954). *The nature of prejudice.* Reading MA: Addison-Wesley.

Ashmore, R. D. (1981). Sex stereotypes and implicit personality theory. In D. L. Hamilton (Ed.), *Cognitive processes in stereotyping and intergroup behavior* (pp. 37–81). Hillsdale, NJ: Erlbaum.

Ashmore, R. D., & Del Boca, F. K. (1981). Conceptual approaches to stereotypes and stereotyping. In D. L. Hamilton (Ed.), *Cognitive processes in stereotyping and intergroup behavior* (pp. 1–33). Hillsdale, NJ: Erlbaum.

Austin, J. L. (1962). *How to do things with words.* Oxford: Clarendon.

Berger, C. R., & Bradac, J. S. (1982). *Language and social knowledge.* London: Edward Arnold.

Berger, P. L., & Luckman, T. (1967). *The social construction of reality.* Harmondsworth UK: Penguin.

Bodenhausen, G. V., & Lichtenstein, M. (1987). Social stereotypes and information processing strategies: The impact of task complexity. *Journal of Personality and Social Psychology,* 52, 871–880.

Bower, G. H. (1981). Mood and memory. *American Psychologist,* 36, 129–148.

Bower, G. H., & Cohen, P. R. (1982). Emotional influences on learning and cognition. In M. S. Clarke & S. J. Fiske (Eds.), *Affect and cognition* (pp. 263–289). Hillsdale, NJ: Erlbaum.

Bowers, J. (1990). All hail the great abstraction: Star Wars and the politics of cognitive psychology. In I. Parker & J. Shotter (Eds.), *Deconstructing social psychology* (pp. 127–140). London: Routledge.

Brewer, M. B., Dull, V., & Lui, L. (1981). Perceptions of the elderly: Stereotypes as prototypes. *Journal of Personality and Social Psychology,* 41(4), 656–670.

Brown, P., & Levinson, S. (1987). *Politeness: Some universals in language use.* Cambridge: Cambridge University Press.

Bulmer, M. (1979). Concepts in the analysis of qualitative data. *Sociological Review,* 27, 653–677.

Carroll, J. S., & Payne, J. W. (1976). *Cognition and social behavior.* Hillsdale, NJ: Erlbaum.

Clark, M. S., & Isen, A. M. (1982). Toward understanding the relationship between feeling states and social behavior. In A. H. Hastorf & A. M. Isen (Eds.), *Cognitive social psychology* (pp. 73–108). New York: Elsevier.

Clifton, A. K., McGrath, D., & Wick, B. (1976). Stereotypes of women: A single category? *Sex Roles,* 2(2), 135–147.

Condor, S., & Henwood, K. (1986). Stereotypes, social cognition and social context. Unpublished manuscript, Psychology Department, University of Lancaster, England.

Coulter, J. (1986). Affect and social context: Emotion defined as a social task. In R. Harre (Ed.), *The social construction of emotions* (pp. 120–134). Oxford: Blackwell.

Coupland, J., Coupland, N., Giles, H., & Wiemann, J. (1988). My life in your hands: Processes of self-disclosure in intergenerational talk. In N. Coupland (Ed.), *Styles of discourse* (pp. 201–253). London: Croom Helm.

Coupland, N., & Coupland, J. (1990). Language and later life: The diachrony and decrement predicament. In H. Giles & P. Robinson (Eds.), *Handbook of language and social psychology* (pp. 451–69). Chichester: Wiley.

Coupland, N., Coupland, J., Giles, H., Henwood, K., & Wiemann, J. (1988). Elderly self-disclosure: Interactional and intergroup Issues. *Language in Society,* 8, 109–133.

Coupland, N., Henwood, K., Coupland, J., & Giles, H. (1990). Accommodating troubles talk: The management of elderly self-disclosure. In G. McGregor and R. White (Eds.), *Reception and response: Hearer creativity and the analysis of written and spoken text* (pp. 112–144). London: Croom Helm.

Deaux, K., Winton, W., Crowley, M., & Lewis, L. L. (1985). Level of categorization and content of gender stereotypes. *Social Cognition, 3,* 145–167.

Dovidio, J. F., Evans, N., & Tyler, R. B. (1986). Racial stereotypes: the contents of their cognitive representations. *Journal of Experimental Social Psychology, 22,* 22–37.

Eiser, J. R. (1980). *Cognitive social psychology: A Guidebook to theory and research.* London: McGraw Hill.

Fishman, J. (1956). An examination of the process and function of stereotyping. *Journal of Social Psychology, 43,* 27–64.

Fiske, S. T. (1982). Schema triggered affect: Applications to social perception. In M. S. Clarke & S. T. Fiske (Eds.), *Affect and cognition: The 17th annual carnegie symposium* (pp. 55–78). Hillsdale, NJ: Erlbaum.

Fiske, S. T., & Taylor, S. E. (1984). *Social cognition.* Reading, MA: Addison-Wesley.

Forgas, J. P. (Ed.). (1981). *Social cognition: Perspectives on everyday understanding.* London: Academic Press.

Forgas, J. P. (1983). What is social about social cognition? *British Journal of Social Psychology, 22,* 129–144.

Freund, T., Kruglanski, A. W., & Shpitzajzen, A. (1985). The freezing and unfreezing of impressional primacy: Effects of the need for structure and the fear of invalidity. *Personality and Social Psychology Bulletin, 11,* 479–487.

Gaertner, S. L., & McLaughlin, J. P. (1983). Racial stereotypes: Associations and ascriptions of positive and negative characteristics. *Social Psychology Quarterly, 46,* 23–30.

Gergen, K. J. (1985). The social constructionist movement in modern psychology. *American Psychologist, 40,* 266–275.

Gergen, K. J., & Davis, K. E. (Eds.). (1985). *The social construction of the person.* New York: Springer-Verlag.

Gergen, K. J., & Shotter, J. (Eds.). (1989). *Texts of identity.* London: Sage.

Gigerenzer, G., & Murray, D. J. (1987). *Cognition as intuitive statistics.* Hillsdale, NJ: Erlbaum.

Glaser, B. G., & Strauss, A. L. (1967). *The discovery of grounded theory.* New York: Aldine.

Hamilton, D. L. (1981). Illusory correlation as a basis for stereotyping. In D. L. Hamilton (Ed.), *Cognitive processes in stereotyping and intergroup behavior* (pp. 115–143). Hillsdale, NJ: Erlbaum.

Hamilton, D. L., & Gifford, R. K. (1976). Illusory correlation in interpersonal perception: A cognitive basis of stereotypical judgments. *Journal of Experimental Social Psychology, 12,* 392–407.

Harding, J., Proshansky, H., Kutner, B., & Chein, I. (1969). Prejudice and ethnic relations. In G. Lindzey & E. Aronson (Eds.), *The handbook of social psychology* (Vol. 5, pp. 1–76). Reading, MA: Addison-Wesley.

Henwood, K. (1987). *The social psychology of stereotypes: A critical assessment.* Unpublished doctoral thesis, Bristol University, England.

Henwood, K. (1992). Stereotyping and self-disclosure: A discourse approach to aging. In M. Featherstone (Ed.), *The future of adult life: Proceedings of the 2nd international conference.* Middlesborough: Teeside Polytechnic Publications.

Henwood, K., Giles, H., Coupland, J., & Coupland, N. (1987). Age identity and social stereotypes. Paper presented at the International Conference on Social Identity, Exeter, England, July.

Hewitt, R., & Stokes, R. (1975). Disclaimers. *American Sociological Review, 40,* 1–11.

Holmes, J. (1984). Hedging your bets and sitting on the fence: Some evidence for hedges as support structures. *Te Reo, 27,* 47–62.

Jones, R. A. (1982). Perceiving other people: Stereotyping as a process of social cognition. In A. G. Miller (Ed.), *In the eye of the beholder: Contemporary issues in stereotyping* (pp. 41–91). New York: Praeger.

Jungermann, H. (1986). The two camps on rationality. In H. R. Arkes & K. R. Hammond (Eds.), *Judgment and decision making* (pp. 627–641). Cambridge: Cambridge University Press.

Katz, D., & Braly, K. (1933). Racial stereotypes of one hundred college students. *Journal of Abnormal and Social Psychology, 30*, 175–193.

Katz, D., & Braly, K. (1935). Racial prejudice and racial stereotypes. *Journal of Abnormal and Social Psychology, 30*, 175–193.

Katz, D., & Braly, K. (1947). Verbal stereotypes and racial prejudice. In E. Macoby, T. M. Newcombe, & E. L. Hartley (Eds.), *Readings in social psychology* (pp. 40–46). New York: Holt, Rinehart, and Winston.

Klineberg, O. (1951). The scientific study of national stereotypes. *International Social Science Bulletin, 3*, 505–515.

Krueger, J., & Rothbart, M. (1988). The use of categorical and individuating information in making inferences about personality. *Journal of Personality and Social Psychology, 55*, 187–195.

Kruglanski, A. W., & Ajzen, I. (1983). Bias and error in human judgment. *European Journal of Social Psychology, 13*, 1–44.

Leventhal, H., & Tomarken, A. J. (1986). Emotion: Today's problems. *Annual Review of Psychology, 37*, 565–610.

Linville, P. W. (1982). The complexity-extremity effect and age-based stereotyping. *Journal of Personality and Social Psychology, 42*, 193–211.

Linville, P. W., & Jones, E. E. (1980). Polarized appraisals of outgroup members. *Journal of Personality and Social Psychology, 38*, 689–703.

Lippa, R. A. (1990). *Introduction to social psychology.* Belmont, CA: Wadsworth.

Lippmann, W. (1922). *Public opinion.* New York: Harcourt, Brace, Jovanovich.

Locksley, A., Hepburn, C., & Ortiz, V. (1982). Social stereotypes and judgments of individuals: An instance of the base-rate fallacy. *Journal of Experimental Social Psychology, 18*, 23–42.

Lopes, L. (1991). The rhetoric of irrationality. *Theory and Psychology, 1*, 65–82.

Mackie, D. (1973). Arriving at 'truth' by definition: The case of stereotype inaccuracy. *Social Problems, 20*, 431–447.

McCauley, C., & Stitt, C. L. (1978). An individual and quantitative measure of stereotypes. *Journal of Personality and Social Psychology, 36*, 929–940.

McCauley, C., Stitt, C. L., & Segal, M. (1980). Stereotyping: From prejudice to prediction. *Psychological Bulletin, 87*, 195–208.

Meenes, M. (1943). A comparison of racial stereotypes of 1935 and 1942. *Journal of Social Psychology, 17*, 327–336.

Miller, A. G. (Ed.). (1982). *In the eye of the beholder: Contemporary issues in stereotyping.* New York: Praeger.

Nisbett, R. E., & Ross, L. (1980). *Human inference: Strategies and shortcomings of social judgment.* Englewood Cliffs, NJ: Prentice Hall.

Park, B., & Hastie, R. (1987). The perception of variability in category development: Instance-versus abstraction-based stereotypes. *Journal of Personality and Social Psychology, 53*, 621–635.

Parker, I., & Shotter, J. (1990). *Deconstructing social psychology.* London: Sage.

Pettigrew, T. F. (1981). Extending the stereotype concept. In D. L. Hamilton (Ed.), *Cognitive processes in intergroup relations* (pp. 303–331). Hillsdale, NJ: Erlbaum.

Potter, J., & Wetherell, M. (1987). *Discourse and social psychology.* London: Sage.

Prothro, E. T., & Melikian, L. H. (1955). Studies in social stereotypes: 5, Familiarity and the kernel of truth hypothesis. *Journal of Social Psychology, 41*, 3–10.

Rasinski, K. A., Crocker, J., & Hastie, R. (1985). Another look at sex stereotypes and social judgments: An analysis of the social perceiver's use of subjective probabilities. *Journal of Personality and Social Psychology, 49*, 317–326.

Richter, U. (1956). The conceptual mechanism of stereotyping. *American Sociological Review,* **21,** 568–571.

Rosch, E., & Mervis, C. B. (1975). Family resemblances: Studies in the internal structure of categories. *Cognitive Psychology, 7,* 573–603.

Rothbart, M. (1981). Memory processes and social beliefs. D. L. Hamilton (Ed.), *Cognitive processes in intergroup relations* (pp. 145–181). Hillsdale, NJ: Erlbaum.

Rothbart, M., & Lewis, D. (1988). Inferring category attributes from exemplar attributes: Geometric shapes and social categories. *Journal of Personality and Social Psychology,* **55,** 861–872.

Rothbart, M., Evans, M., & Fulero, S. (1979). Recall for confirming events: Memory processes and the maintenance of social stereotypes. *Journal of Experimental Social Psychology,* **15,** 343–355.

Schachter, S., & Singer, J. (1962). Cognitive, social and physiological determinants of emotional state. *Psychological Review,* **65,** 379–399.

Sherman, S. J., Judd, C. M., & Park, B. (1989). Social cognition. *Annual Review of Psychology,* **40,** 281–326.

Shotter, J., & Gergen, K. J. (Eds.). (1989). *Texts of identity.* New York: Sage.

Showers, C., & Cantor, N. (1985). Social cognition: A look at motivated strategies. *Annual Review of Psychology,* **36,** 275–305.

Simon, H. A. (1957). *Models of man.* New York: Wiley.

Simpson, G. E., & Yinger, J. (1965). *Racial and cultural minorities.* New York: Harper and Row.

Taylor, S. T., & Crocker, J. (1981). Schematic bases of social information processing. In T. Higgins, C. P. Herman, & M. P. Zanna (Eds.), *Social cognition: The ontario symposium on personality and social psychology* (pp. 89–134). Hillsdale, NJ: Erlbaum.

Tesser, A. (1978). Self-generated attitude change. *Advances in Experimental Social Psychology,* **11,** 289–338.

Tversky, A., & Kahneman, D. (1974). Judgment under uncertainty: Heuristics and biases. *Science,* **185,** 1124–1131.

Van Dijk, T. A. (1987). *Communicating racism: Ethnic prejudice in thought and talk.* London: Sage.

Vinacke, W. E. (1949). Stereotyping among national-racial groups in Hawaii: A study in ethnocentrism. *Journal of Social Psychology,* **30,** 265–291.

Vinacke, W. E. (1956). Explorations in the dynamic process of stereotyping. *Journal of Social Psychology,* **43,** 105–132.

Wilder, D. A. (1984). Intergroup contact: The typical member and the exception to the rule. *Journal of Experimental Social Psychology,* **20,** 177–194.

Zajonc, R. B. (1980). Feeling and thinking: Preferences need no inferences. *American Psychologist,* **35**(2), 151–175.

Zajonc, R. B. (1984). On the primacy of affect. *American Psychologist,* **39**(2), 117–123.

Zawadski, B. (1948). Limitations on the scapegoat theory of prejudice. *Journal of Abnormal and Social Psychology,* **43,** 127–141.

Chapter 13

Social Identity and Social Emotions: Toward New Conceptualizations of Prejudice

ELIOT R. SMITH

Department of Psychological Sciences
Purdue University
West Lafayette, Indiana

Introduction

Stereotyping, prejudice, and discrimination (ranging from economic exploitation of outgroup members through genocide) have been among the central historical themes of the twentieth century. Blacks and whites in Selma, Alabama, Arabs and Israelis in the Middle East, Catholics and Protestants in Northern Ireland—these are just a few reminders of the significance of racial and ethnic conflicts in the course of history. Social psychologists have been at the forefront among social scientists attempting to understand the nature and sources of intergroup conflicts. However, I wish to argue in this chapter that the common social-psychological conceptualization of stereotyping, prejudice, and discrimination in terms of *beliefs, attitudes,* and *attitude-driven behavior,* though it offers many important insights, is inadequate in basic respects. Fortunately, theoretical and empirical advances within social psychology, particularly in the areas of emotions and social identity theory, now allow viewing these phenomena within a new conceptual framework. I believe that they can best be understood as *appraisals, emotions,* and *emotional action tendencies,* based in the perceiver's *social identity.* This chapter will explicate some of the problems in the traditional conceptualization and some of the theoretical strengths and novel hypotheses implicit in the new one. It will also sketch some directions for research that could provide further empirical support for this new viewpoint on prejudice and related phenomena.

Prejudice as Attitude

Current views of intergroup prejudice and the related concepts of stereotype and discrimination build on the fundamental (and prototypically social-psychological) construct of attitude. Stereotypes of an outgroup are conceptualized as the perceiver's *beliefs* about the group's attributes: for example, they may be seen as dirty, clannish, musical, or shrewd. Specific stereotypic beliefs may be positive or negative in evaluative tone, and may be thought to characterize virtually all members of the group or just a few of them. This definition of stereotype is widely accepted. It has the virtue of being closely linked to easily applied measurement techniques, in which subjects are asked about the attributes that they believe characterize a specific group, either in open-ended format or on rating scales (e.g., Katz & Braly, 1933; Deaux & Lewis, 1984).

Somewhat more disagreement exists concerning the appropriate definition of prejudice, but in the social-psychological literature it is consensually defined as an *attitude* toward an outgroup (Dovidio & Gaertner, 1986). Example definitions are "negative attitudes toward social groups" (Stephan, 1985, p. 600); "a favorable or unfavorable predisposition toward any member of the category in question" (Tajfel, 1982, p. 3). Defining prejudice as an intergroup attitude is helpful in allowing social psychologists to bring the whole body of attitude theory and research to bear on issues related to prejudice. Thus, drawing on Fishbein and Ajzen (1975) or related models of the bases of attitudes, we can derive propositions about the relationship of prejudice to stereotypic beliefs. Since the stereotype constitutes the perceiver's beliefs about the object's (the group's) attributes, the perceiver's attitude should be a function of his or her evaluation of the most salient beliefs and the strength with which the beliefs are held (e.g., the proportion of the group presumed to possess the attribute). Eagly and Mladinic (1989) demonstrated such relationships for the groups women, men, Democrats, and Republicans. A group that is stereotypically believed to possess many negative attributes and few positive ones will likely be evaluated negatively, that is, perceivers will tend to be prejudiced against such a group.

More recently Zanna and Rempel (1988) presented a somewhat different viewpoint on attitudes. They hold that an attitude is an evaluation of an object that can be based on any of three broad types of information: beliefs about the object, the perceiver's affective or emotional reactions, or the perceiver's past behaviors. Once an attitude is formed (from any of these bases) it may be cognitively represented and retrieved separately, becoming somewhat autonomous from the information on which it was originally based. This viewpoint thus supplements Fishbein and Ajzen's (1975) belief-centered model with the possibility that attitudes stem from emotional responses (e.g., Abelson *et al.*, 1982) or from the perceiver's past behaviors (Bem, 1972). This model is compatible with my conception of prejudice, as I will discuss later.

The definition of prejudice as an intergroup attitude also provides theoretical leverage for understanding intergroup behaviors including discrimination. Again, Fishbein and Ajzen's (1975) Theory of Reasoned Action is helpful, and leads to a view of intergroup discrimination as *attitude-driven behavior*. This conceptual framework allows the prediction that the individual's overall attitude toward the group (i.e., degree of prejudice) will *not* necessarily correlate with a specific discriminatory behavior (e.g., LaPiere, 1934). However, prejudice should correlate with a broadly aggregated behavioral measure (aggregated across multiple situations or times and across different types of behaviors; Ajzen & Fishbein, 1977). Unfortunately, most research on prejudice and discrimination, like the attitude-behavior research that Wicker (1969) used to argue that attitudes do not relate to behavior, has used narrow, single-act behavioral criteria. This may be one reason why correlations between individual levels of prejudice and discriminatory behavior have generally been found to be disappointingly low (Ehrlich, 1973; Brigham, 1971), though another reason will be suggested below.

The overall model of prejudice and related constructs under the prejudice-as-attitude conceptualization, then, is as follows:

Negative stereotype: *Members of Group A are dirty, hostile, lazy, . . .*
leads to
Prejudiced attitude: *I don't like As*
leads to
Discrimination: *I prefer to avoid As, exclude them from good jobs, . . .*

It has made good sense for social psychologists to treat stereotypes, prejudice, and discrimination within the broad framework of beliefs, attitudes, and attitude-linked behavior. Attitude theory has been one of the central areas of social psychology over the decades, and intensive theoretical and empirical work has produced robust principles and findings that can be applied to understanding and changing intergroup phenomena. And until very recently, no potentially competing theoretical framework could remotely rival the conceptual development and sophistication of attitude theory. But this approach is not without problems.

First, the attitude conceptualization directs attention only to the *evaluative* nature of stereotypic beliefs. Outgroups that are seen as hostile and threatening and those that are seen as dirty and disgusting are assumed to be viewed in the same way: negatively. Similarly, discriminatory behaviors that express hatred versus contempt versus fear for a group are not conceptually distinguished; only the fact that they all reflect negative evaluations is theoretically relevant. The conceptualization presented in this paper allows for a more differentiated view of reactions to groups.

Second, if prejudice is an attitude based on salient stereotypic beliefs about the group's attributes, it should be relatively *constant* across situations or contexts. If a perceiver dislikes the outgroup he or she will attempt to discriminate against them or avoid them on all occasions. Situational specificity of behaviors, as when an outgroup is accepted in menial or servant roles but rejected as co-workers, would be difficult to account for theoretically. Certainly, contact with servants reflects a more intimate level of social distance than contact with co-workers, increasing the puzzle. Moreover, plentiful evidence suggests that attitude change toward an outgroup produced by successful desegregation is generally situation specific. For example, if a workplace is racially desegregated, white workers may become more accepting of black co-workers, but without changing their negative attitudes toward blacks in other contexts (e.g., toward neighborhood or school desegregation; Minard, 1952). The situational specificity of prejudiced reactions may be an important *substantive*—not methodological—reason for the low correlations between prejudice and single discriminatory behaviors.

To account for variation in people's reactions to different outgroup members in different situations, many researchers have turned to the notion of *subtypes*. That is, they assume that people have stereotypes and corresponding attitudes concerning relatively specific types of group members (e.g., sexy woman, career woman, grandmother) rather than toward a social group or category as a whole (women; Brewer *et al.*, 1981). Yet this conceptual advance does not solve all the problems. Researchers have had difficulty arriving at a canonical list of consensual subtypes. More fundamentally, it appears that *persons in situations* rather than *types of persons* are the real target of perceivers' stereotypes and attitudinal and behavioral reactions (cf. Cantor, Mischel, & Schwartz, 1982). The same person who is a career woman at the office may be a sexy woman at a nightclub; the same black who is an acceptable co-worker may be hated as a potential neighbor (Minard, 1952). This observation points to a basic inadequacy in any theory that focuses attention only on the perceiver's conceptions of the outgroup. If a perceiver's attitudes and behaviors toward an outgroup member depend only on general beliefs about the person's group (or subtype), how are situationally specific reactions to be explained? A model incorporating configural cognitive representations of persons together with situational and contextual variables, not just general knowledge about social groups, is required (see Smith, 1990, and Jacoby & Kelley, 1990, for related arguments).

In summary, by assimilating stereotyping, prejudice, and discrimination to the sophisticated and well-developed structure of attitude theory, social psychologists have successfully captured many important aspects of the phenomena. Certainly, the fact that beliefs, evaluations, and behaviors toward social groups are often strongly positive or negative is one key observation that is well reflected in the attitude-based conception. But this conception may obscure other equally important observations, such as the specificity of prejudice and discriminatory behaviors, both the diverse types of feelings directed at different groups (hate, fear, contempt, and the like) and the different feelings that may prevail toward outgroup members in different situations or contexts.

Prejudice as Emotion

An alternative conception of prejudice rests on recent theoretical developments in two rather diverse areas: self-categorization theory and appraisal theories of emotion. These ideas have not previously (as far as I am aware) been combined in this form, though related ideas have been advanced and will be briefly reviewed below.

Self-Categorization as Social Identity

The starting point for this new conceptualization is the notion of a *self-categorization* (Turner, 1987). A self-categorization is a view of oneself as a member of a socially defined group or category (e.g., as female, Canadian, African American, or a "social cognition type"). Turner (1987) drew on earlier versions of social identity theory (Tajfel, 1982) in proposing that when a self-categorization becomes salient, it comprises an aspect of the perceiver's social (as opposed to personal) identity. That is, when personal identity is salient (e.g., when interacting with fellow ingroup members) I will think of myself in terms of my unique individual abilities, goals, personality traits, physical attributes, and so on. However, when a social identity is salient (e.g., in intergroup interaction) I will think of myself *as a group member* and will view myself largely or completely in terms of group-typical attributes.

Turner's theoretical model is complex and extensive, but only a few points need be noted here. The salience of a particular social identity is a function of many factors including (1) the presence (real or imagined) of outgroup members as a focus of social comparison, (2) the perception that significant attributes covary with group membership, and (3) competition or conflict between groups. And one central consequence of the salience of a social identity is perceived within-group homogeneity and between-group differentiation. When the big basketball game between Purdue and Indiana University rolls around, nothing else is as important as one's school identification. As an intergroup situation increases the salience of a particular self-categorization, perceivers are likely to assume that both groups are internally homogeneous (group members think, feel, and act alike) and that the groups are very different from each other.

The salience of a social categorization influences not only the perception of self and others, but also group members' actual attitudes and behaviors. By the process of "auto-stereotyping" (Turner, 1987) group members are motivated to conform to the ingroup stereotype, which functions as a norm, that is, conformity is positively evaluated within the group, while deviance is negatively viewed. Thus, not only will people's perceptions of group members' characteristics exaggerate similarities and downplay heterogeneity, but actual attitudes and behaviors will also tend toward homogeneity when a group identity is salient.

According to self-categorization theory, salient group memberships constitute an integral part of the self. And self-relevant information, whether it pertains to individual characteristics or social categories, is special in many ways (cf. Greenwald & Pratkanis, 1984). Most important, self-relevant information has *affective and motivational significance*. People don't just know things about the self (e.g., that I am ill, or just passed an important examination), but also care about those things, and act with reference to them. To the extent that a self-categorization becomes salient as an element of (social) identity, therefore, it should also possess affective and motivational significance. Thus, people can experience affect on behalf of the group and be moved to act toward group goals. For example, individuals can "bask in reflected glory" of a successful entity (e.g., a college sports team) with which they identify (Cialdini *et al.*, 1976). More generally, fans who feel pride in the home team's successes, guilt when the team displays poor sportsmanship, or painful disappointment at its losses are experiencing social emotions—emotions triggered by events that are *group* relevant, rather than merely personally relevant. The point, then, is that a salient self-categorization, like individual aspects of a person's identity, can elicit emotions and motivational processes.

Appraisals and Emotions

People can experience not only positive or negative moods when their groups succeed or fail, but also experience diverse *specific emotions* with respect to their social as well as personal identities. Specific predictions flow from appraisal theories of emotion, which have been elaborated in various versions by Roseman (1984), Frijda (1986), Scherer (1988), and Smith and Ellsworth (1985), among others. Appraisal theories identify an emotion as a complex syndrome involving cognitions, subjective feelings, and physiological or behavioral action tendencies (e.g., Frijda, Kuipers, & ter Schure, 1989). The syndrome is initially triggered by a configuration of cognitions or beliefs (termed *appraisals*) that are linked to a specific emotion. Appraisals are not necessarily represented in the perceiver's conscious awareness. For example, the emotion of anger might be triggered by appraisals that a motive-inconsistent event was caused by another person and that the perceiver is strong (Roseman, 1984). Note that this configuration includes both appraisals of the target person and of the situation and context. Anger in turn is linked to physiological changes (the "fight-or-flight" reaction) that may be subjectively perceptible, and to motivational urges or action tendencies (e.g., to "move against" the target of the emotion; Frijda *et al.*, 1989).

Appraisals that trigger emotions invariably implicate the self. Thus, Frijda et al. state that an event will lead to emotion if it "appears to favor or harm the individual's concerns: his or her major goals, motives, or sensitivities" (1989, p. 213). An event or situation that does not impinge on the self in some way is unlikely to be affectively significant.[1] However, appraisal theorists have generally considered only the personal, individual aspects of the self. My key point is that to the extent a self-categorization functions as a self-aspect, appraisals of events or situations with respect to that social aspect of identity will also trigger emotions. Thus, ingroup successes will lead to joy, threats to the ingroup to fear, and injustices suffered by the ingroup to anger.

The fact that a fan who is not a team member can feel these emotions based on events that affect the team illustrates that emotions can be experienced with respect to a group and not only with respect to the individual self. We could say that the individual feels emotions (of fear, anger, joy, or pride) on behalf of his or her group, but that formulation misrepresents the psychological nature of the process. We should rather consider that when group membership is salient, the group functions as a part of the self, and therefore that situations appraised as self-relevant trigger emotions just as they always do. Because the self is not limited by the skin, neither are emotions. Moreover, self-categorization theory suggests that insofar as perceivers view themselves in terms of their group membership, these group-relevant beliefs (appraisals) will tend to be shared within the ingroup via motivated conformity to group norms. In an intergroup situation, my

---

[1]Like most emotion theorists, I am leaving aside the problematic issues of empathetic emotions felt on behalf of others. It is worth noting, however, that the insight of self-categorization theory that the self can extend out beyond the skin to encompass our social groups and categories, may constitute a starting point for a theoretically motivated account of empathy. For example, learning of the plight of suffering refugees may activate a common identity (as human beings) that the perceiver shares with them, bringing them within the scope of the social self and making empathy theoretically explicable as self-related (like other emotions).

appraisals of the outgroup's relevance (threat, etc.) to my ingroup are unlikely to be unique to me; instead, all of us in the ingroup are likely to see
things the same way.

Prejudice as Social Emotion

The above formulation concerning social emotions is quite general, applying to such situations as fans' rejoicing or despondency when their team
wins or loses. It has specific application to prejudice and related issues.
Core elements of stereotypes—beliefs about the outgroup's properties and
relation to one's own group—include the types of appraisals that are important in triggering emotions. For example, the belief that an outgroup is
"pushy" and demands more than its fair share of resources is an appraisal
that is related to anger and resentment. But appraisals that induce emotions
rarely focus only on the target person or object; in addition, they refer to
the self and the current situation. For example, judging by the frequency of
newspaper publication of readers' letters on the topic, one situation that
seems to trigger social emotions in many people is a member of an ethnic
minority at the grocery store purchasing items with food stamps. The predominant reaction to this situation seems to be feelings of resentment and
anger directed at the outgroup. The relevant appraisals are not solely or
even mainly those involving the target person's individual characteristics,
but refer to the perceiver's self (e.g., my taxes are burdensome; I work hard
to earn a living; nobody gives me any handouts) and the situation (e.g., she
is using food stamps while I have to pay high prices for my groceries). Even
such situational details as the nature of the items being purchased (e.g.,
hamburger versus sirloin steak) may influence the experience of this social
emotion! Thus, the range of relevant appraisals goes beyond stereotypes
(attributed characteristics of the group or subtype) to include aspects of the
perceiver's self and the situation. Under this model, we would not expect a
perceiver to react in the same way to an outgroup member regardless of the
situation or context of the encounter (cf. Jacoby & Kelley, 1990). This conception of prejudice, then, is highly situation specific and episodic, in contrast to the view of prejudice as a function of highly general belief or
attitude structures (Smith, 1990).

I here define prejudice as *a social emotion experienced with respect to
one's social identity as a group member, with an outgroup as a target.* Social emotions can be positive and prosocial, for example pride in an ingroup's accomplishments or empathetic distress for a suffering outgroup.
But in this paper I follow the tradition of the stereotyping and prejudice literature in focusing on negative intergroup phenomena. Discriminatory behavior is seen as reflecting emotional action tendencies. Examples include
the tendency to aggress against an outgroup that is seen as pushy and there-

fore elicits anger, or to avoid one that is seen as dirty and therefore elicits disgust.

The overall model under the prejudice-as-social-emotion conceptualization, in contrast to that presented earlier, would be something like the following:

> **Appraisals:** *A member of Group A is receiving benefits that are undeserved and paid for by my group's tax dollars*
>
> leads to
>
> **Prejudiced emotion:** *I feel anger and resentment at As*
>
> leads to
>
> **Discrimination:** *I want to harm As by reducing food-stamp and welfare benefits, . . .*

Table I lists some possible intergroup appraisals, the emotions they generate, and corresponding emotional action tendencies (based on Roseman, 1984; Scherer, 1988; Frijda *et al.*, 1989). Note that appraisals of the self (particularly whether the self is strong or weak, reflecting the general significance of psychological control) have been linked to many emotions, along with appraisals of the target and the situation. The table also contains tentative suggestions about the intergroup contexts in which each emotion might be found, to be discussed later in this chapter. As the table emphasizes, the process underlying the generation and expression of social emotions is no different from that assumed by appraisal theories of emotion in general, with the crucial exception that the appraisals are assumed to refer to the (currently salient) *social* rather than individual aspects of the perceiver's identity.

Despite the situationally specific, episodic nature of prejudiced emotions as outlined here, some perceivers do possess relatively general attitudes concerning particular outgroups. This can be understood in terms of two possible mechanisms. (1) Outgroups that are rarely or never encountered in person may be cognitively represented only in terms of the perceiver's *beliefs* about their attributes in the absence of any strong affect or relevant past behaviors. Thus, the Zanna and Rempel (1988) attitude model reduces to the Fishbein and Ajzen (1975) belief-based one, leaving the perceiver with an attitude based on general beliefs about the group. The attitude may for this reason function in a relatively context-free way, being accessed whenever the group is mentioned. (2) As studies by Abelson *et al.* (1982) and Zanna, Haddock, and Esses (1990) suggest, episodic emotional experiences may over time generate an attitude. Generalization and strengthening of the attitude to the point where the outgroup is responded to in an undifferentiated way will depend both on the *consistency* of emotional reactions to the outgroup, and on the *perceived homogeneity* of the group. In the extreme, suppose almost every encounter with a group

TABLE I

Appraisals, Emotions, and Action Tendencies Potentially Relevant to Intergroup Contexts[a]

Appraisals	Emotion	Action tendencies	Potential intergroup context
Motive inconsistent, uncertain/unexpected, caused by others or circumstances, perceiver is weak	Fear	Move away to protect or avoid approach	Members of low-power or minority group feel toward high-power or majority
Motive inconsistent, certain, caused by others or circumstances, others violate ingroup norms (?)	Disgust	Avoid	Members of high-status group feel toward low-status group
Motive inconsistent, unfair, certain, other intentional cause, perceiver is weak	Contempt (dislike)	Move against	Members of any group feel toward outgroup
Motive inconsistent, unfair, certain, other intentional cause, perceiver is strong	Anger	Move against, pay attention	Members of high-power or majority group when lower-power or minority group makes demands or threats
Motive inconsistent, other cause, other has undeserved benefit (?)	Jealousy	Pay attention, demand similar benefit (?)	Members of low-status or low-power group feel toward high-status or high power groups

[a]Appraisals drawn from Roseman (1984), Frijda et al. (1989), and Scherer (1988), and action tendencies from Frijda et al. (1989), except those followed by (?) are speculative. Suggestions for potential intergroup context are speculative.

member leads to similar emotions, and that the ingroup–outgroup distinction is so salient that the outgroup is viewed as quite homogeneous (Turner, 1987). Then the perceiver would end up reacting in the same way to just about any outgroup member ("they're all alike"), even if the context is not particularly conducive to that particular emotion. Evidence for this possibility will be discussed below.

Implications and Unresolved Issues

The conceptualization of prejudice as social emotion has implications for a number of themes and issues in the research literature, very directly in some cases and more speculatively in others. An overview of some of these areas will indicate both the promise for theoretical integration that I see in this new conceptualization, and also some of the many currently unresolved questions and issues.

Evidence Supporting the Role of Social Emotions in Prejudice

Emotions and Prejudice

Several recent treatments of prejudice have included a role for emotions. As mentioned above, Zanna and Rempel (1988) postulate that attitudes can be based on affective reactions, and specifically propose that intergroup attitudes often are (p. 325). Supporting this idea, Zanna et al. (1990) found that subjects' reports of emotions they had experienced during intergroup encounters related to attitudes toward minorities. Dijker (1987) also found correlations between attitudes toward ethnic minorities and four "emotions" (positive mood, anxiety, irritation, and concern) that perceivers reported experiencing when confronted with individual members of the minorities. Action tendencies (self-reports of wishes to physically or verbally aggress against the minorities, or to keep one's distance) also related to the emotions as predicted. Finally, Dijker's data showed that emotional responses depended not only on the target's group membership but also on the conditions under which intergroup contacts took place, for example, encounters with next-door neighbors versus those with more distant others.

Dijker's (1987) study, then, shows that emotional reactions experienced during contacts with outgroup members, and corresponding emotional action tendencies, relate to a traditional (attitudinal) conception of prejudice. It also supports the idea that emotional responses to an outgroup member depend on the situational context and not just the individual characteristics of the target. However, Dijker's work is not tied to appraisal theories of emotion; for example, he identifies positive mood as an emotion though most appraisal theorists would not do so. Dijker also does not focus on the specific content of perceivers' stereotypes or conceive of them as emotion-linked appraisals, simply assuming that outgroup stereotypes will involve negative characteristics. The most significant difference between the model that is implicit in Dijker's (1987) and Zanna et al.'s (1990) work and that developed here, though, is that the former are framed completely at the individual level. The perceiver encounters an outgroup member and feels emotions as an individual—not with respect to a social identity as a group member. As noted above, this individualistic thrust is characteristic of both the prejudice-as-attitude and the appraisal-emotion literatures, but ignores evidence that social rather than individual aspects of identity are more important determinants of political and social attitudes and actions.

Group Identity and Prejudice

Thus, only scattered research currently demonstrates relationships of emotion to intergroup relations. In contrast, there is clear support for the other major component of this conceptualization of prejudice: attitudes and behaviors relevant to intergroup relations are driven by feelings and cognitions that reference the perceiver's *social* rather than individual or personal identity. The clearest illustration is the fact that fraternal relative deprivation—feelings that one's group is not faring as well as it deserves or as well as a comparison group—matters more than "egoistic" or individual-level relative deprivation (Runciman, 1966; Vanneman & Pettigrew, 1972). For example, working-class whites' opposition to busing in Boston in the 1970s was related to their feelings that other groups (e.g., blacks; upper-income professionals) were outstripping their own group, rather than to frustrations in their individual, personal lives (Useem, 1980). And fraternal relative deprivation, though the introduction of the concept predates the development of social identity or self-categorization theory, clearly implicates feelings of resentment or inequity felt on behalf of one's social identity as a group member.

Similarly, there is a large literature centering around the role of "symbolic racism" in predicting various political attitudes and behaviors (e.g., whites voting for or against black mayoral candidates, opposition to busing for school desegregation). Several investigations (e.g., Kinder & Sears, 1981; McConahay, 1982) have powerfully demonstrated that measures of symbolic racism predict such dependent variables better than do measures of the respondents' *individual-level* self-interest (e.g., whether the respondent has school-age children or lives in a district in which busing is likely). However, these findings are open to reconceptualization along the lines argued by Bobo (1983). He suggests that symbolic racism is better thought of as reflecting the *group*-based interests of the respondent, and therefore that the results in the literature show not the unimportance of self-interest but rather that group rather than individual interests are politically relevant. Bobo's conclusions have been challenged by advocates of the symbolic racism concept (Sears & Kinder, 1985), and the resulting debate is too complex and extensive to summarize here (cf. Sniderman & Tetlock, 1986; Weigel & Howes, 1985). I find Bobo's position compelling, and believe that there is reason to identify symbolic racism with group-based, emotion-linked appraisals. For example, symbolic racism has been defined as involving "feelings that blacks violate such traditional American values as individualism and self-reliance, the work ethic, obedience, and discipline" (Kinder & Sears, 1981, p. 416). And scale items used to measure symbolic racism include "Blacks are getting too demanding in their push for equal rights" and "Blacks are getting more economically than they deserve." These items and the definition all involve appraisals of an outgroup as violating ingroup norms or obtaining illegitimate advantages, leading to the emotion of anger (see Table I).

In summary, existing evidence is consistent with the view of prejudice as social emotion. Research by Zanna *et al.* (1990) and by Dijker (1987) demonstrates relationships of episodic, situationally determined emotions to attitudes toward the outgroup (cf. Abelson *et al.*, 1982). And the relative deprivation and symbolic politics literatures provide evidence that individual interests or personally experienced injustices do not impact intergroup attitudes, while perceivers' views of their *group* interests do (Bobo, 1983).

Insights on Related Issues

Situational Specificity of Prejudice

One of the longstanding conceptual puzzles regarding prejudice is the fact that reactions to outgroups are notoriously context and situation specific. For example, racial integration and acceptance of intergroup equality in the workplace may coexist with strict segregation and an ideology of white superiority in all other aspects of life (Minard, 1952). As another example, an old-line racist might accept blacks without any problem in subordinate roles, even roles involving intimate personal contact (e.g., servant, nanny). Observations of such contextual specificity pose a problem if prejudice is viewed as a general negative attitude toward the outgroup. As noted before, subtypes have been proposed to deal with this issue, but they fail to capture the idea that it is not types of *group members* but *specific persons in specific situations* that trigger particular reactions.

However, if we think of prejudice as involving *appraisals that blacks are pushing themselves inappropriately into roles that should be reserved for whites,* with accompanying emotions of anger (if the perceiver feels strong) or fear (if the perceiver feels weak), then episodic, context-specific reactions make sense. Blacks who accept subordinate positions do not trigger these appraisals, so the old-fashioned racist can hate black civil-rights leaders yet accept blacks in menial roles. And for perceivers who endorse equality on the job but strict segregation in residential areas, schools, and churches, the pattern found by Minard (1952) would make sense—while blacks pushing for school desegregation might trigger outrage. The focus in the model advanced here is not the intrinsically negative qualities attributed to blacks themselves (which are the theoretical key in conceptions of prejudice as a negative attitude) but *appraisals of the threats posed by blacks to the perceiver's own group.* The nature and magnitude of these perceived threats will vary from situation to situation, and will depend on the perceiver's conceptions of what is just and fair.

A similar line of argument applies to sexism. It is clear that sexists do not have a generally negative attitude toward women (Eagly & Mladinic,

1989); in fact, they may think highly of women who adhere to traditional sex roles. However, sexists do resent women in certain contexts (e.g., in positions of authority in business or government) or when they make demands that are perceived as unjustified. The situations and actions that sexists find objectionable are probably well captured by appraisals that are theoretically linked to anger/resentment: women are seeking or demanding things that are not legitimately theirs (see Table I).

Emotion Specificity

Another respect in which this conceptualization furnishes a more discriminating view of prejudice is that it allows us to go beyond classifying stereotypes (beliefs) and prejudice (viewed as attitudes) simply as positive versus negative. Perceivers do not *just* like or dislike social groups. A perceiver might appraise Group A as hostile and powerful, so fear will be the predominant emotion. Group B is seen as illegitimately demanding favored treatment, so the perceiver will experience anger and resentment. Group C is perceived to violate ingroup standards of cleanliness or morality (perhaps eating foods that the ingroup classifies as ritually impure, or engaging in sexual conduct that the ingroup proscribes) and therefore triggers feelings of disgust and repulsion. Attitudes toward gays seem often to fall into this category, as illustrated by a Connecticut state representative's reported comment on a fellow legislator's public announcement of his homosexuality: "He demonstrated complete disrespect for common decency. I can't tell you the disgust I had for it. It turned my stomach" (Ravo, 1991). Describing a perceiver as having a negative attitude toward all three groups fails to capture these qualitative differences.

In fact, Kovel (1970) and others have argued that there are different subtypes of racial prejudice, such as dominative versus aversive racism (which might speculatively be linked to appraisals of a racial minority as threatening versus disgusting or dirty, respectively). And Kluegel and Smith (1986), as well as Katz and Hass (1988), have argued that many perceivers simultaneously experience positively and negatively toned feelings (e.g., resentment and sympathy) toward an outgroup. The result is likely to be that overtly expressed feelings will vary over time and context, as subtle situational cues activate appraisals leading to one or the other feeling more strongly. For example, seeing the minority group member using food stamps may elicit appraisals related to undeserved benefits and hence resentment, while reading of the high rate of unemployment for minorities leads to appraisals of their unfortunate situation and hence sympathy. Because discriminatory behavior reflects emotional action tendencies, distinctions can also be made among the types of negative behavior directed at outgroups. Anger will lead to behaviors that harm the outgroup (e.g., attempts to take away their illegitimate benefits) and disgust to attempted avoidance of the group (e.g., restrictions on the roles they may occupy, such as proposals to fire homosexual schoolteachers). Fear may lead to defensive actions supporting the ingroup's own cultural norms and practices, such as the English-only laws that have been proposed in some states with high rates of Hispanic immigration.

The specific nature of intergroup relations within a society is likely to influence the qualitative nature of intergroup appraisals and emotions. For example, Sachdev and Bourhis (1984, 1985, 1987) have found substantial effects of status (high versus low), numbers (majority versus minority), and power (high versus low) on the magnitude of intergroup discrimination in a minimal intergroup situation. Extending their findings, it is certainly plausible that the *content* of typical group stereotypes (appraisals) will depend on these same factors. High- and low-status groups, for example, are likely to view each other in typical ways. High-status groups will be seen as arrogant and snobbish and low-status groups as deviant and immoral; typical emotional responses, correspondingly, should involve resentment versus disgust. These hypotheses should be tested, and similar investigations carried out into the effects of numbers and power on *qualitative* aspects of intergroup stereotypes and emotions. As noted above, measures of symbolic racism and related constructs contain items that can be construed as group-relevant appraisals; perhaps such measures could serve as a source of hypotheses concerning typical patterns of intergroup perceptions. Conversely, this conceptual model might lead to the construction of more clearly theoretically based and/or more empirically effective measures of prejudice.

Several aspects of self-categorization theory concern determinants of the salience of a social identity. These may furnish important hypotheses about the conditions favoring or diminishing intergroup prejudice. For example, the observation that important attributes covary with group membership (for example, attitudinal dissimilarity between groups), the existence of a substantial numerical imbalance that defines a majority and a minority, and the presence of goal conflicts between groups all increase the salience of self-categorization as a group member (Turner, 1987). It is not difficult to map these factors into hypotheses concerning the prevalence of intergroup prejudice. Intergroup prejudice should be stronger when groups differ in significant ways (e.g., in their command of societal resources and power), when they constitute a clear majority and minority rather than being equally numerous, or when the groups' interests clearly diverge (a condition also likely to be created by group differences in power or wealth).

Implications for Reducing Prejudice

Any social-psychological model of prejudice has implications for ways in which prejudice might be altered or reduced. For instance, the conceptualization of prejudice as intergroup emotion suggests why the naive "Brotherhood Week" approach of encouraging individual contacts across group lines is so ineffective in reducing prejudice. Several cognitive and social mechanisms have been described that prevent or limit stereotype change arising from contact (e.g., Rothbart, Dawes, & Park, 1984). In addition, if prejudice is viewed as a social emotion, then two strong reasons will make individual contacts ineffective in reducing it. (1) Contacts across group lines, particularly if they are intimate and positively toned, will often be interpersonal rather than intergroup in nature. That is, both parties will act and react in terms of their individual identities rather than their social identities as group members, making the identity that is responsible for prejudice nonsalient when contact takes place. (2) Prejudice depends on appraisals that the outgroup is hostile, threatening, violates cherished ingroup norms, and the like. Such appraisals will frequently have a "kernel of truth" in realistic intergroup conflicts over resources. Therefore these appraisals probably will not be altered by learning that individual outgroup members have admirable personal characteristics.

What approaches might effectively reduce prejudice under this new conceptualization? Paradoxically, it might be worthwhile to examine the propaganda of racial "hate groups" for clues. Do the appraisals of the target outgroup that they advocate, the underlying emotional reactions, and the actions they propose all fit together in the ways our model would predict (as in Table I)? I suspect that they do. Similarly, in order to reduce prejudice, persuasive materials directed specifically at the relevant group-level appraisals might be the most effective. For example, if an outgroup is viewed as threatening, its peaceful intentions might be stressed. Other types of arguments, such as the idea that outgroup members have positive personal attributes, while potentially relevant to *attitudes* toward the outgroup, would in most cases be irrelevant to the types of appraisals that drive intergroup emotions. In addition, reducing the salience of the ingroup–outgroup distinction, perhaps by manipulations like the "jigsaw classroom" (Aronson, 1990) or an emphasis on cross-cutting distinctions (Deschamps & Doise, 1978), should help ease intergroup conflict. As noted above, if Joe Jones is harmed by Rubén Hernandez's negative behaviors and becomes angry *as an individual,* few if any of the consequences will transcend their dyadic relationship. It is when Jones starts thinking "Those Hispanics always make me mad . . . we should do something about them" that the individual emotion is transformed into social emotion—prejudice—and the prospect of discrimination begins to become real.

These specific suggestions are obviously tentative. But whatever their merits, I believe that the potential value of conceptualizing prejudice as social emotion deserves further exploration. Recent theoretical developments in self-categorization and appraisal-emotion theories now make this exploration possible. While this new conception obviously remains much less fully developed than the notion of prejudice as intergroup attitude, it may ultimately prove to take us further toward the solutions of some of the most basic social problems in the world today.

Acknowledgment

Preparation of this chapter was supported by the National Science Foundation under Grant BNS-8613584.

References

Abelson, R. P., Kinder, D. R., Peters, M. D., & Fiske, S. T. (1982). Affective and semantic components in political person perception. *Journal of Personality and Social Psychology,* **42,** 619–630.

Ajzen, I., & Fishbein, M. (1977). Attitude-behavior relations: A theoretical analysis and review of empirical research. *Psychological Bulletin,* **84,** 888–918.

Aronson, E. (1990). Applying social psychology to desegregation and energy conservation. *Personality and Social Psychology Bulletin,* **16,** 118–132.

Bem, D. J. (1972). Self-perception theory. In L. Berkowitz (Ed.), *Advances in experimental social psychology* (vol. 6, pp. 1–62). New York: Academic Press.

Bobo, L. (1983). Whites' opposition to busing: Symbolic racism or realistic group conflict? *Journal of Personality and Social Psychology,* **45,** 1196–1210.

Brewer, M. B., Dull, V., & Lui, L. (1981). Perceptions of the elderly: Stereotypes as subtypes. *Journal of Personality and Social Psychology,* **41,** 656–670.

Brigham, J. C. (1971). Ethnic stereotypes. *Psychological Bulletin,* **76,** 15–38.

Cantor, N., Mischel, W., & Schwartz, J. (1982). A prototype analysis of psychological situations. *Cognitive Psychology,* **14,** 45–77.

Cialdini, R. B., Borden, R. J., Thorne, A., Walker, M. R., Freeman, S., & Sloan, L. R. (1976). Basking in reflected glory: Three (football) field studies. *Journal of Personality and Social Psychology,* **34,** 366–375.

Deaux, K. K., & Lewis, L. L. (1984). Structure of gender stereotypes: Interrelationships among components and gender label. *Journal of Personality and Social Psychology,* **46,** 991–1004.

Deschamps, J. C., & Doise, W. (1978). Crossed category memberships in intergroup relations. In H. Tajfel (Ed.), *Differentiation between social groups.* (pp. 141–158). London: Academic Press.

Dijker, A. J. M. (1987). Emotional reactions to ethnic minorities. *European Journal of Social Psychology,* **17,** 305–325.

Dovidio, J. F., & Gaertner, S. L. (1986). Prejudice, discrimination, and racism: Historical trends and contemporary approaches. In J. F. Dovidio & S. L. Gaertner (Eds.), *Prejudice, discrimination, and racism* (pp. 1–34). Orlando, FL: Academic Press.

Eagly, A. H., & Mladinic, A. (1989). Gender stereotypes and attitudes toward women and men. *Personality and Social Psychology Bulletin,* **15,** 543–558.

Ehrlich, H. J. (1973). *The social psychology of prejudice.* New York: Wiley.

Fishbein, M. P., & Ajzen, I. (1975). *Belief, attitude, intention, and behavior.* Reading, MA: Addison-Wesley.

Frijda, N. H. (1986). *The emotions.* Cambridge: Cambridge University Press.

Frijda, N. H., Kuipers, P., & ter Schure, E. (1989). Relations among emotion, appraisal, and emotional action readiness. *Journal of Personality and Social Psychology,* **57,** 212–228.

Greenwald, A. G., & Pratkanis, A. R. (1984). The self. In R. S. Wyer & T. K. Srull (Eds.), *Handbook of social cognition* (vol. 3, pp. 129–178). Hillsdale, NJ: Erlbaum.

Jacoby, L. L., & Kelley, C. M. (1990). An episodic view of motivation: Unconscious influences of memory. In E. T. Higgins & R. M. Sorrentino (Eds.), *Handbook of motivation and cognition* (vol. 2, pp. 451–481). New York: Guilford Press.

Katz, D., & Braly, K. (1933). Racial stereotypes in one hundred college students. *Journal of Abnormal and Social Psychology, 28,* 280–290.

Katz, I., & Hass, R. G. (1988). Racial ambivalence and American value conflict: Correlational and priming studies of dual cognitive structures. *Journal of Personality and Social Psychology, 55,* 893–905.

Kinder, D. R., & Sears, D. O. (1981). Prejudice and politics: Symbolic racism versus racial threats to the good life. *Journal of Personality and Social Psychology, 40,* 414–431.

Kluegel, J. R., & Smith, E. R. (1986). *Beliefs about inequality: Americans' views of what is and what ought to be.* Hawthorne, NY: Aldine.

Kovel, J. (1970). *White racism: A psychohistory.* New York: Pantheon.

LaPiere, R. T. (1934). Attitudes vs. actions. *Social Forces, 13,* 230–237.

McConahay, J. B. (1982). Self-interest versus racial attitudes as correlates of anti-busing attitudes in Louisville: Is it the buses or the blacks? *Journal of Politics, 44,* 692–720.

Minard, R. D. (1952). Race relations in the Pocahontas Coal Field. *Journal of Social Issues, 8,* 29–44.

Ravo, N. (1991). Gay legislator in Connecticut welcomes a bill against bias. *The New York Times,* April 23.

Roseman, I. J. (1984). Cognitive determinants of emotion: A structural theory. In P. Shaver (Ed.), *Review of personality and social psychology* (vol. 5). Beverly Hills, CA: Sage.

Rothbart, M., Dawes, R., & Park, B. (1984). Stereotyping and sampling biases in intergroup perception. In J. R. Eiser (Ed.), *Attitudinal judgment* (pp. 109–134). New York: Springer-Verlag.

Runciman, W. G. (1966). *Relative deprivation and social justice.* London: Routledge and Kegan Paul.

Sachdev, I., & Bourhis R. Y. (1984). Minimal majorities and minorities. *European Journal of Social Psychology, 14,* 35–52.

Sachdev, I., & Bourhis, R. Y. (1985). Social categorization and power differentials in group relations. *European Journal of Social Psychology, 15,* 415–434.

Sachdev, I., & Bourhis, R. Y. (1987). Status differentials and intergroup behaviour. *European Journal of Social Psychology, 17,* 277–293.

Scherer, K. R. (1988). Cognitive antecedents of emotion. In V. Hamilton, G. H. Bower, & N. H. Frijda (Eds.), *Cognitive perspectives on emotion and motivation* (pp. 89–126). Dordrecht, The Netherlands: Kluwer.

Sears, D. O., & Kinder, D. R. (1985). Whites' opposition to busing: On conceptualizing and operationalizing group conflict. *Journal of Personality and Social Psychology, 48,* 1141–1147.

Smith, C. A., & Ellsworth, P. C. (1985). Patterns of cognitive appraisal in emotion. *Journal of Personality and Social Psychology, 48,* 813–838.

Smith, E. R. (1990). Content and process specificity in the effects of prior experiences. In T. K. Srull & R. S. Wyer (Eds.), *Advances in social cognition* (Vol. 3, pp. 1–59). Hillsdale, NJ: Erlbaum.

Sniderman, P. M., & Tetlock, P. E. (1986). Symbolic racism: Problems of motive attribution in political analysis. *Journal of Social Issues, 42*(2), 129–150.

Stephan, W. G. (1985). Intergroup relations. In G. Lindzey & E. Aronson (Eds.), *Handbook of social psychology* (vol. 2, pp. 599–658). New York: Random House.

Tajfel, H. (1982). *Social identity and intergroup relations.* Cambridge: Cambridge University Press.

Turner, J. C. (1987). *Rediscovering the social group: A self-categorization theory.* Oxford: Blackwell.

Useem, M. (1980). Solidarity model, breakdown model, and the Boston anti-busing movement. *American Sociological Review, 45,* 357–369.

Vanneman, R. D., & Pettigrew, T. F. (1972). Race and relative deprivation in the urban United States. *Race, 13,* 461–486.

Weigel, R. H., & Howes, P. W. (1985). Conceptions of racial prejudice: Symbolic racism reconsidered. *Journal of Social Issues, 41*(3), 117–138.

Wicker, A. (1969). Attitudes versus action: The relationship of verbal and overt behavioral responses to attitude objects. *Journal of Social Issues, 25,* 1–78.

Zanna, M. P., & Rempel, J. K. (1988). Attitudes: A new look at an old concept. In D. Bar-Tal & A. Kruglanski (Eds.), *The social psychology of knowledge* (pp. 315–334). Cambridge: Cambridge University Press.

Zanna, M. P., Haddock, G., & Esses, V. M. (1990). The determinants of prejudice. Presented at Society of Experimental Social Psychology, Buffalo, New York.

Chapter 14

The Role of Discrepancy-Associated Affect in Prejudice Reduction

PATRICIA G. DEVINE and MARGO J. MONTEITH
Department of Psychology
University of Wisconsin, Madison
Madison, Wisconsin

Introduction

In recent years, the study of social stereotypes and their role in prejudice and intergroup relations has been dominated by efforts to understand the cognitive processes underlying stereotype activation and use. Several reviews of the cognitive approach to stereotyping indicate that cognitive processes and biases seem to ensure the persistence of stereotypes and their resistance to change (see Hamilton, 1981; Hamilton & Trolier, 1986; Stephan, 1985, 1989). Despite progress in understanding the operation of such processes, the exclusive emphasis on the cognitive approach to stereotypes is viewed by many as being too narrow to produce a complete understanding of stereotype activation and use.

The dissatisfaction with exclusively cognitive approaches to studying social stereotypes has been made explicit with calls for theoretical and empirical work that addresses the interface between cognitive and affective processes in intergroup relations (Hamilton, 1981; Hamilton & Trolier, 1986; Pettigrew, 1981). Indeed, it is the interplay between cognitive and affective processes that serves as the focus for the chapters in this volume. For example, one concern has been to examine how affect is represented in stereotypes (see Chapter 7 and 11, this volume). Others have been interested in determining how affect that is associated with stereotype activation influences judgments about members of a stereotyped group (see Chapter 10 and 11, this volume).

Our interest in the interface between affect and stereotype activation and use derives from a different vantage point. In our efforts to understand the experiences of those who reject prejudice and have adopted a nonprejudiced ideology, we have been concerned primarily with the nature of the affect generated by the person in response to his or her own (often inadvertent) use of stereotypes. That is, for nonprejudiced individuals, responding in stereotypic ways violates their nonprejudiced values and thus gives rise to strong affective reactions. In this chapter, we develop and present evidence to support the argument that the self-generated affect that follows from violations of nonprejudiced values plays an important role in the future control and regulation of stereotype-based responses.

In order to delineate this role of affect in people's prejudice reduction efforts, we review our theoretical and empirical efforts over the past several years. In brief, our research indicates that the first step in the prejudice reduction process involves establishing and internalizing nonprejudiced standards and values. However, as the first section of this chapter makes clear, adopting nonprejudiced standards is not equivalent to overcoming prejudice. Despite the fact that stereotype-based responses are viewed as inappropriate once nonprejudiced values are established, such responses are extremely difficult to avoid. The second section of the chapter reviews research relevant to people's experienced difficulties in trying to avoid stereotypical responses and their affective reactions to their failures to avoid such responses. In the third section, we provide the theoretical rationale for understanding why and how affect plays a role in the prejudice reduction process. We also present recent empirical findings to support the contention that self-generated affect arising when people violate their nonprejudiced values facilitates people's prejudice reduction efforts. In the final section, we integrate and synthesize our theoretical and empirical efforts by presenting a model of the prejudice reduction process that applies to the struggles people face once they have defined prejudice as personally unacceptable. This model highlights why the joint consideration of cognitive and affective factors is important for understanding processes underlying prejudice reduction.

Renouncing Prejudice: New versus Old Ways of Responding

The first step in the prejudice reduction process involves developing and internalizing personal beliefs and standards that call for fair and egalitarian treatment of others and rejecting stereotypic ways of thinking. Although people can embrace nonprejudiced values for a variety of reasons (e.g., response to societal changes, personal experiences), our focus is on individuals who have consciously decided that prejudice is personally unacceptable and as such have deliberately renounced prejudice. In renouncing prejudice, these people commit themselves to changing their ways of responding to members of a stereotyped group. That is, they make a commitment to replace "old" unacceptable responses with the "new" nonprejudiced responses. However, such changes are difficult to implement because they require learning to overcome very well learned ways of responding.

Devine's (1989a) discussion of automatic and controlled processes in prejudice provides a theoretical analysis for understanding why "old" ways of responding are not easily overcome by changing one's beliefs. Her analysis focuses on examining exactly what does and does not change when one renounces prejudice. Although renouncing prejudice involves developing new beliefs that are consistent with one's nonprejudiced self-identity, it does not entail the immediate elimination of stereotypes and thus the "old" ways of responding. That is, because stereotypes have been so frequently activated in the past, they are likely to be more accessible than the newly established personal beliefs.[1] More specifically, Devine (1989a,b; Dovidio & Gaertner, 1991; Klinger & Beall, 1992) demonstrated that stereotypes and their associated affect[2] are automatically and involuntarily activated in the presence of members of the stereotyped group (or their symbolic equivalent) both for those who renounce prejudice (i.e., low prejudiced people) and those who do not (i.e., high prejudiced people). Thus, the default response for low prejudiced individuals is a stereotype-based response rather than a nonprejudiced belief-based response (see also Higgins & King, 1981; Jamieson & Zanna, 1989; Kruglanski & Freund, 1983; Sherman & Gorkin, 1980).

However, stereotype use can be avoided if individuals have the time and cognitive capacity to bring their beliefs to mind following stereotype activation but prior to providing a response. In particular, Devine (1989a) found that when a response would conflict with subjects' nonprejudiced identity and they had the opportunity to use controlled processes, low prejudiced subjects successfully inhibited the influence of the stereotype and responded consistently with their nonprejudiced beliefs (see also Jamieson & Zanna, 1989; Kruglanski & Freund, 1983). Thus, overt nonprejudiced responses require (1) the controlled inhibition of the automatically activated stereotype, and (2) the conscious, deliberate activation of nonprejudiced beliefs (but see Gilbert & Hixon, 1991).

The present analysis, which emphasizes the distinction between automatic and controlled processes, suggests that low prejudiced people are

---

[1]See Devine (1989a,b) for a full discussion concerning why stereotypes are more accessible than personal beliefs.

[2]Although Devine's (1989a) original statement of her theory considered only stereotype activation, subsequent research (see text) had demonstrated that affect associated with a stereotyped group representation is similarly automatically activated. Perhaps a more precise statement is that the group representation, which involves both cognitive and affective components, is what is automatically activated.

likely to continue to experience stereotype-consistent responses even after they renounce prejudice. Stereotype-consistent responses are thus analogous to habitual responses, and the process of reducing prejudice is analogous to the process involved in breaking a habit (see Devine, 1989a,b). Breaking any habit requires effort, practice, and time. In breaking the prejudice habit, people must first make a decision to eliminate the habit (i.e., renounce prejudice). They must then *learn* to inhibit the habitual (i.e., stereotype-based) responses and to generate responses that are consistent with their beliefs and standards. The implication of this analysis is that during the change process the low-prejudiced person is especially vulnerable to conflict between his or her enduring negative responses and endorsed nonprejudiced beliefs.

Affective Consequences of Coexisting, Conflicting Reactions

The preceding analysis suggests that even after renouncing prejudice, people are likely to respond more negatively to members of stereotyped groups than their beliefs and nonprejudiced standards dictate is appropriate (e.g., see Crosby, Bromley, & Saxe, 1980; Devine, 1989a,b; Gaertner & Dovidio, 1986; Jamieson & Zanna, 1989; Kruglanski & Freund, 1983; McConahay, 1986; Sherman & Gorkin, 1980). Their actual responses, therefore, would be discrepant with how their nonprejudiced standards indicate they should respond to members of stereotyped groups. Thus, the next phase of our research program focused on assessing (1) the extent to which people report (and thus are aware of) discrepancies between their personal standards and their actual responses, and (2) the nature of their affective reactions to such discrepancies (see Devine, Monteith, Zuwerink, & Elliot, 1991).

On the basis of a number of theoretical frameworks, we expected that affective reactions would be generated in response to personal standard–actual response discrepancies. First, several contemporary theories posit that affective consequences are associated with discrepancies between personal standards and actual responses (i.e., Aronson, 1968; Carver & Scheier, 1990; Duval & Wicklund, 1972; Higgins, 1987; Markus & Nurius, 1986). Although these models differ in their level of specificity regarding the qualitative nature of the affect experienced, they share the assumption that transgressing a personal standard creates psychological distress for the individual. Dissonance theorists, for example, suggested that people experience global and diffuse affect (e.g., tension, discomfort) when their behavior is inconsistent with their attitude. Higgins (1987; Higgins, Bond, Klein, & Strauman, 1985), however, argued that qualitatively distinct affects are associated with distinct types of self-inconsistencies. For example, Higgins and his colleagues have demonstrated that feelings of guilt and self-contempt are uniquely associated with discrepancies between people's actual selves and their self-defined standards for who they think they ought to or should be.[3]

Second, within the prejudice literature, Allport (1954) observed that after people deliberately rejected prejudiced beliefs (decided they should not be prejudiced) they continued to respond to members of a stereotyped group in negative or stereotypic ways, often unintentionally. Important for the present concerns, Allport posited that this conflict between how one believes one *should* respond and how one *actually* responds would lead to feelings of compunction (i.e., guilt and self-criticism). Although a few studies were designed to test this prejudice-with-compunction notion, due to methodological shortcomings none of them provided empirical support that compunction is associated with discrepancies between should standards and actual responses (Campbell, 1961; Friedrichs, 1959; Westie, 1965). It is of interest to note that Rokeach (1973) suggested a more general, but conceptually similar, type of analysis. Rokeach argued that conflict between one's responses (e.g., attitudes, values, behaviors) and central aspects of his or her self-conception would constitute a threat to the self-concept and would produce self-dissatisfaction.

A common assumption in many of these theoretical perspectives is that the nature of the violated standard determines the type of affective reaction that follows from transgressions of the standard. More specifically, each perspective assumes that feelings of guilt and self-dissatisfaction (i.e., negative self-directed affect) arise when an important and self-defining (i.e., internalized) standard is violated. When standards are not well internalized, a discrepancy would merely constitute a cognitive inconsistency and would not carry the same type of self-relevant implications. Thus, violations from standards that are not well internalized are likely to lead to more global feelings of discomfort, but not to specific feelings of guilt and self-dissatisfaction (see also Ausubel, 1955; Piers & Singer, 1971; Schwartz, 1977).

In applying such logic to prejudice-relevant discrepancies, it is important to consider the extent to which people have actually internalized their personal standards.[4] Therefore, we (Devine *et al.*, 1991, Study 3) addressed this issue directly by assessing the extent to which low and high prejudiced

---

[3]Our primary concern is with the particular affective consequences of discrepancies between one's actual responses and one's self-defined standards for who one ought to be. However, Higgins's theory (1987; Higgins, Bond, Klein, & Strauman, 1985; Higgins, Klein, & Strauman, 1985) also specifies different types of discrepancies (e.g., actual vs. ideal standards) as being associated with different types of affective reactions (e.g., dejection).

[4]We also believed it was particularly important to examine the extent to which subjects' standards were internalized because many prejudice theorists have implicitly assumed that renouncing prejudice involves establishing and *internalizing* nonprejudiced personal standards (e.g., Allport, 1954; Devine, 1989a; Sherman & Gorkin, 1980). Despite the intuitive nature of this assumption, it had never been empirically verified.

subjects had internalized their personal standards for how they should respond toward members of a stereotyped group. In particular, in this research subjects were asked about the extent to which they had internalized their standards for how they should *feel* in contact situations involving homosexuals. The findings from this study revealed that low prejudiced subjects had, indeed, strongly internalized their nonprejudiced "should" standards. That is, low prejudiced subjects reported that (1) it is important to respond consistently with their standards, (2) they are committed to responding consistently with their standards, and (3) their standards are central to their self-concepts. In contrast, compared to low-prejudiced subjects, high prejudiced subjects' should standards were not as important or central to their self-concepts.

Given the difference in the extent to which subjects' personal standards are internalized, feelings of guilt and dissatisfaction would arise from awareness of discrepancies for low-, but not high prejudiced subjects. That is, awareness of discrepancies from internalized nonprejudiced standards is likely to threaten the low-prejudiced person's nonprejudiced self-identity (Allport, 1954; Devine, 1989a; Sherman & Gorkin, 1980). Because high-prejudiced subjects' standards are less well internalized, and thus less self-relevant, their self-concepts presumably would not be threatened by transgressions of their standards. As a result, such discrepancies should lead to feelings of global discomfort, but not to feelings of guilt and self-criticism.

To examine the relation between discrepancies and affect within the prejudice domain, we (Devine *et al.*, 1991) first measured high and low prejudiced subjects' personal standards for how they *should* respond in a number of different contact situations with members of a particular group (e.g., homosexuals). We then measured how subjects believed they actually *would* respond in these contact situations. The particular types of responses for which subjects indicated their should standards and their actual responses concerned feeling-related responses. For example, in one contact situation, subjects were asked to imagine themselves going to a job interview and finding out that the interviewer was gay. For this situation, subjects indicated the extent to which they *should feel uneasy* about the interviewer being gay, based on their personal standards (not what others would think). Subjects then considered the situations again, but this time they indicated the extent to which they *actually would feel uneasy* about the interviewer being gay.

Following their *should* and *would* ratings, subjects reported how they felt about the match between their *shoulds* and *woulds*. Our interest centered on determining whether the nature of the affect that follows from discrepancies was global and diffuse or more specific and self-directed. Thus, embedded in the affect measure were items theoretically relevant to global discomfort (e.g., tense, bothered, uncomfortable, anxious) and to more specific feelings of compunction (e.g., guilty, angry at myself, dissatisfied with myself, self-critical).

Several key findings emerged from this research. First, the location of subjects' self-reported personal standards differed for low- and high-prejudiced subjects. The *should* ratings indicated that high-prejudiced subjects' personal standards permitted higher levels of prejudice than was true for the low-prejudiced subjects. Second, high-prejudiced subjects' reports of their actual responses also revealed higher levels of prejudice than was reported by the low prejudiced subjects. From these *should* and *would* ratings a discrepancy measure was calculated by subtracting *should* from *would* ratings for each contact situation and summing the differences. A third important finding is that over three quarters of the subjects reported discrepancies between their *should* and *would* ratings such that their actual responses were more prejudiced than their personal standards indicated was appropriate or acceptable. The finding that the clear majority of our subjects recognized and acknowledged the presence of their discrepancies is important because it is inconsistent with a central assumption of many contemporary theoretical perspectives. For example, the finding is inconsistent with Gaertner and Dovidio's (1986) aversive racism framework and McConahay's (1986) theory of modern racism because both models suggest that, after renouncing prejudice, people develop strategies to exclude their lingering negative reactions from conscious awareness.

The key issue for the present analysis concerns not just awareness of discrepancies but how people react to these discrepancies. That is, the central interest of this research was to examine the relation between the magnitude of subjects' discrepancies and their affective reactions to their discrepancies. It is important to note that despite the fact that the location of the *should* standards differed for low and high prejudiced subjects, the *magnitude* of discrepancies reported by low and high prejudiced subjects did not differ. That is, the degree of the discrepancies between the *should* and *would* ratings was equivalent for low and high prejudiced subjects. As a result, we could examine the affective consequences of small and large discrepancies from *should* standards for both low and high prejudiced subjects. Small discrepancies between *should* standards and actual responses were not associated with elevated levels of negative affect for either low or high-prejudiced subjects. Large discrepancies, however, were associated with elevated levels of negative affect for both low and high prejudiced subjects, but the specific nature of affective reactions differed for low and high prejudiced subjects. Although large discrepancies between personal standards and actual responses were related to feelings of global discomfort for both high and low prejudiced subjects, only low prejudiced subjects experienced the more specific feelings of guilt and self-criticism. Thus, discrepancies only led to feelings of compunction when the discrepancies reflected transgressions from internalized, self-defining personal standards. Because high prejudiced subjects had standards that were less well internalized and thus less self-relevant, their self-concepts presumably were not threatened by transgressions of their standards.

We have extended this line of work in a number of directions and in each case we replicated the general pattern of findings observed by Devine *et al.* (1991). For example, the findings generalized when Blacks (Devine *et al.*, 1991, Study 1; Zuwerink, Devine, & Cook, 1992) and when women (Pressly & Devine, 1992) constituted the target group.

Our earlier research only examined discrepancies with regard to feeling responses (e.g., feeling uneasy that one's job interviewer is gay). In another recent extension we have examined discrepancies and their associated affect across a number of different response domains (Monteith, Devine, & Zuwerink, in press). More specifically, we examined discrepancies in the thought and behavior domains (e.g., thinking stereotypic thoughts or behaving in prejudiced ways) in addition to the feeling domain. In this research we were interested in the location of subjects' standards in each of the response domains and the affective consequences of discrepancies from those standards. Not surprisingly, in all three response domains, low prejudiced subjects reported nonprejudiced personal standards. In addition, large discrepancies from those standards were associated with feelings of compunction for low prejudiced subjects. For high prejudiced subjects, however, the location of the personal standard differed as a function of response domain. In comparison to their feeling and thought standards, high prejudiced subjects did report relatively nonprejudiced standards for their behaviors toward homosexuals. However, despite the relatively nonprejudiced nature of high prejudiced subjects' behavioral standards, these standards still were not as nonprejudiced or as well internalized (i.e., important, self-defining, involving commitment) as low prejudiced subjects' behavioral standards. Replicating our previous findings, regardless of the response domain, high prejudiced subjects reported global discomfort in connection with large discrepancies but did not report feelings of guilt and self-criticism.

This study revealed one other interesting finding that may shed some light on the nature of high prejudiced subjects' personal standards. Although high prejudiced subjects did not internalize their global affect (i.e., direct the negative affect toward themselves), there was evidence to suggest that they externalized their affect. That is, large discrepancies for high prejudiced subjects were associated with elevated levels of negative affect directed toward *others* (e.g., anger, irritation), particularly directed toward members of the stereotyped group (in this case homosexuals). Thus, high and low prejudiced subjects experience distinct types of agitated discomfort following their discrepancies.

This empirical outcome suggests that high and low prejudiced subjects' standards may reflect a difference in the "standpoint" (*own* versus *other*) for the should standard (cf. Higgins, 1987). Whereas low prejudiced subjects' standards involve their "own" personal standpoint, high prejudiced subjects' standards may involve the standpoint of "others," such as significant others or societal norms. That is, high prejudiced subjects may derive their personal standards from their perceptions of what important others think their standards should be (see Devine *et al.*, 1991, for supporting evidence). Indeed, the type of affect experienced by both our low and high prejudiced subjects is generally consistent with this analysis and Higgins's (1987) self-discrepancy theory. Specifically, low prejudiced subjects experience feelings of guilt and self-criticism following discrepancies, the type of affect associated with discrepancies from *own should* standpoints in Higgins's self-discrepancy theory. In addition, the type of affect experienced by our high prejudiced subjects with large discrepancies, anger at others, is exactly the type of affect experienced by subjects who fall short of meeting the *should* or *ought* standards established for them by important "others" (see Higgins, 1987, for a comprehensive review).

Despite the insights gleaned from this program of research, there are potential limitations of the procedures used in these studies. First, each of the previously described studies examined subjects' reactions to imagined discrepancies rather than to actual behavioral discrepancies. Second, our procedure for assessing discrepancies may not reflect the natural circumstances under which discrepant responses occur. That is, subjects' should standards were made accessible prior to asking subjects to consider their actual responses. When people manifest discrepant responses under more natural conditions, it is possible that they may not even consider the extent to which their actual responses match their *should* standards. Third, in the previous studies, subjects were explicitly instructed to consider the match between their personal standards and their actual responses when making their affect ratings. In everyday settings, however, people are not likely to be instructed to consider their affect in connection with their discrepancies. To address these issues, Monteith (1991, Study 1; see also Pressly & Devine, 1992) created a new experimental situation with the following features: (1) subjects' personal standards were not made accessible in the experimental context; (2) subjects generated *behavioral* responses that were discrepant from their standards; and (3) subjects were not instructed to consider the match between their standards and their actual response when making their affect ratings.

In Monteith's research subjects were led to believe that they had engaged in a particular behavior that both high and low prejudiced subjects defined as more prejudiced than their personal standards dictated was appropriate (see following section). However, this behavior violated a well-internalized standard only for the low prejudiced subjects. It is important to realize that subjects' personal standards were not made accessible prior to the behavioral transgression. In addition, subjects made their affect ratings as part of an ostensibly unrelated task, without being reminded of or encouraged to think about their previous discrepancy experience when making the ratings. Monteith's findings closely replicated the pattern of affective reactions reported in our previous studies. Most important, low- but not high-prejudiced subjects experienced guilt and self-criticism after engaging in the discrepant response.

The empirical research presented in this section suggests that in the early phases of the prejudice reduction process, low prejudiced people are likely to fail to inhibit stereotype-consistent responses. Such failures activate a discrepancy between internalized nonprejudiced standards and actual responses. These discrepancy experiences threaten the low prejudiced person's nonprejudiced self-identity and lead to feelings of negative self-directed affect (i.e., guilt and self-criticism). In order for additional progress to be made in the prejudice reduction process, low prejudiced individuals must somehow learn to inhibit or to *control* their stereotypical responses. Without such progress, individuals would be fated not only to continually manifesting prejudice-like responses but also to experiencing the compunction-related feelings that arise in connection with their discrepant responses.

The Functional Significance of Discrepancy-Associated Affect

In this section, we review recent work suggesting that the experience of discrepancies and their associated negative self-directed affect play a functional role in low prejudiced peoples' prejudice reduction efforts. In particular, we summarize the details of Monteith's (1991) theoretical and empirical work, which suggests that discrepancies combined with negative self-directed affect instigate a variety of control mechanisms among low prejudiced individuals, all of which are aimed at inhibiting stereotypic (i.e., discrepant) responses on future occasions. By achieving such control over stereotype-based responses, individuals can generate belief-based responses instead. Monteith derived her theoretical analysis from a number of different theoretical perspectives, the details of which are reviewed to set the context for positing that discrepancies and their associated negative self-directed affect facilitate control over stereotypic responses.

Theoretical Background

Monteith's analysis was derived in part from several social psychological perspectives suggesting that discrepancies between standards and actual responses serve to motivate discrepancy reduction efforts (e.g., Aronson, 1968; Carver & Scheier, 1981, 1990; Duval & Wicklund, 1972; Festinger, 1957; Pyszczynski & Greenberg, 1986, 1987; Rokeach, 1973; Scheier & Carver, 1988). Implicit in many of these analyses is the notion that the motivation for discrepancy reduction arises in connection with discrepancies from *well-internalized* (or self-defining) standards, and that the affect arising from such discrepancies is the actual cause of heightened motivation. For example, Rokeach (1973) emphasized these issues in his discussion of the motivational significance of discrepancies that violate one's self-conception. Pyszczynski and Greenberg (1986, 1987) argued, likewise, that self-relevant discrepancies and their associated negative affect increase discrepancy reduction efforts.

In addition to emphasizing the motivational nature of violating self-relevant standards, Pyszczynski and Greenberg (1986, 1987) posited a *mechanism* that should facilitate discrepancy reduction. Specifically, they suggested that self-relevant discrepancies heighten self-focus, and this inward focus activates a self-regulatory cycle aimed at reducing the discrepancies.

Other research directly addresses additional self-regulatory mechanisms that are engaged by discrepancies. In particular, Gray's (e.g., 1981, 1982) neuropsychological model of motivation and learning posits the existence of three arousal systems: a behavioral activation system, a behavioral inhibition system (BIS), and a nonspecific arousal system. In the context of explaining the operation of the BIS, Gray (1982) provided a detailed account of the mechanisms involved in learning to inhibit discrepant responses, particularly responses that have been associated with aversive consequences in the past. More specifically, the BIS functions to inhibit responses in the presence of cues indicating aversive consequences will occur if a particular response is made. Thus, Gray's portrayal of the BIS provides a useful conceptual heuristic when attempting to understand how individuals can come to control or inhibit responses that conflict with their personal beliefs.

Briefly, Gray (1982) argued that the BIS compares actual to expected environmental events. In the absence of discrepancies, the system operates in a "just checking" mode. However, whenever unexpected or aversive stimuli are detected (i.e., "mismatches") the BIS shifts to a "control" mode, which has several consequences. When a mismatch is detected, arousal increases, ongoing behavior is interrupted, and the sequence of responses occurring when the mismatch was detected is tagged with a "faulty, needs checking" indicator. Gray (1982) suggested that the tagged motor program then is allotted enhanced attention (e.g., rehearse stimuli and responses that appeared to predict the mismatch). In addition to the enhanced attention to discrepancy-relevant stimuli, the organism engages in exploratory-investigative behavior for indications of the mismatch, searching for stimuli or cues that can be associated with the mismatch. Considered jointly, the enhanced attention and exploratory-investigative processes enable the organism to identify stimuli and responses that predict the aversive event.

Gray (1982) further argued that the BIS should be activated whenever cues that were previously associated with response-contingent punishment are presented. The consequence of this BIS activation is that the sequence of responses previously tagged as faulty is executed with greater restraint (e.g., more slowly, more readily abandoned so that alternative responses can be executed). According to Gray, then, the organism learns to inhibit or control responses that previously resulted in aversive consequences (see also Fowles, 1988; Patterson, Kosson, & Newman, 1987; Nichols & Newman, 1986).

Although Gray's (1982) model was derived from animal research, it has been applied frequently in human research as well (see Fowles, 1987, 1988; Gray, 1985; Nichols & Newman, 1986; Patterson et al., 1987; Wallace, Bachorowski, & Newman, 1990). This research has indicated that BIS activation can be measured successfully in humans, and also that the system is not invariably engaged in the experience of mismatches. Rather, it seems that the effect of stimuli on BIS activation can be amplified or attenuated by individual differences in the appraised significance of the stimuli (see Fowles, 1988).

Noting the conceptual parallels between Gray's concept of mismatches and prejudice-related discrepancies, Monteith (1991) used the description of the BIS to understand the specific mechanisms that might mediate the effect of prejudice-related discrepancies on learning to control stereotype-based responses. It is important to note that the development of her theoretical analysis entailed two extrapolations from Gray's (1982) work. First, in line with the notion that the appraised significance of a discrepancy should affect the activation of the BIS, she reasoned that the influence of prejudice-related discrepancies on the activation of inhibitory mechanisms should be pronounced when the discrepancies are from well-internalized (i.e., important, self-defining) standards. Thus, because the prejudice-related standards of low but not high prejudiced subjects are well internalized (see discussions above), discrepancy experiences should instigate inhibitory mechanisms only among low prejudiced individuals.

Another way in which Monteith (1991) extrapolated from Gray's (1982) general model was to identify the specific types of observations that would serve as reasonable indicators of the activation of an inhibitory system following prejudice-related discrepancy experiences. For example, Gray suggested that animals respond to discrepancies by allotting enhanced attention to discrepancy-relevant environmental stimuli. Monteith reasoned that such enhanced attention would be primarily cognitive in humans (e.g., generating thoughts relevant to one's personal discrepancy experiences).

Theoretical Analysis Applied to Prejudice-Related Discrepancies and Relevant Empirical Research

Monteith's (1991) analysis posited that prejudice-related discrepancies from well-internalized standards and their associated negative self-directed affect have several consequences that should facilitate control over future discrepant responses. First, awareness of a discrepant response should immediately interrupt ongoing behavior. Second, a regulatory cycle aimed at accomplishing discrepancy reduction should be engaged. This regulatory cycle should entail heightened self-focus (in line with Pyszczynski & Greenberg, 1986, 1987) and a particular preoccupation with personal discrepancy experiences (in line with Gray, 1982). Based on Gray's work, exploratory and investigative behavior also should be initiated. For example, Monteith reasoned that subjects should pay particular attention to information relevant to understanding why prejudice-related discrepancies are hard to avoid and how to reduce their future occurrence. Through the experience of discrepancies, individuals should establish an association between cues (e.g., group labels) and their discrepant (e.g., stereotypic) responses with discrepancy-related "punishment" (i.e., negative self-directed affect). On future occasions when such cues are presented again, the inhibitory system should be activated. Functionally, this should enable low prejudiced individuals to inhibit stereotypic responses and give them the opportunity to replace stereotypic responses with other responses that are consistent with their personal beliefs. In sum, the several consequences associated with discrepancies should serve the adaptive function of facilitating the inhibition of discrepant responses on future occasions when a discrepant response is possible.

These ideas were investigated in two studies which together provided strong support for the theoretical analysis. In the first study (Monteith, 1991, Study 1), already referred to above, low and high prejudiced subjects either were or were not induced to experience a prejudice-related discrepancy. Most important, the subjects in the discrepancy-activated condition were led to believe that they had rejected a law school applicant because of his sexual orientation. This type of discrepant response was chosen because pretesting indicated that both low and high prejudiced subjects believed that evaluating law school applicants based on their sexual orientation constituted a response that was *inconsistent* with (i.e., more prejudiced than) their personal standards. However, consistent with previous work (Devine *et al.*, 1991; Monteith *et al.*, in press), low-prejudiced subjects' standards for engaging in this response were less prejudiced and better *internalized* than were high-prejudiced subjects' standards. Subjects in the discrepancy-not activated condition evaluated and accepted a heterosexual law school applicant.[5]

Shortly after the discrepancy manipulation, but ostensibly as part of a separate task, subjects completed the affect measure. Subjects were asked to complete a mood evaluation form which they were told is "typically included in most psychological research." Subjects indicated the extent to which each item (e.g., guilty, tense) applied to how they were feeling at that moment. No mention of the previous law school evaluation task was made either before or after subjects completed the affect measure. The results summarized Table I reveal that low and high prejudiced subjects for whom a discrepancy was not activated reported relatively low levels of negative self-directed affect, as did high prejudiced subjects for whom a discrepancy was activated. Low prejudiced subjects for whom a discrepancy was activated reported the highest levels of negative self-directed affect, significantly higher than subjects in any of the other conditions. These affect findings are completely consistent with our previously summarized research.

Subjects then were asked to read through a summary of a proposal for a workshop concerning issues of stereotyping and prejudice with the goal of providing feedback on the workshop ideas. The workshop proposal had two sections. The first focused on why it is difficult to avoid negative responses toward homosexuals (e.g., stereotypes can be automatically used) and the second focused on strategies people can use to eliminate their negative responses toward homosexuals. The experimenter unobtrusively measured subjects' reading time to obtain a measure relevant to the degree of attention subjects paid to information concerning why discrepancies are hard to avoid and how to reduce their occurrence. Next, subjects listed the thoughts that had occurred to them as they read the workshop proposal. From subjects' thought protocols, two measures were extracted. One concerned the number of self-related thoughts subjects generated, which served as a measure of self-focus. These self-focused thoughts were further differentiated into those that referred to personal discrepancy experiences (e.g.,

---

[5]Subjects positive evaluations were made concerning a heterosexual, rather than a homosexual, applicant because low and high prejudiced people are likely to interpret a clearly positive evaluation of a homosexual applicant in different ways. The goal of this study was to compare the reactions of subjects experiencing a discrepancy with those not experiencing any discrepancy. In other studies (e.g., Monteith, 1991, Study 2), we examined low and high prejudiced subjects' reactions to prejudice-related discrepancies relative to low and high prejudiced subjects experiencing a discrepancy, but one that is unrelated to prejudice. These studies show the same pattern of affective consequences described in the text.

TABLE I

Mean Negself Feelings, Proportion of Self and Discrepancy-Focused Thoughts, and Recall
Score as a Function of Prejudice and Discrepancy Activation[a]

| | Discrepancy | | | |
| | Low prejudice | | High prejudice | |
	Activated	Not activated	Activated	Not activated
Negself feelings	5.36[a]	2.03[c]	3.37[b]	2.73[bc]
Self-focused thoughts	.42[a]	.16[b]	.22[b]	.28[ab]
Discrepancy-focused thoughts	.63[a]	.21[b]	.31[b]	.29[b]
Reading time	4.37[a]	3.80[b]	4.07[ab]	4.30[a]
Recall score	2.31[a]	1.19[bc]	.75[c]	1.62[b]

[a]For each dependent measure, means not sharing common superscripts differ significantly from each other ($p < .05$ at least, by Fisher's Least Significant Difference tests). (Data from Monteith, 1991.)

wondering how to avoid stereotype-based responses, thinking about when and why discrepancy experiences occur) and those that did not concern discrepancies. Thus, this second measure indexed the extent to which subjects' self-focused thoughts more specifically reflected attention directed toward subjects' discrepancy experiences. Finally, the participants completed a recall measure concerning the information summarized in the workshop proposal. This provided a second measure of attention to discrepancy-relevant information.

Subjects' self-focused thoughts, discrepancy-focused thoughts, reading time, and recall data are summarized in Table I. The results provided clear evidence supporting the notion that the discrepancy experience engaged a self-regulatory cycle that theoretically should be aimed at discrepancy reduction for low prejudiced subjects. First, the low prejudiced subjects in the discrepancy-activated condition listed a greater proportion of self-focused to total thoughts than their counterparts in the discrepancy-not activated condition, whereas this comparison was not significant for the high prejudiced subjects. Second, the analysis of the proportion of discrepancy to self-focused thoughts revealed that the low prejudiced subjects in the discrepancy-activated condition were more focused on their discrepancy experiences than subjects in the other conditions.

The discrepancy activation also appeared to heighten low prejudiced subjects' attention to discrepancy-relevant information, which provided a third indicator that a regulatory cycle had been engaged following the discrepancy activation. Evidence of attention to discrepancy-relevant information is revealed, in part, by the results concerning the time subjects spent reading the workshop summary. The reading times for low prejudiced subjects in the discrepancy-activated condition were longer than the times for their counterparts in the discrepancy-not activated condition, whereas this difference was not obtained for the high prejudiced subjects. The recall data concerning the workshop summary provided additional evidence that low prejudiced subjects in the discrepancy-activated condition were carefully exploring discrepancy-relevant information. In particular, subjects in this condition recalled significantly more information from the first portion of the essay (concerning why stereotypical responses are difficult to avoid) than any of the other experimental groups.

In sum, Study 1 indicated that the discrepancy activation heightened low prejudiced subjects' self-focus and more specifically prompted them to become preoccupied with their personal discrepancy experiences. The discrepancy activation also appeared to instigate investigative-exploratory behavior aimed at understanding why the discrepancy occurred and how to avoid it in the future. These findings provided evidence of the activation of a self-regulatory cycle that entailed the engagement of inhibitory mechanisms (see also Monteith, 1991, Study 2). In contrast to low prejudiced subjects, no evidence of the activation of regulatory mechanisms was found when high prejudiced subjects transgressed their personal standards for responding to homosexuals. Thus, discrepancy experiences apparently instigate a self-regulatory cycle only when nonprejudiced well-internalized standards are violated and a state of self-dissatisfaction is consequently created.

However, the critical question of Monteith's (1991) research was whether the discrepancy-associated consequences observed among low prejudiced subjects would facilitate their ability to control discrepant responses in a subsequent situation. The central goal of Study 2 (Monteith, 1991) was to address this question. This study consisted of two phases, which were presented as ostensibly unrelated studies.[6] A discrepancy was activated in all subjects during Phase 1, but the nature of this discrepancy was varied. Some of the low and high prejudiced subjects were induced to experience a prejudice-relevant discrepancy (which led to negative self-directed affect among low-prejudiced subjects in a pilot study, suggesting that the discrepancy violated a well-internalized standard). Specifically, subjects were led to believe that their responses to a questionnaire revealed higher levels of subtle prejudice than their standards dictated was appropriate. The remaining subjects were induced to experience a discrepancy unrelated to prejudice (and unrelated to their self-concepts).

---

[6]The procedures for Study 2 were quite complicated. Therefore, only the essential characteristics of the study are summarized herein (see Monteith, 1991, for additional details).

All subjects then participated in the "second" study that supposedly investigated various aspects of humor. Subjects were asked to rate a series of jokes on several dimensions (i.e., how funny, witty, and creative they perceived each joke to be). Several of the jokes were mildly distasteful, and two of the jokes employed humor at the expense of homosexuals. Monteith's reasoning was that individuals often have spontaneous reactions to jokes and thus, by default, would respond more favorably to the homosexual jokes than their personal standards would suggest was appropriate. Supporting this reasoning, pilot testing indicated that both low and high prejudiced subjects were prone to discrepancies concerning the homosexual jokes (i.e., they actually responded to them more favorably than they thought they should). However, for the low prejudiced subjects, Monteith predicted that the prejudice-relevant discrepancy experience would activate a self-regulatory cycle and thus facilitate these subjects' ability to control their spontaneous stereotypical responses to the jokes. Thus, low prejudiced subjects in the prejudice-relevant discrepancy condition were expected to evaluate the homosexual jokes less favorably than their counterparts in the prejudice-irrelevant discrepancy condition. She further expected that the discrepancy manipulation would not affect high-prejudiced subjects' evaluations of the homosexual jokes, because prejudice-related discrepancies did not activate self-regulatory mechanisms among high prejudiced subjects.

The joke rating data are summarized in Table II. The data in the top half of the table provide evidence that the prejudice-related discrepancy experience did facilitate low-prejudiced subjects' subsequent ability to control their stereotypical responses. More specifically, low prejudiced subjects in the prejudice-relevant discrepancy condition consistently provided less favorable joke ratings than their counterparts in the prejudice-irrelevant discrepancy condition. As expected, high prejudiced subjects' evaluations of the jokes were not affected by the discrepancy manipulation. This is apparent from the data in the bottom half of Table II.

The joke rating findings for the low prejudiced subjects suggest that the self-regulatory mechanisms instigated following the experience of discrepancies from well-internalized standards play a crucial role in the process of learning how to inhibit discrepant responses. In line with Gray's (1982) work, Monteith's (1991) analysis suggests that these mechanisms facilitate subsequent control over discrepant responses because they help in building an association between cues present during the discrepancy experience (e.g., group labels) and stereotypic responses with negative self-directed affect. Thus, discrepant responses are more likely to be inhibited on subsequent occasions, because when these cues are present again the inhibitory system is activated and one's responses regulated more effectively. Through this process, low prejudiced individuals can learn to inhibit discrepant (stereotypic) responses and replace them with belief-based responses.

TABLE II
Mean Ratings of Homosexual-Related Jokes as a Function of Prejudice for
Low and High Prejudiced Subjects[a]

	Discrepancy type	
	Prejudice relevant	Prejudice irrelevant
Low-Prejudice		
Joke 1	2.50[a]	3.70[b]
Joke 2	2.39[a]	3.71[b]
Overall index	2.45[a]	3.71[b]
High-prejudice		
Joke 1	5.44[a]	5.59[a]
Joke 2	5.33[a]	4.82[a]
Overall index	5.38[a]	5.21[a]

[a]For both low and high prejudiced subjects, means for each dependent measure that do not share a common superscript differ significantly from each other ($p < .05$ at least, by t tests). The Joke 1 index consists of the average of the funny, witty, and creative ratings for the first homosexual joke presented to subjects. The Joke 2 index consists of the average of these three ratings made in connection with the second homosexual joke presented. The Overall index is the average of all homosexual-relevant joke ratings. (Data from Monteith, 1991.)

A Model of Prejudice Reduction

At this point we would like to draw the reader's attention to Figure 1, which presents our model of prejudice reduction. At the outset, we would like to make two issues clear. First, the processes identified in this model are relevant to those who have renounced prejudice and are committed to responding to members of stereotyped groups in fair and nonprejudiced ways. Second, we would like to underscore our assumption that prejudice reduction, which involves rejecting old ways of responding and adopting new ways of responding, is not easily accomplished. It is a process that occurs over time and with learning. Despite the difficult nature of the task, the findings in our research program suggest that with effort and practice people can learn to respond consistently with their nonprejudiced personal standards.

Drawing from our theoretical and empirical work, we argue that the entry point for the model is the establishment and internalization of nonprejudiced standards. However, establishing and internalizing nonprejudiced personal standards does not imply that change is complete. During the early phases of the prejudice reduction process, we would expect people to follow the path indicated by the solid lines in Figure 1. That is, contact with members of a stereotyped group will lead to the automatic activation of the stereotype and its associated affect. Moreover, during these early

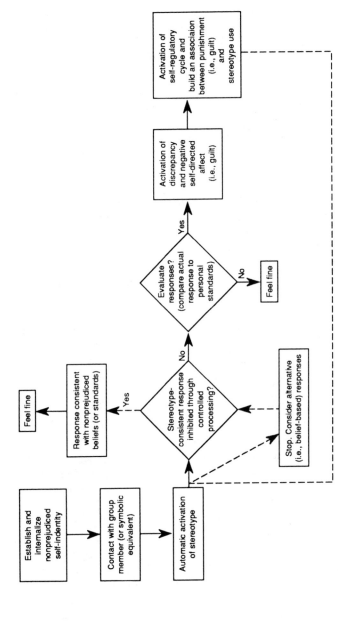

Figure 1 Process model of prejudice reduction.

phases of the prejudice reduction process, low prejudiced people are not expected to be particularly effective or efficient at using controlled processes to inhibit this activation. As a consequence, low prejudiced people would be particularly likely to experience discrepancies between their nonprejudiced standards and their actual responses. If low prejudiced people do not evaluate their actual responses in light of their personal standards, they will exit the process and will not experience any negative affect. If, however, they do evaluate their actual responses and recognize them as being more prejudiced than their personal standards dictate is appropriate, they will experience a threat to their nonprejudiced self-identity. This is indicated in the figure by the activation of a discrepancy and its associated negative self-directed affect.

The model indicates that discrepancies from well-internalized standards combined with negative self-directed affect instigate self-regulatory mechanisms. These mechanisms appear to include self-focused attention that specifically concerns prejudice-related discrepancy experiences, and enhanced attention to discrepancy-relevant information. The operation of these mechanisms enables low prejudiced individuals to build an association between cues present when the discrepancy occurred and the discrepant response with negative self-directed affect. The consequence of building these associations is that on future occasions, the dashed lines shown in the figure should be followed (see Monteith *et al.*, 1992, for additional details). That is, prior to generating a response following stereotype activation, people should stop and consider belief-based alternative responses. Thus, in the later phases of the change process, this additional event should enable individuals to avoid discrepancies and to generate responses that are, instead, consistent with their nonprejudiced beliefs and standards. The encouraging aspect of this model is that it suggests that people can benefit from their failure experiences and can make progress in learning to respond consistently with their nonprejudiced standards. Although it is not easy and clearly requires effort, time, and practice, prejudice appears to be a habit that can be broken.

Having outlined the model, we see two high priorities for future research. First, we need to continue to test and develop the implications of the model for our understanding of the challenges and experiences of low prejudiced people. For example, one portion of the model that has not been systematically investigated concerns the conditions under which people will evaluate their actual responses in light of their personal standards and when they will fail to do so. This type of evaluation is necessary for the discrepancy to be recognized and the subsequent regulatory mechanisms to be engaged (and thus for progress to be made). In terms of the implications of the model, it will be important to examine how a delay between the discrepancy experience and the future situation in which one can inhibit a discrepant response will influence whether people will exert the control needed to generate responses consistent with their standards. In addition, it is possible that people may seek alternative ways to bolster or reaffirm their nonprejudiced self-identity following discrepancy experiences (e.g., Dutton & Lake, 1973; Sherman & Gorkin, 1980; Steele, 1988). Seeking out such self-identity-affirming opportunities could short circuit the activation of the self-regulatory mechanisms that Monteith (1991) described and, as such, actually obstruct rather than contribute to people's progress in learning to inhibit future discrepant responses.

Specifically relevant to these issues is a series of clever experiments designed by Dutton and his colleagues (Dutton & Lake, 1973; Dutton & Lennox, 1974) in which they experimentally induced a "threat" to low-prejudiced subjects' nonprejudiced self-concepts by giving them (false) feedback suggesting that they might be prejudiced. Subjects were then provided with an opportunity to donate money to either a black or white panhandler. In these studies, subjects were found to donate larger sums of money to black than to white panhandlers. Dutton (1976; Dutton & Lake, 1973) suggested that this "reverse discrimination" is motivated by the desire to restore or protect subjects' nonprejudiced self-images. Taking the analysis one step further, Dutton and Lennox (1974) explored the long-term implications of having access to such opportunities to restore a nonprejudiced self-image following a threat experience. That is, on a subsequent occasion subjects were asked to donate time to an interracial "brotherhood" campaign. They found that subjects who were provided with an opportunity to restore their nonprejudiced self-images (i.e., panhandled by a black person) donated more time to the brotherhood campaign than did subjects who did not have an opportunity to restore their self-images (i.e., panhandled by a white person or not panhandled at all).

Dutton and Lennox (1974) suggested that the positive effects (i.e., positive behavior toward minority group members) of threats to one's nonprejudiced self-concept may be transitory and that the long-term consequences for prejudice reduction may be negative (i.e., at minimum may maintain the prejudice). That is, reestablishing one's egalitarian self-image may lead to complacency regarding the need for future positive behaviors concerning the minority group. This type of analysis suggests that the positive effects of discrepancies on prejudice reduction efforts may be fleeting rather than long lasting. However, more work is needed before accepting this conclusion.

Although subjects who had not previously had an opportunity to restore their nonprejudiced self-images donated more time to the campaign (and this presumably was their attempt to restore a nonprejudiced self-image) than did subjects who had restored their nonprejudiced self-image, subjects in the latter group still donated more time to the campaign than did control subjects who never experienced a "threat" to their self-concepts. A detailed analysis of the similarities and differences between the conceptual

frameworks offered by Dutton and colleagues (1973, 1974) and by us is beyond the scope of this chapter. However, there is one point on which we all
would agree. Any complete model of prejudice reduction would have to
specify the duration of the effects of discrepancy experiences and the self-
concept threat they engender (i.e., short lived or long lasting) and the specific nature of those effects (i.e., alleviate or maintain prejudice).

A second priority for future research is to expand our analysis to more
fully incorporate high-prejudiced people. To date, our analysis of the
change process focuses on those who have already decided to renounce
prejudice, which functionally eliminates high-prejudiced individuals. Additional theorizing and research relevant to understanding the nature of high-
prejudiced subjects' standards is needed before we can speculate about how
to go about the task of changing their standards. Based on our work with
low prejudiced individuals, however, it might be reasonable to suggest that
a potentially effective strategy for encouraging high prejudiced people to re-
vise their standards so as to establish and internalize nonprejudiced standards would involve inducing self-dissatisfaction in connection with their
current standards.

A number of both classic and more contemporary theorists have argued
that high prejudiced people possess egalitarian values and that these values
are integral to their self-conceptions (Dovidio & Gaertner, 1986; McConahay, 1986; Myrdal, 1944; Rokeach, 1973). Prejudice, it can be argued, is
inconsistent with egalitarian values. Rokeach's theorizing in the early 1970s
suggests that when prejudice is personally recognized as contradicting fundamental egalitarian values the stage is set for the initiation of prejudice
reduction efforts. Following from Rokeach, then, if it is empirically demonstrated that high-prejudiced people's egalitarian values are self-defining and
important, an effective change strategy might be to encourage high prejudiced people to confront the inconsistency between their egalitarian values
and their more specific prejudiced personal standards. Making this type of
discrepancy salient could threaten high prejudiced people's egalitarian self-
conceptions and may lead to negative self-directed affect (cf. Rokeach,
1973). This affect may then provide the motivation for reconsidering their
prejudiced standards and thus initiating the prejudice reduction process depicted in Figure 1.

Concluding Remarks

The emphasis in this volume is on the interface of cognition and affect
in the analysis of stereotypes—their formation, representation, modification, and use. The study of the control and regulation of stereotype-based
responses has proven to be an area rich for examining the interface of affec-

tive and cognitive processes. In our closing remarks, we comment on two themes common in the prejudice literature that have troubled us and have served, in part, as a motivation for our interests in developing a detailed analysis of the role affect plays in the prejudice reduction process.

Interpreting Discrepancies: True Conflict or Self-Presentation?

Legislators, social scientists, and lay people alike have long been concerned with the paradox of racism in a nation founded on the fundamental value of human equality (see Gaertner & Dovidio, 1986; Katz, Wackenhut, & Hass, 1986; McConahay, 1986; Myrdal, 1944). Legislators responded with the landmark legal decisions of the 1950s and 1960s (e.g., Supreme Court ruling on school segregation and the Civil Rights Laws) which made overt discrimination based on race illegal and functionally made admitting to prejudices socially taboo. In the wake of these changes at the societal level, social scientists have been interested in the extent to which changes at the individual level have followed suit. The literature addressing this issue has produced a conflicting set of findings. That is, although overt expressions of prejudice have declined over the years (based on verbal reports), more subtle indicators (based on nonverbal measures) continue to reveal prejudice even among those who claim to have renounced prejudice (see Crosby *et al.*, 1980, for a review).

A common theme in the prejudice literature is that these conflicting reactions indicate that prejudice has not been reduced at the individual level and that claims of being nonprejudiced merely reflect compliance with (rather than internalization of) society's nonprejudiced values (Crosby *et al.*, 1980; Dovidio & Fazio, 1992; Dovidio & Gaertner, 1991). According to this analysis, prejudice has not truly been reduced, but rather overt expressions of prejudice have simply been replaced with more covert, subtle forms of prejudice. For example, to assess racial attitudes, Crosby *et al.* (1980) clearly favored nonconsciously monitored responses, arguing that the strength of such measures is that they do not involve careful, deliberate, and intentional thought (see also Dovidio & Fazio, 1992). Thus, their analysis centered on the assumption that the less controllable nonconscious responses were inherently more trustworthy than the more controllable verbal responses. This type of analysis seems to assume that change has truly occurred only if all of one's responses are consistent with one's overtly expressed nonprejudiced beliefs.

In contrast to these analyses, our model of prejudice reduction views change as a process and details how negative responses can persist (due to their relatively automatic nature) in the face of changes in one's beliefs. Despite this inconsistency, the present work suggests that less controllable responses are not necessarily more trustworthy than more controllable responses. Indeed, controllable verbal reports may be the more trustworthy responses—or at least they may be more representative of the person's central values.[7]

In addition, we believe that the findings that low prejudiced subjects' discrepancies from their strongly internalized nonprejudiced standards lead to feelings of compunction and instigate a self-regulatory cycle suggest that these individuals have sincerely rejected a prejudiced ideology and have embraced nonprejudiced, egalitarian beliefs and standards. Moreover, discrepancies and their associated self-directed affect can actually facilitate the prejudice reduction process by engaging self-regulatory mechanisms and then bringing one's actual responses closer to one's standards. Indeed, we interpret the pattern of findings across these research programs to suggest that many people appear to be embroiled in the difficult, long-term task of breaking the prejudice habit.

The Inevitability of Prejudice Assumption

A common theme in the prejudice literature, and a theme that was fueled by the cognitive approach to the study of social stereotypes, is that prejudice is an inevitable consequence of ordinary stereotyping or categorization processes (see Billig, 1985, for a review). This inevitability of prejudice perspective essentially equates stereotypes with prejudice and suggests that so long as stereotypes exist, prejudice will follow. This type of analysis fails to consider that people who have internalized nonprejudiced standards regard stereotype-consistent responses as unacceptable, and that these people may be particularly motivated to eliminate their personally unacceptable responses.

A purely cognitive analysis assisted in our understanding of why even those who renounce prejudice may be prone to experiencing discrepancies between their self-defined personal standards and their actual responses (cf. Devine, 1989a). However, the key issue, it appears, is not the discrepancy per se, but how the person responds to that discrepancy. Our subsequent work, which highlights the interface between cognition and affect (Devine *et al.*, 1991; Monteith, 1991; Monteith et al., in press), suggests that prejudice need not be an inevitable consequence of ordinary stereotyping processes. Indeed, by exploring the implications of the self-generated affect that follows from discrepancies, we have gleaned some insights about the processes involved in learning to control and regulate stereotype-based re-

---

[7]We want to be clear here, however, that we are not suggesting that all people's verbal reports are trustworthy. That is, some people may actually engage in strategic self-presentation so as to present a nonprejudiced social image. What we would like to emphasize is that our analysis allows for the possibility that those who report being low in prejudice are in reality low in prejudice.

sponses. Perhaps most importantly, we have demonstrated that these control efforts can be successful (Monteith, 1991).

In conclusion, we believe that by expanding our analysis of the implications of stereotype activation and use to consider the interface between cognition and affect, we have enriched our understanding of the prejudice reduction process. Indeed, the analysis is more complete than would have been possible by pursuing an exclusively cognitive approach. Our analysis is at present an individual level analysis and although we are encouraged by the progress some individuals are making in reducing prejudice, we do not believe that intergroup prejudice is no longer a problem. However, we also are sanguine that the struggle to control prejudice at the personal level may have implications for the amelioration of intergroup tensions.

Acknowledgments

We would like to thank Sophia Evett, David Hamilton, Diane Mackie, and Julia Zuwerink for their comments and suggestions on an earlier draft of this chapter.

References

Allport, G. W. (1954). *The nature of prejudice.* Reading, MA: Addison-Wesley.

Aronson, E. (1968). The theory of cognitive dissonance: A current perspective. In L. Berkowitz (Ed.), *Advances in experimental social psychology* (Vol. 4, pp. 1–34). New York: Academic Press.

Ausubel, D. P. (1955). Relationships between shame and guilt in the socializing process. *Psychological Review, 62,* 378–390.

Billig, M. (1985). Prejudice, categorization, and particularization: From a perceptual to a rhetorical approach. *European Journal of Social Psychology, 15,* 79–103.

Campbell, E. Q. (1961). Moral discomfort and racial segregation—an examination of the Myrdal hypothesis. *Social Forces, 39,* 228–234.

Carver, C. S., & Scheier, M. F. (1981). *Attention and self-regulation: A control theory approach to behavior.* New York: Springer-Verlag.

Carver, C. S., & Scheier, M. F. (1990). Origins and functions of positive and negative affect: A control process view. *Psychological Review, 97,* 19–35.

Carver, C. S., Blaney, P. H., & Scheier, M. F. (1979). Reassertion and giving up: The interactive role of self-directed attention and outcome expectancy. *Journal of Personality and Social Psychology, 37,* 1859–1870.

Crosby, F., Bromley, S., & Saxe, L. (1980). Recent unobtrusive studies of black and white discrimination and prejudice: A literature review. *Psychological Bulletin, 87,* 546–563.

Devine, P. G. (1989a). Stereotypes and prejudice: Their automatic and controlled components. *Journal of Personality and Social Psychology, 56,* 5–18.

Devine, P. G. (1989b). Automatic and controlled processes in prejudice: The role of stereotypes and personal beliefs. In A. R. Pratkanis, S. J. Breckler, & A. G. Greenwald (Eds.), *Attitude structure and function* (pp. 181–212). Hillsdale, NJ: Erlbaum.

Devine, P. G. Monteith, M. J., Zuwerink, J. R., & Elliot, A. J. (1991). Prejudice with and without compunction, *Journal of Personality and Social Psychology, 60,* 817–830.

Dovidio, J. F., & Fazio, R. H. (1992). New technologies for the direct and indirect assessment of attitudes. In J. M. Tanur (Ed.), *Questions about questions: Inquiries into the cognitive bases of surveys* (pp. 204–237). New York: Russel Sage Foundation.

Dovidio, J. F., & Gaertner, S. L. (1986). Prejudice, discrimination, and racism: Historical trends and contemporary approaches. In J. F. Dovidio & S. L. Gaertner (Eds.), *Prejudice, discrimination, and racism* (pp. 1–34). New York: Academic Press.

Dovidio, J. F., & Gaertner, S. L. (1991). Changes in the nature and assessment of racial prejudice. In H. Knopke, J. Norrell, & R. Rogers (Eds.), *Opening doors: An appraisal of race relations in contemporary America* (pp. 201–241). Tuscaloosa, AL: University of Alabama Press.

Dutton, D. G. (1976). Tokenism, reverse discrimination, and egalitarianism in interracial behavior. *Journal of Social Issues, 32,* 93–107.

Dutton, D. G., & Lake, R. A. (1973). Threat of own prejudice and reverse discrimination in interracial situations. *Journal of Personality and Social Psychology, 28,* 94–100.

Dutton, D. G., & Lennox, V. L. (1974). Effect of prior "token" compliance on subsequent interracial behavior. *Journal of Personality and Social Psychology, 29,* 65–71.

Duval, S., & Wicklund, R. A. (1972). *A theory of objective self-awareness.* New York: Academic Press.

Ehrlich, H. J. (1973). *The social psychology of prejudice.* New York: Wiley.

Festinger, L. (1957). *A theory of cognitive dissonance.* Stanford, CA: Stanford University Press.

Fowles, D. C. (1987). Application of a behavioral theory of motivation to the concepts of anxiety and impulsivity. *Journal of Research in Personality, 21,* 417–435.

Fowles, D. C. (1988). Psychophysiology and psychopathology: A motivational approach. *Psychophysiology, 25,* 373–391.

Friedrichs, R. W. (1959). Christians and residential exclusion: An empirical study of a Northern dilemma. *Journal of Social Issues, 15,* 14–23.

Gaertner, S. L., & Dovidio, J. F. (1986). The aversive form of racism. In J. F. Dovidio & S. L. Gaertner (Eds.), *Prejudice, discrimination, and racism* (pp. 61–89). New York: Academic Press.

Gilbert, D., & Hixon, J. G. (1991). The trouble with thinking: Activation and application of stereotypic beliefs. *Journal of Personality and Social Psychology, 60,* 509–517.

Gray, J. A. (1981). A critique of Eysenck's theory of personality. In H. J. Eysenck (Ed.), *A model for personality* (pp. 246–276). Berlin: Springer-Verlag.

Gray, J. A. (1982). *The neuropsychology of anxiety: An enquiry into the functions of the septo-hippocampal system.* New York: Oxford University Press.

Gray, J. A. (1985). Issues in the neuropsychology of anxiety. In A. H. Tuma & J. P. Maser (Eds.), *Anxiety and the anxiety disorders* (pp. 5–25). Hillsdale, NJ: Erlbaum.

Hamilton, D. L. (1981). Stereotyping and intergroup behavior: Some thoughts on the cognitive approach. In D. L. Hamilton (Ed.), *Cognitive processes in stereotyping and intergroup behavior* (pp. 333–353). Hillsdale, NJ: Erlbaum.

Hamilton, D. L., & Trolier, T. (1986). Stereotypes and stereotyping: An overview of the cognitive approach. In J. F. Dovidio & S. L. Gaertner (Eds.), *Prejudice, discrimination, and racism* (pp. 127–163). New York: Academic Press.

Higgins, E. T. (1987). Self-discrepancy theory: A theory relating self and affect. *Psychological Review, 94,* 319–340.

Higgins, E. T., & King, G. (1981). Accessibility of social constructs: Information processing consequences of individual and contextual variability. In N. Cantor & J. F. Kihlstrom (Eds.), *Personality and social interaction* (pp. 69–121). Hillsdale, NJ: Erlbaum.

Higgins, E. T., Bond, R. N., Klein, R., & Strauman, T. J. (1985). Self-discrepancies and emotional vulnerability: How magnitude, accessibility, and type of discrepancy influence affect. *Journal of Personality and Social Psychology, 51,* 5–15.

Higgins, E. T., Klein, R., & Strauman, T. J. (1985). Self-concept discrepancy theory: A psychological model for distinguishing among different aspects of depression and anxiety. *Social Cognition, 3,* 51–76.

Jamieson, D. W., & Zanna, M. P. (1989). Need for structure in attitude formation and expression. In A. R. Pratkanis, S. J. Breckler, & A. G. Greenwald (Eds.), *Attitude structure and function* (pp. 383–406). Hillsdale, NJ: Erlbaum.

Katz, I., Wackenhut, J., & Hass, R. G., (1986). Racial ambivalence, value duality, and behavior. In J. F. Dovidio & S. L. Gaertner (Eds.), *Prejudice, discrimination, and racism* (pp. 35–60). New York: Academic Press.

Klinger, M., & Beall, P. (1992). Conscious and unconscious effects of stereotype activation. Paper presented at the 64th annual meeting of the Midwestern Psychological Association, Chicago, May.

Kruglanski, A. W., & Freund, T. (1983). The freezing and unfreezing of lay inferences: Effects on impressional primacy, ethnic stereotyping and numerical anchoring. *Journal of Experimental Social Psychology, 19*, 448–468.

Markus, H., & Nurius, P. (1986). Possible selves. *American Psychologist, 41*, 954–969.

McConahay, J. G. (1986). Modern racism, ambivalence, and the modern racism scale. In J. F. Dovidio & S. L. Gaertner (Eds.), *Prejudice, discrimination, and racism* (pp. 91–125). New York: Academic Press.

Monteith, M. J. (1991). Self-regulation of stereotypical responses: Implications for progress in prejudice reduction efforts. Unpublished doctoral dissertation, University of Wisconsin - Madison.

Monteith, M. J., Devine, P. G., & Zuwerink, J. R. (in press). Self-directed vs. other-directed affect as a consequence of prejudice-related discrepancies. *Journal of Personality and Social Psychology.*

Monteith, M. J., Zuwerink, J. R., Devine, P. G. (1992). Stereotypes and prejudice: Replacing the old with the new. In P. G. Devine, D. L. Hamilton, & T. M. Ostrom (Eds.), *Social cognition: Contributions to classic issues in social psychology.* New York: Springer-Verlag.

Myrdal, G. (1944). *An American dilemma.* New York: Harper & Row.

Nichols, S., & Newman, J. P. (1986). Effects of punishment on response latency in extraverts. *Journal of Personality and Social Psychology, 50*, 624–630.

Patterson, C. M., Kosson, D. S., & Newman, J. P. (1987). Reaction to punishment, reflectivity, and passive avoidance learning in extraverts. *Journal of Personality and Social Psychology, 52*, 565–575.

Pettigrew, T. F. (1981). Extending the stereotype concept. In D. L. Hamilton (Ed.), *Cognitive processes in stereotyping and intergroup behavior* (pp. 303–331). Hillsdale, NJ: Erlbaum.

Piers, G., & Singer, M. B. (1971). *Shame and guilt.* New York: Norton.

Pressly, S. L., & Devine, P. G. (1992). Sex, sexism, and compunction: Group membership or intenatization of standards? Paper presented at the 64th annual meeting of the Midwestern Psychological Association, Chicago, May.

Pyszczynski, T., & Greenberg, J. (1986). Persistent high self-focus after failure and low self-focus after success: The depressive self-focusing style. *Journal of Personality and Social Psychology, 50*, 1039–1044.

Pyszczynski, T., & Greenberg, J. (1987). Self-regulatory perseveration and the depressive self-focusing style: A self-awareness theory of reactive depression. *Psychological Bulletin, 102*, 122–138.

Rokeach, M. (1973). *The nature of human values.* New York: Free Press.

Scheier, M. F., & Carver, C. S. (1988). A model of behavioral self-regulation: Translating intention into action. In L. Berkowitz (Ed.), *Advances in experimental social psychology* (Vol. 21, pp. 303–346). New York: Academic Press.

Schwartz, S. (1977). Normative influences on altruism. In L. Berkowitz (Ed.), *Advances in experimental social psychology* (Vol. 10, pp. 221–279). New York: Academic Press.

Sherman, S. J., & Gorkin, L. (1980). Attitude bolstering when behavior is inconsistent with central attitudes. *Journal of Experimental Social Psychology, 16*, 388–403.

Steele, C. M. (1988). The psychology of self-affirmation: Sustaining the integrity of the self. In L. Berkowitz (Ed.), *Advances in experimental social psychology* (Vol. 21, pp. 261–346). New York: Academic Press.

Stephan, W. G. (1985). Intergroup relations. In G. Lindzey & E. Aronson (Eds.), *The handbook of social psychology,* (3rd Ed., Vol. 2, pp. 559–658). Hillsdale, NJ: Erlbaum.

Stephan, W. G. (1989). A cognitive approach to stereotyping. In D. Bar-Tal, C. F. Gaumann, A. W. Kruglanski, & W. Stroebe (Eds.), *Stereotyping and prejudice: Changing conceptions* (pp. 37–57). New York: Springer-Verlag.

Tajfel, H. (1981). *Human groups and social categories: Studies in social psychology.* Cambridge: Cambridge University Press.

Wallace, J. F., Bachorowski, J., & Newman, J. P. (1990). Failures in response modulation: Impulsive behavior in anxious and impulsive individuals. *Journal of Research in Personality,* **25,** 23–44.

Westie, F. R. (1965). The American dilemma: An empirical test. *American Sociological Review,* **30,** 527–538.

Wicklund, R. A. (1975). Objective self-awareness. In L. Berkowitz (Ed.), *Advances in experimental social psychology* (Vol. 8, pp. 233–275). New York: Academic Press.

Zuwerink, J. R., Devine, P. G., & Cook, D. (1992). Prejudice with and without compunction: A replication in Arkansas. Paper presented at the 64th annual meeting of the Midwestern Psychological Association, Chicago, May.

Chapter 15

Social Stigma: The Consequences of Attributional Ambiguity

BRENDA MAJOR and JENNIFER CROCKER
Department of Psychology
State University of New York at Buffalo
Buffalo, New York

Introduction

For more than four decades, social psychologists have studied and documented the existence and consequences of stereotypes about various groups in society. This research has demonstrated that many individuals and social groups in our society are stigmatized. By stigmatized, we mean individuals who, by virtue of their membership in a particular social group, or by their possession of particular characteristics, are targets of negative stereotypes, are vulnerable to being labeled as deviant, and are devalued in society (cf. Goffman, 1963; Jones *et al.*, 1984). People who are stigmatized or members of stigmatized groups are often targets of prejudice, discrimination, and oppression (Jones *et al.*, 1984). Stereotypes of the stigmatized frequently justify and contribute to prejudice and discrimination against the stigmatized, and hence represent an important social problem.

A great deal of social psychological research has been devoted to understanding stereotyping and prejudice, as the chapters in this volume testify. The dominant focus of this research has been on the beliefs and reactions of the nonstigmatized, or dominant groups in society, toward those who are members of stigmatized or oppressed groups. In contrast, relatively little work has taken the perspective of the person or group who is the target of stereotypes or prejudice. Our concern in this chapter is with the subjective experience of being stigmatized, from the perspective of the stigmatized person. Specifically, we address the cognitive, affective, motivational, and interpersonal consequences of prejudice for members of stigmatized groups.

We propose that cognitions held by the stigmatized about their stigma, including their awareness of stereotypes associated with their stigma or group, their beliefs about the content of these stereotypes, and especially the attributions they make for the treatment and outcomes they receive, have important affective, motivational, and interpersonal consequences for the stigmatized individual. In particular, our central thesis is that the stigmatized exist in a chronic state of *attributional ambiguity* with regard to the causes of others' behavior toward them. That is, the stigmatized frequently are uncertain as to why they are treated the way they are and why they receive the outcomes they do. This attributional ambiguity occurs because when the stigmatized and the nonstigmatized interact, the behavior of the nonstigmatized individual may be in response to the individual, personal qualities or behavior of the stigmatized person, or it may reflect the stereotypes and prejudices that the nonstigmatized person holds about the stigma. Reactions of the nonstigmatized toward the stigmatized may also reflect relatively automatic responses such as of pity or disgust (cf. Jones *et al.*, 1984). We propose that this attributional ambiguity experienced by the stigmatized has important consequences for their affect, self-esteem, self-evaluations, motivation, and interpersonal strategies.

Consider, for example, the attributional possibilities of a black candidate who applies for but is turned down for a job. One set of attributions he might make for this rejection is that it was due to his lack of qualifications, experience, or other job-related skills. An alternative attribution he might make, however, is that he was turned down for the job because of prejudice and discrimination against his race. Which type of attribution he makes has important implications for his feelings, self-evaluations, and motivation. Attributional ambiguity may also surround positive outcomes, particularly if they occur in certain contexts. For example, consider the subjective experience of a black job candidate who applies to and is hired by a company which is pursuing a vigorous affirmative action program. On one hand, our candidate may attribute his success to his superior qualifications, experience, job-related skills, and the like. On the other hand, our candidate may believe that he was given his job not because of his individual merits, but because of his race. Again, his feelings, self-evaluations, and motivation should be affected by which type of attribution he makes.

In this chapter we first describe the attributional ambiguity associated with negative and positive outcomes for the stigmatized. We then discuss the affective and self-evaluative implications of this attributional ambiguity. Following this, we consider implications of attributional ambiguity for motivation and the interpersonal strategies adopted by the stigmatized. We conclude with a discussion of determinants and sources of attributional ambiguity.

The Attributional Ambiguity of Stigma

Some uncertainty usually accompanies causal attributions for all individuals. All of us are at times unsure as to whether the outcomes or treatment we receive are due to internal factors, such as our own abilities or efforts, or to external factors, such as characteristics of the particular situation or task in which we are engaging. We propose, however, that this is particularly true for the stigmatized because their outcomes, both negative and positive, could be affected by, or be seen as being affected by, another factor: others' reactions to their stigma or their membership in a stigmatized group. Consequently, those who are stigmatized may experience considerably more attributional ambiguity than the nonstigmatized with regard to the causes of their treatment.

There is evidence that a stigma often assumes a central role in the way a stigmatized individual construes his or her social world (see Jones *et al.*, 1984). The stigmatized often take it for granted that their stigma affects all of the behaviors of those who interact with them (cf. Goffman, 1963; Wright, 1960). In an ingenious experiment, Kleck and Strenta (1980) demonstrated that this perception may persist even when the stigma in fact has no effect on the treatment the stigmatized receive. Women in this experiment were led to believe that the purpose of the experiment was to assess how another person would react to a facially disfiguring scar. To create the scar, theatrical makeup was applied to the women's faces, running from the ear to the mouth. After the women had examined the scar in a mirror, the experimenter applied moisturizer, ostensibly to "keep the scar from cracking," which, unbeknownst to the women, removed the scar. Subjects then interacted with another individual, who saw no disfigurement and who knew nothing of what had gone before. Compared to women in a control condition, who were led to believe their conversational partner thought they had an allergy, women who (falsely) believed that they possessed a physically deviant characteristic were much more sensitive to how their partners reacted to them. They rated their partners as more tense, distant, and patronizing, even though observers who later analyzed the videotapes could find no differences in treatment between the supposedly disfigured women and the control women. Thus, these results suggest that people who are self-conscious about being stigmatized may sometimes misinterpret mannerisms, comments, and behaviors from others and misattribute them to their stigma.

Of course, the stigmatized often have good reason to suspect that the behavior of others toward them is influenced by their stigma. This suspicion applies to negative as well as positive feedback and treatment. Because our analysis of responses to negative and positive feedback differs, these will be considered separately here.

The Attributional Ambiguity of Negative Feedback

There is considerable theory and evidence that people who are stigmatized, or are members of stigmatized groups, often are perceived and treated more negatively than those who are not so stigmatized (cf. Crosby, Bromley & Saxe, 1980; Goffman, 1963). For example, people hold negative stereotypes about blacks, women, the physically handicapped, and facially disfigured, mentally retarded, homosexual, and mentally ill persons (see Crocker & Major, 1989). Furthermore, it is well documented that members of these groups are often discriminated against, both interpersonally and economically (see Crocker & Major, 1989). Members of stigmatized groups frequently are aware of prejudice and discrimination directed against their group (cf. Crosby, 1982; Taylor, Wright, Moghaddam, & Lalonde, 1990). Consequently, when members of stigmatized groups are treated negatively by others, or are the recipients of negative outcomes, the causes of their treatment or outcomes may be ambiguous. On the one hand, it may be an accurate reflection of their personal abilities or attributes. Alternatively, a plausible, and frequently accurate, explanation for this negative feedback is that it is a result of prejudice and discrimination based on their stigma. Attributions to prejudice may enable the stigmatized to discount (Kelley, 1972) the personal implications of negative feedback (Crocker & Major, 1989).

But the stigmatized do not receive uniformly negative feedback from nonstigmatized others. Although attitudes and behavior toward the stigmatized may be predominantly negative, they may coexist with feelings of sympathy, pity, concern, or even genuine admiration. For example, research indicates that attitudes toward the physically handicapped are ambivalent. Feelings of revulsion and disgust toward the handicapped are often mixed with feelings of sympathy and concern (Katz, 1981). Furthermore, research on responses to the handicapped indicates that people often behave more positively toward the handicapped than toward the nonhandicapped (Kleck, Ono, & Hastorf, 1966).

Attitudes toward blacks also tend to be ambivalent; negative attitudes are often mixed with feelings of sympathy and concern (cf. Katz, Wackenhut, & Hass, 1986; Gaertner & Dovidio, 1986). Research indicates that white subjects sometimes respond more favorably to blacks than whites who are in need (Gaertner & Dovidio, 1977), or evaluate black targets more positively than white targets (cf. Linville & Jones, 1980). For example, Carver, Glass, Snyder, & Katz (1977) found that college students evaluated both black and physically handicapped interviewees more favorably than nonstigmatized interviewees, especially when the interviewee was portrayed in an unfavorable light. How is this positive feedback interpreted by the stigmatized?

The Attributional Ambiguity of Positive Feedback

Positive feedback may be even more attributionally complex than negative feedback for the stigmatized because it may be viewed as occurring either *in spite of,* or *because of,* their stigma.

Augmenting

On one hand, the stigmatized may view positive feedback as occurring in spite of the prejudice and discrimination that accompanies their stigma. Following Kelley's (1972) augmenting principle, this may lead them to be especially likely to attribute positive feedback or outcomes to their own deservingness. Just this pattern was observed by Major, Carrington, & Carnevale (1984). In this study, attractive and unattractive college students wrote an essay that was evaluated positively by a (bogus) opposite-sex peer, who the subjects believed could either see them (blinds on a one-way mirror were up) or could not see them (blinds were down). The students believed that the evaluator was currently unattached, and was looking for someone to become involved with. Consistent with the augmentation principle, unattractive students were more likely to believe that the positive evaluation was due to the high quality of their essay when they could be seen by the evaluator, than when they could not be seen. Attractive individuals, on the other hand, appeared to discount the positive feedback. They were less likely to attribute the positive evaluation to the quality of their essay when they could be seen than when they could not be seen by the evaluator (see also Sigall & Michela, 1976). Apparently, the attractive students felt that an opposite-sex evaluator who saw them might have ulterior reasons for evaluating their essay positively, whereas the unattractive students harbored no such illusions.

Discounting

An alternative response the stigmatized might show when they receive positive feedback, however, is to discount it. That is, under some circumstances people who are members of stigmatized groups may believe that they received favorable treatment because of their stigma, rather than their own deservedness. The validity or genuineness of positive feedback might be doubted for several reasons. One reason is that positive responses toward the stigmatized may be motivated by social desirability or self-presentational concerns, specifically, the desire *not* to appear prejudiced (cf. Carver, Glass, & Katz, 1978; Gaertner & Dovidio, 1986). Most people think of themselves as nonprejudiced or egalitarian, supporting equal rights for blacks (cf. Gaertner & Dovidio, 1986), as well as for other stigmatized groups (cf. Katz et al., 1986). In order to avoid appearing prejudiced, either to themselves or to others, people may sometimes "bend over backward" to act in exaggeratedly positive ways toward the stigmatized (cf. Gaertner & Dovidio, 1986; Katz, 1981; Katz et al., 1986). For example, Gaertner and Dovidio (1986) suggest that whites are particularly likely to respond in exaggeratedly positive ways toward blacks under conditions in which a negative response could be clearly attributed to prejudice.

The social desirability of not being or appearing prejudiced against the stigmatized seems to be particularly relevant in the case of blacks. This was demonstrated convincingly in a study by Carver et al. (1978). These authors used the bogus pipeline technique to lead people to believe their true attitudes were being assessed. Carver et al. (1978) asked college women to indicate their impressions of a handicapped, black, or nonstigmatized interviewee. These impressions were assessed either via a standard self-report questionnaire, or while subjects were hooked up to electronic equipment that supposedly assessed their "true" feelings. Carver et al. found that evaluations of both the black and handicapped interviewee were more favorable than those of the nonstigmatized interviewee when assessed via a standard questionnaire. In contrast, when subjects believed that the experimenter could access their "true" feelings, evaluations of the black interviewee were substantially more negative than those of the nonstigmatized interviewee. Evaluations of the physically handicapped interviewee, however, continued to be more positive than those of the nonstigmatized interviewee. Thus, this study suggests that positive evaluations of blacks often do reflect social desirability concerns, whereas positive evaluations of the physically handicapped may not.

Positive responses to the stigmatized may also be motivated by other concerns, such as sympathy or pity either for the stigmatizing condition, or for its consequences. For example, a nonstigmatized person might be especially kind to a person who is blind, out of sympathy for their plight. Weiner and his colleagues (Weiner, Perry, & Magnusson, 1988) have suggested that stigmas for which people are not held responsible (e.g., a physical handicap, a heart condition) tend to elicit sympathy or pity, and consequently provoke less anger and elicit greater help from others than stigmas for which people are held responsible. Sympathy is often considered a positive response to the stigmatized (cf. Katz, 1981; Weiner, 1990). However, this contributes to attributional ambiguity for the stigmatized, who may wonder whether a kindness indicates that the other genuinely cares for them as an individual, or simply feels sorry for them because of their stigma.

Helping is also considered to be a positive response to the stigmatized by the nonstigmatized (cf. Weiner, 1990). For the stigmatized, however, any situation in which help is received from a nonstigmatized person, especially if the help is unsolicited, may carry with it inherent ambiguity as to *why* the help is being offered, and what it implies for the self. Although unsolicited help may indicate that one is cared for, it may also suggest that the helper assumes the recipient is inferior or deficient. The motives behind help should be most suspect when an offer of help appears to be based solely on one's stigma or group membership. In addition, helping should be perceived as revealing prejudiced attitudes most when the type of help offered is stereotypically associated with a deficit or problem of the stigmatized group (e.g., academic help for blacks, who are stereotyped as academically inferior).

Summary

We have argued that the patterns of feedback and treatment that stigmatized individuals receive from the nonstigmatized create attributional ambiguity for the stigmatized. In the case of negative treatment or outcomes, the stigmatized may be uncertain as to whether the feedback was due to their own personal failings or due to prejudice against them based on their stigma. The case of positive feedback may be even more attributionally ambiguous for the stigmatized. On one hand, they may augment the personal implications of positive feedback or outcomes, believing that it occurred despite the prejudice and discrimination associated with their stigma. Alternatively, they may discount the personal implications of positive feedback, believing that it was motivated by concerns directly linked to their stigma, such as sympathy or pity, the desire not to appear prejudiced, or beliefs that one's stigmatized group is inferior. In the following sections we discuss the affective, self-evaluative, interpersonal, and motivational implications of this attributional ambiguity.

Implications of Attributional Ambiguity

Consequences of Attributional Ambiguity for Affect and Self-Evaluation

We believe that attributional ambiguity has important affective and self-evaluative implications for the stigmatized. By affect we mean temporary states or changes in mood, such as feelings of depression, anxiety, or hostility. By self-evaluation, we refer to both domain-specific evaluations of the self (e.g., evaluations of competence, ability, likability) as well as global self-esteem. We believe that the attributional ambiguity associated with stigma has very different affective and self-evaluative implications, depending on whether the feedback is negative or positive. Accordingly, reactions to negative and positive feedback are discussed separately below.

Reactions to Negative Feedback

Because the stigmatized can attribute negative feedback, treatment, or outcomes to an external cause—prejudice against their stigmatized group— we propose that they may be buffered from the negative affective and self-evaluative implications of this feedback (Crocker & Major, 1989). This hypothesis is consistent with a number of theories of emotion which posit that internal attributions for negative outcomes result in more negative affect and lowered self-esteem than external attributions for negative outcomes (see Abramson, Seligman, & Teasdale, 1978; Scheier & Carver, 1988; Weiner, 1980, 1982, 1985). Empirical research is also consistent with this prediction (e.g., Brewin & Furnham, 1986; Crocker, Alloy, & Kayne, 1988; MacFarland & Ross, 1982; Tennen & Herzberger, 1987; Weiner, Russell, & Lerman, 1978).

Furthermore, results of several studies are supportive of our hypothesis that attributing negative feedback to one's membership in a stigmatized group, rather than to oneself, may buffer or attenuate the affective implications of this feedback (see Dion, 1986, for a review). For example, in one study, females received negative feedback from a male evaluator. Following receipt of this feedback, those women who believed that they had been discriminated against were higher in self-esteem than were those who did not believe that they had been discriminated against (Dion, 1975; see also Dion & Earn, 1975). The results of this internal analysis are consistent with the notion that attributing negative outcomes to prejudice against one's group protects self-esteem. They are also consistent, however, with the hypothesis that people who are initially high in self-esteem are more likely to attribute negative outcomes to prejudice against their group. More direct evidence was provided in two recent studies by Crocker, Voelkl, Testa, & Major (1991).

In our first study, female students were asked to write an essay that they believed would be subsequently evaluated by a male peer. Prior to writing the essay, the subjects exchanged "opinion questionnaires" with the evaluator. For some students, the evaluator's answers to several items in the questionnaire indicated that he had negative attitudes toward women, whereas for other students, he indicated positive attitudes. For example, in the "prejudiced" condition, the evaluator indicated agreement with statements such as "women should avoid fields like engineering because they lack mathematical ability," "women benefit more from divorce than men do because they receive child support and alimony," and "women, who are less serious about their jobs, are taking jobs away from men with families to support." The "nonprejudiced evaluator" disagreed with these statements.

Women later heard the evaluator give either a positive or a negative evaluation of their essay over an audio system (it was actually prerecorded). We then measured attributions for the feedback, changes in global self-esteem [assessed with the Rosenberg Self-esteem Scale (Rosenberg, 1965)], and affect [depression, anxiety, and hostility, assessed with the Multiple Affect Adjective Checklist (Zuckerman & Lubin, 1965)]. Consistent with our attribution predictions, a negative essay evaluation was more likely to be attributed to the evaluator's attitudes toward women if he had expressed negative attitudes toward women ($M = 4.15$ on a 7-point scale) than if he had expressed positive attitudes toward women ($M = 2.33$, $p < .05$).

Furthermore, consistent with our hypothesis that being able to attribute negative feedback to prejudice would buffer or attenuate the affective implications of this feedback, women who received negative feedback experienced less depressed affect if the evaluator had unfavorable attitudes toward women ($M = 8.54$) than if he had favorable attitudes ($M = 11.53$, $p < .05$). Self-esteem also tended to drop when negative feedback was received from a nonprejudiced evaluator, but not when received from a prejudiced evaluator, although these means did not differ significantly. Regardless of whether the evaluator was prejudiced or not, however, women who received negative feedback were more hostile and derogated the evaluator more than women who received positive feedback. Thus, it appeared that all women who received negative feedback felt angry, but only those who could not attribute the feedback to prejudice internalized the feedback.

Our second study provided a conceptual replication and extension of this study (Crocker *et al.*, 1991, Experiment 2). Black and white students were led to believe they were participating in a study on friendship development with a white same-sex evaluator, who either could see them (blinds on the one-way mirror were up) or could not see them (blinds were down). After exchanging self-description forms with their (bogus) partner, students received either a very favorable or very unfavorable response from the "other subject." We reasoned that when they received negative feedback, and could be seen by the evaluator, the black students would attribute the feedback to prejudice. We further predicted that in this condition their self-esteem would not suffer, compared to when they could not be seen by the evaluator, and hence could not attribute the negative feedback to prejudice.

The results generally supported our hypotheses. Among black students, the feedback was significantly more likely to be attributed to prejudice when it was negative, rather than positive, and when the blinds were up (and the evaluator could see them) than when the blinds were down (both *F*s were significant for blacks but not for whites). Furthermore, black students were more likely to attribute *both* positive and negative feedback to their personality when they could not be seen ($M = 3.80$) than when they could be seen ($M = 2.89$, $p < .05$). This effect was nonsignificant and in the opposite direction for white students. Thus, these data suggest that black students tend to discount interpersonal feedback from white evaluators when they know that the evaluator is aware of their race, and are especially likely to do so if the feedback is negative. Furthermore, consistent with our self-esteem prediction, analysis of changes in self-esteem indicated that for black students who received negative feedback, self-esteem decreased if they could not be seen by the evaluator, but did *not* decrease when they could be seen by the evaluator (although post-hoc tests did not show a significant difference between these two conditions). No such trend was observed among white students.

Together, these studies provide the clearest evidence to date that the stigmatized will attribute negative outcomes to prejudice against their group when such an attribution is plausible (e.g., when they know that the evaluator has negative attitudes toward their group, and/or when the evaluator is aware of their group membership). Furthermore, this discounting of negative feedback appears to have self-protective consequences for the stigmatized. We would caution, however, that attributing negative outcomes to stigma or to prejudice against one's group may not always be self-protective. For example, when attributing negative feedback to prejudice also produces feelings of helplessness, greater depression may result even though self-esteem may not suffer (Luhtanen, Blaine, & Crocker, 1991). Furthermore, when the stigmatized individual feels that the stigma is justified or feels responsible for the stigma (e.g., when one is stigmatized for being a child abuser, or being alcoholic) then attributions to the stigma or to prejudice may not be self-protective. Following this line of reasoning, a study by Crocker, Cornwell, & Major (1992) found that overweight women were more likely than normal weight women to attribute rejection by an attractive male to their weight, but this did not protect them from feeling depressed. Finally, when stereotypes associated with the stigma are internalized and accepted by the stigmatized individual, attributing negative feedback to the stigma is unlikely to be self-protective (cf. Crocker & Major, 1989).

Reactions to Positive Feedback

Positive feedback is also attributionally ambiguous for the stigmatized. Theory and research suggest that internal attributions for positive outcomes are associated with positive affect and higher self-esteem, whereas external attributions for positive outcomes are associated with more negative affect and lowered self-esteem (cf. Weiner, 1985; MacFarland & Ross, 1982). Thus, when the stigmatized believe they got positive feedback in spite of prejudice against their group, attributions to personal merit may be augmented, and more positive affect, more favorable self-evaluations, and higher self-esteem may result. However, when the stigmatized attribute positive outcomes to aspects of their stigma, rather than to their own personal merits, positive feedback may not only lose its beneficial effects, but actually have detrimental consequences for affect, self-evaluation, and self-esteem.

Results supportive of this latter hypothesis were observed in our study of black and white students' responses to feedback from a white peer, described above (Crocker et al., 1991, Experiment 2). Recall that black students attributed interpersonal feedback (even positive feedback) more to prejudice and less to their own personality when the evaluator could see them than when he/she could not. Consistent with the discounting hypothesis, we found that following positive feedback, the self-esteem of blacks increased when they could not be seen by the evaluator ($M = .40$), but decreased if they could be seen ($M = -.50, p < .05$). This pattern was not observed for whites. Apparently, the black students discounted positive feedback from a white evaluator who knew their race as due to prejudice, and this actually led to decreases in self-esteem. In contrast, the responses of women to positive feedback from a male peer in our first study did not show this pattern (Crocker et al., 1991, Experiment 1). In that study, regardless of whether the evaluator had expressed favorable or unfavorable attitudes toward women, women who received positive feedback were equally unlikely to attribute his evaluation to his attitudes toward women. Furthermore, when the feedback was positive, the evaluator's attitudes had no effect on women's depressed affect or self-esteem. Taken together, the results of these two studies suggest that the stigmatized may be particularly vulnerable following positive feedback, but only when the cause of that feedback is attributed to one's stigmatized status, such as prejudice against one's group.

One implication of our analysis is that behaviors of the nonstigmatized toward the stigmatized that are well intentioned or genuinely supportive, but which are seen as based on stigma or attributed to membership in a stigmatized group, may have unintended negative consequences for the stigmatized. For example, being the object of pity or sympathy may be a mixed blessing. A study by Graham (1984) is consistent with this hypothesis. She manipulated how black and white children were responded to by an evaluator after failing a task. She found that regardless of race, children who were responded to with sympathy made lower ability self-ascriptions and showed a greater decline in expectancy for future success than children who were responded to with either anger or no affective reaction. This study suggests that if the stigmatized attribute positive reactions of others to sympathy or pity, this may result in more negative self-evaluations and more depressed affect.

Reactions to Being Helped

Like pity, help may also be a mixed blessing. On one hand, help may be supportive, transmitting the positive message that the helper genuinely cares for and is concerned about the recipient or that the recipient has earned the help through his or her merits (such as a scholarship). On the other hand, being helped may threaten the self-esteem of the recipient, because it suggests the inferiority of the recipient. Nadler and Fisher (1986) demonstrated that help that is perceived as supportive leads to an increase in positive feelings about the self, whereas help perceived as threatening leads to negative feelings about the self and a variety of defensive behaviors.

As we noted above, the motives behind help should be most suspected when an offer of help appears to be based solely on stigma or group membership and/or when the type of help offered is associated with a stereotyped deficit or problem of the stigmatized group. These types of help may also be most likely to threaten the self-concept and self-esteem of a stigmatized individual. For example, in a recent paper discussing the problems of black children in American schools, Claude Steele (1992) has argued that recruitment and admission policies to schools that emphasize minority status and services that are based solely on minority status imply to their recipients that they are an "at risk" group. Furthermore, he proposes that programs intended to be helpful but which emphasize first and foremost the need for remediation create a climate of "suspicion of inferiority" for their recipients. Hence, unless helping occurs in unambiguously supportive contexts, free of the suspicion of inferiority, receiving help may threaten the self-concept of the stigmatized more than the nonstigmatized.

Schneider, Major, Luhtanen, & Crocker (1991) recently found support for this hypothesis. In this study, black and white students were led to believe they were paired with a white same-sex partner via an exchange of picture student ID cards. All were told they were participating in a study assessing verbal-spatial abilities and that they would work individually on a first test, and jointly with their partner on a second test. Subjects were informed that neither partner would learn each other's score on the first test. Subjects then completed the first test, which involved unscrambling as many anagrams as they could in 10 minutes, and were subsequently told that their score on the first test was "OK." Thus, in this study, unlike prior studies of recipients' reactions to help (see Nadler & Fisher, 1986), the subjects' own score was adequate rather than inferior to the partner's, and the partner did not know the subjects' score. All subjects then completed a "student interest" questionnaire, and were given the same questionnaire ostensibly completed by their partner. This contained the help/no help manipulation. For half of the subjects, the "partner" handwrote a note at the bottom of the questionnaire stating "You might do better next time if you knew there was a pattern to the anagrams on this last task—all the odd ones unscramble in the same way, and so do all the even ones." For the other half of the students no note was included from the partner, thus no help was received.

We predicted that more negative affect and lowered self-esteem would be observed among black students who received unsolicited help compared to white students who received unsolicited help. Analyses of subsequent self-esteem and depression scores were consistent with this hypothesis. Black students who received help had significantly lower self-esteem and tended to be more depressed than black students who did not receive help, whereas white students' self-esteem and depression scores did not vary as a function of whether or not they were helped. Self-esteem was lowest and depressed affect highest among black students who received help. Thus, this study suggests that unsolicited help may backfire if the help is attributed to stigma or is believed to reflect the helper's assumptions that one is inferior because of one's stigma.

Recent research on women's reactions to preferential selection policies based on sex also is consistent with this hypothesis. Certain programs and policies, such as affirmative action, are designed to overcome past histories of discrimination against certain groups. Although there are many effective ways in which such programs may be implemented (see Blanchard & Crosby, 1989), one way in which such programs are sometimes believed to be implemented is by giving individuals who are members of disadvantaged groups preferential treatment based primarily on their group membership. Our analysis suggests that this policy may have some unintended negative consequences in addition to the obvious positive consequences for its beneficiaries. Results of several studies are consistent with this hypothesis. For example, Chacko (1982) found that women managers who believed that they were hired for their positions because of their sex had lower organizational commitment and job satisfaction and higher role stress than women who did not attribute their positions to their sex. The correlational nature of this study, however, does not demonstrate that attributions to group membership caused less organizational commitment among these women.

Several role-play studies have explored this question more directly. Nacoste (1985) asked women to imagine themselves in the position of a female professor who received a grant over a male professor under one of several conditions. Some subjects were told that sex was the primary criterion for selection; others were told that both sex and qualifications were taken into account. Subjects who were told that sex was the primary criterion reported significantly less positive affect than those who were told that both sex and qualifications mattered. Taylor and Dube (1986) asked subjects to place themselves in the position of an actor in a series of vignettes, and to imagine how they would feel in response to receiving either positive or negative feedback directed against a component of personal identity (i.e., attributes unique to the individual) or social identity (i.e., gender, race, or ethnolinguistic group). For example, subjects indicated how angry and satisfied they would feel if they were denied (or given), a position because of their race (or personal qualifications). Regardless of whether the feedback was positive or negative, subjects said they would feel more anger and less satisfaction when feedback was directed at their social identity than at their personal identity; this difference, however, was especially pronounced in the case of positive feedback. Taylor and Dube observed that, "subjects note subtle distinctions about the meaning of positive feedback and tend to ignore subtleties in negative feedback" (p. 90). It is possible, however, that both the role-play nature of the experiment and the particular affective measures used may have masked differences in response to negative feedback based on personal versus social identity characteristics.

Several recent experiments by Heilman and her colleagues have examined recipients' reactions to preferential selection based on sex without using a role-playing methodology. Heilman, Simon, & Repper (1987) led men and women to believe that they were selected for a leadership role over an opposite-sex confederate either because they had scored higher than the confederate on a pretest measure of leadership ability, or because the experimenter needed more males (or females) in the leadership position. Subjects subsequently were led to believe that they either succeeded or failed on the leadership task. Heilman et al. (1987) found that women's, but not men's, self-perceptions and self-evaluations were negatively affected by the sex-based preferential selection method relative to the merit-based method. When selected only on the basis of sex, women devalued their leadership performance, reported less interest in persisting as a leader, and characterized themselves as more deficient in general leadership skills, regardless of whether they had succeeded or failed. Men's self-evaluations were generally unaffected by method of selection.

In a second study, Heilman, Lucas, & Kaplow (1990) tested the hypothesis that preferential selection procedures create ambiguity about competence and most adversely affect those who initially lack confidence in their ability to perform the job well. This study repeated the sex versus merit conditions of their first study, but added two additional selection conditions. In one, men and women privately received high scores on the pretest measure of leadership ability, thereby leading them to have high confidence in their ability. In a second condition, men and women privately received low scores on the pretest ability measure. Results replicated the findings of Heilman et al. (1987) in that in the absence of ability feedback, preferential selection based only on sex had detrimental effects on women's evaluation of their leadership ability compared to selection based on merit, but did not affect men's self-evaluations. Importantly, however, this study also showed the critical role of self-perceptions of ability in producing these effects. When provided with positive information about task-related ability, women selected preferentially did not differ in self-view from those selected on the basis of merit. And when provided with negative information about task-related ability, men selected preferentially did evidence more negative self-views than those selected on the basis of merit. This study is important because it suggests that preferential selection policies will not be detrimental for the self-evaluations of their recipients if they are combined with clear feedback that the recipient is competent for the job. The gender differences observed by Heilman *et al.* (1987, 1990) are consistent with our argument that positive outcomes (in this case being awarded the leadership role) are particularly likely to have negative self-evaluative implications for recipients when they are perceived to be based on group membership and are accompanied by the perception that one's group is (or is believed to be) inferior on the dimension on which help is offered.

Summary

In summary, we have argued that the attributional ambiguity that accompanies being stigmatized can have both positive and negative affective and self-evaluative implications for the stigmatized. Attributing negative feedback or treatment to one's stigma or membership in a stigmatized group may buffer the affective and self-evaluative implications of negative outcomes. Affective and self-evaluative reactions to positive feedback or treatment, however, depend on whether the feedback or treatment is seen as having occurred in spite of or because of one's stigma or membership in a stigmatized group. In the former case, positive affect and favorable self-evaluations should be enhanced. When positive feedback or treatment is seen as occurring because of one's stigma or membership in a stigmatized group, however, the affective and self-evaluative implications of positive outcomes may be attenuated and perhaps even undercut.

Although the primary focus of our analysis and of our research thus far has been on the implications of stigma for affect and self-evaluation, the framework that we have proposed also has interesting implications for motivation and the management of interpersonal interactions. We will consider each of these briefly in the next sections.

Consequences of Attributional Ambiguity for Interpersonal Interaction Strategies

The stigmatized do not merely react passively to the behaviors of others toward them. They may manage their interpersonal interactions in a variety of ways to minimize potentially negative consequences of their stigma. For example, they may avoid situations in which they are particularly likely to be disadvantaged due to their stigmatizing condition, or selectively affiliate with others who share their stigma. We suggest that the stigmatized may also under some circumstances manage their interactions so as to take advantage of the attributional ambiguity that stigma affords in an effort to regulate their affect and protect their self-esteem.

One way the stigmatized may manage the attributional implications of their stigma is by revealing it to or concealing it from others. Stigmas differ considerably in the extent to which they are easily concealed from others (see Jones et al., 1984). Some, such as a learning disability or a past history of mental illness, may be quite concealable; others, such as race or severe physical handicaps, may be readily apparent. Interaction settings also differ in the extent to which they allow a stigma to be concealed from others (Jones et al., 1984). In some situations, such as in applications materials for schools or jobs, or other written communications, even individuals with obvious stigmas may be able, if they choose, to withhold information about their stigmatizing condition. In other situations, such as face-to-face interactions, some stigmatizing conditions cannot be concealed.

Whether it is preferable to conceal or reveal a stigma is a matter of some debate. Some research suggests that individuals with concealable stigmas experience (and expect) more satisfactory social encounters than those whose stigmas are visible (Kleck, 1968). For example, Farina, Gliha, Boudreau, Allen, & Sherman (1971) found that individuals who believed that their interaction partner was aware of their stigma behaved less competently (i.e., were more tense and uncomfortable and acted so as to alienate the partner) than individuals who believed their stigma was not known to their partner. Other researchers (e.g., Shears & Jensema, 1969; English, 1971), however, have suggested that visible stigmas are preferable to concealed ones. Individuals whose stigmas are concealed are denied the benefits of the attributional self-protective strategy, should negative feedback or outcomes occur (Crocker & Major, 1989). That is, if an evaluator who is unaware of one's stigma evaluates one negatively, the ability to discount this feedback as due to stigma is blocked. This analysis suggests that stigmatized individuals who anticipate negative feedback or outcomes may sometimes choose to reveal their stigma to others, and risk rejection, in order to provide an "excuse" for the anticipated negative outcomes.

A substantial amount of research (e.g., DeGree & Snyder, 1985; Smith, Snyder, & Handelsman, 1982; Smith, Snyder, & Perkins, 1983; Snyder, Smith, Augelli, & Ingram, 1985) has shown that individuals who fear failure on an impending performance may claim symptoms (such as shyness, test anxiety) as handicaps unless they are told that these excuses are not plausible (see Arkin & Baumgardner, 1985; Leary & Shepperd, 1986, for reviews). We hypothesize that membership in a stigmatized group may also be used self-protectively under similar circumstances. It is important to note that group membership may serve as a plausible excuse for both stigmatized and nonstigmatized individuals. However, this is probably a more prevalent self-protective strategy among the stigmatized, because people are more likely to make the assumption that their stigma inhibits rather than enhances their performance (at least in the eyes of others).

But what if a stigmatized individual expects positive outcomes, feedback, or treatment? Based on the analysis we have presented here, we predict that under some circumstances (such as when positive outcomes may be attributable to stigmatized group membership, or to the ulterior motives of another, such as the desire to avoid appearing prejudiced), the stigmatized may go to great pains to conceal their stigma, so that positive outcomes will not be discounted and will be unambiguously attributed to personal deservedness. Under other conditions (such as when it is clear that positive outcomes will be seen as occurring in spite of stigmatized status), the stigmatized may be particularly eager to make their stigmatized status known, and hence exploit the augmenting principle.

Consequences of Attributional Ambiguity for Motivation

The attributional ambiguity created by stigma may also have a variety of implications for motivation. First, when the stigmatized suspect that positive feedback or outcomes are due to their stigma (such as their membership in a disadvantaged group, or the desire of an evaluator to avoid appearing prejudiced), rather than to their true ability, they may be particularly vulnerable to engaging in self-handicapping behaviors. According to the self-handicapping framework, individuals who are uncertain as to why they have succeeded and who fear failure may sometimes handicap their performance, rather than risk the more esteem-damaging attribution that they have low ability (see Arkin & Baumgardner, 1985, for a review). Research has shown that males who receive noncontingent positive feedback, or who are uncertain about their ability to maintain a positive performance, will sometimes engage in behavior, such as taking performance-inhibiting drugs (e.g., Berglas & Jones, 1978) that actually decreases their chances of successful outcomes.

Our analysis suggests that a similar process may apply when the stigmatized receive positive feedback that is ambiguous as to its cause. That is, the ambiguity of positive feedback for the stigmatized may be akin to uncertainty surrounding positive outcomes. For example, recall that Crocker *et al.* (1991, Experiment 2) found that blacks who received positive feedback with the blinds up felt a high degree of uncertainty regarding the reasons for this positive feedback, whereas blacks who received positive feedback with the blinds down appeared quite certain that the feedback was due to their positive qualities. Thus, for blacks in this situation, getting positive feedback from a white evaluator who knew their race may be analogous to receiving noncontingent success feedback. Similarly, individuals who are unsure as to whether they have been hired, promoted, or admitted to an organization or school on the basis of their own merits or because of their group membership might also be vulnerable to self-handicapping if they are uncertain of their ability to maintain a successful performance.

Second, because the feedback and treatment they receive from others is often attributionally ambiguous, the stigmatized may find it difficult to predict their future outcomes, and to select tasks of a difficulty level that is appropriate to their ability.[1] That is, because alternative attributions may exist both for negative outcomes and for positive outcomes, the stigmatized may regard feedback and outcomes as not particularly diagnostic of their true ability. When positive or negative outcomes are attributed to stigma or membership in a stigmatized group, the stigmatized may be less certain of how they will do on other tasks, and be less responsive to the feedback they receive. This should not be true, however, when feedback is not attributed to group membership, such as when it is received from an evaluator who is unaware of one's stigmatized status.

Third, to the extent that the stigmatized believe that their outcomes are determined by their stigma or membership in a stigmatized group, rather than by their own efforts or abilities, their motivation may be undermined. Although the attribution of negative feedback to causes that are external and not under one's personal control (such as the prejudice of others) may protect self-esteem, it may also undermine the belief that greater personal effort will lead to better outcomes. A large literature demonstrating behavioral deficits associated with learned helplessness is consistent with this proposition (cf. Abramson et al., 1978). The attribution of positive outcomes to one's membership in a stigmatized group, rather than to one's personal deservedness, may also undermine motivation. As noted above, Chacko (1982) found that women managers who attributed their managerial position to their sex reported lower organizational commitment than those who did not, and Heilman et al. (1987) found that women who were awarded a leadership role based on their sex reported less interest in persisting as a leader than women who were awarded the role based on their merit. Claude Steele's (1992) recent analysis of black children's school achievement is consistent with these findings. As noted above, he has argued that programs aimed at disadvantaged groups which are intended to be supportive but which convey to their recipients that they are an inferior and "at risk" group stigmatize the recipients of these programs. Furthermore, he has argued that stigmatization based on group membership can break black students' identification with school and undermine their motivation to achieve at school. Attributing positive outcomes to sympathy or pity may exert a similar effect. Graham (1984) found that children whose prior failures were responded to with sympathy had lower expectancies for subsequent success than children whose failures were met with anger or no affective reaction. Taken together, these studies are consistent with the hypothesis that the attributional ambiguity experienced by the stigmatized may have detrimental consequences for their motivation.

[1]We are grateful to Russell Fazio for this suggestion.

Determinants of Attributional Ambiguity

In the preceding sections we have argued that compared to the nonstigmatized, the stigmatized are more likely to experience attributional ambiguity as to the causes of the interpersonal treatment and feedback they receive. Furthermore, we have suggested that this state of attributional ambiguity may be fairly chronic, in that stigmatized individuals may show a consistent tendency to see others' reactions to them as affected by their stigma (Goffman, 1963; Wright, 1960). A variety of factors, however, are likely to affect the extent to which treatment, feedback, or outcomes will be attributed to one's stigma, or membership in a stigmatized group.

One factor is whether or not the person responsible for the feedback is believed to be aware of one's stigmatized status. Without such awareness, an attribution to stigma is implausible. Awareness of the stigma might be due to characteristics of the interaction situation. Experimental manipulations such as raising or lowering blinds on a one-way mirror, or exchanging or not exchanging photographs, attempt to capture this factor (e.g., Major et al., 1984; Crocker et al., 1991). In a related vein, some stigmas are more visually obvious than others. Stigmas such as those due to sexual orientation, learning disabilities, or a past history of mental illness cannot be seen by others; hence others are frequently unaware of the stigma. Other stigmas, such as facially disfiguring conditions, obesity, or a physical disability that requires a wheelchair are visible to others. In general, because others are more likely to be aware of clearly visible stigmas, they should be associated with more attributional ambiguity than concealed stigmas.

Another factor that affects the likelihood of attributing feedback to one's stigma is whether or not the agent responsible is believed to have ulterior motives for responding in a particular way. For example, negative feedback or outcomes are more easily attributable to stigmatized group status if the giver is known to be prejudiced against one's group (Crocker et al., 1991, Experiment 1), or if an organization has a known history of discrimination against one's group. Similarly, positive feedback may be more readily attributed to stigmatized status if the giver is assumed to have ulterior motives for giving this feedback, such as a desire not to appear prejudiced (Crocker et al., 1991, Experiment 2). Positive feedback is unlikely to be attributed to one's stigma, and may be augmented if the giver has no apparent ulterior motives for giving positive feedback (e.g., Major et al., 1984). This analysis suggests that attributional ambiguity may be more pronounced among individuals who are members of stigmatized groups which have experienced a strong history of prejudice and discrimination coupled with salient social norms prohibiting prejudice and discrimination against that group. For members of these groups, both negative and positive feedback are ambiguous.

Although the relationship between treatment or outcomes and one's membership in a stigmatized group is often ambiguous, sometimes it is fairly explicit. The more explicit the relationship, the more outcomes should be attributed to stigma or group membership. For example, some types of intellectual tests are widely believed to be biased against certain ethnic and racial groups and/or women. Members of these groups should discount poor performances on tests believed to be culturally biased and augment successes on such tests. In addition, the more that selection procedures explicitly give preference to members of certain disadvantaged groups, the more that positive outcomes should be attributionally ambiguous for members of these groups. Being admitted, hired, or promoted under these programs may be attributed to one's group status rather than one's personal deservedness, leading members of these groups to discount their success (e.g., Heilman *et al.*, 1987). Alternatively, positive outcomes that occur in the face of blatant prejudice against one's group should be augmented, leading members of disadvantaged groups who "succeed against the odds" to feel especially deserving of their outcomes.

In sum, although attributional ambiguity is generally more characteristic of the stigmatized than the nonstigmatized, certain situational and stigma-related factors may exacerbate or attenuate it.

Alternative Sources of Attributional Ambiguity

Thus far we have focused on the subjective experience of being a member of a stigmatized or oppressed social category. We have proposed that people who are stigmatized or members of stigmatized groups experience more attributional ambiguity about the causes of the interpersonal treatment and outcomes they receive than do those who are not so stigmatized. Although we believe that the stigmatized may experience more chronic attributional ambiguity than those who are not stigmatized, the theoretical framework that we have proposed may be more broadly applied to people who are members of other types of social categories, or who are responded to on the basis of their membership in a social group.

For example, our attributional ambiguity framework may be applied to understand the subjective experiences of those who are statistically deviant in the larger culture by virtue of having a culturally valued, rather than stigmatized, characteristic (e.g., the exceptionally attractive, athletic, or wealthy; see Frable, Blackstone, & Scherbaum, 1990). Like stigmas, culturally valued "marks" are associated with valenced stereotypes (in this case generally positive stereotypes), and often trigger stereotype-consistent behavior (cf. Berscheid & Walster, 1978). For individuals who possess culturally valued marks, positive feedback may be especially attributionally ambiguous. That is, these individuals may be uncertain whether others' favorable reactions to them are genuine or reflect ulterior motives. Similarly, they may be unsure whether they have earned their positive outcomes through their personal efforts or talents, or were accorded them because of their culturally valued mark.

For example, Sigall and Michela (1976) found that physically attractive women were more disparaging of the character of a male evaluator who rated them positively when he had seen them than when he had not. Similarly, Major *et al.* (1984) found that highly attractive individuals of both sexes were less likely to attribute a positive essay evaluation from an opposite-sex evaluator to the quality of their work when they had been seen by the evaluator than when they had not been seen by him or her. These studies suggest that for individuals with culturally valued marks, positive feedback is ambiguous and is likely to be discounted. Similarly, Berglas (1986) has argued that the very rich and very famous have difficulty forming trusting relationships with those they come in contact with because they fear that people may feign liking them in order to benefit from their power or influence. Likewise, he noted the attributional ambiguity that surrounds the achievements of those who are children or spouses of famous people, or who are exceptionally beautiful, commenting that for these individuals there are "very obvious explanations for desired outcomes apart from their personal or "inner" attributes" (p. 104). Berglas (1986) proposed that these individuals, in part because of the uncertainty and ambiguity surrounding their successes, are particularly vulnerable to engaging in self-handicapping behaviors.

Our analysis may also be applied to situations in which people feel they are being responded to on the basis of their membership in a particular social group, rather than on the basis of their personal deservedness. For example, attributional ambiguity may characterize many situations in which individuals from different social groups interact, regardless of the stigmatized status of the groups. Research on ingroup bias reveals that categorization of individuals into groups often leads to the tendency to evaluate the ingroup more positively than the outgroup, and to discriminate in favor of ingroup members and against outgroup members (cf. Brewer, 1979; Wilder, 1986, for reviews). Consequently, in intergroup interactions, it may be unclear whether feedback or treatment received from outgroup members is based on one's individual characteristics (personal identity) or one's group membership (social identity). Because ingroup bias is more pronounced when group boundaries are salient to the interactants, the more salient the group boundaries, the more attributional ambiguity should result.

Simply being different from others, however, should not be enough to generate attributional ambiguity. Rather, the analysis that we have proposed assumes that attributional ambiguity arises because a particular attribute or group membership is associated with a set of stereotyped beliefs which are valenced, that is, which make a person more or less valued.

Individuals experience attributional ambiguity in their interactions with others when they are aware of others' stereotypes about their attributes or group membership and have some knowledge of the content and valence of these stereotypes. Thus, for example, it is unlikely that a student majoring in Art would experience attributional ambiguity in her interactions with students majoring in Psychology unless she believed that Psychology majors held particular positive or negative stereotypes about Art majors. Similarly, differences in group membership will not necessarily produce attributional ambiguity unless there is a belief that one is being devalued (or preferred) simply because of one's group membership.

In sum, central to our framework is a distinction between feedback, treatment, or outcomes that are attributed to "inner" attributes such as personality, effort, or ability versus those that are attributed to more "external" or "superficial" attributes such as membership in a particular social category or physical characteristics. Whenever situational or personal factors make it unclear whether feedback or outcomes should be attributed to "external" features of a person (e.g., stigma, family wealth, group membership), or to personal deservedness based on "inner" attributes, attributional ambiguity is heightened.

Conclusions and Directions

Most research on social stigma has been devoted to understanding the reactions of the nonstigmatized to the stigmatized. Relatively little research has focused on the subjective experience of members of stigmatized groups. We believe that a full understanding of social stigma requires an understanding of the phenomenology of being stigmatized. In this chapter we have argued that an important consequence of membership in a stigmatized group is ambiguity regarding whether one's outcomes are due to one's personal characteristics and deservedness, or to one's stigmatizing condition. Furthermore, we have argued that this ambiguity can have a variety of affective, motivational, and interpersonal consequences for the stigmatized individual. Although some of these consequences are beneficial, such as the protection of self-esteem afforded by attributing negative feedback or outcomes to prejudice, others are not, such as the affective and motivational decrements that may accompany attributing positive feedback to external rather than internal factors.

Research is needed to better understand how the negative implications of attributional ambiguity can be overcome. For example, one major question for future research is how help can be offered to the disadvantaged without threatening their views of their own competence or undermining their self-esteem or motivation. Clearly, help has many beneficial consequences. For example, without affirmative action programs and special academic and financial support programs, many talented women and minorities would not have had an opportunity to realize their talents and excel at school or work. One key to answering this question, according to Steele (1992), is the establishment of a "wise" environment, that is, a place where the stigmatized feel free from suspicion of inferiority and feel like valued people with good prospects. In the context of the schooling of black children, Steele argues that schools should emphasize students' potential and value *as individuals,* not their membership in a category of people explicitly or implicitly in need of remediation. Similarly, Heilman *et al's.,* (1990) research suggests that preferential help may not hurt if it is accompanied by the perception that one is individually qualified irrespective of group membership. Another issue for future research concerns the long-term implications of attributional ambiguity for the stigmatized. Although our research has focused on short-term implications of attributional ambiguity for affect and self-evaluation, we believe that attributional ambiguity also will have long-term implications for affect and motivation and for the interpersonal interaction strategies adopted by the stigmatized.

To conclude, we believe that recognizing attributional ambiguity, clarifying the conditions that foster and reduce it, and understanding the implications of this ambiguity may help to facilitate interactions between the stigmatized and the nonstigmatized, and assist in the design of more effective interventions intended to benefit the stigmatized.

Acknowledgment

Preparation of this manuscript was supported by National Science Foundation Grant BNS 9010487 to J. Crocker and B. Major.

References

Abramson, L. Y., Seligman, M. E. P., & Teasdale, J. (1978). Learned helplessness in humans: Critique and reformulation. *Journal of Abnormal Psychology, 87,* 49–74.

Arkin, R. M., & Baumgardner, A. H. (1985). Self-handicapping. In J. Harvey & G. Weary (Eds.), *Attribution: Basic issues and applications* (pp. 169–202). New York: Academic Press.

Berglas, S. (1986). *The success syndrome.* New York: Plenum.

Berglas, S., & Jones, E. E. (1978). Drug choice as a self-handicapping strategy in response to noncontingent success. *Journal of Personality and Social Psychology, 36,* 405–417.

Berscheid, E., & Walster, E. (1978). *Interpersonal attraction.* Reading, MA: Addison-Wesley.

Blanchard, F. A., & Crosby, F. J. (Eds.). (1989). *Affirmative action in perspective.* New York: Springer-Verlag.

Brewer, M. B. (1979). Ingroup bias in the minimal intergroup situation: A cognitive-motivational analysis. *Psychological Bulletin, 86,* 207–224.

Brewin, C. R., & Furnham, A. (1986). Attributional versus preattributional variables in self-esteem and depression: A comparison and test of learned helplessness theory. *Journal of Personality and Social Psychology, 50,* 1013–1020.

Carver, C. S., Glass, D. C., Snyder, M. L., & Katz, I. (1977). Favorable evaluations of stigma-tized others. *Personality and Social Psychology Bulletin, 3,* 232–235.

Carver, C. S., Glass, D. C., & Katz, I. (1978). Favorable evaluations of blacks and the handi-capped: Positive prejudice, unconscious denial, or social desirability? *Journal of Applied Social Psychology, 8,* 97–106.

Chacko, T. I., (1982). Women and equal employment opportunity: Some unintended effects. *Journal of Applied Psychology, 67,* 119–123.

Crocker, J., & Major, B. (1989). Social stigma and self-esteem: The self-protective properties of stigma. *Psychological Review, 96,* 608–630.

Crocker, J., Alloy, L. B., & Kayne, N. T. (1988). Attributional style, depression, and percep-tions of consensus for events. *Journal of Personality and Social Psychology, 54,* 840–846.

Crocker, J., Cornwell, B., & Major, B. (1992). The stigma of overweight: The affective conse-quences of attributional ambiguity. Manuscript in preparation.

Crocker, J., Voelkl, K., Testa, M., & Major, B. (1991). Social stigma: The affective conse-quences of attributional ambiguity. *Journal of Personality and Social Psychology, 60,* 218–228.

Crosby, F. J. (1982). *Relative deprivation and working women.* New York, NY: Oxford Uni-versity Press.

Crosby, F. J., Bromley, S., & Saxe, L. (1980). Recent unobtrusive studies of black and white discrimination and prejudice: A literature review. *Psychological Bulletin, 87,* 546–563.

DeGree, C. E., & Snyder, C. R. (1985). Adler's psychology of use today: Personal history of traumatic life events as a self-handicapping strategy. *Journal of Personality and Social Psychology, 48,* 1512–1519.

Dion, K. L. (1975). Women's reactions to discrimination from members of the same or oppo-site sex. *Journal of Research in Personality, 9,* 294–306.

Dion, K. L. (1986). Responses to perceived discrimination and relative deprivation. In J. M. Olson, C. P. Herman, & M. P. Zanna (Eds.), *Relative deprivation and social comparison: The Ontario symposium* (Vol. 4, pp. 159–179). Hillsdale, NJ: Erlbaum.

Dion, K. L., & Earn, B. M. (1975). The phenomenology of being a target of prejudice. *Journal of Personality and Social Psychology, 32,* 944–950.

English, R. W. (1971). Correlates of stigma towards physically disabled persons. *Rehabilita-tion Research and Practice Review, 2,* 1–17.

Farina, A., Gliha, D., Boudreau, L. A., Allen, J. G., & Sherman, M. (1971). Mental illness and the impact of believing others know about it. *Journal of Abnormal Psychology, 77,* 1–5.

Frable, D., Blackstone, T., & Scherbaum, C. (1990). Marginal and mindful: Deviants in social interaction. *Journal of Personality and Social Psychology, 59,* 140–149.

Gaertner, S. L., & Dovidio, J. F. (1977). The subtlety of white racism, arousal, and helping be-havior. *Journal of Personality and Social Psychology, 35,* 691–707.

Gaertner, S. L., & Dovidio, J. F. (1986). The aversive form of racism. In J. F. Dovidio & S. L. Gaertner (Eds.), *Prejudice, discrimination, and racism* (pp. 61–90). Orlando, FL: Acade-mic Press.

Goffman, E. (1963). *Stigma: Notes on the management of spoiled identity.* Englewood Cliffs, NJ: Prentice-Hall.

Graham, S. (1984). Communicating sympathy and anger to black and white children: The cognitive (attributional) consequences of affective cues. *Journal of Personality and Social Psychology, 47,* 40–54.

Heilman, M. E., Simon, M. C., & Repper, D. P. (1987). Intentionally favored, unintentionally harmed? Impact of sex-based preferential selection on self-perceptions and self-evalua-tions. *Journal of Applied Psychology, 72,* 62–68.

Heilman, M. E., Lucas, J. A., & Kaplow, S. R. (1990). Self-derogating consequences of prefer-ential selection: The moderating role of initial self-confidence. *Organizational Behavior and Human Decision Process, 46,* 202–216.

Jones, E. E., Farina, A., Hastorf, A. H., Markus, H., Miller, D. T., & Scott, R. A. (1984). *Social stigma: The psychology of marked relationships*. New York: Freeman.

Katz, I. (1981). *Stigma: A social psychological analysis*. Hillsdale, NJ: Erlbaum.

Katz, I., Wackenhut, J., & Hass, R. G. (1986). Racial ambivalence, value duality, and behavior. In J. F. Dovidio & S. L. Gaertner (Eds.), *Prejudice, discrimination, and racism* (pp. 35–60). Orlando, FL: Academic Press.

Kelley, H. H. (1972). Causal schemata and the attribution process. In E. E. Jones, D. E. Kanouse, H. H. Kelley, R. E. Nisbett, S. Valins, & B. Weiner (Eds.), *Attribution: Perceiving the causes of behavior*, (pp. 151–176). Morrison, NJ: General Learning Press.

Kleck, R. E. (1968). Self-disclosure patterns of the nonobviously stigmatized. *Psychological Reports, 23*, 1239–1248.

Kleck, R. E., & Strenta, A. (1980). Perceptions of the impact of negatively valued physical characteristics on social interaction. *Journal of Personality and Social Psychology, 39*, 861–873.

Kleck, R., Ono, H., & Hastorf, A. H. (1966). The effects of physical deviance upon face-to-face interaction. *Human Relations, 19*, 425–436.

Leary, M. R., & Shepperd, J. A. (1986). Behavioral self-handicaps versus self-reported handicaps: A conceptual note. *Journal of Personality and Social Psychology, 51*, 1265–1268.

Linville, P., & Jones, E. E. (1980). Polarized appraisals of outgroup members. *Journal of Personality and Social Psychology, 38*, 689–703.

Luhtanen, R., Blaine, B., & Crocker, J. (1991). *Personal and Collective Self-esteem and Depression in African-American and White Students*. Paper presented at the annual meeting of the Eastern Psychological Association, New York.

MacFarland, C., & Ross, M. (1982). Impact of causal attributions on affective reactions to success and failure. *Journal of Personality and Social Psychology, 43*, 937–946.

Major, B., Carrington, P. I., & Carnevale, P. (1984). Physical attractiveness and self esteem: Attributions for praise from an other-sex evaluator. *Personality and Social Psychology Bulletin, 10*, 43–50.

Nacoste, R. W. (1985). Selection procedure and responses to affirmative action: The case of favorable treatment. *Law and Human Behavior, 9*, 225–242.

Nadler, A., & Fisher, J. D. (1986). The role of threat to self-esteem and perceived control in recipient reaction to help: Theory development and empirical validation. In L. Berkowitz (Ed.), *Advances in experimental social psychology*. (Vol. 9, pp. 81–122). Orlando, FL: Academic Press.

Rosenberg, M. (1965). *Society and the adolescent self-image*. Princeton, NJ: Princeton University Press.

Scheier, M. F., & Carver, C. S. (1988). A model of behavioral self-regulation: Translating intention into action. In L. Berkowitz (Ed.), *Advances in experimental social psychology*. (Vol. 21, pp. 303–346). New York: Academic Press.

Schneider, M., Major, B., Luhtanen, R., & Crocker, J. (1991). *Social Stigma and Reactions to Help*. Manuscript presented at the meeting of the American Psychological Society, Washington, D.C.

Shears, L. M., & Jensema, C. J. (1969). Social acceptability of anomalous persons. *Exceptional Children, 36*, 91–96.

Sigall, H., & Michela, J. (1976). I'll bet you say that to all the girls: Physical attractiveness and reaction to praise. *Journal of Personality, 44*, 611–626.

Smith, T. W., Snyder, C. R., & Handelsman, M. M. (1982). On the self-serving function of an academic wooden leg: Test anxiety as a self-handicapping strategy. *Journal of Personality and Social Psychology, 42*, 314–321.

Smith, T. W., Snyder, C. R., & Perkins, S. C. (1983). On the self-serving function of hypochondrial complaints: Physical symptoms as self-handicapping strategy. *Journal of Personality and Social Psychology, 44*, 787–797.

Snyder, C. R., Smith, T. W., Augelli, R. W., & Ingram, R. E. (1985). On the self-serving function of social anxiety: Shyness as a self-handicapping strategy. *Journal of Personality and Social Psychology*, **48**, 970–980.

Steele, C. (1992). Race and the schooling of Black Americans. The Atlantic, **269**, No. 4, 68–78.

Taylor, D. M., & Dube, L. (1986). Two faces of identity: The "I" and the "We." *Journal of Social Issues*, **42**, 81–98.

Taylor, D. M., Wright, S. C., Moghaddam, F. M., & Lalonde, R. N. (1990). The personal/group discrimination discrepancy: Perceiving my group, but not myself, to be a target for discrimination. *Personality and Social Psychology Bulletin*, **16**, 254–262.

Tennen, H., & Herzberger, S. (1987). Depression, self-esteem, and the absence of self-protective attributional biases. *Journal of Personality and Social Psychology*, **52**, 72–80.

Weiner, B. (1980). *Human motivation*. New York: Holt, Reinhart, Winston.

Weiner, B. (1982). The emotional consequences of causal attributions. In M. Clark and S. T. Fiske (Eds.), *Affect and cognition: The seventeenth annual Carnegie symposium on cognition*. Hillsdale, NJ: Erlbaum.

Weiner, B. (1985). An attributional theory of achievement motivation and emotion. *Psychological Review*, **92**, 548–573.

Weiner, B. (1990). On perceiving the other as responsible. *Nebraska Symposium on Motivation*. (Vol. 38, pp. 165–198). Lincoln, NE: University of Nebraska Press.

Weiner, B., Russell, D., & Lerman, D. (1978). Affective consequences of causal ascriptions. In J. H. Harvey, W. J. Ickes, & R. F. Kidd (Eds.), *New directions in attribution research*. (Vol. 2, pp. 59–90). Hillsdale, NJ: Erlbaum.

Weiner, B., Perry, R., & Magnusson, J. (1988). An attributional analysis of reactions to stigmas. *Journal of Personality and Social Psychology*, **55**, 738–748.

Wilder, D. A. (1986). Social categorization: Implications for creation and reduction of intergroup bias. In L. Berkowitz (Ed.) *Advances in Experimental Social Psychology* (Vol. 19, pp. 291–355). Orlando, FL: Academic Press.

Wright, B. (1960). *Physical disability: A psychological approach*. New York: Harper & Row.

Zuckerman, M., & Lubin, B. (1965). *Manual for the Multiple Affect Adjective Checklist*. San Diego, CA: Educational and Industrial Testing Service.

Chapter 16

Affect, Cognition, and Stereotyping: Concluding Comments

DIANE M. MACKIE and DAVID L. HAMILTON

Department of Psychology
University of California, Santa Barbara
Santa Barbara, California

In the introduction to this volume, we expressed optimism for the benefits of focusing on affective and cognitive processes as they interacted during social perception, social evaluation, and social behavior. We believe that the richness of the theoretical and empirical advances described in the chapters in this volume justify this optimism. In this concluding commentary we forego the temptation (or challenge) to try to summarize these advances. Instead, our goal in this chapter is to highlight some thoughts and questions about the roles of cognition and affect in intergroup perception that impressed or puzzled us as we thought about these chapters. Our discussion focuses on four issues that, it seems to us, arise from thinking about affect and cognition in combination. Reflecting, perhaps inevitably, the newness of the enterprise, our commentary raises as many questions as it provides answers.

Developing the Interface: Affect and Cognition in Constant Interaction

Taken together, the chapters in this volume portray a complex interplay within the intergroup perception context, with affective and cognitive processes in continuous mutual interaction. Indeed, the accumulated research findings reported here demonstrate the joint effects of cognition and affect at various phases of an intergroup encounter. That is, some of these effects derive from factors that a perceiver brings to the social perception situation; others arise as a person or group is perceived or an intergroup interaction evolves; still others reflect reactions to or consequences of elements of the situation that has already transpired. As a whole, this portrayal begins to convey some of the complexity of intergroup relations. What have we learned about this complexity?

To begin, the distinction introduced by Bodenhausen (Chapter 2) between affect that is incidental to and affect that is integral in the intergroup context seems to us to be a central organizing principle. Incidental affect is generated by some unrelated event before participants even enter the intergroup situation. This affect, which in principle is unrelated to intergroup issues, may nevertheless carry over and influence the way information about groups and group members is processed. The intergroup context itself can activate a variety of cognitive processes. These processes include those arising from the activation of generalized distinctions between ingroup and outgroup and from the activation of preexisting stereotypes about particular groups. They also include information processing mechanisms that are engaged when observers gather information about the central tendencies and variability of groups and their members. And they include the various processing goals that are brought into play when intergroup interaction is marked by competition or cooperation. Any of these three processes—involving stereotype activation, social perception, and social interaction—can be influenced by the presence of incidental affect, as the evidence reported by Bodenhausen (Chapter 2), Hamilton, Stroessner, and Mackie (Chapter 3) Stroessner and Mackie (Chapter 4), and Wilder (Chapter 5) clearly documents.

These cognitive factors can also play a role in the generation of integral affect—affect that arises in the context of the intergroup encounter itself. For example, stereotype activation might bring with it associated affect; learning new material about the group may prompt affective reactions; and interacting with group members can produce the frustration of blocked goals and of thwarted intentions. Many of these outcomes are demonstrated in the chapters by Dovidio and Gaertner (Chapter 8), Bornstein (Chapter 9), Vanman and Miller (Chapter 10), Fiske and Ruscher (Chapter 11), and Henwood et al., (Chapter 12). Once generated, this integral affect can then influence subsequently occurring cognitive processes—those that feed back on the participants' concepts of their selves as well as those that concern ongoing perceptions of others. In Chapter 14, for example, Devine and Monteith track affective outcomes (distress at discrepancy from the ideal self) that in turn stimulate heightened vigilance in subsequent cognitive processing. These processes can in turn have affective consequences, as when the outcome of attributional processing raises or lowers self esteem (see Major & Crocker, Chapter 15). Those affective outcomes no doubt influence further cognitive processing, and so on, and so on. Thus we begin to appreciate the continuing interplay of processes that can shape and guide the course of intergroup perceptions and interactions.

When viewed within this context, it becomes clear that any single research enterprise necessarily creates arbitrarily defined starting and stopping points in the ongoing sequence of interaction. Similarly, any attempt to describe the sequence conceptually or schematically would also be constrained by its focus and the boundaries on that focus. However, some of the theoretical richness manifested in these chapters arises in part from how this sequence is sliced. Each slicing, inevitably but incompletely, reflects a particular relationship between affect, cognition, and intergroup processes that can be explored and investigated. Perhaps most important, where in the sequence different approaches focus has implications for models of intergroup behavior.

For some researchers, the important focus is on the link from emotion or affect to behavior. For example, approach to or avoidance of groups and group members can follow more or less directly from the experience of affect (as when anger prompts attack, or when fear prompts withdrawal). From this point of view (see Vanman & Miller, Chapter 10 and Smith, Chapter 13 for descriptions of this perspective), research interest should be focused on this direct impact of affect on behavior, and on the role of cognition in increasing or decreasing the affective experience. This affective reaction then prompts, in a relatively straightforward manner, intergroup behavior.

For other approaches, cognitive factors are the important antecedents of behavior. Here, approach or avoidance is initially determined by the activation of beliefs that have positive or negative evaluative implications (see Chapters 2 through 5; Bodenhausen; Hamilton et al., Stroessner & Mackie; Wilder, for this approach). In this case, the interesting causal pathways to explore are those that link cognition directly to behavior (e.g., expectancy confirmation processes), and the role of affect in producing differences in cognitive processing outcomes, assuming that behavior follows in a rather straightforward manner from those cognitively rooted effects.

Both of these approaches are evident in the research literature, and clearly the choice of approach is not one of right versus wrong. Nevertheless, adopting one approach and a corresponding research strategy orients the researcher to certain issues and effects, to the possible exclusion of others. It is here that the eclecticism of the present collection of chapters is particularly instructive. Viewing the intergroup encounter as involving constantly interacting cognitive and affective processes reveals the arbitrariness of any distinction between emotion-to-cogniton and cognition-to-emotion models of behavior. Instead, it becomes evident that intergroup behavior reflects the joint influence of both kinds of processes, and attention might profitably turn to determining how these processes combine to exert their joint effects and to delineating the circumstances under which one or the other process might dominate.

This interactive perspective has another benefit, and one that strikes us as not particularly obvious or expected. Specifically, this approach highlights certain similarities in how affective and cognitive processes appear to operate. At any given stage, the occurrence of one process can facilitate or inhibit the influence of the other process. For example, the presence of affect may exacerbate the output of a cognitive process, or it may diminish it. Thus, the presence of some affective states can undermine stereotyping based on processing of new information but it can increase stereotyping that depends on the use of stereotyped preconceptions (see Bodenhausen, Chapter 2; Hamilton et al., Chapter 3; Stroessner & Mackie, Chapter 4). Cognitive processes can have similar impacts on affect. Thus, how a situation is appraised can fuel or dampen the experience of emotion (Smith, Chapter 13) attributional processing can raise or lower self-esteem (Major & Crocker, Chapter 15). Moreover, both cognition and emotion can apparently function as "justifications" for the operation of the other process, such as when stereotypes are negotiated to explain discomfort (Henwood et al., Chapter 12) or when prejudice arises as a "rational" response to perceived violations of ingroup values (Stephan & Stephan, Chapter 6; Esses et al., Chapter 7; but particularly Smith, Chapter 13). And although the research programs reported in these chapters have not included intense manipulations of either affective or cognitive factors, it appears that extreme activation of one processing system can overwhelm the other completely: intense emotion can disrupt information processing (Mandler, 1984), while extensive cognitive activity can short-circuit the experience of affect (Erber & Tesser, 1992).

In sum, the chapters in this volume raise a variety of issues about the mutually interacting roles of affect and behavior in intergroup relations. These ideas seem rich in possibilities for future research.

Changing Conceptualizations of Stereotype and Prejudice

More generally, the clearly interactive nature of affective and cognitive processes in producing intergroup behavior raises interesting new questions about the ways in which social scientists might view the relationships among stereotyping, prejudice, and discrimination. Historically, discrimination has typically been assumed to flow from prejudice, which in turn has been assumed to arise from group stereotypes. The interactive view that permeates this volume raises new questions about this conceptualization, suggesting the possibility that some rethinking of these concepts and their relationships may be in order.

Certainly the link between stereotypes and prejudicial attitudes has come under new scrutiny. Stereotypes, traditionally conceptualized as a set of traits associated with group membership, and prejudice, traditionally conceptualized as a generalized evaluative attitude toward a group, have been assumed to be closely related to each other. Yet evidence reported by Stephan and Stephan (Chapter 6) and Esses *et al.* (Chapter 7) questions the effectiveness of even individually held stereotypes in predicting measures of prejudice toward various groups. Indeed, measures of emotional reactions generated to various groups seem to play a powerful role in determining one's overall evaluative responses to those groups. How, then, do stereotypes feed into this process?

In a parallel manner, the link between prejudice and discrimination has been subjected to the same kind of criticisms leveled at the link between attitudes and behavior more generally. Much more is now known about the conditions under which attitudes impact behavior (see Fazio, 1990), and making the same kinds of qualifications may also be important for understanding the relationship between prejudice and discrimination. For example, the study of aversive racism indicates that discrimination depends on norms as well as prejudice (Gaertner & Dovidio, 1986), just as behavior depends on norms as well as attitudes. However, recent conceptualizations of the relationships between emotion and behavior pose a more fundamental threat to the concept of prejudice. It is possible, for example, that specific emotions arising in the intergroup encounter elicit behavioral reactions directly (Frijda, 1986; see Smith, Chapter 13). If so, the need for a concept of generalized prejudice as a determinant of intergroup behavior becomes questionable (see Vanman & Miller, Chapter 10; Smith, Chapter 13).

Both of these developments have prompted an ongoing reevaluation of the concepts of stereotyping and prejudice, some of which is represented in this volume. The concept of stereotypes has gradually been broadened to include not only the trait attributes considered characteristic of a group but also information about a group's appearance, beliefs, attitudes, feelings, and preferences, as well as specific behavioral instances (see Messick & Mackie, 1989, for a review). Beyond these developments, the findings reported by Esses *et al.* (Chapter 7) suggest that the concept of stereotyping needs to incorporate the notion of symbolic values, those beliefs that are associated with an outgroup's position relative to the ingroup on cherished and deeply ingrained ways of viewing and valuing the world. How is saying that someone violates the Protestant work ethic different from saying that he or she is lazy? Do traits commonly associated with stereotypes differ in their social significance for the relationship between groups? What stereotypic information predicts behavior toward groups? These are some of the questions prompted by the research reported here.

At the same time, the concept of prejudice is evolving. The first step in this evolution would reflect changes in the conception of prejudice as an attitude, changes based on advances in the theoretical definition of attitude. In the attitude literature, attitudes are now seen as global evaluations based on cognitive, affective, and behavioral components. Thus prejudice could be described as an intergroup attitude based on some (changing) combination of cognitive, affective, and behavior component information, a view put forward by Esses *et al.* in Chapter 7. This view has several implications. First, it assigns affect a role within the cognitive process model. And as Esses and her colleagues point out, under many circumstances affect may be a better predictor of global intergroup evaluations than are beliefs alone. Second, this more recent view allows for flexibility in the prejudice concept. No longer monolithic and unchanging, prejudice could vary not only in intensity but perhaps even in direction as the situational context activates different aspects of the stereotype and different emotional reactions. But even this extra flexibility may not be sufficient. In Chapter 13, Smith argues that the concept of prejudice is limited by its bidirectionality: intensity aside, only two evaluations of groups, positive or negative, are possible. Viewing prejudice in terms of appraisal conceptions of emotion allows for more differentiated reactions to groups; presumably we do not act in the same manner toward an outgroup we fear as we do toward an outgroup we despise.

Whether the traditional concepts of stereotyping and prejudice, and the traditional view of their relationships, can evolve to incorporate the kinds of ideas and findings generated by this more interactive perspective remains to be seen. At minimum, the contributors to this volume have posed some interesting challenges for future conceptual developments in this area.

From Individual to Intergroup Concepts
of Cognition and Emotion

One theme that appears in several of the chapters, and that impresses us as having far-reaching implications, is the blurring of the distinction between individual and intergroup concepts of cognition and emotion. The trail blazers in this regard were, of course, the theories of self categorization and social identity (Tajfel & Turner, 1986; Turner, 1987). First, by the process of self categorization, group membership becomes an important part of the individual's sense of self, so that the individual also becomes in some psychological sense "the group," adopting its defining norms and characteristics. In this sense, ingroup and self become entwined. Second, by the process of social identity, the self as group member—and everyone else as group members—become affect laden. To the extent that the group provides an important source of positive self-regard, ingroup outcomes become the outcomes of the individual as well.

This perspective opens up new possibilities for intergroup conceptualizations of stereotyping and prejudice, as well as of cognitive and emotional processes. Stereotypic beliefs associated with group membership become important to the extent that they have consequences for the ingroup relative to other groups. Perhaps this helps explain the greater impact of beliefs concerned with "symbolic" values on prejudice (Stephan & Stephan, Chapter 6; Esses *et al.*, Chapter 7) as well as the fact that intergroup behavior may be better explained by appeal to group interest rather than self interest (Crosby, 1982; Sears, 1988). Of course, it is possible that all stereotypic traits are symbolic to some degree. White Anglo-Saxon Protestants might not have developed stereotypes of outgroups as lazy if such behavior did not violate the Protestant work ethic, or as dirty if cleanliness were not next to Godliness. Thus cognitive appraisal processes may proceed by evaluating situations not only in terms of consequences for the self (I am in danger; I am disgusted) but also in terms of their consequences for one's group (my group is in danger; my group sensibilities are offended). Because of self categorization and social identification, those consequences are experienced as sharply on behalf of the group as they would be if they applied only to the individual. Thus prejudice toward groups, or how group members are evaluated, depends on their contextual ability to threaten, repulse, cower, or enhance not only the individual but also the individual's ingroup.

The influence of group-based belief and evaluation is reflected in several of the chapters of the book. The importance of symbolic values is made clear by Esses *et al.* in Chapter 7; Dovidio and Gaertner show that the mere activation of the concepts "we" and "they" produce robust evaluative outcomes in Chapter 8; stereotypes are negotiated until ingroup discomfort is diminished (Henwood *et al.*, Chapter 12); and the idea of expanding the concepts of appraisal and emotion beyond the individual to encompass the group is the central focus of Smith's Chapter 13. As research at the interface of cognition and affect continues, and as further pressure is put on the explanatory adequacy of current conceptualizations of stereotype and prejudice, the interdependence of individual and group level processes should become more apparent and have increasing impact on theory development in intergroup perception.

In this regard, we want to draw special attention to the need to study intergroup issues in multigroup contexts. No doubt for historical reasons, research has been concerned most extensively with the mutual perceptions, evaluations, and behavior of White Americans and African Americans. Trying to understand these relationships has of course meant trying to understand the relationship between a majority and a minority group. But increasingly, the ebb and flow of intergroup relations takes place in a context of multiple groups jockeying for positive social identities and material resources. One particularly poignant example of the need to understand such relations comes in the wake of the 1992 Los Angeles riots. The incidents were sparked by tensions between Whites and Blacks, but Korean shopkeepers felt targeted for much of the subsequent violence, reflecting the enduring tensions between Blacks and Koreans in this community. In this context, not only are relationships between the (for now) majority White population and a wide range of minority groups of interest, but also relationships among the different minority groups need to be understood. How are interminority group relations affected by majority–minority group relations? How are majority–minority perceptions, evaluations, and behavior influenced by the presence of other minority groups? If cognitive processes (like appraisal) and emotional processes (like self-esteem maintenance) are to be viewed as intergroup phenomena, the full complexity of the intergroup context will soon have to be taken into account.

Further Difficulties for the Contact Hypothesis

Almost from the moment of its inception, the contact hypothesis—the idea that intergroup interaction will reduce intergroup prejudice—has suffered a rather ignoble history. Its initial rather expansive promise of helping reduce prejudice has been further and further curtailed and constrained by qualifications. First came the laundry list of conditions necessary for contact to work: equal status, personalized contact, positive affect, cooperative interaction (Stephan, 1987; Pettigrew, 1986). More recently came more theoretically based attacks, spearheaded by demonstrations of the self-protective functioning of stereotypes even in the face of inconsistent information (Rothbart & John, 1985) and by arguments for the limited usefulness of interpersonal encounters that had little relevance for changing group-level perceptions and evaluations (Hewstone & Brown, 1986). Perhaps not surprising, when we explicitly begin to recognize the place of affect in this mosaic, it seems that the claims of the contact hypothesis must become even more constrained.

First, it is clear that both the idea (Vanman & Miller, Chapter 10; Fiske & Ruscher, Chapter 11) and the practice (Vanman & Miller, Chapter 10; Fiske & Ruscher, Chapter 11; Henwood et al., Chapter 12) of intergroup contact are affect laden, and that the affect with which they are laden typically is negative. Second, research evidence described in Chapters 2 through 5 (Bodenhausen; Hamilton et al.; Stroessner & Mackie; Wilder) supports the idea that unpleasant affect—anger, anxiety, and, at least in some cases, sadness—has negative consequences for intergroup perception. These consequences include increased use of stereotypes, more probable formation of expectancy-based illusory correlations, reductions in perceived intragroup variability, and the inability to recognize behavior that is inconsistent with expectancies and stereotypes. Third, and perhaps most unfortunate, even the presence of pleasant incidental affect during intergroup encounters does not guarantee positive outcomes. As the research in Chapters 2 through 5 documents, induced happiness can also increase reliance on stereotype-based judgments and decrease perceived group variability. Fourth, even specific recommendations for ensuring a positive outcome for contact come under some fire. The importance of intergroup comparisons in many aspects of interaction (the activation of "we" versus "they" categories, the role of violation of ingroup values in outgroup derogation, the negotiation of outgroup stereotypes in ingroup conversation, the idea that discrimination may reflect group-based rather than individually based emotion) makes the prospect of individualized contact seem all but impossible, and makes equal status contact seem unlikely. We have already seen that the presence of positive affect need not facilitate change. In addition, as Fiske and Ruscher argues in Chapter 11, interdependence may not be the assumed cure-all for impaired intergroup relations. As their analysis makes clear, interdependence may be first and foremost a cause of disruption, irritation, annoyance, and hostility. And finally, Major and Crocker's elegant analysis of attributional ambiguity indicates that minority group members cannot straightforwardly accept positive feedback as a sign of improved intergroup relations. Even positive interaction that is effective in reducing the prejudices of the majority member may not be beneficial for the minority member. That is, interaction that culminates in praise, reward, or compliments may not improve participants' relations if those positive outcomes are discounted.

Nevertheless, some research findings offer a modicum of relief from such unrelenting pessimism regarding the effects of intergroup contact. First, Bodenhausen (Chapter 2) suggests that incidentally induced sadness can often induce careful thought and reduce reliance on stereotypes in making judgments (although whether sadness induces more or less careful thought is an issue still open to considerable debate). Second, Hamilton and his colleagues (Chapter 3) suggest that under some conditions affect can interfere with the kinds of cognitive processes upon which stereotypes are formed. Thus distinctiveness-based illusory correlations did not develop when information processing was undermined by either positive or negative affect. Third, Stroessner and Mackie (Chapter 4) and Wilder (Chapter 5) offer suggestions about ways in which the fact that affect undermines perceptions of group variability could be used to promote, rather than prevent, favorable intergroup relations.

Fourth, Bornstein's (Chapter 9) focus on the impact of mere exposure offers some possibility for optimism. In the laboratory at least, mere exposure seems to increase liking for outgroups. Of course this process usually works to the advantage of the ingroup, to whom we are usually more

frequently exposed. Even here, however, some aspects of the mere exposure process give pause. First, mere exposure effects may be more robust
when people are unaware of their frequency of exposure (Bornstein,
1989). This may be typically easier to attain for the ingroup, whom we
often see in individualized rather than group terms, than for the outgroup,
with whom all encounters might be more consciously processed. Once increased exposure becomes obvious, its benefits may decline. Second, the
impacts of mere exposure appear more promising inside than outside the
laboratory. This may suggest that in actual interaction, situational determinants of cognitive appraisal and emotional experience disrupt the mere
exposure effect.

Fifth, Devine and Monteith's Chapter 14 extends Devine's (1989) earlier ideas that unprejudiced individuals can overcome the automatic aspects
of prejudice with controlled processing. In this chapter they develop the
idea that affect arising from discrepancies between idealized positions (race
neutrality for the nonprejudiced person) and actual prejudiced judgments
can motivate processing that induces vigilance against further prejudice.
This suggests that when contact results in prejudiced judgments or behaviors, at least some individuals will attempt to bring their responses in line
with their nonprejudiced beliefs. Of course the problem here for amelioration of intergroup relations is that only the already unprejudiced suffer
from these discrepancies, and only the already unprejudiced are motivated
to reduce these discrepancies. Thus, in a sense, these processes preach to the
converted. However, Devine and Monteith offer some suggestions as to
how more evenhanded processing could be induced even in those who still
endorse negative views of other groups.

The majority of findings militate against looking for easy answers or
quick benefits from intergroup contact. However, it is too soon to draw the
conclusion that the contact hypothesis has outlived its usefulness. First,
there are ways in which affect can facilitate change, as we have seen. Second, much of the research suggesting that positive affect has negative implications for intergroup judgments involves manipulations of incidental
affect. It is still possible, as suggested by the contact hypothesis, that positive affect arising out of the interaction will be more likely to have positive
effects. Finally, attempts to put intergroup contact into practice can only be
facilitated by knowing what potential pitfalls can arise from the presence of
affective states during the intergroup encounter.

An Opportunity for Social Change?

We began the introductory chapter to this volume by noting that two
developments in psychology—the predominance of cognition and the revitalization of affect in social psychological research—have converged to

make the research described in this volume possible. We believe that there is a third development that might also make the potential contribution of the book particularly timely. This development, occurring outside of the formal boundaries of psychology, reflects the broader, sociopolitical climate in society. Specifically, we believe that intergroup relations, in this country and in Europe, presently "hang in the balance," as these societies for the first time in recent decades are marked by real ambivalence toward these issues.

Documenting the continued dominance of cognition and the resurgence of interest in affect in psychology is relatively easy. However, we have much more difficulty, and feel much greater uncertainty, in positing this third development. Part of our argument—that American society has endured a period of relative neglect of intergroup concerns—seems clear enough. Following the civil rights advances of the 1960s and early 1970s, we seem to have pulled back from social commitments and focused instead on self-interest and individual economic well-being. This shift was first evident in the 1970s when, faced with oil embargoes and rising inflation, people became increasingly concerned with their own economic stability, their ability simply "to make ends meet." However, this soon evolved, during the Reagan years, from a concern with economic stability to the economic excesses of the 1980s. Correspondingly, interest in and concern for social issues waned: feelings of social responsibility were assuaged by a popular belief in the presence of a "safety net," a convenient political image that in reality had numerous holes and tears in the mesh.

In this context, we see several signs that concern for and commitment to improving intergroup relations are at a critical stage. On the negative side, we see and hear a steady flow of headlines documenting intergroup strife between racial groups, nationalities, and religious sects, as well as groups with differing lifestyle preferences. The incidence of "hate crimes" has increased, gains by some minority groups in higher education have decreased. Blatantly racist tactics have been used for political gain. Moreover, the current membership of the United States Supreme Court seems more likely to erode than shore up affirmative action and school integration policies. By these indicators, intergroup conflicts are as prominent and pervasive today as ever before.

On the other hand, and at the risk of appearing to be the proverbial eternal optimists, we propose that there at least are reasons for hope. After a decade or more of focusing on self-interest, individual economic gain, and personal happiness (the "me" generation), there may be indications that American society is once again returning to an awareness of its social complexity, its multicultural fabric, and the intergroup problems that always seem to impede our attaining the American ideal of equality. For example, whereas affirmative action was previously advocated as a means of redressing an unjust past, we now stress diversity as a positive value. And whereas the civil rights movements of the 1960s focused attention on certain groups (first Blacks, then women), current societal concerns highlight the problems faced by numerous and diverse groups, including Mexican American, Asian Americans, gays, the elderly, the homeless, the obese, the unemployed, carriers of the HIV virus, as well as other more specific groups such as abused children, battered women, and the terminally ill.

Admittedly, expressions of public concerns for these groups are, to some extent, the products of institutional and/or political rhetoric. Nevertheless, many of those concerns do seem to be genuine and, we hope, reflect a shift in social priorities. Moreover, our impression is that, where it exists, the public concern includes a more sophisticated recognition of the complex and multifaceted nature of underlying problems, as well as a corresponding cognizance that simple, singularly focused remedies are unlikely to provide satisfactory solutions.

If so, then the broader impact of societal sentiment may foster and support a fresh and renewed attack on intergroup research. And it may be particularly compatible with the emphasis in this volume that intergroup problems—whether they be biases in intergroup perceptions or instances of outright conflict—represent the convergence of multiple forces that combine in complex ways to produce specific outcomes. With their focus on the interface and interaction of cognitive and affective processes, we hope that the research reported in the chapters in this volume can begin to help generate some new solutions to the age-old puzzle of intergroup relations.

References

Bornstein, R. F. (1989). Exposure and affect: Overview and meta-analysis of research, 1969–1987. *Psychological Bulletin, 106*, 265–289.

Crosby, F. (1982). *Relative deprivation and working women.* New York: Oxford University Press.

Devine, P. T. (1989). Stereotypes and prejudice: Their automatic and controlled components. *Journal of Personality and Social Psychology, 56*, 5–18.

Erber, R., & Tesser, A. (1992). Task effort and the regulation of mood: The absorption hypothesis. *Journal of Experimental Social Psychology, 28*, 339–359.

Fazio, R. H. (1990). Multiple processes by which attitudes guide behaviors: The MODE model as an integrative framework. In M. P. Zanna (Ed.), *Advances in Experimental Social Psychology* (Vol. 23, pp. 75–110). New York: Academic Press.

Frijda, N. H. (1986). *The emotions.* New York: Cambridge University Press.

Gaertner, S. L., & Dovidio, J. F. (1986). The aversive form of racism. In J. F. Dovidio & S. L. Gaertner (Eds.), *Prejudice, discrimination, racism: Theory and research* (pp. 61–89). New York: Academic Press.

Hewstone, M., & Brown, R. (1986). Contact is not enough: an intergroup perspective on the contact hypothesis. In M. Hewstone & R. Brown (Eds.), *Contact and conflict in intergroup encounters* (pp. 1–44). New York: Basil Blackwell.

Mandler, G. (1984). *Mind and body: Psychology of emotion and stress.* New York: Norton.

Messick, D. M., & Mackie, D. M., (1989). Intergroup relations. *Annual Review of Psychology, 40*, 45–81.

Pettigrew, T. F. (1986). The intergroup contact hypothesis reconsidered. In M. Hewstone & R. Brown (Eds.), *Contact and conflict in intergroup encounters* (pp. 169–95). New York: Basil Blackwell.

Rothbart, M., & John, O. P. (1985). Social categorization and behavioral episodes: a cognitive analysis of the effects of intergroup contact. *Journal of Social Issues, 41,* 81–104.

Sears, D. O. (1988). Symbolic racism. In P. E. Katz & D. A. Taylor (Eds.), *Eliminating racism: profiles in controversy* (pp. 31–52). New York: Plenum.

Stephan, W. G. (1987). The contact hypothesis in intergroup relations. *Review of Personality and Social Psychology, 9,* 13–40.

Tajfel, H., & Turner, J. C. (1986). An integrative theory of intergroup relations. In S. Worchel & W. G. Austin (Eds.), *Psychology of intergroup relations* (pp. 7–24). Chicago: Nelson-Hall.

Turner, J. C. (1987). *Rediscovering the social group: A self-categorization theory.* New York: Basil Blackwell.

Index